Bear's Guide to Earning College Degrees Non-Traditionally

11th Edition

by John Bear, Ph.D.

PRESIDENT

GREENWICH UNIVERSITY

Greenwich University Press

HILO, HAWAII, U.S.A.

For Marina

TO REACH THE DISTRIBUTOR:
K. & F. Costedoat
P. O. Box 826
Benicia, California 94510
(707) 746-8535

TO REACH THE AUTHOR:
John Bear, Ph.D.
P. O. Box 1717
Hilo, Hawaii 96721

Library of Congress Catalog Number: 88-051086
ISBN: 0-89815-248-8

Printed in the United States of America

Contents

About the Author: His Life, His Biases, and a Request for Help

LIFE

I attended school at a time when non-traditional education virtually did not exist in the United States. I did my best to create my own alternative program within the traditional framework. From my junior year at Reed College through my Master's at Berkeley to my Ph.D. from Michigan State University, I always had at least one demanding off-campus job, often related to my academic studies. I was generally able to integrate my work as a newspaper reporter, prison psychologist, advertising writer, and researcher at a school for the deaf to what I was doing in school, but with little support or encouragement from my school or faculty.

I have taught at major universities (Iowa, Berkeley, Michigan State) and small schools (City College of San Francisco, College of the Redwoods); worked as a business executive (research director for Bell & Howell's educational division; director of communications for the Midas Muffler Shop chain); as director of the Center for the Gifted Child in San Francisco; and as consultant to organizations as diverse as General Motors, Xerox Corporation, Encyclopaedia Britannica, and The Grateful Dead. Since 1974, I have been devoting much of my time to investigating and writing about non-traditional higher education.

In 1977, I established Degree Consulting Services, to offer detailed consulting to people seeking more personal advice than a book can provide. While I no longer deal with individual clients, the Service is in good hands, and is described on the last page of this book.

My family has been more non-traditional in their education than I. Twenty years after completing her traditional B.A., my wife, Marina, enrolled in the non-resident M.A. in humanities at California State University, Dominguez Hills and completed that degree in 1986. She is now working on her Ph.D. at Vanderbilt University. Our twin daughters left high school at age 15, midway through 10th grade, and passed the state high school equivalency exam. One went on to college at that early age; the other worked for three years, then entered college at the "traditional" age of 18. Their older sister maintained a demanding job at a major publishing house while finishing her Bachelor's (Phi Beta Kappa) in mass communication.

BIASES

As you read this book, you will learn that I am biased. I have strong opinions about which schools and programs are good and which are not, and I do not hesitate to say so. I have been sued three times: twice for millions of dollars by people who operate what I called (and continue to call) illegal diploma mills; and once, years ago, by a school that I incorrectly identified as a diploma mill.

It is the case that, over the years, I have done consulting or advisory work for various schools, who paid me in money, goods (generally the use of their mailing lists to help sell this book), and in two cases, stock:

- In return for my consulting work in the early 1970s, Columbia Pacific University paid me with a small amount of its stock, which I sold years ago.
- I was one of four founders of Fairfax University, a not-for-profit non-traditional school. Once it was launched, I resigned, and have no connection whatever with Fairfax.
- In 1987, eager to experience non-traditional education from the other side of the desk, as it were, I accepted the presidency of the International Institute for Advanced Studies, a small, older (in this field, being founded in 1972 makes one a true pioneer), non-profit school.

In 1990, I became the full-time president of Greenwich University which evolved from the International Institute, and which, needless to say, I regard as one of the best schools of its kind. I hope you will read its description on page 113 and give it serious consideration. (End of commercial announcement.)

I am confident that these activities have had, and have no bearing on the opinions expressed in this book. Hundreds of excellent schools have never even taken me to lunch, yet I recommend them highly. (I will probably accept if they ever *do* offer lunch.) On the other side of the ledger, there is no way in the world I can be persuaded to say good things about schools I don't like. My biases and opinions are my own, and not subject to outside influence from any direction.

HELP

Over the years, great amounts of feedback from readers have been of immense value. If you are aware of schools or programs I have overlooked, please let me know. If you disagree with my evaluation of a school based on your own experience, please don't hesitate to let me know. I may be biased, but I like to think I am open-minded, and indeed I have changed my opinions on many schools (both up and down) over the years.

Please communicate(preferably in writing), and if you'd like a reply (I can't guarantee it, but I'll do my best.), please enclose a stamped self-addressed envelope or, outside the U.S., two international reply coupons, available at your post office. You can reach me at this address:

John B. Bear, Ph.D.
P. O. Box 1717
Hilo, Hawaii 96721

Thank you.

Drawing by Handelsman; © 1972 The New Yorker Magazine, Inc.

"It is my wish that this be the most educated country in the world, and toward that end I hereby ordain that each and every one of my people be given a diploma."

1. Introduction: What Non-Traditional Education is All About

Education's purpose is to replace an empty mind with an open one.
—Malcolm Forbes

The man on the telephone was so distraught, he was almost in tears. For more than 20 years, he had been in charge of sawing off dead tree branches for a large midwestern city. But a new personnel policy in that city decreed that henceforth, all department heads would have to have a Bachelor's degree. If this man could not earn a degree within two years, he would no longer be permitted to continue in the job he had been performing satisfactorily for more than 20 years.

It is an unfortunate but very real aspect of life today that a college or university degree is often more important (or at least more useful) than a good education, or substantial knowledge in your field, whether that field is nuclear physics or sawing off branches. It doesn't matter if you've been reading or studying and learning all your life. It doesn't matter how good you are at what you do. In many situations, if you don't have a piece of (usually imitation) parchment that certifies you as a Bachelor, Master, or a Doctor, you are somehow perceived as less worthy, and are often denied the better jobs and higher salaries that go to degree-holders.

In fact, as more and more degree-holders, from space scientists to philosophers, are unable to find employment in their specific chosen fields, and move elsewhere in the job market, degrees have become more important than ever. Consider, for instance, a job opening for a high school English teacher. Five applicants with comparable skills apply, but one has a Doctorate while the other four have Bachelor's degrees. Who do you think would probably get the job?

Never mind that a Ph.D. is no more necessary to teach high school English than a B.A. is needed to chop down trees. The simple fact is that degrees are extremely valuable commodities in the job market.

Happily, as the need for degrees has grown, so has their availability. Since the mid-1970s, there has been a virtual explosion in what is now commonly called "alternative" or "non-traditional" or "external" or "off-campus" education—ways and means of getting an education, or a degree (or both, if you wish) without sitting in classrooms day after day, year after year.

The rallying cry was, in fact, sounded in 1973 by Ewald B. Nyquist, then president of the wonderfully innovative University of the State of New York. He said:

> There are thousands of people . . . who contribute in important ways to the life of the communities in which they live, even though they do not have a college degree. Through native intelligence, hard work and sacrifice, many have gained in knowledge and understanding. And yet, the social and economic advancement of these people has been thwarted in part by the emphasis that is put on the possession of credentials . . . As long as we remain a strongly credentialed society . . . employers will not be disposed to hire people on the basis of what they know, rather than on what degrees and diplomas they hold. If attendance at a college is the only road to these credentials, those who cannot or have not availed themselves of this route but have acquired knowledge and skills through other sources, will be denied the recognition and advancement to which they are entitled. Such inequity should not be tolerated.

Non-traditional education takes many forms, including these:

- credit (and degrees) for life experience learning, even if the learning took place long before you entered school
- credit (and degrees) for passing examinations

- credit (and degrees) for independent study, whether or not enrolled in a school at the time
- credit (and degrees) through intensive study (for instance, 10 hours a day for a month instead of 1 hour a day for a year)
- credit (and degrees) through guided private study, at your own pace, and from your own home or office, under the supervision of a faculty member with whom you communicate on a regular basis
- credit (and degrees) for work done on your home or office computer, linked to the computer of your school, wherever in the world it may be
- credit (and degrees) from weekend schools, evening schools, and summer-only schools
- credit (and degrees) entirely by correspondence study
- credit (and degrees) through the use of audio- and videotaped courses, taken when convenient for you, not when scheduled by a school.

This book endeavors to cover all these areas, and more, as completely as possible. Yet this is truly an impossible task. New programs are introduced literally every day. In recent years, an average of one new college or university has opened for business every *week*, while old, established universities are disappearing at the rate of two or three each month.

So, although this book is as current and correct as I can possibly make it, there are bound to be recent changes not covered, as well as, inevitably, errors and omissions. For all of these, I apologize now, and invite your suggestions and criticisms for the next edition. Thank you.

Perhaps the best way to make clear, in a short space, the differences between the traditional (dare I say old-fashioned) approaches to education and degrees and the non-traditional (or modern) approach is to offer the following dozen comparisons.

Traditional education awards degrees on the basis of time served and credit earned.
Non-traditional education awards degrees on the basis of competencies and performance skills.

Traditional education bases degree requirements on the mediaeval formula of some generalized education and some specialized education.
Non-traditional education bases degree requirements on an agreement between the student and the faculty, aimed at helping the student achieve his or her career, personal, or professional goals.

Traditional education awards the degree when the student meets certain numerical requirements.
Non-traditional education awards the degree when the student's actual work and learning reach agreed-upon levels.

Traditional education considers the years from age 18 to age 22 as the period when a first degree should be earned.
Non-traditional education assumes learning is desirable at any age, and that degrees should be available to people of all ages.

Traditional education considers the classroom as the primary source of information and the campus as the center of learning.
Non-traditional education sees any part of the world as appropriate for some learning.

Traditional education believes in printed text materials as the principal learning resource.
Non-traditional education believes the range of learning resources is limitless, from the daily newspaper to personal interviews; from videocassettes to microcomputers to world travel.

Traditional faculty must have appropriate credentials and degrees.
Non-traditional faculty are judged on competency and personal qualities, in addition to credentials and degrees.

Traditional credits and degrees are based primarily on mastery of course content.
Non-traditional credits and degrees also take into consideration learning *how to learn* and the integration of diverse fields of knowledge.

Traditional education cultivates dependence on authority through prescribed curricula, required campus residence, and required classes.

Non-traditional education cultivates self-direction and independence through planned independent study, both on and off campus.

Traditional curricula are generally oriented toward traditional disciplines and well-established professions.
Non-traditional curricula reflect the student's individual needs and goals and are likely to be problem-oriented, issue-oriented, and world-oriented.

Traditional education aims at producing "finished products"—students who are done with their education and ready for the job market.
Non-traditional education aims at producing lifelong learners, capable of responding all through their life to their own evolving needs and those of society.

Traditional education, to adapt the old Chinese saying, gives you a fish and feeds you for a day.
Non-traditional education teaches you how to fish, and feeds you for life.

Traditional education had nothing to offer the dead-tree-limb expert.
Non-traditional education made it possible for him to complete a good Bachelor's degree in less than a year, entirely by correspondence and at a modest cost. His job is now secure.

2. What Are Colleges and Universities and How Do They Work?

A college is a machine that transfers information from the notes of the professor to the notes of the student without it passing through the mind of either.
—Traditional

The question of this chapter title may sound trivial or inconsequential, but it turns out to be be quite a complex issue, for which there is no simple answer at all.

Many state legislatures, mulling over laws that would govern the awarding of degrees, have fought with the problem of producing precise definitions of words like "college" and "university." (One school even tried to sue its state department of education to force them to define "educational process." The state managed to evade the suit.)

Some states have simply given up the problem as unsolvable, which is why *either* they have virtually no laws governing higher education *or* their laws are so restrictive as to prohibit the development of innovative new programs. Needless to say, the former policy encourages the proliferation of degree mills and other bad schools in those states and the latter policy discourages the establishment of any creative new non-traditional schools or programs.

Other states have, from time to time, produced rather ingenious definitions, such as Ohio's (later repealed), stating that a "university" was anything that (a) said it was a university, and (b) had an endowment or facilities worth $1 million dollars. The assumption, of course, was that no degree mill could be so well endowed. California had a similiar law but the sum was only $50,000. But since the late 1980s, much tougher requirements have been instituted in California. California still has more unaccredited schools than any other state, but the number is declining rapidly. Louisiana looks like the next home for many of these schools, some good, some awful.

Many people remember a famous CBS "60 Minutes" episode in 1978, in which the proprietor of a flagrant diploma mill was actually arrested while being interviewed by Mike Wallace. At the time, his school, California Pacific University, was licensed by the state of California. The owner had bought some used books and office furniture, declared it to have a value of $50,000, and consequently received his state authorization to grant Doctorates and all other degrees.

History repeated itself in 1990, when the proprietor of yet another degree mill, North American University, was enjoined from operating by the state of Utah on the very day that the Inside Edition television program arrived to film his nefarious operation.

The problem of definition is made even more complicated by the inconsistent way in which the words "college" and "university" are used.

In the United States, the two words are used almost interchangeably. Before long, they will probably mean exactly the same thing. Historically, a college has been a subdivision of a university. For instance, the University of California has, within its structure, a College of Arts and Sciences, a College of Education, a College of Law, and so on. The University of Oxford is comprised of Balliol College, Exeter College, Magdalen College, and about three dozen others.

But there are many degree-granting colleges that are not part of any university, and there are universities that have no colleges in their structure. Also, there is an ever-growing trend for colleges to rename themselves as universities, either to reflect their growth, to enhance their image, or both. In recent years, dozens of colleges, from Antioch in Ohio to San Francisco State in California, have turned themselves into universities.

To make the situation even more complex, outside the United States, the word "college" rarely refers to a degree-granting institution, and often is used for what Americans call a high school. American personnel managers and admissions officers have been fooled by this fact. An Englishman, for instance, who states on his job application, "Graduate of Eton College," means, simply, that he has completed the high school of that name.

Many readers have told me that they simply will not go to a "college," no matter how good it may be, because the word just doesn't sound real enough to them.

Finally, there are some degree-granting institutions that have chosen a name other than "college" or "university." The most common words used are "school" (e.g., the New School for Social Research; California School of Professional Psychology, etc.) and "institute" (e.g., Fielding Institute, Union Institute, etc.).

HOW COLLEGES AND UNIVERSITIES WORK

The Calendar

There is no uniform pattern to the calendar, or scheduling of classes, from one school to the next. However, most schools tend to follow one of four basic patterns:

1. The Semester Plan A semester is 16 to 18 weeks long and there are usually two semesters per year, plus a shorter summer session. Many classes are one semester long, while others will last two semesters or longer (e.g., Algebra I in the fall semester and Algebra II in the spring).

A class that meets three hours a week for one semester is likely to be worth 3 semester hours of credit. Depending on the amount of homework, additional reading, laboratory time, etc., the *actual* amount of credit could be anywhere from 2 to 6 semester hours for such a class.

2. The Quarter Plan Many universities divide the year into four quarters of equal length, usually 11 or 12 weeks. Many courses require two or more quarters to complete. A course that meets three hours a week for a quarter will probably be worth 3 "quarter hours" or "quarter units," with a range of 2 to 6. One "semester unit" is equal to 1-1/2 "quarter units."

3. The Trimester Plan A much smaller number of schools divide the year into three equal trimesters of 15 or 16 weeks each. A "trimester unit" is usually equal to 1-1/4 semester units.

4. Other Alternatives A model popularized by National University, the University of Phoenix, and other relatively new schools, is that of one course per month. Students can start on the first day of any month. The school offers one or more complete courses, intensively, each month.

Many non-resident programs have no calendar at all. Students can begin on their independent study program as soon as they have been admitted.

How Credit is Earned

In a traditional school, most credit is earned by taking classes. Non-traditional units may be earned in other ways. The most common methods are these four:

1. Life Experience Learning Credit is given for what you have learned, regardless of how or where it was learned. For example, a given university might offer six courses in German worth 4 semester units each. If you can show them that you speak and write German just as well as someone who has taken and passed those six courses, then they will give you 24 semester units of German, whether you learned the language from your grandmother, from living in Germany, or from Berlitz tapes. The same philosophy is applied to business experience, learning to fly an airplane, military training, and dozens of other non-classroom learning experiences.

2. Equivalency Examinations Many schools say that if you can pass an examination in a subject, then you should get credit for knowing that subject, without having to sit in a classroom month after month to "learn" what you already know. More than 100 standard equivalency exams are offered, worth anywhere from 2 to 39 semester units each. In general, each hour of examination is worth anywhere from 2 to 6 semester units. But different schools may award significantly different amounts of credit for the same examinations. Some schools will design examinations in fields in which there are no standard exams.

3. Correspondence Courses More than 70 universities offer thousands of home study courses, most of which may be taken by people living anywhere in the world. These courses are generally worth anywhere from 2 to 6 semester units each, and require anywhere from a month or two to a year or more to complete.

4. Learning Contracts Quite a few schools will negotiate a learning contract with a student. A learning contract is a formal, negotiated agreement between the student and the school, stating that if the student does certain things (for instance, reads these books, writes a paper of this length, does the following laboratory experiments, etc.), then, on their successful completion, the school will award so many units of credit.

Learning contracts can be written for anywhere from a few units up to and including an entire degree program. Often the school will provide a faculty member to guide the course of study.

Each of these four methods of earning credit by alternative means will be discussed in some detail in later chapters.

Grading and Evaluation Systems

Most schools, traditional and non-traditional, make use of one of four common grading systems. Grades are generally given for each separate course taken. Some schools assign grades to equivalency examinations, learning contract work, and correspondence courses. Life experience credit is rarely graded, but rather is assigned a certain number of units, without further evaluation.

The four common systems are these:

1. Letter Grades An "A" is the highest grade; "B" means "good," "C" means "average," "D" stands for "barely passing" (or, in some cases, "failing"). Some schools will use pluses and minuses, so that a "B+" is better than a "B," but not quite as good as an "A-." Some schools use "AB" instead of "B+" or "A-."

2. Number Grades Many schools use a system in which students are graded on a scale of zero (worst grade) to 4 (highest grade). The best students will get a 3.9 or 4.0 Other outstanding students might get a 3.7 or 3.8 Often, a 1.0 (or a 1.5) is the lowest passing score; anything lower is a failing score. Just to make it even more confusing, some schools use a zero to 3 scale, and some a zero to 5, but 4 is the most common.

3. Percentage Grades A smaller number of schools follow the European system and grade each student in each class on a percentage score, from 0% to 100%. In most (but not all) schools, a grade of 90% to 100% is considered excellent, 80% to 90% is good, 70% to 80% is fair, 60% to 70% is either failure or barely passing, and below 60% is failing.

4. Pass/Fail System Quite a few universities have inaugurated a pass/fail option, either for some classes or, more rarely, for all classes. In such a system, there is no specific evaluation of a student's performance—only the statement by the teacher that the student has either passed or failed the course. At many schools using this system, students are given the chance to choose a pass/fail option for one or two out of the four or five courses they might be taking during a given semester or quarter.

Grade Point Average

Most schools report a student's overall performance in terms of the "G.P.A." or Grade Point Average. This is the average of all grades received, weighted by the number of semester or quarter units each course is worth.

For example, if a student gets a 4.0 (or an "A") in a course worth 3 semester units, and a 3.0 (or a "B") in a course worth 2 semester units, his or her G.P.A. would be calculated like this: 3 x 4.0 = 12. And 2 x 3.0 = 6. Then 12 + 6 = 18, divided by a total of 5 semester units results in a G.P.A. of 3.6.

Pass/Fail courses are generally not taken into account in calculating a grade point average.

G.P.A.'s can be very important. Often it is necessary to maintain a certain average in order to earn a degree—typically a 2.0 (in a 4-point system) for a Bachelor's degree, and a 3.0 for a Master's degree and a Doctorate. Honors degrees ["Magna Cum Laude," etc.], scholarships, even permission to play on the football team, are dependent on the G.P.A. (No, non-resident schools do not have football teams. I keep waiting for a chess-by-mail league or a computer game league to spring up, however.)

3. Degrees, Degree Requirements, and Transcripts

It is not titles that honor men, but men that honor titles.
—Niccoló Machiavelli

A degree is a title conferred by a school to show that a certain course of study has been successfully completed. A diploma is the actual document or certificate that is given to the student as evidence of the awarding of the degree.

Diplomas are also awarded for courses of study that do *not* result in a degree, as for example, on completion of a program in real estate management, air conditioning repair, or military leadership. This can lead to confusion, often intentional, as in the case of someone who says, "I earned my diploma at Harvard," meaning that he or she attended a weekend seminar there, at the end of which a Diploma of Completion was awarded.

The following six kinds of degrees are awarded by college and universities in the United States.

1. The Associate's Degree

The Associate's degree is a relatively recent development, reflecting the tremendous growth of two-year community colleges (which is the new and presumably more respectable name for what used to be known as junior colleges).

Since many students attend these schools for two years, but do not continue on to another school for the Bachelor's degree, a need was felt for a degree to be awarded at the end of these two years of full-time study (or their equivalent by non-traditional means). More than 2,000 two-year schools now award the Associate's degree, and a small but growing number of four-year schools also award them to students who leave after two years.

The two most common Associate's degrees are the A.A. (Associate of Arts) and the A.S. (Associate of Science). But more than 100 other titles have been devised, ranging from the A.M.E. (Associate of Mechanical Engineering) to the A.D.T. (Associate of Dance Therapy).

An Associate's degree typically requires 60 to 64 semester hours of credit (90 to 96 quarter hours), which, in a traditional program, normally takes two academic years (four semesters, or six quarters) to complete.

2. The Bachelor's Degree

The Bachelor's degree has been around for hundreds of years. In virtually every nation of the world, it is the first university degree earned. (The Associate's is little used outside the United States.) The traditional Bachelor's degree in America is widely believed to require four years of full-time study (120 to 128 semester units, or 180 to 192 quarter units), although a rather devastating report in 1990 revealed that the average time is closer to six years! In most of the rest of the world, it is three years. But through non-traditional approaches, some people with a good deal of prior learning have earned Bachelor's degrees in as short a time as two or three months.

The Bachelor's degree is supposed to signify that the holder has accumulated a "batch" of knowledge; that he or she has learned a considerable amount in a particular field of study (the "major"), and some broad general knowledge of the world as well (history, literature, art, social science, science, mathematics). This broad approach to the degree is peculiar to traditional American programs. In many non-traditional programs, as well as in most other countries, Bachelor's degrees studies are much more intense in a given field. When someone educated in England says, "I read history at Oxford," it means that for the better part of three years he or she did, in fact, read history and not much else. This is one reason traditional American degrees take longer to acquire than most foreign ones.

More than 300 different Bachelor's degree titles have been used in the last hundred years, but the great majority of the million-plus Bachelor's degrees awarded in the United States each year are either the B.A. (Bachelor of Arts) or the B.S. (Bachelor of Science), sometimes with additional letters to indicate the field (e.g., B.S.E.E. for electrical engineering, B.A.B.A. for business administration, and so on). Other common Bachelor's degree titles include the B.B.A. (business administration), B.Mus. (music), B.Ed. (education), and B.Eng. (engineering). Some non-traditional schools or programs award the B.G.S. (general studies), B.I.S. (independent studies), B.L.S. (liberal studies) and similar titles.

In the late 19th century, educators felt that the title of "Bachelor" was inappropriate for young ladies, so some schools awarded female graduates titles such as Mistress of Arts or Maid of Science.

3. The Master's Degree

Until the 20th century, the Master's and the Doctor's titles were used somewhat interchangeably, as an appropriate title for anyone who had completed work of significance beyond the Bachelor's degree. But now a Master's is almost always the first degree earned after the Bachelor's, and is always considered to be a lower degree than the Doctorate.

The traditional Master's degree requires from one to two years of on-campus work after the Bachelor's. Some non-traditional Master's degrees may be earned entirely through non-resident study, while others require anywhere from a few days to a few weeks on campus.

There are several philosophical approaches to the Master's degree. Some schools (or departments within schools) regard it as a sort of advanced Bachelor's, requiring only the completion of one to two years of advanced-level studies and courses. Other schools or departments see it as a junior Doctorate, requiring a moderate amount of creative, original research, culminating in the writing of a thesis, or original research paper. Some programs give the student the option of choosing either approach: they may choose either to take, for example, 10 courses and write a thesis, or 13 courses with no thesis, to earn the Master's degree.

And in a few world-famous schools, including Oxford and Cambridge, the Master's degree is an almost meaningless award, given automatically to all holders of their Bachelor's degree if they have managed, as the saying goes, to stay out of jail for four years, and are able to afford the small fee. (Most American schools had a similar practice at one time, but Harvard abolished it more than a century ago, and the rest followed suit soon after.)

Master's degree titles tend to follow closely those of Bachelor's degrees. The M.A. (Master of Arts) and M.S. (Master of Science) are by far the most common, along with the standby of American business, the M.B.A. (Master of Busiiness Administration). Other common Master's degrees include the M.Ed. (education), M.Eng. (engineering), M.L.S. (library science), and M.J. (either journalism or jurisprudence).

4. The Doctorate

The term "Doctor" has been a title of respect for a learned person since Biblical times. Moses, in Deuteronomy 31:28 (Douay Version), says, "Gather unto me all the ancients of your tribes and your doctors, and I will speak these words in their hearing."

But it was not until about 800 years ago that the first academic title was used, when outstanding scholars at the University of Bologna and the University of Paris were called either "Doctor" or "Professor" in the mid-12th century.

The first use of the title in America came in the late 17th century, under, as tradition has it, rather amusing circumstances. There had long been a tradition (and, to a large extent, there still is) that "it takes a Doctor to make a Doctor." In other words, only a person with a Doctorate can confer a Doctorate on someone else.

But in all of America, no one had a Doctorate, least of all Harvard's president, Increase Mather who, as a Dissenter, was ineligible for a Doctorate from any English university, all of which were controlled by the Church.

Still, Harvard was eager to get into the Doctorate business, so their entire faculty (that is to say, a Mr. Leverett and a Mr. Brattle) got together and unanimously agreed to award an honorary Doctorate to Mr. Mather, whereupon Dr. Mather was able to confer Doctorates upon his faculty and, subsequently, they were able to doctor their students.

This, in essence, was the start of graduate education in America, and there are those who say things have gone downhill ever since!

America's second doctorate, incidentally, was also awarded under rather odd circumstances. It was the case that a British physician named Daniel Turner was eager to get into the Royal Society of Physicians and Surgeons, for which an M.D. was required. In England, then as now, most doctors have a *Bachelor* of Medicine; the *Doctor* of Medicine is an advanced degree. English universities would not give Turner a Doctorate because he did not belong to the Church. Scottish universities turned him down because he had published some unkind remarks about the quality of Scottish education. And of course no European university would give a degree to an Englishman. So Mr. Turner made a deal with Yale University.

Yale agreed to award Turner the Doctorate in absentia (he never set foot in America), and he, in turn, gave Yale a gift of 50 valuable medical books. Wags at the time remarked that the M.D. he got must stand for the Latin *multum donavit*, or, "he gave a lot."

Nowadays the academic title of "Doctor" (as distinguished from the professional and honorary titles, to be discussed shortly) has come to be awarded for completion of an advanced course of study, culminating in a piece of original research in one's field, known as the Doctoral thesis, or dissertation.

While traditional Doctorates used to require at least two years of on-campus study after the Master's degree, followed by the necessary research for the writing of the dissertation, the trend lately has been to require little more than the dissertation. More and more schools are letting people without a Master's into their Doctoral programs, and awarding the Master's on completion of the course work (and any qualifying exams).

The total elapsed time can be anywhere from three years on up. Indeed, the trend in the 1980sand early 90s has been for Doctorates to take longer and longer. In his splendid book *Winning the Ph.D. Game,* Richard Moore offers evidence that a typical Ph.D. now takes 6 or 7 years, with a range from 3 to 10 (not all of it necessarily spent in residence on campus, however).

Many non-traditional Doctoral programs waive the necessity for on-campus study, on the assumption that the mature candidate already knows a great deal about his or her field. Such programs require little or even no coursework, but are focused on the writing of the dissertation, to demonstrate creativity.

Some non-traditional doctoral programs permit the use of work already done (books written, symphonies composed, business plans created, etc.) as partial (or, in a few cases, full) satisfaction of the dissertation requirement. But many schools insist on all, or almost all, new work.

The most frequently awarded (and, many people feel, the most prestigious) Doctorate is the Doctor of Philosophy (known as the Ph.D. in North America, and the D.Phil. in many other countries). The Doctor of Philosophy need have nothing to do with the study of philosophy. It is awarded for studies in dozens of fields, ranging from chemistry to communication, from agriculture to aviation management.

Until well into the 20th century, the Ph.D. was also given as an honorary degree. But in the late 1930s, Gonzaga University in Spokane, Washington, spoiled the whole thing by handing out an honorary Ph.D. to one Harry Lillis "Bing" Crosby, to thank him for donating some equipment to the football team. Dr. Crosby made great sport about being a Doctor on his popular radio program that week. The academic world rose in distressed anger and that, effectively, was the end of the honorary Ph.D.

More than 500 other Doctorate titles have been identified in the English language alone. After the Ph.D., the most common include the Ed.D. (education), D.B.A. (business administration), D.P.A. (public administration), D.A. (art or administration), Eng.D. (engineering), Psy.D. (psychology), D.Sc. (science), and D.Hum. (humanities). The latter two often, but not always, are honorary degrees in the U.S. and earned degrees elsewhere.

A Bachelor's degree is almost always required for admission to a Doctoral program, and many traditional schools require a Master's as well. However more and more Doctoral programs are admitting otherwise qualified applicants without a Master's degree. Most non-traditional programs will accept equivalent career experience in lieu of a Master's, and, in rare instances, in lieu of a Bachelor's as well.

In the late 1950s, someone submitted a resumé of Eleanor Roosevelt as part of an application to various doctoral programs, changing the name and disguising some of her more obvious remarkable achievements. Mrs. Roosevelt had never attended college. All 12 schools turned her down, most suggesting that she reapply after completing a Bachelor's and a Master's, presumably six to eight years later.

In Europe, but very rarely in America, a so-called "higher Doctorate" (typically the D.Litt. or Doctor of Letters) is awarded solely on the basis of one's life work, with no further studies required. The great majority of those receiving a D.Litt. already have another Doctorate, but this is not essential. In most quarters, the D.Litt. is considered to be an earned, not an honorary degree, but there are those who disagree.

Finally, it should be mentioned that several American schools, concerned with what one called the "Doctoral glut," are reported to be seriously considering instituting a new degree, *higher* than the Doctorate, presumably requiring more years of study and a more extensive dissertation. The name "Chancellorate" has been bandied about. Indeed, the prestigious *Chronicle of Higher Education* devoted a major article to this possibility in early 1990. It may well be that holders of a Chancellorate (Ph.C.?) would not appreciably affect the job market, since most of them will be drawing their Old Age Pension by the time they complete this degree.

5. Professional Degrees

Professional degrees are earned by people who intend to enter what are often called "the professions"—medicine, dentistry, law, the ministry, and so forth. In the United States, these degrees are almost always earned *after* completing a Bachelor's degree, and almost always carry the title of "Doctor" (e.g., Doctor of Medicine,

Doctor of Divinity).

In many other countries, it is common to enter professional school directly from high school, in which case the first degree earned is a Bachelor's. (For instance, there is the British Bachelor of Medicine, whose holders are invariably called "Doctor," unless they have earned the advanced degree of "Doctor of Medicine," in which case they insist on being called "Mister." No one ever said the British were easy to understand.)

One exception in the United States is the D.C. (Doctor of Chiropractic), a program that students used to be able to enter right from high school, but which now requires two years of college, but no Bachelor's degree. This may be one reason so many medical doctors look down their noses at chiropractors.

Another exception used to be the law degree which, until the mid-1960s, was an LL.B., or Bachelor of Laws. Many lawyers objected to working three or four years beyond their Bachelor's degree simply to end up with yet another Bachelor's degree, while optometrists, podiatrists, and others were becoming doctors in the same length of time.

And so now it is the case that virtually every American law school awards a Doctorate as the first law degree. This degree is usually the J.D., which stands either for Doctor of Jurisprudence, or Juris Doctor.

Almost all law schools offered their graduates with Bachelor of Law degrees the option of turning in their old LL.B. diplomas and, in effect, being retroactively Doctored with a J.D. A fair number of lawyers accepted this unprecedented offer, although few actually call themselves "Doctor."

The LL.D., known both as Doctor of Law and Doctor of Laws, is now used almost exclusively as an honorary title in the U.S., but is an earned advanced law degree elsewhere in the world.

The traditional law degree requires three years of study beyond the Bachelor's degree. Some non-traditional approaches will be discussed in chapter 19).

The only widely-accepted medical degree in America is the M.D. (Doctor of Medicine), which requires four years of study beyond the Bachelor's degree, although there are some shorter approaches, and some alternative ones, which will be discussed in chapter 20.

There are other medical or health specialties that have their own respective professional Doctorates. These include, for instance, D.O. (osteopathy), D.P. (podiatry), and O.D. (optometry).

There are no accelerated approaches to the dental degree, and I'm not sure I'd want to go to any dentist who *had* taken shortcuts. The traditional dental degree for many years has been the D.D.S. (Doctor of Dental Surgery), although there has been a strong recent trend toward the D.M.D. (Doctor of Medical Dentistry). Either program requires four years of study beyond the Bachelor's degree.

More than 100 different professional degree titles have been identified in the area of religion. None can be said to be the standard one. There are the S.T.D. (sacred theology), D.Min. (ministry), Th.D. (theology), D.D. (divinity), D.Rel. (religion), D.R.E. (religious education), D.S.R. (science of religion), and so forth, as well as the Ph.D. in religion.

The Canadian mathematician and humorist Stephen Leacock writes that shortly after he received his Ph.D., he was on board a cruise ship. When a lovely young lady fainted, the call went out, "Is there a doctor on board?" Leacock says he rushed to the Captains's cabin, but he was too late. Two D.D.'s and an S.T.D. had gotten there before him.

There are quite a few other degrees that are regarded as honest professional titles by those who hold them, and are regarded with vigorously-raised eyebrows by many others. These include, for example, the N.D. (either naturopathy, naprapathy, or napropathy), D.Hyp. (hypnotism), H.M.D. or M.D.(H.) (homeopathic medicine), D.M.S. (military science), Met.D. (metaphysics), Graph.D. (graphoanalysis) and so forth.

6. Honorary Degrees

The honorary degree is indeed the stepchild of the academic world, and a most curious one at that. In fact, it has no more relationship or connection with academia than the former basketball ace, "Doctor J," has with the world of medicine. It is, purely and simply, a title that some institutions (and some scoundrels) have chosen to bestow, from time to time, and for a wide variety of reasons, upon certain people. These reasons often have to do with the donation of money, or with attracting celebrities to a commencement ceremony.

The honorary Doctorate has no academic standing whatsoever, and yet, because it carries with it the same title, "Doctor," that is used for the earned degree, it has become an extremely desirable commodity for those who covet titles and the prestige they bring. For respectable universities to award the title of "Doctor" via an honorary Doctorate is as peculiar as if the Army were to award civilians the honorary title of "General"—a title the civilians could then use in their everyday life.

More than 1,000 traditional colleges and universities award the honorary Doctorate (anywhere from 1 to 50 per year, each), and a great many Bible schools, spurious schools, and degree mills hand them out with wild abandon to almost anyone willing to pay the price. The subject will be discussed in detail in chapter 23.

TRANSCRIPTS

A transcript is, quite simply, the official record of all the work one has done at a given university. While the diploma is the piece of paper (or parchment) that shows that a given degree has been earned, the transcript is the detailed description of all the work done to earn that degree.

Typically, a transcript will be a typewritten (or, more common nowadays, a computer-printed) sheet of paper listing in columns all the courses taken, when taken, and the grade received. The overall G.P.A. (grade point average) is calculated as of the end of each semester or quarter.

Nearly all non-traditional schools and programs issue transcripts as well. Sometimes they try to make the transcripts look as traditional as possible, listing, for instance, aviation experience as "Aviation 100, 4 units;" "Aviation 101, 3 units;" etc. Other programs offer a *narrative transcript*, in which the procedures used by the school in evaluating the experience are described.

The original copy of a transcript is always kept by the university. Official copies, bearing the raised seal of the university, can be made for the student, other schools, or employers, at the student's request.

Unfortunately, there is a great deal of traffic in forged transcripts. Sometimes students will change a few grades to improve the G.P.A., or add entire classes. Of course such changes would normally be on the copy only. For this reason, most schools and many employers will only accept transcripts that are sent directly from the office of the registrar of the university. But half a dozen scandals in the late 1980s involving tampering with a university's computer, either by hackers having fun or by dishonest employees selling their service, raise questions about the validity of *any* university-produced document.

4. Is a Degree Worth the Effort?

"I'm 38 years old, and thinking about pursuing a Bachelor's degree, but I'm not sure I should, because if I do, I'll be 42 years old when I'm done."
"And how old will you be in four years if you don't do it?"
—Dear Abby

The simple answer to the question in the chapter title is, I would say, this: *Yes* for non-traditional degrees; very likely *No* for traditional degrees.

Let me first elaborate on why I think the non-traditional degree is worth the effort, and then offer arguments on why the old-fashioned way may not be worth it.

WHY THE NON-TRADITIONAL DEGREE MAKES SENSE

Much depends on the degree itself, and on the reasons for wanting it. If, for instance, a Bachelor's degree is required for a job, a promotion, or a salary increase, then the accredited degree of the University of the State of New York, earned 100% by correspondence courses, is exactly as good as any Bachelor's degree earned by sitting in classrooms for four or five or six years at a state university, and the cost would be less than 5% as much (not to mention that one can continue earning a living while pursuing the non-traditional degree).

As another example, a non-resident Doctorate, earned by a combination of life experience credit and new work, from one of the better unaccredited, state-licensed universities may be of minimal value in getting a faculty position at Harvard. But such degrees have proved useful in many cases for advancement in business, government, and industry, not to mention doing wonders for self-image and in gaining the respect of others.

Finally, a Doctorate purchased for a hundred bucks from a no-questions-asked degree mill may ultimately bring shame, public embarrassment, loss of job, and even a fine and imprisonment.

This covers the full range of possible outcomes. Many non-traditional degrees are good for most people in most situations. But there can be major exceptions, which is why it pays to check out the school in advance (this book is a good place to start) and to make as sure as you can that the degree you seek will satisfy any gatekeepers who may appear on your path.

A word of warning. Please do not be misled by the results of a study on the acceptance of non-traditional degrees, sponsored by the National Institute of Education in the late 1970s. This study, by Sosdian and Sharp, is misquoted in the literature of at least 12 non-traditional universities, in a most misleading effort to convince prospective students that their degrees will be accepted in the academic, professional, or business world.

Sosdian and Sharp did determine that there was indeed a high level of acceptance—*but their research was almost entirely on the acceptance level of accredited Bachelor's degrees.* It is totally misleading to imply, as many have done, that results would be comparable for unaccredited degrees, much less Master's and Doctorates. It just isn't so, and those dozen or more schools should be ashamed of themselves.

Now, let's look at the six main reasons why people choose to pursue non-traditional degrees, and the kinds of degrees that may be most appropriate.

1. Job or salary advancement in business. Many job descriptions in business and industry specify that a certain degree is required, or that additional salary will be paid, if a certain degree is held. In many of these situations, a good, unaccredited degree will suffice.

It is crucial to find out in advance, whenever possible, if a given degree will be accepted. While many businesses, large and small, will recognize good unaccredited degrees, many will not. Tragically, I have heard from dozens of people who spent many thousands of dollars on degree programs, only to find that the degree they earned was not acceptable to their employer or potential employer.

2. Job or salary advancement in education. The academic world has been more reluctant to accept unaccredited degrees than has the world of business or government. Even some excellent accredited, non-traditional degrees have occasionally caused problems. However, the situation remains extremely variable. It is almost impossible to draw general rules or conclusions. Many universities refuse to consider hiring a faculty member with an unaccredited degree, or to admit people with such degrees into their graduate programs. Others welcome them. And the most enlightened schools consider each case on its own merits.

Once I surveyed a group of school board presidents, to determine their boards' policies on paying salary increments to district teachers who completed Master's or Doctorates. The results were pretty evenly divided into four categories. About one-fourth said the degrees had to be accredited. Another quarter said they could be unaccredited. Twenty-five percent said they judge each case individually. And the remainder either didn't understand the difference between accredited and unaccredited degrees, or said that no one had ever asked the question so there was no policy.

Once again, the watchword is to check in advance before spending any money with any school.

3. Job or salary advancement in the professions. When a profession must be licensed by the state or a trade organization, that body often has certain degree requirements. Depending on the state, this may apply to psychologists, marriage counselors, engineers, accountants, real estate brokers, social workers, hypnotists, masseurs, and others. There is absolutely no pattern here in the acceptability of non-traditional degrees, other than a clear trend in favor of their increased acceptance.

Nonetheless, in one state, a psychologist must have a traditionally accredited Doctorate while a civil engineer with sufficient career experience may have an unaccredited degree or no degree at all. In another state, it may be just the opposite. Many regulations are exceedingly unclear on this subject, so a judgment is made in each individual case. Once again, it is crucial to determine in advance if a given degree will meet a given need.

4. Admission to traditional graduate schools. The trend is strongly in the direction of increased acceptance of alternative degrees, including the better unaccredited degrees, for admission to Master's and Doctoral programs at traditional universities. For example, one highly regarded, unaccredited program reported that its students have transferred to more than 30 traditional universities, getting credit for their work at the unaccredited school. Another unaccredited university has letters from Harvard, Yale, and Princeton, among others, indicating a willingness to consider their students for admission to graduate school.

5. Self-satisfaction. This is a perfectly good reason for wanting a degree, and no one should ever feel embarrassed for so wanting. Many of my counseling clients seek a degree (generally a Doctorate) for self-satisfaction, to gain respect from others, to feel more comfortable with colleagues, or to "validate" a long and worthwhile career. Such people are generally well satisfied with a degree from one of the better, more respectable unaccredited schools. One of the main criteria to consider here is avoidance of potential embarrassment. More than one holder of a degree from a legitimate, but not especially good, non-traditional school has suffered extreme discomfort or embarrassment when newspaper articles or television stories on the school made big local waves.

One of my favorite consulting clients wrote to me that his doctoral dissertation had been rejected by Columbia University in 1910, and now he'd like to finish the degree. I wrote back offering suggestions, and mentioned what I thought was an amusing typographical error in his letter; he said 1910. No, he wrote back, that's correct. He was now 96 years old, and these events had happened seventy years earlier. He was accepted by a good non-traditional external program, and completed his Ph.D. shortly before his 100th birthday.

6. Fooling people. An alarming number of people want fake degrees for all manner of devious purposes. After CBS broadcast its degree mill report on "60 Minutes," they received a huge number of telephone calls from people simply wanting to know the addresses and phone numbers of the fake schools they had just seen exposed!

Almost every week I hear from people who would like "a Doctorate from Harvard University, please, with no work required, and can it be back-dated to 1974, and I need it by next Tuesday." The best I can do is warn these people that they are endangering their reputations (and possibly their freedom) by considering such a course. Then I usually suggest that if they must have a degree by return mail, they consider a degree from a far-less-dangerous, second-rate Bible college. Nothing to be especially proud of, but less hazardous to one's health.

WHY THE TRADITIONAL DEGREE MAKES LESS SENSE THAN THE NON-TRADITIONAL

People attend traditional colleges for a great many different reasons, as Caroline Bird writes in her fascinating book, *The Case Against College* :

> A great majority of our nine million post-secondary students who are 'in college' are there because it has become the thing to do, or because college is a pleasant place to be . . . because it's the only way they can get parents or taxpayers to support them without working at a job they don't like; because Mother wanted them to go; or for some reasons utterly irrelevant to the course of studies for which the college is supposedly organized.

Basically, I think, there are two main reasons people go to college: either to get an education or to get a degree. The two can be quite independent. There are those who only care about the training; there are those who only want the degree; and there are those who want or need both.

Sadly, there is a strong trend in America toward what David Hapgood calls *Diplomaism* in his book of that title. He writes:

> We are well on our way to repealing the American dream of individual accomplishment and replacing it with a system in which the diploma is the measure of a man, a diploma which bears no relation to performance. The career market is closing its doors to those without degrees . . . . Diplomaism zones people into a set of categories that tends to eliminate the variety and surprise of human experience. In a system run by diplomas, all avenues to personal advancement are blocked except one: the school that gives the diploma . . . . when we leave the institution, like carcasses coming off a packing plant's assembly line, an anonymous hand affixes an indelible stamp . . . which thereafter determines what we can do, and how we shall be rewarded. And that stamp, unlike the imprint on a side of beef, reflects neither our personal value to the society, nor the needs of the economic system.

There are, in fact, three major problem areas with traditional schools and traditional degree programs:

1. There may be little connection between degrees earned traditionally and on-the-job performance.
2. There is much evidence that vast numbers of students are spending huge amounts of time being trained for jobs that simply do not exist.
3. It may well be that the cash investment in a traditional college education is an extremely poor investment indeed.

Let us consider each of these three problem areas.

Traditional College Training Versus On-The-Job Performance

Many studies have found little or no relationship between these two factors, and some have even found a negative relationship. One extensive study, by Ivar Berg of Columbia University, published under the delightful title, *Education and Jobs: The Great Training Robbery*, looked at various jobs in which people with degrees and people without were doing identical work. In many situations, there was no difference in performance by the degreed and non-degreed people, and in a few jobs (including air traffic controllers and pants makers), the people without degrees were doing a better job!

Sadly, Berg also found that many bosses either ignored or refused to believe the evidence that had been collected in their own offices and factories. For instance, in one big chemical firm where the laboratory workers without degrees were out-performing those with degrees, the management steadfastly maintained its policy of promoting only those employees with degrees.

Hapgood believes that personnel practices at such firms are not likely to be changed in the forseeable future, because "employers made it clear they were demanding diplomas for reasons that had little to do with job performance." The real reasons, he thinks, had to do with conformity to the dominant culture and with the "ability" to stay in school for four or more years. "It proves that he was docile enough (or good or patient or stupid enough; choose your own adjective) to stay out of trouble for 13 or 17 or 20 years in a series of institutions that demand a high degree of unthinking conformity."

I was given similar responses when I surveyed the personnel managers of major airlines. Almost all require an accredited Bachelor's degree, but they don't care whether the degree is in aviation or Chinese history. The important thing, they say, is the discipline of being able to complete a degree program. You may have been flying for 10 years for the navy or the air force. But that doesn't count. And if the hypocrisy needed to be underlined, in times when pilot trainees are in short supply, the degree requirement mysteriously disappears.

Whatever the reasons, the system is a confused and disarrayed one, with the one strongly positive note being the increasing acceptance of non-traditional degrees, whose holders often have far more practical knowledge and experience through on-the-job training than those who learned about the subject in the college classroom.

There are ever-growing numbers of employers who will say, for instance, that you learn more about practical journalism in your first two weeks working on a daily newspaper than in four years of journalism school. (The same goes for law, advertising, and dozens of other fields.) And the person who has both the experience and the non-traditional degree based, at least in part, on that experience may be in the best situation of all.

It used to be the case that many employers denied jobs to people without degrees, even if the degree had nothing to do with the ability to perform the job. But following a key decision by the Supreme Court (*Griggs vs. Duke Power Company, 1971*), employers must now prove that a degree is required to do a certain job, or they cannot discriminate against those without them. This is equally true for high school diplomas, Doctorates, and everything in between.

Is a Traditional College Degree Useful in Today's Marketplace?

Once I worked as an assistant to the psychologist in a large state prison. (No, I was a graduate student, not an inmate!) The prison was very proud of its vocational training program. It operated a large cotton mill, where the inmates learned how to run the equipment and, in fact, made their own prison uniforms. But when they got out of prison, they learned that not only was the equipment they had learned to operate hopelessly out-of-date, but the nearest large cotton mill was 2,000 miles away! No wonder many of them returned to a life of crime.

Much the same sort of thing goes on in traditional colleges and universities. As an example, through the 1960s, hundreds of thousands of students were told about the great teacher shortages that were coming, so they graduated with degrees in education. But, as Alexander Mood wrote in a report for the Carnegie Commission:

> It has been evident for some time to professors of education that they were training far more teachers than would ever find jobs teaching school, but few of them bothered to mention that fact to their students. That is understandable, of course, since their incomes depend on having students.

Much the same thing happened with the study of space science and astrophysics in the 1970s, and again with computer science in the 1980s and into the 90s.

And so we find thousands of people with Doctorates teaching high school; people with Master's degrees teaching first grade; and an awful lot of people with Bachelor's degrees in education waiting on tables and doing office work.

The business world is not exempt. A survey by the *Wall Street Journal* found copious numbers of highly disillusioned M.B.A. students and recent graduates. "I wouldn't have come here and spent all that money if I had known it would be this tight," said one jobless M.B.A. "Graduate school was a waste of time," said another, after 10 months of fruitless searching for a business job. But cheer up. The president of the Association of MBA Executives, Inc., says things will be much better later in the 1990s. Any bets?

These problems are by no means confined to education and business. In virtually any field you look at, from psychology to civil engineering, you find lots of well-trained and unemployed practitioners. In one recent year, for instance, there were over 100,000 graduates in the field of communications, and about 14,000 new jobs in the communications industries. Five thousand anthropology graduates are finding about 400 job openings in their field. And so it goes. Or doesn't go.

According to Bird, "Law schools are already graduating twice as many new lawyers every year as the Department of Labor thinks will be needed . . . ." Mood says that

> in the past, the investment in higher education did at least pay off for most students; that is, they did get access to higher-status jobs; now for the first time in history, a college degree is being judged by many parents and students as not worth the price. They see too many of last year's graduates unable to find work, or taking jobs ordinarily regarded as suitable for high school graduates. . . . Moreover, this is not a temporary phenomenon.

The Bureau of Labor Statistics says that about 25% of college graduates entering the labor market are getting jobs previously held by people without degrees. That doesn't mean the degrees are needed to perform those jobs, of course, but only that there are millions of job-seekers with degrees who cannot find jobs requiring their degrees.

So the outlook for the traditional degree is rather bleak. People will continue to pursue them for the wrong reasons, and industry will continue to require them for the wrong reasons. And enlightened people of all ages will, more and more, come to realize that a non-traditional degree can do just about anything a traditional one can—with a much smaller expenditure of time, effort, and money.

Is Pursuing a Traditional Degree Worth the Cost?

Just what is the cost? Anything I write today will be out of date tomorrow, because traditional college costs are escalating so fast. In 1990, the average cost of attending a private college for four years in the United States was in excess of $60,000, including tuition, room and board, books, etc. At public colleges, the average cost is "only" around $35,000 to $40,000.

Based on a highly conservative rate of academic inflation of 6% (most schools do try to hold the line, but there are limits to how much they can do), here is how things look in years to come with regard to college costs:

YEAR	4 YRS. PRIVATE COLLEGE	4 YRS.PUBLIC COLLEGE
1993	72,000	41,000
1998	87,000	52,851
2003	116,000	66,050

It seems more than likely that a child born in 1990, who will enter college in 2008, can expect to pay well over $100,000 for a traditional college education!

The time has come when many people are simply not able to afford to pursue a traditional degree. And yet the value of the degree, in terms of higher salary, increased likelihood of getting better jobs, and personal satisfaction, is well demonstrated. For a while, the gap seemed to be narrowing. In the early 1970s, the average Bachelor's degree-holder was earning about 53% more than the average high school graduate. Within a decade, this was down to a 35% advantage. But the Reagan and Bush years brought about major changes in the other direction. The data available in 1990 show that the average Bachelor's degree-holder is earning a whopping 76% more than an average high school graduate.

Here are average lifetime earnings based on levels of education. The amount shown is total lifetime earnings, from the year of entering the job market (18 for high school graduates, 22 for Bachelor's degree-holders, etc.) until age 65:

Attended high school, did not graduate:	$407,000
High school graduate, did not go to college:	589,000
Attended college for 1 to 3 years:	645,000
Bachelor's degree:	950,000
Master's degree:	1,126,000
Doctorate:	1,449,000
Professional degree:	1,625,820

Here are some enlightening differences in earnings between sexes and races. These figures are all for people with Master's degrees, where the most data were available:

	PER YEAR	LIFETIME
All persons with Master's	$27,456	$1,125,696
Men with Master's	34,116	1,398,756
Women with Master's	19,740	809,340
Whites with Master's	27,444	1,125,204
Blacks with Master's	23,592	967,272

(Who did I hear saying that the Equal Rights Amendment and civil rights legislation is unnecessary?)

From these figures, it may look, to an 18-year-old on the brink of either college or a job, as if taking four years off to earn a Bachelor's degree is going to be worth more than $360,000 in the long run. However, Caroline Bird thinks that if the only reason people go to college is to make more money, then higher education is a truly dumb financial investment.

She argues this way (I have adapted her 1976 figures to the reality of the higher interest rates of the early 1990s): The average Princeton graduate will have spent about $70,000 to get a degree, including tuition, room and board, books, travel, etc. If that sum of money were put, instead, into certificates of deposit earning 10% interest, by the age of 65, never having done a day's work, that person would have over $10 million dollars! That, needless to say, is about 50 times more than the "mere" $360,000 additional that the average Bachelor's degree-holder makes in a lifetime.

Of course, most people wouldn't have the $70,000 to invest at age 18. But Bird argues that if one enters the job market at 18, the earnings over the next four years, plus, presumably, some advance from parents on what they would otherwise have spent on college tuition, wisely invested, would produce a similar result.

A study by Drs. J. H. Hollomon of the Massachusetts Institute of Technology and Richard Freeman of Harvard University concludes that "in the brief span of about five years, the college job market has gone from a major boom to a major bust. Large numbers of young people, for the first time, are likely to obtain less schooling and potentially lower occupational status than their parents."

All well and good, I suppose. But none of these people takes non-traditional education and degrees into account. Bird and others have produced some powerful reasons not to pursue a *traditional* degree. But it is now possible, and will become increasingly easier, to earn degrees at a low cost while remaining fully employed, thereby having the best of both worlds.

Whether pursuing a degree for the sake of the learning or the sake of the diploma, or both, the alternative student seems far more likely

- to be motivated to complete his or her program;
- to select courses and programs that are appropriate and relevant to his or her needs;
- to avoid cluttering up campuses and dormitories (which, in the words of former Columbia University president William McGill, are in danger of becoming "storage houses for bored young people");
- to save years over the time of traditional programs (or, alternatively, to pursue educational objectives without giving up job or family), and, perhaps most importantly for most people, to save a tremendous amount of time and money, compared with the demands and costs of a traditional degree program.

Many non-traditional programs, in fact, come very close to John Holt's ideal educational system, which he describes by analogy with a public library: you go whenever you want something it has to offer; no one checks your credentials at the door; you leave when you have gotten what you wanted; and it is you, not the librarian, who decides if it has been a worthwhile experience.

WHERE, THEN, ARE THINGS GOING?

One message of Charles Reich's fascinating book, *The Greening of America*, is that things are happening now that have never happened before; that for the first time, the standards and lessons of the past may have no relevance for the future.

Things are indeed changing almost amazingly fast in higher education. The direction in which they are changing is away from traditional education and degrees toward alternative higher education and non-traditional degrees.

It is always difficult—and challenging—to live in a time of great change. On one hand, we have universities that have refused (or were unable, by law) to invite people like Eleanor Roosevelt, Buckminster Fuller, Andrew Wyeth, or Eric Hoffer to lecture, because they never earned a college degree. And on the other hand, we have people earning higher degrees entirely by correspondence, entering prestigious Doctoral programs without even a high school diploma, and earning law degrees without ever seeing the inside of a law school.

Thirty years ago, if you wanted to earn a degree without sitting in classrooms for three or four years, and wanted to remain in North America, you had exactly two legal alternatives: the University of London and the University of South Africa, both of which offered (and still offer) non-resident programs, from the Bachelor's level through the Doctorate and professional degrees.

At the same time, predictably, many traditional universities and colleges are really hurting financially, due to decreased enrollments and rising costs. Unprecedented numbers of traditional schools are simply going out of business, and many others are almost frantically implementing non-traditional programs as a last resort to stay afloat financially. Things can only grow worse for traditional schools, as the declining birth rate of the late 1960s and 1970s starts showing up at college age level during the late 1980s and early 1990s.

Alternative education and the non-traditional degree seem, indeed, to be the wave of the educational future.

5. Using Titles

Question: What do you call the person who finishes last in his or her medical school class?
Answer: Doctor.

There is a question that arises regularly in the degree consulting practice I established: "If I earn a degree, especially an alternative or non-traditional degree, in what way am I entitled to use the degree, and the title that comes with it (in the case of Doctorates), in my life and career?"

There is no simple answer to this question, since rules and regulations vary from state to state, and from profession to profession. But the basic philosophy of whatever laws there are regulating degrees is essentially the same: *You can probably do almost anything you want in the way of titles, as long as you do not do it with the intent of deceiving anyone.*

No one ever had Colonel Sanders arrested for pretending to be a military officer, nor is Doc Severinsen in danger of prosecution for impersonating a physician. However, when a man gets a job as a meteorologist for a big-city television station, using the title of "Doctor," and that is a degree he never earned, then there is a major problem, because it can be reasonably assumed that the title helped him get the job—even if he was performing his duties satisfactorily without benefit of doctoral training. (The meteorologist lost his job after the exposure.)

In general, as long as the degree comes from an unquestionably legal and legitimate school, there is usually no problem in using that degree in public life, as long as all local and licensing requirements are met.

In some states, a "quickie" Doctorate from a one-room Bible School is sufficient to set up practice as a marriage counselor and psychotherapist. In other states, with stiffer licensing requirements, this same behavior could result in major legal problems.

The use of degree titles varies considerably from profession to profession, and from nation to nation. Most people in the United States do not append a Bachelor's degree notation to their letterhead or signature, while in most of the rest of the world, it is quite common to see, for instance, "David Pozerycki, B.A." The name or abbreviation of the school is often appended, as well: "Felipe Lujan, B.A. (Oxon)" or "B.A. (Cantab)," indicating that the degree is from Oxford or Cambridge.

Master's degrees are more commonly used in print in the United States, especially the M.B.A. (e.g., "Joseph Judd, M.B.A.").

Holders of a Doctorate almost always use it in their public or professional lives—with the curious exception of politicians. (Most prominent politicians with earned Doctorates, from Woodrow Wilson to George McGovern, seem to have gone to great lengths to avoid public disclosure of the degree. Perhaps there is merit to columnist Herb Caen's belief that people will never vote for anyone they think is more intelligent than they are!)

There are, and probably always will be, educational conservatives who decry the use of non-traditional (and particularly unaccredited non-traditional) titles. A typical situation has occurred in the field of electrical engineering, where a gentleman in New York formed the "Committee of Concerned E.E.'s" for the purpose of carrying on a vigorous campaign against the right of electrical engineers with unaccredited Doctorates to use the title of "Doctor." The journals in this field often carry articles and letters from people on various sides of this issue.

Despite the complaints of Thomas Carlyle regarding the "peculiar ambition of Americans to hobble down to posterity on crutches of capital letters," Americans are far less likely than Europeans and Asians to use all the letters at their command. Whereas a typical Englishman will list all his degrees, and perhaps a few fellowships besides (e.g., "Lowell James Hicks, B.A., M.A., Ph.D., F.R.S., L.C.P."), most Americans would only use their highest degree (e.g., "John Walsh, Ph.D."), unless they have more than one Doctorate, in which case both would be listed (e.g., "Pauline Butler, M.D., Ph.D.").

Not everyone agrees with this. The former president of a California religious school, for instance, regularly used all nine of his claimed Doctorates, with his civil service rank (G.S.9) thrown in between Doctorates number four and five, for good measure. And then there was the chap who wrote to me from Massachusetts, using these letters after his name: L.R.A., M.N.G.S., B.S.A. When I asked, he explained that the letters stood for Licensed Real Estate Agent, Member of the National Geographic Society, and Boy Scouts of America.

Holders of honorary Doctorates are treading on far more dangerous ground when they use their degrees in public, especially if such degrees were purchased "over the counter," no matter how legally. Still, public figures from Dr. Billy Graham to Dr. Edward Land, founder of Polaroid, regularly use the title "Doctor" based on honorary degrees from major universities.

Nonetheless, if an insurance agent makes a sale, if a clergyman makes a convert, or if a teacher makes a salary increase that can be attributed, even in part, to the prestige of being called "Doctor," and if that Doctorate is unearned, then the claim can always be made that that person is acting, at least in part, on false pretenses.

There is also the matter of whether a Doctorate-holder chooses to call herself Carla Yamada, Ph.D. or Dr. Carla Yamada. Although either form would appear to be acceptable in many circumstances, an audiologist in New York suffered legal repercussions for calling himself Dr. So-and-so rather than So-and-so, Ph.D. The prosecution's claim was that the use of the word "Doctor" in a near-medical field such as fitting hearing aids was done to deceive clients into thinking he was a medical doctor.

Another category of title abusers are those people who use degrees they never earned. What surprises me is how many of them there are. When the head of a major motion picture studio got into legal troubles a few years back, a sidelight of the case was that the degree he said he had from Yale University turned out to be non-existent. At the same time, Yale revealed that they keep files on all cases of publicly-claimed Yale degrees that are lies, and that to date they had logged more than 7,000 such claims!

It seems reasonable to hypothesize that these 7,000 are just the tip of the iceberg. Untold thousands of others are going about free, only because so few people ever bother to check up on other people's degrees. Most exposures happen in connection with other events, often when something good happens to a person. For instance, there is the case of the Arizona "Teacher of the Year" for 1987 who, after he entered the public eye, was discovered to have falsified his claim to a Doctorate. Two of the 1988 presidential hopefuls, Biden and Robertson, got a lot of press coverage when it turned out their academic credentials were not as they had represented. And the chairman of the board of a major university in the South resigned when it became known his Doctorate was from a "school" whose founder was in federal prison for selling degrees.

The young woman whose 1981 Pulitzer Prize was taken away when it turned out she had falsified her story on a young drug addict also turned out to have two fake degrees listed on her *Washington Post* job application. During the 1984 elections, candidates in three states were discovered to be claiming degrees they did not earn. After the ensuing publicity, all lost!

People rarely check up on other people's degrees. Do you know, for instance, where your own doctor, lawyer, and accountant earned their degrees? Have you checked with the schools just to be sure? A diploma on the wall is not sufficient evidence. I know of three different places that have sold fake diplomas from any school, printed to order for a modest sum. I have a fake Harvard medical degree hanging on my wall, alongside my real Ph.D. It cost $50 from a mail order distributor. What if your family doctor knows the same place? (No, I am not going to give out their names and addresses; they do enough damage in the world as it is.)

This topic moves very rapidly from the abstract to the concrete when something happens nearby. It was clearly brought home to me some years ago when a locally prominent "certified public accountant," living just down the road from us, hurriedly packed his shingle and left town. One of his clients had decided to check, and found out that he simply did not have the credentials he said he had.

So then, common sense should be sufficient to make your decision on how to use a degree in almost any situation that may arise. Where there is any doubt at all about using a given degree or title, it may be wise to seek legal advice, or at the very least to check with the relevant state agencies—generally the state education department (see chapter 6), or the appropriate licensing agencies.

And, in general, it isn't a bad idea to worry just a little about other people's degrees and titles. A lot of fakes and frauds are out there right now, practicing medicine, teaching classes, practicing law, counseling troubled families, building bridges, pulling teeth, and keeping books, without benefit of a degree, a license, or proper training. If more people would ask a few more questions about the title before the name, or the document on the wall, these dangerous phonies would be stopped before they do more harm to us all. Almost all schools will confirm, either by mail or by telephone, whether or not a given person has indeed earned a degree from them. This is not an invasion of privacy, since the facts are known as "directory information" available to the public through printed directories or publicly accessible university information files.

(Glad you asked. My own Ph.D. was awarded by Michigan State University, East Lansing, Michigan, on March 19, 1966, and you are most welcome to check it out with them.)

NON-ACADEMIC TITLES

I am often asked, "Well, if I can't become a Doctor overnight, what about becoming a baron or a knight or something?" Indeed, it has been suggested that one reason honorary Doctorates are so popular in America is that we don't have titles of nobility, as many other countries do. This topic is really not within the scope of the book, but let me share a few opportunities of which I have become aware over the years. Please understand that I know nhing about any of this stuff; I am simply passing along other peoples's information. Please don't blame me if you are arrested for impersonating a Baron, or drafted into the Bosnian army.

Baron of Bosnia

The Royal and Imperial House of Serbia and Bosnia, represented by His Royal Highness, King Marcijan II, is willing to grant the "fully inheritable" noble titles of Baron, Viscount, or Count of Serbia and Bosnia upon a contribution of from $10,000 to $20,000. Since the King insists that recipients be able to "represent this honour," a resumé is required as well, to be sure one is suitable. Information from The Cultural Counsel for the Royal and Imperial House of Serbia and Bosnia, Winfried Heffner, Ralf Count Huber, Schloss Wiedergrun, D7601 Durbach, West Germany.

Ambassador of the Byzantine Empire

According to the Permanent Diplomatic Delegation of the Byzantine Empire, the last recognized heir, Prince Pietro III, Paleologo, is interested in granting various titles of nobility, upon proper remuneration. The Empire claims to have "diplomatic relations with more than 70 governments." Details from Joseph Baier, Director for External Relations and International Cooperation of the Byzantine Empire, POB 8, A-9500 Villach, Austria.

Knight of Malta

There are at least 19 separate organizations calling themselves Knights of Malta. Some of them offer knighthood in return for a donation. The original order was established in the year 1113, and is officially called the Sovereign Military Hospitaller Order of St. John of Jerusalem of Rhodes and Malta. Catholics may be nominated by their bishop, and if the top people in Rome approve, nominees pay $1,500 and are entitled to put the letters K.M. after their names, but no title before the name. See your bishop. Then there is the Sovereign Military and Hospitaller Order of Saint John of Jerusalem, Knights of Malta, which may be an offshoot the original, established for non-Catholics by the Czar of Russia in 1798. This order will seriously consider knighthood to appropriate people, many of whom are said to have made non-tax-deductible donations of $10,000 and up. Further information from Grand Sovereign Master Prince Khimchiachvili, Duke de l'Eliseni, Knights of Malta Chancellery, 116 Central Park South, New York, NY 10019.

Patriarchate of Antioch

This church offers appointments to the Patriarchal Nobility and Diplopmatic Corps and Orders of Chivalry in exchange for donations. They range from $375 for the Order of the STar of the Nile to $1,000 for Prince, Baron or Knight to $5,000 for creation of a Grand Dukedom with qualification to $10,000 for "recognition of claims to thrones (by treaty)." An Ambassadorship ($5,000) comes with diplomatic ID cards and Lettres de Chancellerie. Full details from The Church Coadjutor, Patriarchate of Antioch, BM3254, 27A Old Gloucester Street, London WC1N 3XX, England. (The address is a mail forwarding service, so be cautious about sending money.)

6. How to Evaluate a School

Judge, lest ye be judged.
—Not Matthew 7:1

Once, I was walking down a city street with an investigative reporter for a large newspaper. "You know," he said, "I could go into any building on this block—that office, that hospital, that laundromat, that factory—and given enough time and money, I would find a story there that would probably make page one."

The same is very likely true of virtually every school in this book, from Harvard on down. Some simply have a lot more skeletons in a lot more closets than others.

There are many times, indeed, when I wish I had an army of trained investigators and detectives at my disposal. With very limited resources and manpower, I cannot do a detailed and intensive investigation of every single school. Happily, I have received a great deal of assistance from readers of this book, who have followed my advice on checking out a school and have reported their findings to me.

Here, then, is the four-step procedure I recommend for investigating schools that are not covered in this book, or looking further into those that are. And please, if you do this, share your research with me. The address appears at the front of the book. (Thank you.)

STEP ONE: CHECK IT OUT IN THIS BOOK

If it isn't here, it may be because the school is very new, or because I didn't consider it sufficiently non-traditional for inclusion—or quite possibly because I simply missed it. And even if it *is* listed here, don't take my opinions as the Gospel Truth. Hardly a day passes that I don't get a letter challenging my opinions. Sometimes they begin, "You idiot, don't you know that . . ." and sometimes they begin, "I beg to differ with you in regard to . . . ." Whatever the tone, I am always glad to have these opinions. There have been quite a few instances where such a letter spurred me to look more closely at a school, resulting in a revised opinion, either upward or downward.

STEP TWO: CHECK IT OUT WITH FRIENDS, COLLEAGUES, OR EMPLOYERS

If the degree is needed for a new job, a salary increase, or a state license, be sure to find out specifically if this degree will suffice before you invest any money in any school. Many schools will gladly enter into correspondence with employers, state agencies, or others you may designate, to explain their programs and establish their credentials.

In my consulting practice, I used to hear regularly from people who had lost thousands of dollars, and wasted incredible amounts of time, in completing a degree that was useless to them. "But the school said it was accredited," they lament.

STEP THREE: CHECK IT OUT WITH THE GOVERNMENT AGENCY

Every state and every nation has an agency which oversees higher education. Check the school out with the agency in your state or in the state or country in which the school is located. A list of these agencies is given at the end of the chapter. Some correspondence schools are well known (positively or negatively) to the Better Business Bureau as well. And all other nations of the world have either a department, bureau, or ministry of education that may be able to supply information on a school. They also all have embassies in Washington DC and United Nations delegations in New York, where questions may be addressed.

STEP FOUR: CHECK OUT THE SCHOOL ITSELF

Visit the campus or the offices if at all possible, or if you have any doubts. If the school's literature does not make clear the precise legal or accreditation status, and if you still have any questions, check with the appropriate accrediting agency. They are all listed in chapter 7. If the accreditor is not listed in chapter 7, be careful. There are a lot of phony accrediting agencies in operation.

Here are some of the questions you may wish to ask. **I would ask you not to make up a form letter and just send it to 50 or more schools, as more than a few readers have done.** Being more selective, both about schools and questions, will save both you and the schools time and money.

- How many students are currently enrolled? (Curiously, quite a few schools seem reluctant to reveal these numbers. Sometimes it is because they are embarrassed about how large they are, as, for instance, in the case of one alternative school that at one time had more than 3,000 students and a faculty of five! Sometimes it is because they are embarrassed about how small they are, as is the case with one heavily-advertised school, with impressive literature, extremely high tuition, and fewer than 50 students.)

- How many degrees have been awarded in the last year?
- What is the size of the faculty? How many of these are full-time and how many are part-time or adjunct faculty? If the catalogue doesn't make it clear, from which schools did the faculty earn their degrees?
- From which school(s) did the president, the dean, and other administrators earn their own degrees? (There is nothing inherently wrong with staff members earning degrees from their own school, but when the number doing so is 25% or more, as is the case at some institutions, it starts sounding a little suspicious to me.)
- May I have the names and addresses of some recent graduates in my field of study, and/or in my geographical area?
- May I look at the work done by students? (Inspection of Master's theses and Doctor dissertations can often give a good idea of the quality of work expected, and the caliber of the students. But you may either have to visit the school [not a bad idea] or offer to pay for making and sending copies.)
- Will your degree be acceptable for my intended needs (state licensing, certification, graduate school admission, salary advance, new job, whatever)?
- What exactly is your legal status, with regard to state agencies and to accrediting associations? If accreditation (or candidacy for accreditation) is claimed, is it with an agency that is approved either by the U.S. Department of Education or the Council on Postsecondary Accreditation? If not accredited, are there any plans to seek accreditation?

No legitimate school should refuse to answer questions like these. Remember, you are shopping for something that may cost you several thousand dollars, or more. It is definitely a buyer's market, and the schools all know this. If they see that you are an informed customer, they will know that they must satisfy you or you will take your business elsewhere.

Remember, too, that alternative education does not require all the trappings of a traditional school. Don't expect to find a big campus with spacious lawns, an extensive library, or a football team. Some outstanding nontraditional schools are run from relatively small suites of rented offices.

Another thing I've learned is that you cannot go by the catalogue or other school literature alone. Some really poor schools and some outrageous degree mills have hired good writers and designers, and have produced very attractive catalogues, albeit ones that are full of lies and misleading statements. A common trick, for instance, is to show a photograph of a large and impressive building, which may or may not be the building in which the school rents a room or two, but the implication is that "This is our world headquarters." Another common device is to list a large number of names of faculty and staff, sometimes with photographs of their smiling faces. My files are full of certified, deliver-to-addressee-only letters sent to these people, that have been returned as undeliverable.

Finally, be very suspicious of schools with no telephones, or, perhaps even more of a red flag, schools where you can't call them, they have to call you. For instance, in 1989, I was attempting to check out a new and heavily-advertised school called North American University. The people who answer their toll-free phone line were cheerful, but after many calls, I was never put through to anyone. It was always, "Dr. Peters will call you back." "Dr. Peters" turned out to be an alias for the school's owner, a convicted felon, who would return calls from his home in another state.

On the other side of the ledger, it is also the case that some good, sincere, legitimate schools have issued typewritten and mimeographed catalogues, either to save money or to go along with their low-key images, and a few sincere, very low-budget schools have even operated without a telephone for a while.

STATE AND FOREIGN AGENCIES FOR HIGHER EDUCATION

These are the agencies in each state, and the District of Columbia, that oversee higher education. If you have any concerns about the legality of an institution, or its right to award degrees, these are the places to ask.

STATE AGENCIES

Alabama
Department of Postsecondary Education
419 South Perry Street
Montgomery AL 36104 (205) 834-2200
Dr. Charles L. Payne, Chancellor

Commission on Higher Education
1 Court Square, Suite 221
Montgomery AL 36197 (205) 269-2700
Dr. Joseph T. Sutton, Executive Director

Alaska
Commission on Postsecondary Education,
P. O. Box FP, 400 Willoughby Ave.
Juneau AK 99811 (907) 465-2854
Dr. Kerry D. Romesburg

Arizona
Arizona Commission for Postsecondary Education
1645 West Jefferson, Suite 127
Phoenix AZ 85007 (602) 255-3109
Dr. R. Ross Erbschloe, Executive Director

Arkansas
Department of Education
1301 West 7th St.
Little Rock AR 72201 (501) 371-1441
Dr. Paul Marion, Director

California
Postsecondary Education Commission
1020 12th St.
Sacramento CA 95814 (916) 445-7933
Elizabeth Testa, Senior Librarian

Colorado
Commission on Higher Education
Colorado Heritage Center, 2nd Floor,
1300 Broadway
Denver CO 80203 (303) 866-2723
Dr. Charles W. Manning,
Interim Executive Director

Connecticut
Board of Governors for Higher Education
61 Woodland St.
Hartford CT 06105 (203) 566-5766
Dr. Norma Foreman Glasgow,
Commissioner of Higher Education

Delaware
Postsecondary Education Commission
Carvel State Office Building,
820 N. French St.
Wilmington DE 19801 (302) 571-3240
Dr. John F. Corrozi, Executive Director

Distric of Columbia
Office of Postsecondary Education,
Research and Assistance
1331 H Street NW, Suite 600
Washington DC 20005 (202) 727-3685
Mrs. Eloise C. Turner, Chief

Florida
Postsecondary Education Planning Commission
Florida Department of Education,
W.V. Knott Building,
Tallahassee FL 32301 (904) 488-6029
Dr. Patrick H. Dallet, Asst. Executive Director

Georgia
Governor's Committee on Postsecondary Education
2 Martin Luther King Jr. Drive, Suite 812,
West Tower
Atlanta GA 30334 (404) 656-2526
Dr. David M. Morgan, Director

Hawaii
Office of Consumer Protectiom
Department of Commerce and Consumer Affairs
250 S. King St.
Honolulu HI 96813 (808) 548-2560
Philip Doi, Director

Idaho
State Board of Education
650 West State St.,
Len B. Jordan Bldg., Room 307
Boise ID 83720 (208) 334-2270
Richard Sperring, Executive Director

Illinois
Illinois Board of Higher Education
500 Reisch Bldg., 4 W. Old Capital Square

Springfield IL 62701 (217) 782-2551
Dr. Richard D. Wagner, Executive Director

Indiana
Commission for Higher Education
143 W. Market St., Suite 400
Indianapolis IN 46204 (317) 232-1900
Dr. Clyde R. Ingle, Commissioner for Higher Education

Iowa
Board of Regents
Lucas State Office Building
Des Moines IA 50319 (515) 281-3934
Mr. R. Wayne Richey, Executive Secretary

Kansas
Kansas Board of Regents
Suite 609, Capitol Tower,
400 S.W. Eighth Street
Topeka KS 66603 (913) 296-3421
Mr. Stanley Z. Koplik, Executive Director

Kentucky
Council on Higher Education
West Frankfort Office Complex,
U.S. 127 South, Frankfort KY 40601 (502) 564-3553

Dr. Gary S. Cox, Executive Director

Louisiana
Board of Regents
161 Riverside Mall
Baton Rouge LA 70801 (504) 342-4253
Dr.William Arceneaux,
Commissioner of Higher Education

or

Louisiana Proprietary School Commission
P.O. Box 94064
Baton Rouge LA 70814 (504) 342-3543
Andrew Gasperecz, Director

Maine
Dept. of Education & Cultural Services,
Division of Higher Education Services
State House Sta. #119
Augusta ME 04333 (207) 289-2183
Mr. Fred Douglas, Director

Maryland
State Board for Higher Education
Jeffery Bldg., 16 Francis St.
Annapolis MD 21401 (301) 974-2971
Dr. Sheldon H. Knorr,
Commissioner of Higher Education

Massachusetts
Board of Regents
1 Ashburton Pl., Room 1401,
McCormack Bldg.
Boston MA 02108 (617) 727-7785
Neil J. Harrington, Admin.
Assistant to the Chancellor

Michigan
Department of Education
Higher Education Management Services,
P.O. Box 30008
Lansing MI 48909 (517) 373-3820
Ronald L. Root, Director

Minnesota
Higher Education Coordinating Board,
Suite 400, Capitol Square Bldg., 550 Cedar St.
St. Paul, MN 55101 (612) 296-3974
Dr. David A. Longanecker, Executive Director

Mississippi
Board of Trustees of State Institutions of Higher Learning
P.O. Box 2336
Jackson MS 39225 (601) 982-6611
Dr. George Carter, Deputy Commissioner

Missouri
Coordinating Board for Higher Education
101 Adams St.
Jefferson City MO 65101 (314) 751-2361
Dr. Robert Jacob,
Assistant Commissioner

Montana
Montana University System
33 S. Last Chance Gulch
Helena (isn't this a wonderful address!),
MT 59620 (406) 444-6570
Dr. Carol Krause, Commissioner of Higher Education

Nebraska
Coordinating Commission for Postsecondary Education,
6th Floor, Capitol Bldg., P. O. Box 95005
Lincoln NE 68509 (402) 471-2847
Sue Gordon–Gessner, Executive Director

Nevada
Commission on Postsecondary Education
1000 E. William, Suite 102

Carson City, NV 89710 (702) 885-5690
Mr. John V. Griffin, Administrator

New Hampshire
Postsecondary Education Commission
61 S. Spring St.
Concord NH 03301 (603) 271-2555
Dr. James A. Busselle, Executive Director

New Jersey
Dept. of Higher Education
225 W. State St.,
Trenton NJ 08625 (609) 292-4310
Dr. T. Edward Hollander, Chancellor

New Mexico
Commission of Higher Education
1068 Cerillos Rd.
Santa Fe NM 87501 (505) 827-8300
Dewayne Matthews, Executive Director

New York
Division of Academic Program Review
State Education Department
Empire State Plaza
Albany NY 12234 (518) 474-8299
Dr. Denis F. Paul, Assistant Commissioner

North Carolina
Commission on Higher Education Facilities
UNC General Administration,
910 Raleigh Rd., P.O. Box 2688
Chapel Hill, NC 27515 (919) 962-1000
Mr. Charles L. Wheeler, Director

North Dakota
State Board of Higher Education
State Capitol Bldg.
Bismarck ND 58505 (701) 224-2960
Dr. John A Richardson, Commissioner of Higher Education

Ohio
Board of Regents,
30 E. Broad St.
Columbus OH 43215 (614) 466-6000
Dr. Jonathan Tafel, Director, Certificates of Authorization and Continuing Education

Oklahoma
State Regents for Higher Education
500 Education Bldg., State Capitol Complex
Oklahoma City OK 73105 (405) 521-2444
Dr. Melvin R. Todd, Vice Chancellor for Academic Administration

Oregon
Office of Educational Policy and Planning
Oregon Educational Coordinating Commission
225 Winter St. NE
Salem, OR 97310 (503) 378-3921
Dr. David A. Young, Administrator

Pennsylvania
Division of Postsecondary Education Services
Department of Education, 9th Floor,
333 Market St.
Harrisburg PA 17126 (717) 783-6769
Dr. Warren D. Evans, Chief

Rhode Island
Office of Higher Education
199 Promenade St., Suite 222
Providence RI 02908 (401) 277-6560
Dr. Eleanor M. McMahon, Commissioner of Higher Education

South Carolina
Commision on Higher Education
1333 Main St., Suite 650
Columbia SC 29201 (803) 253-6260
Mr. Fred R. Sheheen, Commissioner

South Dakota
Dept. of Education and Cultural Affairs
Richard Kneip Bldg.
Pierre SD 57501 (605) 773-3134
Roxie Thielen, Administrative Aide

Tennessee
Higher Education Commission,
Parkway Towers, Suite 1900,
404 James Robertson Pkwy.
Nashville TN 37219 (615) 741-3605
Dr. George M. Roberts, Director of Licensure

Texas
Higher Education Coordinating Board
P.O. Box 12788, Capitol Station
Austin TX 78711 (512) 475-0718
Dr. David T. Kelley, Director of Institutional Certification

Utah
Utah System of Higher Education
355 West North Temple, Suite 560
Salt Lake City UT 84180 (801) 538-5247
Dr. Sterling R. Provost, Assistant Commissioner

Vermont
Vermont Higher Education Council
Box 70
Hyde Park, VT 05655 (802) 888-7771
Ann Turkle, Executive Director

Virginia
State Council of Higher Education
101 North 14th St., 9th Floor
Richmond VA 23219 (804) 225-2137
Dr. Gordon K. Davies, Director

Washington
Council for Postsecondary Education
908 E. 5th St.
Olympia WA 98504 (206) 753-3241
Dr. Carl A. Trendler, Executive Coordinator

West Virginia
Board of Regents
P.O. Box 3368
Charleston WV 25333 (304) 348-2101
Dr. Leon H. Ginsberg, Chancellor

Wisconsin
State Educational Approval Board
P. O. Box 7874
Madison, WI 53707 (608) 266-1996
David R. Stucki, Executive Secretary

Wyoming
Coordinating Council for Postsecondary Education
1720 Carey Ave., 5th Floor
Cheyenne WY 82001 (307) 777-7763
Russell A. Hansen, Executive Officer

Guam
Pacific Post-Secondary Education Council
P. O. Box 23067
G M F Guam 96921 (617) 734-2962
William A. Kinder, Executive Director

Puerto Rico
Council on Higher Education
Univ. of Puerto Rico Station, Box F
San Juan PR 00931 (809) 765-6590
Ismael Ramirez-Soto, Executive Secretary

FOREIGN AGENCIES

Australia
Department of Education
MLC Tower, Keltie St.,
Phillip, ACT 2606
(062) 891333; telex 62116
Minister for Education

Belgium
Ministry of National Education
(Flemish Sector)
Centre Arts Lux., 4th and 5th Floors,
58 Ave des Arts, BP5 1040 Brussels
(02) 512-66-60
Minister of Education

Brazil
Ministry of Education and Culture
Esplanada dos Ministerios, Bloco L,
70.047 Brasilia, DF;
(061) 214-8432; telex 2259105
Minister of Education

Bulgaria
Ministry of Education
Blvd A. Stamboliski 18;
Sofia 1000
84-81
Minister of Education

Cuba
Ministry of Higher Education
Calle 23y F, Vedado, Havana
3-6655; telex 511253
Minister of Education

Denmark
Ministry of Education
Frederiksholms Kanal 21-25,
1220 Copenhagen K.;
(01) 92-50-00
Minister of Education

Egypt
Ministry of Education
Sharia El Falaky,
Cairo
(02) 27363
Minister of National Education

Finland
Ministry of Education
Kirkkokat U3, 00170 Helsinki;
(90) 171636; telex 122079
First Minister of Education for Veteran's Education and Proprietary Schools

France
Ministry of National Education
110 Rue De Grenelle 75700 Paris
(1) 45-50-10-10
Minister of National Education

Germany
Ministry of Education and Science
5300 Bonn 2, Heinemannstr. 2
(0228) 571; telex 885666
Minister of Education

Greece
Ministry of Education and Religion
Odos Mihalakopoulou 80, Athens;
(21) 3230461; telex 216059
Minister of Education and Religion

Hungary
Ministry of Culture and National Education
1055 Budapest, Szalay u. 10/14;
530-600
Minister of Culture and National Education

India
Ministry of Education
Shastri Bhavan, New Delhi 110011
(11) 3012380
Minister of Education

Indonesia
Ministry of Education and Culture
Jalan Jenderal Sudirman,
Senayan, Jakarta Pusat
(021) 581618
Minister of Education and Culture

Ireland
Ministry of Education
Marlborough St.,
Dublin 1
(01) 717101; telex 31136
Minister of Education

Israel
Ministry of Education and Culture
Hakirya, 14 Klausner St.,
Tel Aviv
414155
Minister of Education

Italy
Ministry of Education
Viale Trastevere 76A,
00100 Rome
Telex 4759841
Minister of Education

Japan
Ministry of Education
3-2, Kasumigaseki, Chiyoda–Ku,
Tokyo
(3) 581-4211
Minister of Education

Mexico
Secretariat of State for Public Education
Republica de Argentina y Gonzales
Obregon 28, 06029 Mexico, DF;
5103029
Secretary of Public Education

Netherlands
Ministry of Education and Science
Europaweg 4, POB 25000
2700 LZ Zoetermeer;
(079) 531911; telex 32636
Minister of Eucation and Science

New Zealand
Department of Education
Private Bag Wellington
(04) 735499
Minister of Education

Norway
Ministry of Church and Education
POB 8119, Dep., 0520 1;
Oslo
(2) 11-90-90
Minister of Church and Education

Philippines
Ministry of Education, Culture, and Sports
Palacio del Gobernador,
Gen. Luna St, Cnr Aduana St,
Intramuros,Manila
(02) 402949
Minister of Education

Portugal
Ministry of Education
Av. 5 de Outubro 107
1000 Lisbon
731291
Minister of Education and Culture

Republic of Korea (South Korea)
Ministry of Education
77-6 Sejong–no, Chongno–Ku,
Seoul;
720-3315; telex 24758

South Africa
Ministry of Home Affairs and National Education
Civitas BLDG, Struben St, Private Bag X114, Pretoria
282551
Minister of National Education

Spain
Ministry of Education and Science
Ministerios de Educacion y Ciencia,
Alcala 34,
Madrid 14
2321300
Minister of Education and Science

Sweden
Ministry of Education and cultural Affairs
Mynttorget 1
103 33 Stockholm
(8) 736-10-00; telex 13284
Minister of Education and Cultural Affairs

Turkey
Ministry of Education, Youth and Sports
Milli Egitim, Genclik ve Spor
Bakanligi, Ankara
(41) 231160
Minister of Education, Youth and Sports

United Kingdom
Department of Education and Science
Elizabeth House, York Rd.,
London SE1 7PH
(01) 928-9222; telex 23171
Secretary of State for Education and Science

Venezuela
Ministry of Education
Edif. Educacion, esq. El Conde,
Caracas
562-5444
Minister of Education

7. Accreditation

It's right because I say it's right.
It's good because I say it's good.
It's legit because I say it's legit.
—attributed to Al Capone

Accreditation is perhaps the most complex, confusing, and important issue in higher education. It is surely the most misunderstood and the most misused concept—both intentionally and unintentionally.

In selecting a school, there are three important things to know about accreditation: what it is, why it may be important for certain situations, and what are the different kinds of accrediting associations?

WHAT IS ACCREDITATION?

Quite simply, it is a validation—a statement by a group of persons who are, theoretically, impartial experts in higher education—that a given school, or department within a school, has been thoroughly investigated and found worthy of approval.

Accreditation is a peculiarly American concept. In every other country in the world, all colleges and universities either are operated by the government, or gain the full right to grant degrees directly from the government. In the United States, accreditation is an *entirely voluntary process*, done by private, non-governmental agencies. As a result of this lack of central control or authority, there have evolved good accrediting agencies and bad ones, recognized ones and unrecognized ones, legitimate ones and phony ones.

So when a school says, "We are accredited," that statement alone means nothing. The question must always be asked, "Accredited by whom?" Unfortunately, many consumer-oriented articles and bulletins simply say that one is much safer dealing only with accredited schools, but they do not attempt to unravel the complex situation. I hear regularly from distressed people who say, about the degrees they have just learned are worthless, "But the school was accredited; I even checked with the accrediting agency." The agency, needless to say, turned out to be as phony as the school.

The wrong kind of accreditation can be a lot worse than none at all.

Normally a school wishing to be accredited will make application to the appropriate accrediting agency. After a substantial preliminary investigation to determine that the school is probably operating legally and is run legitimately, it may be granted correspondent or provisional status. Typically this step will take anywhere from several months to several years or more, and when completed does not imply any kind of endorsement or recommendation, but is merely an indication that the first steps on a long path have been taken.

Next, teams from the accrediting agency, often composed of faculty of already-accredited institutions, will visit the school. These "visitations," conducted at regular intervals throughout the year, are to observe the school in action, and to study the copious amounts of information that the school must prepare, relating to its legal and academic structure, educational philosophy, curriculum, financial status, planning, and so forth.

After these investigations and, normally, at least two years of successful operation (sometimes a great deal more), the school may be advanced to the status of "candidate for accreditation." Being a candidate means, in effect, "Yes, you are probably worthy of accreditation, but we want to watch your operation for a while longer." This "while" can range from a year or two to six years or more. The great majority of schools that reach candidacy status eventually achieve full accreditation. Some accreditors do not have a candidacy status; it is an all-or-nothing situation. (The terms "accredited" and "fully accredited" are used interchangeably.)

Once a school is accredited, it is visited by inspection teams at infrequent intervals (5 to 10 years is common) to see if it is still worthy of its accreditation. The status is always subject to review at any time, should new programs be developed or should there be any significant developments, positive or negative, in the life of the school.

THE IMPORTANCE OF ACCREDITATION

Although accreditation is undeniably important to both schools and students or would-be students, this importance is undermined and confused by three factors:

1. There are no national standards for accreditation. What is accreditable in New York may not be accreditable

in California, and vice versa. The demands and standards of the group that accredits schools of chemistry may be very different from the people who accredit schools of forestry. And so on.

2. Many very good schools (or departments within schools) are not accredited, either by their own choice (since accreditation is a totally voluntary and often very expensive procedure), or because they are too new (all schools were unaccredited at one time in their lives), or too experimental (many would say too innovative) for the generally conservative accreditors.

3. Many very bad schools claim to be accredited—but it is always by unrecognized, sometimes non-existent accrediting associations, often of their own creation.

Still, accreditation is the only widespread system of school evaluation that we have. A school's accreditation status can be helpful to the potential student in this way: while many good schools are not accredited, it is very unlikely that any very bad or illegal school is authentically accredited. (There have been exceptions, but they are quite rare.)

In other words, authentic accreditation is a pretty good sign that a given school is legitimate. But it is important to remember that *lack of accreditation need not mean that a school is either inferior or illegal.*

I stress the term *authentic* accreditation, since there are very few laws or regulations anywhere governing the establishment of an accrediting association. Anyone can start a degree mill, then turn around and open an accrediting agency next door, give his school its blessing, and begin advertising "fully accredited degrees." Indeed, this has happened many times.

The crucial question, then, is this: Who accredits the accreditors?

WHO ACCREDITS THE ACCREDITORS?

There are two agencies, one private and one governmental, that have responsibility for evaluating and approving or recognizing accrediting agencies.

The Council on Postsecondary Accreditation (known as COPA), is a nationwide non-profit corporation, formed in 1975, to evaluate accrediting associations and award recognition to those found worthy.

Within the Department of Education is the Eligibilty and Agency Evaluation Staff (EAES), which is required by law to "publish a list of nationally recognized accrediting agencies which [are determined] to be reliable . . . as to the quality of training offered." This is done as one measure of eligibility for federal financial aid programs for students.

EAES also has the job of deciding whether unaccredited schools can qualify for federal aid programs, or their students for veterans' benefits. This is done primarily by what is called the "four-by-three" rule: Proof that credits from at least four students have been accepted by at least three accredited schools (twelve total acceptances). If they have, then the unaccredited school is recognized by the Department of Education for that purpose. Schools qualifying under the four-by-three rule must regularly submit evidence of continued acceptance of their credits by accredited schools in order to maintain their status.

An already complex situation is confused almost beyond belief by several other factors.

- One is the Republican party's former intention to dissolve the Department of Education entirely. While President Reagan was unable to accomplish this during his administration, the wish remains in some circles, although "Education President" Bush has not echoed it. One effect of all those years of uncertainty has been that many of the 50 states have considered going into the accreditation business and/or the accrediting agency recognition business.
- Another is a proposal being entertained by the Department of Education that it get entirely out of the evaluation process, and leave recognition of accrediting agencies up to each state.
- And a third is the disputes that have gone on between COPA and EAES as to who has jurisdiction in various situations, although a period of extreme confrontation seems to have evolved into a mellower relationship.

One example of how all this confusion impacts the public is the matter of the accrediting of medical schools, in which there are two unrelated accrediting agencies. One has jurisdiction over accreditation from July 1 to June 30 of even-numbered years; the other has jurisdiction for odd-numbered years.

ACCREDITATION AND NON-TRADITIONAL EDUCATION

One of the frequent complaints levied against the recognized accrediting agencies is that they have, in general, been slow to acknowledge the major trend to alternative or non-traditional education.

A few years ago, the Carnegie Commission on Higher Education conducted research on the relationship between accreditation and non-traditional approaches. Their report, written by Alexander Mood, confirmed that a serious disadvantage of accreditation is "in the suppression of innovation. Schools cannot get far out of line without risking loss of their accreditation—a penalty which they cannot afford."

Also, the report continues,

> loss of accreditation implies that the curriculum is somewhat inferior and hence that the degree is inferior. Such a large penalty...tends to prevent colleges from striking out in new directions.... As we look toward the future, it appears likely that accrediting organizations will lose their usefulness and slowly disappear. Colleges will be judged not by what some educational bureaucracy declares but by what they can do for their students. Of much greater relevance would be statistics on student satisfaction, career advancement of graduates, and data like that.

Faced with high-powered criticism of this sort, some accrediting agencies sponsored (with a major grant from the Kellogg Foundation) a large-scale study of how the agencies should deal with non-traditional education.

The four-volume report of the findings of this investigation said, in summary, very much what the Carnegie report had to say. The accreditors were advised, in effect, not to look at the easy quantitative factors (percentage of Doctorate-holders on the faculty, books in the library, student-faculty ratio, acres of campus, etc.), but rather to evaluate the far more elusive qualitative factors, of which student satisfaction and student performance are the most crucial.

In other words, if the students at a non-traditional, non-resident university regularly produce research and dissertations that are as good as those of traditional schools or if graduates of non-traditional schools are as likely to gain admission to graduate school or high-level employment and perform satisfactorily there—then the non-traditional school may be just as worthy of accreditation as the traditional school.

Accrediting agencies move slowly. Various committees and commissions are studying this Kellogg report, and others like it, and perhaps some of its recommendations will one day be implemented. Most non-traditional schools are not holding their collective breaths awaiting any such action, although eventually either it must come, or, as the Carnegie report predicts, the traditional accreditors will fade away.

In 1987, Secretary of Education William Bennett voiced similar complaints about the failure of accrediting agencies to deal with matters such as student competency and satisfaction. "Historically," he said, "accrediting agencies have examined institutions in terms of the resources they have, such as the number of faculty with earned doctorates and the number of books in the library. Now [we] are considering the ways agencies take account of student achievement and development."

In 1990, Bennett's successor, Lauro F. Cavazos said almost exactly the same thing, while managing to split an infinitive: "Despite increasing evidence that many of our schools are failing to adequately prepare our chilren, either for further study or for productive careers, the accreditation process still focuses on inputs, such as the number of volumes in libraries or percentage of faculty with appropriate training. It does not examine outcomes—how much students learn."

John W. Harris, chairman of the National Advisory Committee on Accreditation echoed these concerns: "It is not enough to know that teachers have certain degrees and that students have spent so much time in the classroom. The question is, can institutions document the achievement of students for the degrees awarded?"

The accrediting agencies were quick to respond, assuring us that they *do* deal with such matters. And the battle goes on.

THE APPROVED ACCREDITING AGENCIES

There are six regional associations, each with responsibility for schools in one region of the United States and its territories. Each one has the authority to accredit an entire college or university. There are also about 80 professional associations, each with authority to accredit either specialized schools or specific departments or programs within a school.

Thus, it may be the case, for instance, that the North Central Association (one of the six regional associations) will accredit Dolas University. When this happens, the entire school is accredited, and all its degrees may be called accredited degrees, or more accurately, degrees from an accredited institution.

Or it may be the case that just the art department of Dolas University has been accredited by the relevant professional association, in this case the National Association of Schools of Art. If this happens, then only the art majors at Dolas can claim to have accredited degrees.

So if an accredited degree is important for you, the first question to ask is, "Has the school been accredited by one of the six regional associations?" If the answer is no, then the next question is, "Has the department in which I am interested been accredited by its relevant professional association?"

There are those jobs (psychology and nursing are two examples) in which professional accreditation is more important than regional accreditation. In other words, even if a school is accredited by its regional association, unless its psychology department is also accredited by the American Psychology Association, its degree will be less useful for psychology majors. (One of the legends about accreditation has arisen because of these matters: the widespread belief that Harvard is not accredited. Harvard University *is* duly accredited by its regional agency, but its psychology department (and many others) are not accredited by the relevant professional agencies.

Yet another aspect of confusion in this matter is that some accrediting agencies are officially recognized by the U.S. Department of Education; some are recognized by the Council on Postsecondary Accreditation (the private non-government agency), some by both, and some by neither. There actually are situations where it is important to know which national agency has recognized an accreditor, although by and large, if either one has, that is good enough.

Totally unrecognized agencies may still be quite legitimate, or they may be quite phony. Some of the unrecognized ones will be discussed after the following listing of the recognized ones. Each of the approved accreditors will gladly supply lists of all the schools (or departments within schools) they have accredited, and those that are candidates for accreditation and in correspondent status. They will also answer any questions pertaining to any school's status (or lack of status) with them.

THE TWO AGENCIES THAT RECOGNIZE ACCREDITING AGENCIES

- Department of Education, Division of Eligibilty and Agency Evaluation, Bureau of Postsecondary Education, Washington, DC 20202, (202) 245-9875
- Council on Postsecondary Accreditation, 1 Dupont Circle N., #760, Washington, DC 20036, (202) 452-1433

RECOGNIZED ACCREDITING AGENCIES

All agencies are recognized by both the Department of Education and COPA, the Council on Post secondary Accreditation, unless otherwise indicated.

REGIONAL ACCREDITING AGENCIES

Middle States Association of Colleges and Schools,
Commission on Higher Education
3624 Market St.
Philadelphia, PA 19104
(215) 662-5606
Delaware, District of Columbia, Maryland, New Jersey, New York, Pennsylvania, Puerto Rico, Virgin Islands.

New England Association of Schools and Colleges
15 High St.
Winchester, MA 01890
(617) 729-6762
Connecticut, Maine, Massachusetts, New Hampshire, Rhode Island, Vermont.

North Central Association of Colleges and Schools
159 Dearborn St.
Chicago, IL 60601
(800) 621-7440
Arizona, Arkansas, Colorado, Illinois, Indiana, Iowa, Kansas, Michigan, Minnesota, Missouri, Nebraska, New Mexico, North Dakota, Ohio, Oklahoma, South Dakota, West Virginia, Wisconsin, Wyoming.

Northwest Association of Schools and Colleges
7300B University Way N.E.
Seattle, WA 98105
(206) 543-0195
Alaska, Idaho, Montana, Nevada,, Oregon, Utah, Washington.

Southern Association of Colleges and Schools
795 Peachtree St., NE
Atlanta, GA 30365
(404) 897-6125
Alabama, Florida, Georgia, Kentucky, Louisiana, Mississippi, North Carolina, South Carolina, Tennessee, Texas, Virginia.

Western Association of Schools and Colleges
Box 9990, Mills College
Oakland, CA 94613
(415) 632-5000
California, Hawaii, Guam, Trust Territory of the Pacific.

PROFESSIONAL ACCREDITING AGENCIES

Architecture
National Architecture Accrediting Board
1735 New York Ave. NW
Washington, DC 20006 (202) 783-2007

Art
National Association of Schools of Art and Design
11250 Roger Bacon Drive, No. 21
Reston, VA 22090 (703) 437-0700

Bible College Education
American Association of Bible Colleges
P.O. Box 1523
Fayetteville, AR 72701 (501) 521-8164

Blind and Visually Handicapped Education
National Accreditation Council for Agencies Serving Blind and Visually Handicapped (not COPA)
15 West 65th St., 9th Fl.
New York, NY 10023 (212) 496-5880

Allied Health
Accrediting Bureau of Health Education Schools
Oak Manor Office, 29089 U.S. 20 West
Elkhart, IN 46514 (219) 293-0124

Business
American Assembly of Collegiate Schools of Business
605 Old Ballas Road, Suite 220
St. Louis, MO 63141 (314) 872-8481

Association of Independent Colleges and Schools (not COPA)
1 Dupont Circle N.W., Suite 350
Washington , DC 20036 (202) 659-2460

Chiropractic
The Council on Chiropractic Education
3209 Ingersoll Ave.
Des Moines, IA 50312 (515) 255-2184

Clinical Pastoral Education
Association for Clinical Pastoral Education, Inc.
1549 Claremont Rd., Suite 103
Decatur, GA 30033 (404) 320-1472

Construction Education
American Council for Constrution Education, (COPA only)
1015 15th St. NW, Suite 700
Washington, DC 20005 (202) 347-5875

Cosmetology
National Accrediting Commission of Cosmetology Arts and Sciences (not COPA),
1333 H St. NW, Suite 710
Washington, DC 20005 (202) 289-4300

Dentistry
American Dental Association
211 E. Chicago Ave.
Chicago, IL 60611 (312) 440-2500

Dance
National Association of Schools of Dance
11250 Roger Bacon Drive, #21
Reston, VA 22090 (703) 437-0700

Dietetics
American Dietetic Association
208 S. LaSalle St., Suite 1100
Chicago, IL 60604 (312) 899-4870

Engineering
Accrediting Board for Engineering and Technology
345 E. 47th St.
New York, NY 10017 (212) 705-7685

Marriage and Family Therapy
American Association for Marriage and Family Therapy
1717 K St. NW, Suite 407
Washington, DC 20036 (202) 429-1825

Forestry
Society of American Foresters
5400 Grosvenor Lane
Bethesda, MD 20814 (301) 897-8720

Funeral Service Education
American Board of Funeral Service Education (not COPA)
23 Crestwood Rd.
Cumberland, ME 04201 (207) 829-5715

Health Services Administration
Accrediting Commission on Education for Health Services Administration
1911 N. Fort Myer Dr., Suite 503
Arlington, VA 22209 (703) 524-0511

Home Economics
American Home Economics Association (COPA only)
2010 Massachusetts Ave. NW
Washington, DC 20036 (202) 862-8355

Home Study Education
National Home Study Council
1601 18th St. NW
Washington, DC 20009 (202) 234-5100

Interior Design Education
Foundation for Interior Design Research
322 8th Ave., Suite 1501
New York, NY 10001 (212) 929-8366

Journalism
Accrediting Council on Education in Journalism and Mass Communications
University of Kansas School of Journalism, Stauffer-Flint Hall
Lawrence, KS 66045 (913) 864-3973

Landscape Architecture
American Society of Landscape Architects
1733 Connecticut Ave. NW
Washington, DC 20009 (202) 466-7730

Law
American Bar Association
Indiana University, 735 W. New York St.
Indianapolis, IN 46202 (312) 264-8071

Association of American Law Schools (COPA only)
One Dupont Circle NW, Suite 370
Washington, DC 20036 (202) 296-8851

Librarianship
American Library Association
50 E. Huron St.
Chicago, IL 60611 (312) 944-6780

Medical Assistant/Medical Laboratory Technician

Accrediting Bureau of Health Education Schools
Oak Manor Office, 29089 U.S. 20
West Elkhart, IN 46514 (219) 293-0124

Medicine
American Medical Association
535 N. Dearborn St.
Chicago, IL 60610 (312) 751-6610
They are the accreditor only in odd-numbered years, beginning on July 1.

Association of American Medical Colleges
One Dupont Circle NW, Suite 200
Washington, DC 20036 (202) 828-0670
They are the accreditor in even-numbered years, beginning on July 1.

Music
National Association of Schools of Music
11250 Roger Bacon Drive, No. 21
Reston, VA 22090 (703) 437-0700

Nursing
American Association of Nurse Anesthetists (not COPA)
216 Higgins Rd.
Park Ridge, IL 60068 (312) 692-7050

National League for Nursing
10 Columbus Circle
New York, NY 10019 (212) 582-1022

Occupational Therapy
American Occupational Therapy Association
1383 Picard Dr., Suite 300
Rockville, MD 20850 (301) 948-9626

Occupational, Trade, and Technical Education
National Association of Trade and Technical Schools
2251 Wisconsin Ave., NW, Suite 200
Washington, DC 20007 (202) 333-1021

Optometry
American Optometric Association
243 N. Lindbergh Blvd.
St. Louis, MO 63141 (314) 991-4100

Osteopathic Medicine
American Osteopathic Association
212 E. Ohio St.
Chicago, IL 60611 (312) 280-5800

Paramedical Fields
The American Medical Association
535 N. Dearborn St.
Chicago, IL 60610 (312) 645-4660
The American Medical Association has separate accreditation programs for each of sixteen paramedical areas. The appropriate address is The American Medical Association, in care of one of the following programs: Programs for the Blood Bank Technologist, Programs for the Cytotechnologist, Programs for the Histologic Technician, Medical Assistant Programs, Medical Laboratory Technician Programs, Programs for the Medical Record Administrator and Medical Record Technician, Programs for the Medical Technologist, Programs for the Nuclear Medicine Technologist, Programs for the Occupational Therapist, Programs for the Physical Therapist, Programs for the Assistant to the Primary Care Physician, Programs for the Radiation Therapist, Technologist Programs for the Radiographer, Programs for the Respiratory Therapist, Programs for the Surgeon's Assistant, Programs for the Surgical Technologist.

Pharmacy
American Council on Pharmaceutical Education
311 W. Superior
Chicago, IL 60610 (312) 664-3575

Physical Therapy
American Physical Therapy Association
1111 N. Fairfax St.
Alexandria, VA 22314 (703) 684-2782
(see also PARAMEDICAL)

Podiatry
American Podiatric Medical Association
9312 Old Georgetown Rd.
Bethesda, MD 20814 (301) 571-92000

Psychology
American Psychological Association
1200 17th St. NW
Washington, DC 20036 (202) 955-7671

Public Health
Council on Education for Public Health
1015 15th St. NW, Suite 403
Washington, DC 20005 (202) 789-1050

Rabbinical and Talmudic Education
Association of Advanced Rabbinical and Talmudic Schools (not COPA)
175 Fifth Avenue, Room 711
New York, NY 10010 (212) 477-0950

Rehabilitation Counseling
Council on Rehabilitation Education (COPA only)
185 N. Wabash St., Rm. 1617
Chicago, IL 60601 (312) 346-6027

Social Work
Council on Social Work Education
1744 R Street, NW
Washington, DC 20009 (202) 667-2300

Speech pathology
American Speech Language and Hearing Association
10801 Rockville Pike
Rockville, MD 20852 (301) 897-5700

Teacher Education
National Council for the Accreditation of Teacher Education
1919 Pennsylvania Ave. NW, Suite 202
Washington, DC 20006 (202) 466-7496

Theology
The Association of Theological Schools in the United States and Canada
P.O. Box 130
Vandalia, OH 45377 (513) 898-4654

Theater
National Association of Schools of Theater
11250 Roger Bacon Dr., #21
Reston, VA 22090 (703) 437-0700

Veterinary Medicine
American Veterinary Medical Association
930 N. Meacham Road
Schaumburg, IL 60196 (312) 885-8070

Recognized State Agencies
New York State Board of Regents
State Department of Education,
University of the State of New York
Albany, NY 12224 (518) 457-3300

UNRECOGNIZED ACCREDITING AGENCIES

There are a great many so-called accrediting agencies that are not approved or recognized either by COPA or by the Department of Education. A small number are clearly sincere and legitimate; many others are not.

Accrediting Commission for Specialized Colleges
Gas City, Indiana. Established by "Bishop" Gordon Da Costa and associates (one of whom was Dr. George Reuter, who left to help establish the IACSCTS, described in this section), from the address of Da Costa's Indiana Northern Graduate School (a dairy farm in Gas City). According to their literature, the accrediting procedures of ACSC seem superficial at best. The only requirement for becoming a candidate for accreditation was to mail in a check for $110.

Accrediting Commissional International for Schools, Colleges and Theological Seminaries
Beebe, Arkansas. See "International Accrediting Commission for Schools, Colleges and Theological Seminaries" in this section. After the IAC was fined and closed down by authorities in Missouri in 1989, Dr. Reuter retired, and turned the work over to a colleague, who juggled the words in the name and opened up one state over. All IAC schools were offered automatic accreditation by the ACI. I am not aware of any that turned it down.

Alternative Institution Accrediting Association
Allegedly in Washington, DC, and the accreditor of several phony schools.

American Association of Accredited Colleges and Universities
Another unlocatable agency, the claimed accreditor of Ben Franklin Academy.

Arizona Commission of Non-Traditional Private Postsecondary Education.
Established in the late 1970s by the proprietors of Southland University, which claimed to be a candidate for their accreditation. The name was changed after a complaint by the real state agency, the Arizona Commission on Postsecondary Education (see Western Council, below).

Association of Career Training Schools
A slick booklet sent to schools suggests, "Have your school accredited with the Association. Why? The Association Seal...could be worth many $$$ to you! It lowers sales resistance, sales costs, [and] improves image." Nuff said.

Commission for the Accreditation of European Non-Traditional Universities
The University de la Romande, in England, used to claim accreditation from this agency, which I could never locate.

Council for the Accreditation of Correspondence Colleges
Several curious schools claimed their accreditation; the agency is supposed to be in Louisiana.

Council on Postsecondary Alternative Accreditation
An accreditor claimed in the literature of Western States University. Western States never responded to requests for the address of their accreditor. The name seems to have been chosen to cause confusion with the reputable Council on Postsecondary Accreditation.

International Accreditation Association
The literature of the University of North America claims that they are accredited by this association. No address is provided, nor could one be located.

International Accrediting Association
The address in Modesto, California is the same as that of the Universal Life Church, an organization that awards Doctorates of all kinds, including the Ph.D., to anyone making a "donation" of $5 to $100.

International Accrediting Commission for Schools, Colleges and Theological Seminaries
Holden, Missouri. More than 150 schools, many of them Bible schools, were accredited by this organization. In 1989, the Attorney General of Missouri conducted a clever "sting" operation, in which he created a fictitious school, the "East Missouri Business College," which rented a one-room office in St. Louis, and issued a typewritten catalogue, with such executives as "Peelsburi Doughboy" and "Wonarmmed Mann." Their marine biology text was *The Little Golden Book of Fishes.* Nonetheless, Dr. George Reuter, Director of the IAC, visited the school, accepted their money, and duly accredited them. Soon after, the IAC was enjoined from operating, slapped with a substantial fine, and the good Dr. Reuter decided to retire. (But, see above, the almost identical "Accrediting Commission International" immediately arose in Arkansas.)

Before he was apprehended, when someone wrote to Dr. Reuter to ask why I felt as I felt about his Association, Dr. Reuter replied, "Some of us do not rate Dr. John Bear very high. We think he is really a traditionalist and really favors those colleges and universities, and, at the same time, strives to plant dissent with others." Oh, dear.

International Association of Non-Traditional Schools
The claimed accreditor of several British degree mills; allegedly located in England.

International Commission for the Accreditation of Colleges and Universities
Established in Gaithersburg, Maryland, by a diploma mill called the United States University of America (now defunct) primarily for the purpose of accrediting themselves.

Middle States Accrediting Board
A non-existent accreditor, made up by Thomas University and other degree mills, for the purpose of self-accreditation. The name was chosen, of course, to cause confusion with the Middle States Association of Colleges and Schools in Philadelphia, one of the six regional associations.

National Accreditation Association
Established in Riverdale, Maryland by Dr. Glenn Larsen, whose Doctorate is from a diploma mill called the Sussex College of Technology. His associate is Dr. Clarence Franklin, former president and chancellor of American International University (described in the chapter on diploma mills). In a mailing to presidents of unaccredited schools, the NAA offered full accreditation by mail, with no on-site inspection required.

National Association for Private Post-Secondary Education
Washington, DC. Mentioned, in 1990, in the literature of Kennedy-Western University. When I telephoned and asked questions about the organization, the woman on the telephone said, unsolicitedly, "Are you interested in Kennedy-Western University?" I deduce there may be some connection between the school and the Association.

National Association of Alternative Schools and Colleges
Western States University claimed in their literature that they had been accredited by this organization, which I have never been able to locate.

National Association of Open Campus Colleges
Southwestern University of Arizona and Utah (which closed after its proprietor was sent to prison as a result of the FBI's diploma mill investigations) claimed accreditation from this agency. The address in Springfield, Missouri, was the same as that of Disciples of Truth, an organization that operated a chain of diploma mills.

National Association for Private Nontraditional Schools and Colleges
182 Thompson Rd., Grand Junction, CO 81503, (303) 243-5441
The National Association for Private Nontraditional Schools and Colleges (formerly the National Association for Schools and Colleges) appears to be a serious effort to establish an accrediting agency specifically concerned with alternative schools and programs. It was established in the 1970s by a group of educators associated with Western Colorado University, a non-traditional school that has since gone out of business. Although NAPNSC's standards for accreditation have grown stiffer and stiffer over the years, they are still not recognized by either the Department of Education or by COPA. The National Association had announced plans to make a third application for such recognition in late 1989, but withdrew the application at the last minute, saying they would try again later.

National Council of Schools and Colleges
Accreditation by this agency was claimed by International University, formerly of New Orleans, later of Pasadena, California, and now out of existence. Despite many inquiries, the proprietors of the school never provided information on their accreditor.

West European Accrediting Society
Established from a mail forwarding service in Liederbach, West Germany by the proprietors of a chain of diploma mills such as Loyola, Roosevelt, Lafayette, Southern California, and Oliver Cromwell Universities, for the purpose of accrediting themselves.

Western Association of Private Alternative Schools
One of several accrediting agencies claimed in the literature of Western States University. No address or phone number has ever been provided, despite many requests.

Western Association of Schools and Colleges
This is the name of the legitimate regional accreditor for California and points west. However it is also the name used by the aforementioned proprietors of Loyola, Roosevelt, etc., from a Los Angeles address, to give accreditation to their own diploma mills.

Western Council on Non-Traditional Private Post Secondary Education
The name of an accrediting agency started by the founders of Southland University, presumably for the purpose of accrediting themselves and others (see Arizona Commission, above).

Worldwide Accrediting Commission
Operated from a mail forwarding service in Cannes, France, for the purpose of accrediting the fake Loyola University (Paris), Lafayette University, and other American-run degree mills.

BIBLE SCHOOL ACCREDITING AGENCIES

There are four recognized accreditors of religious schools, previously listed. There are also a great many unrecognized ones. Since many Bible schools readily acknowledge that their degrees are not academic in nature, accreditation of them has quite a different meaning. These associations may well be quite legitimate, but their accreditation has no academic relevance. Some accreditors are apparently concerned primarily with doctrinal soundness; others may have other motivations. Among the Bible school accreditors are:

Accreditation Association of Christian Colleges and Seminaries, Morgantown, KY
Accrediting Association of Christian Colleges and Seminaries, Sarasota, FL
AF Sep (I don't know what this means, but Beta International University claims it is the name of their accrediting association), address unknown
American Association of Accredited Colleges and Universities, address unknown
American Association of Theological Institutions, address unknown
American Educational Accrediting Association of Christian Schools, address unknown
Association of Fundamental Institutes of Religious Education (AFIRE), address unknown
International Accrediting Commission, Kenosha, WI
International Accrediting Association of Church Colleges, address unknown
National Educational Accrediting Association, Columbus, OH
Southeast Accrediting Association of Christian Schools, Colleges and Seminaries, Milton, FL

THE LAST WORD ON ACCREDITATION

Don't believe everything anyone says. It seems extraordinary that any school would lie about something so easily checkable as accreditation, but it is done. For instance, a degree mill once unabashedly sent out thousands of bulletins announcing their accreditation by a recognized agency. The announcement was totally untrue.

I have heard salespeople, while trying to recruit students, make accreditation claims that are patently false. Quite a few schools ballyhoo their "fully accredited" status but never mention that the accrediting agency is unrecognized, and so the accreditation is of little or (in most cases) no value.

One accrediting agency (the aforementioned International Accrediting Association for Schools, Colleges and Theological Seminaries) boasted that two copies of every accreditation report they issue are "deposited in the Library of Congress." But for $20, anyone can copyright anything and be able to make the identical claim.

WORDS THAT DO NOT MEAN "ACCREDITED"

Some unaccredited schools use terminology in their catalogues or advertising that might have the effect of misleading unknowledgeable readers. Here are six of the common ways this is done:

1. Pursuing accreditation. A school may state that it is "pursuing accreditation," or that it "intends to pursue accreditation." But that says nothing whatever about its chances for achieving same. I can state just as accurately that I am practicing my tennis game, with the intention of playing Boris Becker in the finals at Wimbledon. Don't hold your breath.

2. Chartered. In some places, a charter is the necessary document that a school needs to grant degrees. A common ploy by diploma mill operators is to form a corporation, and state in the articles of incorporation that one of the purposes of the corporation is to grant degrees. This is like forming a corporation whose charter says that it has the right to appoint the Pope.

3. Licensed or Registered. This usually refers to nothing more than a business license, granted by the city or county in which the school is located, but which has nothing to do with the legality of the school, or the usefulness of its degrees.

4. Recognized. This can have many possible meanings, ranging from some level of genuine official recognition at the state level, to having been listed in some directory often unrelated to education, perhaps published by the school itself. One ambitious degree mill once published an entire book as thick as this one, solely for the purpose of being able to devote a lengthy section to itself as "the finest school in America."

5. Authorized. In California, this has had a specific meaning (see below). Elsewhere, the term can be used to mean almost anything the school wants it to—sometimes legitimate, sometimes not. A Canadian degree mill once claimed to be "authorized to grant degrees." It turned out that the owner had authorized his wife to go ahead and print the diplomas.

6. Approved. In California, this has a specific meaning (see below). In other locations, it is important to know who is doing the approving. Some not-for-profit schools call themselves "approved by the U.S. Government," which means only that the Internal Revenue Service has approved their non-profit status for income taxes—and nothing more. At one time, some British schools called themselves "Government Approved," when the approval related only to the school lunch program.

THE SITUATION IN CALIFORNIA

Until 1990, California had more unaccredited colleges and universities than the other 49 states combined: over 200 at one time. But in 1989, a series of laws were passed and signed by the governor which appear to change drastically the way California will handle the matter of school licensing, particularly with regard to unaccredited schools.

There used to be a three-tiered system: authorized schools, approved schools, and accredited schools, but the new legislation does away with the 'authorized' status, after a period of time, and severely restricts the amount of credit an unaccredited school can give for prior learning.

Authorization, for many years, was a joke. The primary requirement for authorization was owning $50,000 in assets, and even this was not strictly enforced. By the early 1980s, there were over 200 "authorized" schools, more than a few of them less than wonderful.

Then the state got tougher, adding some fairly strict criteria with regard to curriculum, methods of operation, and faculty, as well as financial responsibility. Most importantly, an on-site inspection by a state team was required. In the late 1980s, more than 100 schools either closed, merged, or moved to other, less strict places. And the president of one of California's largest authorized schools predicted, in early 1990, that within two years, there would only be half a dozen unaccredited schools left in the state.

Approval (or "full institutional approval") means the state has inspected the academic programs at the school and found them worthy.

Until 1984, "approval" was granted only for individual programs within a school, not for the entire school. So, for instance, an authorized school could also have some approved programs. Then, by mandate of the state senate, and over some vigorous objections from people in the Postsecondary Education Commission, the commission was ordered to approve entire institutions rather than individual programs.

At that time, the senate directed the superintendent of public instruction to determine that the curriculum of an approved institution "is consistent in quality with curricula offered by appropriate established accredited institutions."

Thus until 1990, the state senate required the superintendent to declare that approval is comparable to accreditation, but the Department of Education did not wish to do this. Indeed, a Postsecondary Education Commission report says that "while existing statute states that the curricula of approved institutions is consistent in quality with the curricula of accredited institutions, questions remain about the rigor and thoroughness of the state approval process and its ability to permit the licensure of only quality institutions."

Translation: The senate may have ordered us to say certain things, but we're not sure we're ready to do so.

Another confusion in California is that the senate said that holders of approved degrees should be permitted to take relevant state licensing exams, such as those in marriage, family, and child counseling. But the state board of professional licensing refused to go along, saying that the standards for approval and the standards for certain exams were not at all the same.

The best advice in dealing with an unaccredited California school is to be a bit more cautious. Ask them what their plans are, as a result of the Morgan Bill and the Greene Bill. Do they have plans to move? merge? close? (Since the legislation passed, more than a few California schools have either moved to other states, or established offices in other, less restrictive states, merged, or simply gone out of business.)

8. Scholarships and Other Financial Aid

If you think education is expensive, try ignorance.
—Derek Bok, President of Harvard University

Financial assistance comes in four forms.

Outside Scholarships: an outright gift of money, paid to you or the school by an outside source (government, foundation, corporation, etc.).

Inside Scholarships: the school itself reduces your tuition and/or other expenses.

Fellowship: money either from the school or an outside source, in return for certain work or services to be performed at the school (usually teaching or research).

Loans: from outside lenders, or from the school itself, to be paid back over a period of anywhere from 1 to 10 years, generally at interest rates lower than current prime rate.

Sadly, it is the case that as college costs continue to rise substantially, the amount of money available for financial aid has diminished dramatically. Many loan and scholarship programs were either funded or guaranteed by the federal government, and much of this money was eliminated as part of the Reagan administration's cutbacks, and has not been restored. After all, 300,000 cancelled full-tuition scholarships can buy one nuclear-powered aircraft carrier. And already have. [Because of this remark in previous editions, I have received three stern letters from veterans asking me, in effect, if I would rather be protected from a Commie invasion by a nuclear battleship or by 300,000 scholars.]

Still, billions of dollars are available to help pay the college costs of people who need help. The vast majority of it goes to full-time students under age 25, pursuing residential degrees at traditional schools.

Tapping into that particular fount is outside the scope of this book. There are several very useful books on this subject, which are described in the reference section, including my own book, *Finding Money for College,* published by Ten Speed Press.

My book is the only one I know of that is specifically oriented to the non-traditional student, the older student, and the student in quest of Master's and Doctorate degrees. It covers a wide range of non-traditional strategies, ranging from bartering skills (gardening, athletic coaching, etc.) for tuition; recruiting new students on a commission basis; and real estate and tax angles.

There are some computerized services that have collected data on tens of thousands of individual scholarships. These match their clients' needs and interests with donors for a modest fee. All but a few of these services are licensees, and tap into the same computer, so there is no point in getting more than one report.

The company that licenses is Academic Guidance Services, 300 S. Route 73, Suite 2A, Marlton, NJ 08053. If you are buying more than one report, you should confirm that they are not *both* AGS licensees.

Here are two independent scholarship search services:

- College Student Financial Aid Services, Shady Grove Road and Route 355, 16220 S. Frederick Rd., Suite 208, Gaithersburg, MD 20877.
- National Scholarship Research Service, 86 Belvedere St., San Rafael, CA 94901.

Some of the scholarships available are, admittedly, awfully peculiar: for rodeo riders with high grades, for Canadian petunia fanciers, for reformed prostitutes from Seattle, for people named Baxendale or Murphy, for people born on certain dates and/or in certain towns, and so on. But many are quite general, and a fair number do not depend on financial need or net worth.

Many students enrolled in non-traditional, even non-residential programs have their expenses paid, all or in part, by their employer. Thousands of large corporations, including nearly all of the Fortune 500, have tuition plans for their employees. But *billions* of dollars in corporate funds go unclaimed each year, simply because people don't ask for them.

Many, but not all, corporations will pay for unaccredited programs. Some unaccredited schools list in their literature the names of hundreds of corporations as well as U.S. and foreign government agencies that have paid students' tuition costs.

Most non-traditional schools, accredited and unaccredited, offer inside scholarships to their students who need them. In other words, they will award a partial scholarship, in the form of tuition reduction (10% to 30% is the usual range), rather than lose a student altogether. Quite a few schools also offer an extended payment plan, in which the tuition can be paid in a series of smaller monthly installments, or even charged to a MasterCard or Visa credit card.

There are schools, traditional and non-traditional, that offer tuition reduction in the form of commissions, or finders' fees, for bringing in other students. This quite ethical procedure can result in a tuition reduction of from $50 to several hundred dollars for each referral, when the referred student enrolls.

But the biggest factors, by far, in financial aid for students at non-traditional schools are the speed of their education and the possibility of remaining fully employed while pursuing the degree. If even one year can be cut from a "traditional" four-year Bachelor's degree program, the savings (including revenue from a year of working for pay) are greater than 99% of all scholarship grants. And, as mentioned earlier, the average "four year" Bachelor's degree now takes six years, which should be taken into account in figuring time lost from jobs.

So, while it is nice to "win" money from another source, it is surely the case that to be able to complete an entire degree program for an out-of-pocket cost of from $2,000 to $5,000 (the typical range at non-traditional schools) is one of the great financial bargains of these difficult times.

9. Applying to Schools

Admissions Standards, Harvard College, c. 1650:
When any Scholar is able to read Tully or such like classical Latin Author ex tempore, *and to make and speak true Latin in verse and prose . . . and decline perfectly the paradigms of Nouns and verbs in the Greek tongue, then may he be admitted into the College, nor shall any claim admission before such qualifications.*

HOW MANY SCHOOLS SHOULD YOU APPLY TO?

There is no single answer to this question that is right for everyone. Each person will have to determine his or her own best answer. The decision should be based on the following four factors:

1. Likelihood of admission

Some schools are extremely competitive or popular and admit fewer than 10% of qualified applicants. Some have an "open admissions" policy and admit literally everyone who applies. Most are somewhere in between.

If your goal is to be admitted to one of the highly competitive schools (for instance, Harvard, Yale, Princeton, Stanford), where your chances of being accepted are not high, then it is wise to apply to at least four or five schools that would be among your top choices, and to at least one "safety valve," an easier one, in case all else fails.

If your interest is in one of the good, but not world-famous, non-resident programs, your chances for acceptance are probably better than nine in ten, so you might decide to apply only to one or two.

2. Cost

There is a tremendous range of possible costs for any given degree. For instance, a respectable Ph.D. could cost around $3,000 at a good non-resident school, or more than $50,000 at a well-known university—not even taking into account the lost salary. In general, I think it makes sense to apply to no more than two or three schools in any given price category.

3. What they offer you

Shopping around for a school is a little like shopping for a new car. Many schools either have money problems, or operate as profit-making businesses, and in either case, they are most eager to enroll new students. Thus it is not unreasonable to ask the schools what they can do for you. Let them know that you are a knowledgeable "shopper," and that you have this book. Do they have courses or faculty advisors in your specific field? If not, will they get one for you? How much credit will they give for prior life experience learning? How long will it take to earn the degree? Are there any scholarship or tuition reduction plans available? Does tuition have to be paid all at once, or can it be spread out over time? If factors like these are important for you, then it could pay to shop around for the best deal.

You might consider investigating at least two or three schools that appear somewhat similar, because there will surely be differences.

> **CAUTION:** Remember that academic quality and reputation are probably the most important factors—so don't let a small financial saving be a reason to switch from a good school to a less-good school.

4. Your own time

Applying to a school can be a time-consuming process—and it costs money, too. Many schools have application fees ranging from $25 to $100. Some people get so carried away with the process of applying to school after school that they never get around to earning their degree!

Of course once you have prepared a good and detailed resume, Curriculum Vitae, or life experience portfolio, you can use it to apply to more than one school.

Another time factor is how much of a hurry you are in. If you apply to several schools at once, the chances are good that at least one will admit you, and you can begin work promptly. If you apply to only one, and it turns you down, or you get into long delays, then it can take a month or two to go through the admission process elsewhere.

SPEEDING UP THE ADMISSIONS PROCESS

The admissions process at most traditional schools is very slow; most people apply nearly a year in advance; and do not learn if their application has been accepted for four to six months. Non-traditional programs vary immensely in their policies in this regard. Some will grant conditional acceptance within a few weeks after receiving the application. ("Conditional" means that they must later verify the prior learning experiences you claim.) Others take just as long as traditional programs.

The following three factors can result in a much faster admissions process:

1. Selecting schools by policy

A school's admissions policy should be stated in its catalogue. Since you will find a range among schools of a few weeks to six months for a decision, the simple solution is to ask, and then apply to schools with a fast procedure.

2. Asking for speedy decisions

Some schools have formal procedures whereby you can request an early decision on your acceptance. Others do the same thing informally, for those who ask. In effect what this does is put you at the top of the pile in the admissions office, so you will have the decision in, perhaps, half the usual time. Other schools use what they call a "rolling admissions" procedure, which means, in effect, that each application is considered soon after it is received instead of being held several months and considered with a large batch of others.

3. Applying pressure

As previously indicated, many schools are eager to have new students. If you make it clear to a school that you are in a hurry and that you may consider going elsewhere if you don't hear from them promptly, they will usually speed up the process. It is not unreasonable to specify a time frame. If, for instance, you are mailing in your application on September 1, you might enclose a note saying that you would like to have their decision mailed or phoned to you by October 1. (Some schools routinely telephone their acceptances; others do so if asked; some will only do so by collect call; and others will not, no matter what.)

HOW TO APPLY TO A SCHOOL

The basic procedure is essentially the same at all schools, traditional or non-traditional:

1. You write (or telephone) for the school's catalogue or bulletin or other literature, and admissions forms.
2. You complete the admissions forms and return them to the school, with application fee, if any.
3. You complete any other requirements the school may have (exams, transcripts, letters of recommendation, etc.).
4. The school notifies you of their decision.

It is step three that can vary tremendously from school to school. At some schools all that is required is the admissions application. Others will require various entrance examinations to test your aptitude or knowledge level, transcripts, three or more letters of reference, a statement of financial condition, and possibly a personal interview, either on the campus or with a local representative in your area.

Happily, the majority of non-traditional schools have relatively simple entrance requirements. And all schools supply the materials that tell you exactly what they expect you to do in order to apply. If it is not clear, ask. If the school does not supply prompt, helpful answers, then you probably don't want to deal with them anyway. It's a buyer's market.

It is advisable, in general, *not* to send a whole bunch of stuff to a school the very first time you write to them. A short note, asking for their catalogue, should suffice. You may wish to indicate your field and degree goal ("I am interested in a Master's and possibly a Doctorate in psychology...") in case they have different sets of literature for different programs. It probably can do no harm to mention that you are a reader of this book; it might get you slightly prompter or more personal responses. (On the other hand, I have gotten more than a few grouchy letters from readers saying, "I told them I was a personal friend of yours, and it still took six months for an answer." Oh, dear. Well, if they hadn't said that, it might have been even longer. Or perhaps shorter. Who knows?)

ENTRANCE EXAMINATIONS

Many non-resident degree programs, even at the Master's and Doctoral levels, do not require any entrance examinations. On the other hand, the majority of residential programs *do* require them. The main reason for this appears to be that non-traditional schools do not have to worry about overcrowding on the campus, so they can admit more students. A second reason is that they tend to deal with more mature students who have the ability to decide which program is best for them.

There are, needless to say, exceptions to both reasons. If you have particular feelings about examinations—positive or negative—you will be able to find schools that meet your requirements. Do not hesitate to ask any school about their exam requirements if it is not clear from the catalogue.

Bachelor's Admission Examinations

Most residential universities require applicants to take part or all of the "ATP" or Admissions Testing Program, run by a private agency, the College Entrance Examination Board (888 7th Ave., New York, NY 10019). The main component of the ATP is the SAT, or Scholastic Aptitude Test, which measures verbal and mathematical abilities. There are also achievement tests, testing knowledge levels in specific subject areas: biology, European history, Latin, etc. These examinations are given at centers all over North America several times each year, at modest fees, and by special arrangement in many foreign locations.

A competing private organization, ACT (American College Testing Program, P.O. Box 168, Iowa City, IA 52240) offers a similar range of entrance examinations.

The important point is that very few schools have their own exams; virtually all rely on either the ACT or the ATP.

Graduate Degrees

Again, many non-residential schools do not require any entrance examinations. Many, but by no means all, residential Master's and Doctoral programs ask their applicants to take the GRE, or Graduate Record Examination, administered by the Educational Testing Service (P.O. Box 955, Princeton, NJ 08541). The basic GRE consists of a 3 1/2-hour aptitude test (verbal, quantitative, and analytical abilities). Some schools also require GRE subject-area exams, which are available in a variety of specific fields (chemistry, computer science, music, etc.).

Professional Schools

Most law and medical schools also require a standard examination, rather than having one of their own. The MSAT (Medical School Admission Test is given several times a year by ACT while the LSAT (Law School Admission Test) is given five times a year by ETS.

There are many excellent books available at most libraries and larger bookstores on how to prepare for these various exams, complete with questions and answers. Some of these are listed in the bibliography of this book. Also, the testing agencies themselves sell literature on their tests as well as copies of previous years' examinations.

The testing agencies used to deny vigorously that either cramming or coaching could affect one's scores. In the face of overwhelming evidence to the contrary, they no longer make those claims. Some coaching services have documented score increases of 25% to 30%. Check the Yellow Pages or the bulletin boards on high school or college campuses.

10. Equivalency Examinations

In an examination, those who do not wish to know
ask questions of those who cannot tell.
—Walter Raleigh

The non-traditional approach to higher education says that if you have knowledge of an academic field, then you should get credit for that knowledge, regardless of how or where you acquired the knowledge. The simplest and fairest way of assessing that knowledge is through an examination.

More than 2,000 colleges and universities in the United States and Canada, many of whom would deny vigorously that there is anything "non-traditional" about them, award credit toward their Bachelor's degrees (and, in a few cases, Master's and Doctorates) solely on the basis of passing examinations.

Many of the exams are designed to be equivalent to the final exam in a typical college class, and the assumption is that if you score high enough, you get the same amount of credit you would have gotten by taking the class—or, in some cases, a good deal more.

While there are many sources of equivalency exams, including a trend toward schools developing their own, two independent national agencies are dominant in this field. They offer exams known as CLEP and PEP.

CLEP and PEP

CLEP (the College-Level Examination Program) and PEP (the Proficiency Examination Program) administer more than 75 exams. They are given at hundreds of testing centers all over North America and, by special arrangement, many of them can be administered almost anywhere in the world.

CLEP is offered by the College Entrance Examination Board, known as "the College Board" (CN 6600, Princeton, NJ 08541-6600). Military personnel who want to take CLEP should see their education officer or write DANTES, CN, Princeton, NJ 08541.

PEP is offered in the state of New York by the Regents External Degree–College Proficiency Programs (Cultural Education Center, Albany, NY 12230), and everywhere else by the American College Testing Program (P.O. Box 168, Iowa City, IA 52243).

Many of the tests offered by CLEP are available in two versions: just multiple-choice questions, or multiple choice plus an essay. Some colleges require applicants to take both parts, others just the multiple choice. There are five general exams, each 90 minutes long, and only multiple choice, except English, which has the option of a 45-minute multiple choice and a 45-minute composition.

CLEP offers 30 subject-area exams, each of them 90 minutes of multiple-choice questions, with the option of an additional 90 minutes for writing an essay. The cost is around $30 per test.

PEP offers 43 subject-area exams, most of them three hours long, but a few are four hours. The fees range from $40 to $125 per exam.

Each college or university sets its own standards for passing grades, and also decides for itself how much credit to give for each exam. Both of these factors can vary substantially from school to school. For instance, the PEP test in anatomy and physiology is a three-hour multiple-choice test. Hundreds of schools give credit for passing this exam. Here, for instance, are three of them:

- Central Virginia Community College requires a score of 45 (out of 80), and awards 9 credit hours for passing.
- Edinboro University in Pennsylvania requires a score of 50 to pass, and awards 6 credit hours for the same exam.
- Concordia College in New York requires a score of 47, but awards only 3 credit hours.

Similar situations prevail on most of the exams. There is no predictability or consistency within a given school. For instance, at the University of South Florida, a three-hour multiple-choice test in maternal nursing is worth 18 units while a three-hour multiple-choice test in psychiatric nursing is worth only 9 units.

So, with dozens of standard exams available, and more than 2,000 schools offering credit, it pays to shop around a little and select both the school and the exams where you will get the most credit.

CLEP exams are offered in five general subject areas, which are

- Social Science and History
- Humanities
- Natural Science
- English Composition
- Mathematics

Specific-subject area exams are offered in the following fields:

American Government
Educational Psychology
Human Growth and Devopment
Introductory Macroeconomics
Western Civilization I and II
German I and II
American Literature
College Composition
Freshman English
Algebra and Trigonometry
General Chemistry
Introduction to Management
Introductory Business Law
College Algebra
American History I and II
General Psychology
Introductory Marketing
Introductory Sociology
French I and II
Spanish I and II
Analysis and Interpretation
English Literature
Trigonometry
General Biology
Computers and Data Processing
Introductory Accounting
Calculus and Elementary Functions

PEP exams are offered in these fields:

Abnormal Psychology
Earth Science
Microbiology
Statistics
Cost Accounting
Advanced Accounting
Federal Income Taxation
Corporate Finance
Organizational Behavior
Labor Relations
Management, Human Resources
Production/Operations Management
Reading Instruction
Fundamentals of Nursing
Anatomy and Physiology
Foundations of Gerontology
Physical Geology
Accounting I and II
Auditing
Intermediate Business Law
Business Policy
Principles of Management
Personnel Administration
Marketing
Statistics
Educational Psychology
Remedial Reading
15 more nursing exams

HOW EXAMS ARE SCORED

CLEP exams are scored on a scale of either 20 to 80 or 200 to 800. This is done to maintain the fiction that no score can have any intrinsic meaning. It is not obvious, for example, whether a score of 514 is either good or bad. But any college-bound high school senior in America can tell you that 400 is pretty bad, 500 is OK, 600 is good, and 700 is great. Still, each college sets its own minimum score for which they will give credit, and in many cases all that is necessary is to be in the upper half of those taking the test.

PEP gives standard numerical or letter grades for its tests.

Anywhere from 1-2/3 to 6 credits may be earned for each hour of testing. For example, the five basic CLEP tests (90 minutes of multiple choice questions each) are worth anywhere from 8 to 30 semester units, depending on the school. Thus it is possible to complete the equivalent of an entire year of college—30 semester units—in two days, by taking and passing these five tests.

CLEP tests are given over a two-day period once each month at more than 1,000 centers, most of them on college or university campuses. PEP tests are given for two consecutive days on a variable schedule in about 100 locations, nationwide.

Persons living more than 150 miles from a test center may make special arrangements for the test to be given nearer home. There is a modest charge for this service. And for those in a big hurry, the CLEP tests are given twice each week in Washington, DC.

There is no stigma attached to poor performance on these tests. In fact, if you wish, you may have the scores reported only to you, so that no one but you and the computer will know how you did. Then, if your scores are high enough, you can have them sent on to the schools of your choice. CLEP allows exams to be taken every six months; you can take the same PEP exam twice in any 12-month period.

HOW HARD ARE THESE EXAMS?

This is, of course, an extremely subjective question. However, I have heard from a great many readers who have attempted CLEP and PEP exams, and the most common response is "Gee, that was a lot easier than I had expected." This is especially true of more mature students. The tests are designed for 18-to-20-year-olds, and there appears to be a certain amount of knowledge of facts, as well as experience in dealing with testing situations, that people acquire in ordinary life situations as they grow older.

PREPARING (AND CRAMMING) FOR EXAMS

The testing agencies issue detailed syllabuses describing each test and the specific content area it covers. CLEP also sells a book that gives sample questions and answers from each examination.

At least four educational publishers have produced series of books on how to prepare for such exams, often with full-length sample tests. These can be found in the reference section of any good bookstore or library.

For years, the testing agencies vigorously fought the idea of letting test-takers take copies of the test home with them. But consumer legislation in New York has made the tests available, and a good thing, too. Every so often, someone discovers an incorrect answer, or a poorly-phrased question that can have more than one correct answer, necessitating a recalculation and reissuance of scores to all the thousands of people who took that test.

In recent years, there has been much controversy over the value of cramming for examinations. Many of my counseling clients have told me they were able to pass four or five CLEP exams in a row by spending an intensive few days (or weeks) cramming for them. Although the various testing agencies used to deny that cramming can be of any value, in the last few years there have been some extremely persuasive research studies that demonstrate the effectiveness of intensive studying. These data have vindicated the claims made by people and agencies that assist students in preparing for examinations. Such services are offered in a great many places, usually in the vicinity of college campuses, by graduate students and moonlighting faculty. The best place to find them is through the classified ads in campus newspapers and on bulletin boards around the campus.

For example, one testing service The Princeton Review, claims that their preparation materials, in person or through their book, increase scores by an average of 150 points. [Princeton Review, P.O. Box 3354, Princeton, NJ 08540, (609) 683-0082.] A nationwide chain of preparation centers is operated by the Stanley H. Kaplan Educational Centers. They offer intensive preparation for dozens of different tests, ranging from college admissions to national medical boards. Although the main method of preparation involves a good deal of classroom attendance at a center (from 20 to over 100 hours), almost all the materials can be rented for home study. Residential tuition for most examination preparation courses is in the range of $150 to $300, but the cost goes as high as $850 for some medical exams. Rental of most sets of materials for home study costs from $100 to $200 for most sets of materials. Kaplan Centers operate in 40 states, the District of Columbia, Puerto Rico, and in Canada. [Stanley H. Kaplan Educational Center, Ltd., 131 West 56th St., New York, NY 10019, (212) 977-8200; outside New York, (800) 223-1782.]

Probably the best strategy is to take a sample self-scoring test from one of the various guidebooks. If you do very well, you may wish to take the real exam right away. If you do very badly, you may conclude that credit by examination is not your cup of hemlock. And if you score anywhere in between, consider cramming on your own, or with the help of a paid tutor or tutoring service.

OTHER EXAMINATIONS

Here are some other examinations that can be used to earn substantial credit toward many non-traditional degree programs.

Graduate Record Examination

The GRE is administered by the Educational Testing Service [P.O. Box 955, Princeton, NJ 08541, (212) 966-5853] and is given at nationwide locations four times each year. The GRE Advanced Test is a three-hour multiple-choice test, designed to test knowledge that would ordinarily be gained by a Bachelor's degree holder in that given field. The exams are available in the fields of biology, chemistry, computer science, economics, education, engineering, French, geography, geology, German, history, English literature, mathematics, music, philosophy, physics, political science, psychology, sociology, and Spanish.

Schools vary widely in how much credit they will give for each GRE. The range is from none at all to 30 semester units in the case of Regents College of the University of the State of New York.

I once met a National Guard sergeant who had crammed for, taken, and passed three GRE exams in a row, thereby earning 90 semester units in nine hours of testing. Then he took the five basic CLEP exams in two days, and earned 30 more units, which was enough to earn an accredited Bachelor's degree, start to finish, in 16-1/2 hours, starting absolutely from scratch with no college credit.

MLA Foreign Language Proficiency Tests

Although many schools will give credit for foreign language skills, the most credit is available through the MLA tests. Unfortunately they are normally given only under the auspices of three outstanding non-resident schools, at those schools' offices: the University of the State of New York, Thomas Edison State College of New Jersey, and Charter Oak College in Connecticut. (I have heard from a few readers who were able to arrange for schools in other locations to administer these tests, but there is no regular program for so doing.)

The MLA exams consist of two "batteries." Battery A is a half-day exam in either French, German, Italian, Russian, or Spanish, covering comprehension, speaking, reading, and writing. It is worth 24 semester hours at the University of the State of New York, somewhat less at most other schools. Battery B covers linguistics, civilization and culture, and language-teaching techniques. It also requires a half a day, and is worth 9 semester units at various schools.

DANTES

The Defense Activity for Non-Traditional Education Support, or DANTES, administers its own exams, as well as CLEP and PEP exams. The exams are for active military personnel, who can obtain information from their base education officers.

University End of Course Exams

Several schools offer the opportunity to earn credit for a correspondence course solely by taking (and passing) the final exam for that course. One need not be enrolled as a student in the school to do this. Two schools with especially large programs of this kind are Ohio University (Course Credit by Examination, Tupper Hall, Athens, OH 45701) and the University of North Carolina (Independent Study, Abernethy Hall 002A, Chapel Hill, NC 27514).

Advanced Placement Examinations The College Board offers exams specifically for high school students who wish to earn college credit while still in high school. Exams in 13 subject areas are offered. (College Board Advanced Placement Program, 888 7th Ave., New York, NY 10106)

Special Assessments

For people whose knowledge is both extensive and in an obscure field (or at least one for which no exams have been developed), some schools are willing to develop special exams for a single student. At the University of the State of New York, both for its students and for Regents Credit Bank depositors (see the chapter on the Credit Bank), this takes the form of an oral exam. They will find at least two experts in your field, be it Persian military history, paleontology, French poetry, or whatever. Following a three-hour oral exam, conducted at everyone's mutual convenience in Albany, New York, the examiners decide how many credits to award for that particular knowledge area.

11. Correspondence Courses

The postman is the agent of impolite surprises.
Every week, we ought to have an hour for receiving letters—
and then go and take a bath.
—Friedrich Nietzsche

There are two kinds of correspondence study, or home study, courses—vocational and academic. Vocational courses (meat cutting, locksmithing, appliance repair, etc.) often offer useful training, but rarely lead to degrees, so they are not relevant for this book. The National Home Study Council (1601 18th St. NW, Washington, DC 20009) offers excellent free information on the sources of vocational home study courses in many fields.

Seventy major universities and teaching institutions offer academic correspondence courses—more than 12,000 courses in hundreds of subjects, from accounting to zoology. Virtually all of these courses can be counted toward a degree at almost any college or university. However, most schools have a limit on the amount of correspondence credit they will apply to a degree. This limit is typically around 50%, but the range is from zero to 100%.

"One hundred percent" means that it is indeed possible to earn an accredited Bachelor's degree entirely through correspondence study. This may be done, for instance, at the University of the State of New York, Thomas Edison State College of New Jersey, and Western Illinois University. Courses taken at any of the 70 schools can be applied to these degrees.

Each of the 70 institutions publishes a catalogue or bulletin listing their available courses. Some offer just a few while others have hundreds. All of the schools will accept students living anywhere in the United States, although some schools charge more for out-of-state students. About 80% accept foreign students, but all courses are offered only in English.

There is a helpful directory that is, in effect, a master catalogue to all 70 schools. It lists the course titles of every course at each school. The abbreviated one-line course titles are surprisingly informative: "Hist & phil of phys ed," "Fac career dev in schools," and 12,000 more.

The directory is called *The Independent Study Catalog*, and it is revised approximately every three years by the publisher, Peterson's Guides (P.O. Box 3601, Princeton, NJ 08540).

Of course you can also write directly to the schools. All of them will send you their catalogue without charge. Many of the schools have popular subjects like psychology, business, and education, but some of the more esoteric topics may only be available at one or two schools, and this directory points you to them.

Correspondence courses range from 1 to 6 semester hours worth of credit, and can cost anywhere from less than $40 to more than $100 per semester hour. The average is around $60, so that a typical 3-unit course would cost $180. Because of the wide range in costs, it pays to shop around.

A typical correspondence course will consist of from 5 to 20 lessons, each one requiring either a short written paper, answers to questions, or an unsupervised test graded by the instructor. There is almost always a supervised final examination. These can usually be taken anywhere in the world where a suitable proctor can be found (usually a high school or college teacher).

People who cannot go to a testing center, either because they are handicapped, live too far away, or are in prison, can usually arrange to have a test supervisor come to them. Schools can be extremely flexible. One correspondence program administrator told me he had two students—a husband and wife—working as missionaries on a remote island where they were the only people who could read and write. He allowed them to supervise each other.

Many schools set limits on how fast and how slow you can complete a correspondence course. The shortest time is generally three to six weeks, while the upper limit ranges from three months to two years. Some schools limit the number of courses you can take at one time, but most do not. Even those with limits are concerned only with their own institution. There is no cross-checking, and in theory one could take simultaneous courses from all 70 institutions.

A sidelight: I would have thought that correspondence programs would remain quite stable, since so much time and effort is required to establish one. However in the three years between the two most recent

Peterson's Guides, 6 schools (1 in 12) dropped their programs, and 5 new ones (Ball State, Governors State, Old Dominion, Saint Joseph's, and Weber State) started new ones.

THE 70 SCHOOLS
Coding as follows:
✔ = one of the dozen schools with the most college-level courses
❤ = school that welcomes students from outside the U.S.
◆ = school that prefers not to deal with foreign students but treats each case on its own merits
× = school that will not accept foreign students

Adams State College ❤
Extension Division,
Alamosa, CO 81102
(303) 589-7671
Approximately 7 college-level courses
Math courses only.

Arizona State University ❤
Correspondence Study Office, ASB 112,
Tempe, AZ 85287
(602) 965-6563
Approximately 90 college-level courses

Athabasca University ×
Student Services Office, Box 10000,
Athabasca, Alberta, Canada T0G 2R0
(403) 645-6111
Approximately 125 college-level courses

Auburn University ❤
Independent Study Program, Mell Hall,
Auburn, AL 36849
(205) 826-5103
Approximately 45 college-level courses

Ball State University ×
School of Continuing Education,
Carmichael Hall, Muncie, IN 47306
(317) 285-1581
Approximately 80 college-level courses

Brigham Young University ❤ ✔
Independent Study, 206 Harmon Continuing
Education Building, Provo, UT 84604
(801) 378-2868
Approximately 280 college-level courses

California State University ❤
Office of Water Programs,
6000 J Street, Sacramento, CA 95819
(916) 454-6142
Approximately 6 college-level courses
All courses deal with wastewater management

Central Michigan University ❤
Office of Independent Study, Rowe Hall 125,
Mt. Pleasant, MI 48859
(517) 774-7140
Approximately 70 college-level courses

Colorado State University ❤
Correspondence Program Coordinator,
C102 Rockwell Hall, Fort Collins, CO 80523
(303) 491-5288
Approximately 40 college-level courses
Graduate courses in adult education, grantsmanship

Department of Agriculture Graduate School ❤
U. S. Department of Agriculture, 1404 South Bldg.,
14th and Independence Ave. SW ,
Washington, DC 20250
(202) 447-7123
Approximately 80 college-level courses
Many fields are covered, but not agriculture.

East Tennessee State University ❤
Department of Environmental Health,
P. O. Box 22960-A, , Johnson City, TN 37614
(615) 929-4462
Approximately 9 college-level courses
All courses in environmental health, rodent control, sanitation.

Eastern Kentucky University ❤
Dean of Extended Programs, Perkins 217,
Richmond, KY 40475
(606) 622-2001
Approximately 45 college-level courses

Eastern Michigan University ◆
Coordinator of Independent Study,
329 Goodison Hall,, Ypsilanti, MI 48197
(313) 487-1081
Approximately 12 college-level courses

Governors State University ❤
Independent Study by Correspondence,
Stuendel Road, University Park, IL 60466
(312) 534-5000, Ext. 2121
Approximately 20 college-level courses
Six graduate courses in ethnic studies, urban politics.

Home Study International ❤
6940 Carroll Ave.,
Takoma Park, MD 20912
(202) 722-6572
Approximately 70 college-level courses

Indiana State University ❤
Director of Independent Study,
Alumni Center 124,
Terre Haute, IN 47809
(812) 237-2555
Approximately 60 college-level courses

Indiana University ❤
Independent Study Program, Owen Hall,
Bloomington, IN 47405
(812) 335-3693
Approximately 90 college-level courses

Louisiana State University ❤ ✔ 8/8/96
Office of Independent Study,
Baton Rouge, LA 70803
(504) 388-3171
Approximately 160 college-level courses

Mississippi State University ❤
Continuing Education, P. O. Drawer 5247,
Mississippi State, MS 39762
(601) 325-3473
Approximately 75 college-level courses

Murray State University ◆
Center for Continuing Education,
15th at Main, Murray, KY 42071
(502) 762-4159
Approximately 35 college-level courses
Includes animal, poultry, swine and crop science.

Ohio University ❤ ✔ 8/8/96.
Director of Independent Study,
303 Tupper Hall, Athens, OH 45701
(614) 594-6721
Approximately 185 college-level courses

Oklahoma State University ❤
Correspondence Study Department,
001P Classroom Building,
Stillwater, OK 74078
(405) 624-6390
Approximately 120 college-level courses

Old Dominion University ❤
Office of Continuing Education,
Education Building, Room 145, Norfolk, VA 23508
(804) 440-3163
Approximately 9 college-level courses
All courses in pharmacology and allied areas.

Oregon State System of Higher Education ❤
Office of Independent Study,
Portland State University, P. O. Box 1491,
Portland, OR 97207
(800) 547-8887, Ext. 4865
Approximately 100 college-level courses

Pennsylvania State University ❤ ✔
Director of Independent Learning,
128 Mitchell Building,
University Park, PA 16802
(814) 865-5403
Approximately 150 college-level courses

Purdue University ❤
Division of Media-Based Programs,
116 Stewart Center
West Lafayette, West Lafayette, IN 47907
(317) 494-7231
Approximately 8 college-level courses
Courses in food service, pest control, pharmacology.

Roosevelt University ❤
College of Continuing Education,
430 S. Michigan Avenue,
Chicago, IL 60605
(312) 341-3866
Approximately 60 college-level courses
Includes three graduate courses in psychology.

Saint Joseph's College ❤
Continuing Education, White's Bridge Road,
North Windham, ME 04062
(207) 892-6766
Approximately 50 college-level courses

Savannah State College ❤
Correspondence Study Office, P. O. Box 20372Savan-
nah, GA 31404
(912) 356-2243
Approximately 25 college-level courses

Southern Illinois University ❤
Division of Continuing Education,
Washington Square C,
Carbondale, IL 62901
(618) 536-7751
Approximately 14 college-level courses

Texas Tech University ❤
Continuing Education, P. O. Box 4110,
Lubbock, TX 79409
(806) 742-1513
Approximately 90 college-level courses

University of Alabama ❤ ✔
Independent Study Department, P. O. Box 2967, University, AL 35486
(205) 348-7642
Approximately 175 college-level courses

University of Alaska ❤
Correspondence Study, 115 Eielson Bldg., 403 Salcha St., Fairbanks, AK 99701
(907) 474-7222
Approximately 65 college-level courses

University of Arizona ❤
Continuing Education, Babcock Bldg, Suite 1201, 1717 E. Speedway, Tucson, AZ 85719
(602) 621-3021
Approximately 110 college-level courses

University of Arkansas ❤
Department of Independent Study, 2 University Center, Fayetteville, AR 72701
(501) 575-3647
Approximately 120 college-level courses

University of California ❤ ✔
Independent Study, 2223 Fulton St., Berkeley, CA 94720
(415) 642-4124
Approximately 200 college-level courses

University of Colorado ❤
Division of Continuing Education, Campus Box 178, Boulder, CO 80309
(303) 492-5145
Approximately 85 college-level courses

University of Florida ❤
Department of Independent Study by Correspondence, 1938 W. University Ave., Room 1, Gainesville, FL 32603
(904) 392-1711
Approximately 115 college-level courses

University of Georgia ❤
Center for Continuing Education, 1197 South Lumpkin St., Athens, GA 30602
(404) 542-3243
Approximately 130 college-level courses

University of Idaho ❤
Correspondence Study in Idaho, Continuing Education Building, Room 116, Moscow, ID 83843
(208) 885-6641
Approximately 100 college-level courses

University of Illinois ◆
Guided Individual Study, 1046 Illini Hall, 725 S. Wright St., Champaign, IL 61820
(217) 333-1321
Approximately 140 college-level courses

University of Iowa ❤ ✔
Center for Credit Programs, W400 Seashore Hall, Iowa City, IA 52242
(319) 353-4963
Approximately 140 college-level courses

University of Kansas ❤
Independent Study, Continuing Education Building, Lawrence, KS 66045
(913) 864-4792
Approximately 120 college-level courses

University of Kentucky ◆
Independent Studies, Frazee Hall, Room 1, Lexington, KY 40506
(606) 257-3466
Approximately 125 college-level courses

University of Michigan ❤
Department of Independent Study, 200 Hill St., Ann Arbor, MI 48104
(313) 764-5306
Approximately 30 college-level courses

University of Minnesota ❤ ✔
Independent Study, 45 Wesbrook Hall, 77 Pleasant St. SE, Minneapolis, MN 55455
(612) 373-3803
Approximately 265 college-level courses

University of Mississippi ❤
Department of Independent Study, Division of Continuing Education, University, MS 38677
(601) 232-7313
Approximately 135 college-level courses
Offers non-credit French and German for Ph.D. candidates.

University of Missouri ❤
Center for Independent Study,
400 Hitt St.,
Columbia, MO 65211
(314) 882-6431
Approximately 120 college-level courses

University of Nebraska ❤
269 Nebraska Center for Continuing Education,
33rd and Holdrege,
Lincoln, NE 68583
(402) 472-1926
Approximately 75 college-level courses

University of Nevada ❤
Independent Study Department, Room 333,
College Inn, 1001 S. Virginia St.,
Reno, NV 89557
(702) 784-4652
Approximately 65 college-level courses

University of North Carolina ❤ ✔
Independent Study,
201 Abernethy Hall 002A,
Chapel Hill, NC 27514
(919) 962-1106
Approximately 160 college-level courses

University of North Dakota ✕
Department of Correspondence Study,
Box 8277, University Station,
Grand Forks, ND 58202
(701) 777-3044
Approximately 90 college-level courses

University of Northern Colorado ❤
Frasier Hall, Room 11,
Greeley, CO 80639
(303) 351-2944
Approximately 16 college-level courses

University of Northern Iowa ❤
Coordinator of Credit Programs,
144 Gilchrist, Cedar Falls, IA 50614
(319) 273-2 121
Approximately 55 college-level courses

University of Oklahoma ❤ ✔
Independent Study Department,
1700 Asp Ave., Room B-1,
Norman, OK 73037
(405) 325-1921
Approximately 200 college-level courses

University of South Carolina ❤
Correspondence Study, 915 Gregg St.,
Columbia, SC 29208
(803) 777-2188
Approximately 130 college-level courses

University of South Dakota ❤
126 Center for Continuing Education,
414 E. Clark,
Vermillion, SD 57069
(605) 677-5281
Approximately 95 college-level courses

University of Southern Mississippi❤
Department of Independent Study,
P. O. Box 5056, Southern Station,
Hattiesburg, MS 39406
(601) 266-4860
Approximately 90 college-level courses

University of Tennessee ❤ ✔
Center for Extended Learning,
420 Communications Bldg.,
Knoxville, TN 37996
(615) 974-5134
Approximately 180 college-level courses
Many non-credit courses in pharmacology, creative writing, Bible study.

University of Texas ❤
Correspondence Study,
Education Annex F38, P. O. Box 7700,
Austin, TX 78713
(512) 471-5616
Approximately 100 college-level courses

University of Utah ❤
Division of Continuing Education,
1152 Annex Building, Salt Lake City, UT 84112
(801) 581-6485
Approximately 140 college-level courses

University of Washington ❤ 8/8/96
University Extension—Distance Learning
GH-23, 5001 25th Ave. NE, Room 109,
Seattle, WA 98195
(206) 543-2350
Approximately 130 college-level courses
Many foreign language courses.

University of Wisconsin ❤ ✔
Independent Study, 432 N. Lake St.,
Madison, WI 53706
(608) 263-2055
Approximately 195 college-level courses
Many foreign language courses.

University of Wyoming ❤
Correspondence Study Department,
Box 3294, University Station,
Laramie, WY 82071
(307) 766-5631
Approximately 100 college-level courses

Utah State University ❤
Independent Study Division,
Eccles Conference Center,
Logan, UT 84322
(801) 750-2131
Approximately 100 college-level courses

Washington State University ❤
Independent Study, 208 Van Doren Hall,
Pullman, WA 99164
(509) 335-3557
Approximately 100 college-level courses

Weber State College ❤
Division of Continuing Education,
3750 Harrison Blvd.,
Ogden, UT 84408
(801) 626-6600
Approximately 60 college-level courses

Western Illinois University ◆
Independent Study Program, 318 Sherman Hall,
West Adams Road,
Macomb, IL 61455
(309) 298-2496
Approximately 70 college-level courses

Western Michigan University ◆
Self-Instructional Programs, Ellworth Hall,
Room B-102, West Michigan Ave.,
Kalamazoo, MI 49008
(616) 383-0788
Approximately 75 college-level courses

Western Washington University ◆
Independent Study, Old Main 400,
Bellingham, WA 98225
(206) 676-3320
Approximately 40 college-level courses

12. Credit for Life Experience Learning

Experience is the name everyone gives to their mistakes.
—Oscar Wilde

The philosophy behind "credit for life experience learning" can be expressed very simply: Academic credit is given for what you know, without regard for how, when, or where the learning was acquired.

Consider a simple example. Quite a few colleges and universities offer credit for courses in typewriting. For instance, at Western Illinois University, Business Education 261 is a basic typing class. Anyone who takes and passes that class is given 3 units of credit.

Advocates of credit for life experience learning say: "If you know how to type, regardless of how and where you learned, or even if you taught yourself at the age of nine, you should still get those same 3 units of credit, once you demonstrate that you have the same skill level as a person who passes Business Education 261."

Of course not all learning can be converted into college credit. But many people are surprised to discover how much of what they already know is, in fact, credit-worthy. With thousands of colleges offering hundreds of thousands of courses, it is a rare subject, indeed, that someone hasn't determined to be worthy of some credit. There is no guarantee that any given school will honor any given learning experience, or even accept another school's assessment for transfer purposes. Yale might not accept typing credit. But then again, often the course title sounds much more academic than the learning experience itself, as in "Business Education" for typing, "Cross-cultural Communication" for a trip to China, or "Fundamentals of Physical Education" for golf lessons.

Here are eight major classifications of life experiences that may be worth college credits, especially in non-traditional, degree-granting programs:

1. **Work.** Many of the skills necessary in paid employment are also skills that are taught in colleges and universities. These include, for instance, typing, filing, shorthand, accounting, inventory control, financial management, map reading, military strategy, welding, computer programming or operating, editing, planning, sales, real estate appraisals, and literally thousands of other skills.

2. **Homemaking.** Home maintenance, household planning and budgeting, child raising, child psychology, education, interpersonal communication, meal planning and nutrition, gourmet cooking, and much more.

3. **Volunteer work.** Community activities, political campaigns, church activities, service organizations, volunteer work in social service agencies, hospital volunteering, and so forth.

4. **Non-credit learning in formal settings.** Company training courses, in-service teacher training, workshops, clinics, conferences and conventions, lectures, courses on radio or television, non-credit correspondence courses, etc.

5. **Travel.** Study tours (organized or informal), significant vacation and business trips, living for periods in other countries or cultures, participating in activities related to subcultures or other cultures.

6. **Recreational activities and hobbies.** Musical skills, aviation training and skills, acting or other work in a community theater, sports, arts and crafts, fiction and non-fiction writing, public speaking, gardening, attending plays, concerts, movies, visiting museums, designing and making clothing, and many other leisure-time activities.

7. **Reading, viewing, listening.** Any subject area in which a person has done extensive or intensive reading and study, and for which college credit has not been granted. This category has, for instance, included viewing various series on public television.

8. **Discussions with experts.** A great deal of learning can come from talking to, listening to, and working with experts, whether in ancient history, carpentry, or theology. Significant, extensive, or intensive meetings with such people may also earn credit.

THE MOST COMMON ERROR PEOPLE MAKE

The most common error people make when thinking about getting credit for life experience is to confuse time spent with learning. Being a regular church-goer for 30 years is not worth any college credit in and of itself. But the regular church-goer who can document that he or she has prepared for and taught Sunday school classes, worked with youth groups, participated in leadership programs, organized fund raising drives, studied Latin or

Greek, taken tours to the Holy Land, or even engaged in lengthy philosophical discussions with a clergyman, is likely to get credit for those experiences. Selling insurance for 20 years is worth no credit—unless you describe and document the learning that took place in areas of marketing, banking, risk management, entrepreneurial studies, etc.

It is crucial that the experiences can be documented to the satisfaction of the school. Two people could work side by side in the same laboratory for five years. One might do little more than follow instructions in running routine experiments, setting up and dismantling apparatus, and heading home. The other, with the same job title, might do extensive reading in the background of the work being done, get into discussions with supervisors, make plans and recommendations for other ways of doing the work, propose or design new kinds of apparatus, or develop hypotheses on why the results were turning out the way they were.

It is not enough just to say what you did, or to submit a short resumé. The details and specifics must be documented. The two most common ways this is done are by preparing a life experience portfolio (essentially a long, well-documented, annotated resumé), or by taking an equivalency examination to demonstrate knowledge gained.

PRESENTING YOUR LEARNING

Most schools that give credit for life experience learning require that a formal presentation be made, usually in the form of a life experience portfolio. Each school will have its own standards for the form and content of such a portfolio, and many, in fact, offer either guidelines or courses (some for credit, some not) to help the non-traditional student prepare the portfolio.

Several books on this subject have been published by the Council for Adult and Experiential Learning, 10840 Little Patunxent Pkwy., Columbia, MD 21044. They will send a list of current publications.

CAEL also offers a set of sample portfolios. The cost is $65 for introductory materials plus four large sample portfolios, or $80 for nine portfolios, representing seven schools. This is the sort of thing that it may be worth trying to convince a local public or community college library to acquire.

The University of the State of New York offers a most helpful guide called the *Self-Assessment and Planning Manual,* specifically geared by their Regents College programs, but useful anywhere. The cost is $8, including postage, from Regents College, Cultural Education Center, SD45, Albany, NY 12230.

Here are 24 other means by which people have documented life experience learning, sometimes as part of a portfolio, sometimes not:

official commendations
slides
bills of sale
programs of recitals and performances
awards and honors
copies of speeches made
certificates
interviews with others
official job descriptions
military records
samples of writing
works of art
audiotapes
course outlines
exhibitions
videotapes
mementos
licenses (pilot, real estate, etc.)
testimonials and endorsements
newspaper articles
copies of exams taken
samples of arts or crafts made
designs and blueprints
films and photographs

HOW LIFE EXPERIENCE LEARNING IS TURNED INTO ACADEMIC CREDIT

It isn't easy. In a perfect world, there would be universally accepted standards, by which it would be as easy to measure the credit value in a seminar on refrigeration engineering as it is to measure the temperature inside a refrigerator. Indeed, some schools and national organizations are striving toward the creation of extensive "menus" of non-traditional experiences, such that anyone doing the same thing would get the same credit.

There continues to be progress in this direction. Many schools have come to agree, for instance, on aviation experience: a private pilot's license is worth 4 semester units; an instrument rating is worth 6 additional units; and so forth.

The American Council on Education, a private organization, regularly publishes a massive multi-volume set of books, in two series: *The National Guide to Educational Credit for Training Programs* and *Guide to the Evaluation of*

Educational Experiences in the Armed Forces. See Bibliography for details.

Many schools use these volumes to assign credit directly, and others use them as guidelines in doing their own evaluation. A few examples will demonstrate the sort of thing that is done:

The Red Cross nine-day training course in The Art of Helping is evaluated as worth 2 semester hours of social work.

The John Hancock Mutual Life Insurance Company's internal course in technical skills for managers is worth 3 semester hours of business administration.

Portland Cement Company's five-day training program in kiln optimization, whatever that may be, is worth 1 semester hour.

The Professional Insurance Agents' three-week course in basic insurance is worth 6 semester units: 3 in principles of insurance and 3 in property and liability contract analysis.

The army's 27-week course in ground surveillance radar repair is worth 15 semester hours: 10 of electronics and 5 more of electrical laboratory.

The army legal clerk training course can be worth 24 semester hours, including 3 in English, 3 in business law, 3 in management, etc.

There are hundreds of additional business and military courses that have been evaluated already, and thousands more that will be worth credit for those who have taken them, whether or not they appear in these A.C.E. volumes.

THE CONTROVERSY OVER GRADUATE CREDIT FOR LIFE EXPERIENCE LEARNING

As Norman Somers writes, "Powerful forces in graduate education have declared the granting of credit for prematriculation experiences anathema. Many professors and graduate deans have spoken out against the assessment of learning experiences which have occurred prior to a student's formal enrollment."

The policy of the Council of Graduate Schools is that "no graduate credit should be granted for experiential learning that occurs prior to the student's matriculation." It should, they insist, be given "only when a graduate faculty and dean of an accredited institution have had the opportunity to plan the experience, to establish its goals, and to monitor the time, effort and the learning that has taken place."

In other words, if I enroll in a school and then study and master advanced statistical techniques, they should give me, say, 9 units of credit. But if I learned those techniques on the job as chief statistician for the Bureau of the Census for 20 years, no credit should be given.

Fortunately, many schools and organizations, including the influential American Council on Education disagree with this policy. Their guidelines, described earlier, regularly include recommendations for graduate credit, based on "independent study, original research, critical analysis, and the scholarly and professional application of the specialized knowledge or discipline."

SOME INSPIRATION

There are always some people who say, "Oh, I haven't ever done anything worthy of college credit." I have yet to meet anyone with an IQ higher than room temperature who has not done at least some credit-worthy things, assuming they were presented properly in a portfolio. Just to inspire you, then, here is a list of 100 things that *could* be worth credit for life experience learning. The list could easily be ten or a hundred times as long.

Playing tennis
Leading a church group
Speaking French
Studying gourmet cooking
Building model airplanes
Learning shorthand
Navigating a small boat
Buying a Persian carpet
Decorating a home or office
Being a counselor at camp
Bicycling across Greece
Living in another culture
Throwing a pot
Preparing for natural childbirth
Taking a body-building class
Selling real estate
Reading *War and Peace*
Touring through Belgium
Starting a small business
Writing a book
Watching public television
Attending a convention
Studying Spanish
Interviewing senior citizens
Writing advertising
Repairing a car

Performing magic
Welding and soldering
Negotiating a contract
Planning a trip
Appraising an antique
Studying first aid or C.P.R.
Researching international laws
Designing a playground
Devising a marketing strategy
Designing a home
Playing the piano
Reading about the Civil War
Helping a dyslexic child
Pressing flowers
Writing public relations releases
Running the P.T.A.
Flying an airplane
Taking photographs
Developing an inventory system
Helping in a political campaign
Painting a picture
Serving on a jury
Visiting a museum
Sewing and designing clothes
Having intensive talks with a doctor
Reading the Bible
Learning Braille
Eating in an exotic restaurant
Planning a balanced diet
Learning sign language of the deaf
Training an apprentice
Hooking a rug
Laying bricks
Being Dungeonmaster
Developing film
Applying statistics to gambling
Taking care of sick animals
Attending art films
Designing and weaving a rug
Editing a manuscript
Steering a ship
Writing a speech
Organizing an union
Listening to Shakespeare's plays
Planning a garden
Reading the newspaper
Attending a seminar
Studying a new religion
Taking ballet lessons
Riding a horse
Keeping tropical fish
Writing for the local newspaper
Acting in little theater
Designing a quilt
Building a table
Programming a home computer
Playing a musical instrument
Playing political board games
Volunteering at the hospital
Attending a great books group
Playing golf
Teaching the banjo
Leading a platoon
Operating a printing press
Running a store
Reading *All and Everything*
Teaching Sunday School
Being an apprentice
Learning yoga
Making a speech
Negotiating a merger
Learning calligraphy
Doing circle dancing
Reading this book

13. Credit by Learning Contract

An oral agreement isn't worth the paper it's written on.
—Samuel Goldwyn

A mainstay of many non-traditional degree programs is the learning contract, also known as a study plan, study contract, degree plan, etc. It is, essentially, a formal agreement between the student and the school, setting forth a plan of study the student intends to undertake, goals he or she wishes to reach, and the action to be taken by the school once the goals are reached—normally the granting either of a certain amount of credit, or of a degree.

A well-written learning contract is a good thing for both student and school, since it reduces greatly the chances of misunderstandings or problems after the student has done a great deal of work and the inevitable distress that accompanies such an event.

In my counseling practice, there were many cases when people had become distressed, even devastated, to have discovered that some project on which they had been working for many months was really not what their faculty advisor or school had in mind, and so they would be getting little or no credit for it.

Indeed, I had a similar sort of experience myself. After I had worked for nearly two years on my Doctorate at Michigan State University, one key member of my faculty guidance committee suddenly died, and a second transferred to another school. No one else on the faculty seemed interested in working with me, and without a binding agreement of any sort, there was no way I could make things happen. I simply dropped out. (Three years later, a new department head invited me back to finish my degree, and I did so. But a lot of anguish could have been avoided if I had had a contract with the school.)

A learning contract is a legally binding contract, for both the student and the school. If the student does the work called for, then the school must award the predetermined number of credits. In case of disputes arising from such a contract, there are usually clauses calling for binding arbitration by an impartial third party.

Looking at examples of a simple, and then a somewhat more complex learning contract should make clear how this concept works.

A SIMPLE LEARNING CONTRACT

The Background

In the course of discussing the work to be done for a Bachelor's degree, the student and her faculty advisor agree that it would be desirable for the student to learn to read in German. Rather than take formal courses, the student says that she prefers to study the language on her own, with the help of an uncle who speaks the language. If the student had taken four semesters of German at a traditional school, she would have earned 20 semester hours of credit. So the learning contract might consist of these eight simple clauses:

The Contract

1. Student intends to learn to read German at the level of a typical student who has completed four semesters of college-level German.

2. Student will demonstrate this knowledge by translating a 1000-word passage from one of the novels of Erich Maria Remarque.

3. The book and passage will be selected and the translation evaluated by a member of the German faculty of the college.

4. The student will have three hours to complete the translation, with the assistance of a standard German-English dictionary.

5. If the student achieves a score of 85% or higher in the evaluation, then the college will immediately award 20 semester hours of credit in German.

6. If the student scores below 85%, she may try again at 60-day intervals.

7. The fee for the first evaluation will be $100, and, if necessary, $50 for each additional evaluation.

8. If any dispute shall arise over the interpretation of this contract, an attempt will be made to resolve the dispute by mediation. If mediation fails, the dispute will be settled by binding arbitration. An arbitrator shall be chosen jointly by the student and the school. If they cannot agree in choosing an arbitrator, then each party will

choose one. If the two arbitrators cannot agree, they shall jointly appoint a third, and the majority decision of this panel of three shall be final and binding. The costs of arbitration shall be shared equally by the two parties.

This contract has the four basic elements common to any learning contract:

1. The objectives or goals of the student.
2. The methods by which these goals are to be reached.
3. The method of evaluation of the performance.
4. What to do in case of problems or disagreement.

The more precisely each of these items can be defined, the less likelihood of problems later. For instance, instead of simply saying, "The student will become proficient in German," the foregoing agreement defines clearly what "proficient" means.

A MORE COMPLEX LEARNING CONTRACT

What follows is an abridgement of a longer learning contract, freely adapted from some of the case histories provided in a catalogue of the late, lamented Beacon College.

Goals

At the end of my Master's program, I plan to have the skills, experience, and theoretical knowledge to work with an organization in the role of director or consultant, and to help the organization set and reach its goals; to work with individuals or small groups as a counselor, providing a supportive or therapeutic environment in which to grow and learn.

I want to acquire a good understanding of and grounding in group dynamics, how children learn, why people come together to grow, learn, and work.

I am especially interested in alternative organizations. I want to have the skills to help organizations analyze their financial needs, and to locate and best utilize appropriate funding.

Methods

- ***Theory and Skill Development (40% of work)***

I shall take the following three courses at Redwood Community College [courses listed and described] = 20% of program.

After reading the following four books [list of books], and others that may be suggested by my faculty advisor, I shall prepare statements of my personal philosophy of education and growth, as a demonstration of my understanding of the needs of a self-directed, responsible, caring human = 10% of program.

I shall attend a six-lesson workshop on power dynamics and assertiveness, given by [details of the workshop] = 10% of program.

- ***Leadership and Management Practicum (30% of work)***

I shall work with the Cooperative Nursery School to attempt to put into practice the things I have learned in the first phase of my studies, in the following way: [much detail here]. Documentation shall be through a journal of my work, a log of all meetings, a self-assessment of my performance, and commentary supplied by an outside evaluator = 15% of program.

I shall donate eight hours a week for 20 weeks to the Women's Crisis Center, again endeavoring to put into practice the ideas which I have learned [much detail here on expectations and kinds of anticipated activities] = 15% of program.

- ***Organizational Development, Analysis, and Design (30% of work)***

I shall study one of the above two groups (nursery school or crisis center) in great detail, and prepare an analysis and projection for the future of this organization, including recommendations for funding, management, and development = 20% of program.

Documentation will be in the form of a long paper detailing my findings and recommendations and relating them to my philosophy of growth and organization development. This paper will be read and evaluated by [name of persons or committee] = 10% of program.

Outcome

Upon completion of all of the above, the college will award the degree of Master of Arts in organization development. [Arbitration clause.]

Learning contracts are truly negotiable. There is no right or wrong, no black or white. So a skillful negotiator might well get more credit for the same amount of work, or the same degree for a lesser amount of work, when compared with a less-skillful negotiator.

Some schools will enter into a learning contract that covers the entire degree program, as in the second example. Others prefer to have separate contracts, each one covering a small portion of the program: one for the language requirement, one for science, one for humanities, one for the thesis, and so forth.

It is uncommon, but not unheard of, to seek legal advice in the preparation or the evaluation of a learning contract, especially for a long or complex one covering an entire Master's or Doctoral program. As lawyers often say, "It is better to invest a small amount of money in my time now, rather than get into an expensive and protracted battle later, because of an unclear agreement." Dozens of colleges and universities are sued every year by students who claim that credits or degrees were wrongfully withheld from them. Many of these suits could have been avoided by the use of well-drawn learning contracts.

14. Credit for Foreign Academic Experience

How much a dunce that has been sent to roam
Excels a dunce that has been kept at home.
—William Cowper

There are many thousands of universities, colleges, technical schools, institutes, and vocational schools all over the world, whose courses are at least the equivalent of work at American universities. In principle, most universities are willing to give credit for work done at schools in other countries.

But can you imagine the task of an admissions officer faced with the student who presents an Advanced Diploma from the Wysza Szkola Inzynierska in Poland, or the degree of Gakushi from the Matsuyama Shoka Daigaku in Japan? Are these equivalent to a high school diploma, a Doctorate, or something in between?

Until 1974, the U.S. Office of Education offered the service of evaluating educational credentials earned outside the United States and translating them into approximately comparable levels of U.S. achievement. But this service is no longer available from the government which has chosen, instead, to recognize some private non-profit organizations who perform the evaluation service.

These services are used mostly by the schools themselves to evaluate applicants from abroad, or with foreign credentials, but individuals may deal with them directly, at relatively low cost.

Depending on the complexity of the evaluation, the costs run from $60 to $150. Some of the services are willing to deal with non-school-based experiential learning as well. The services operate quickly. Less than two weeks for an evaluation is not unusual. While many schools will accept the recommendations of these services, others will not. Some schools do their own foreign evaluations.

It may be wise, therefore, to determine whether a school or schools in which you have interest will accept the recommendations of such services before you invest in them.

Typical reports from the services will give the exact U.S. equivalents of non-U.S. work, both in terms of semester units earned, and of any degrees or certificates earned. For instance, they would report that the Japanese degree of Gakushi is almost exactly equivalent to the American Bachelor's degree.

Organizations performing these services include:

Credentials Evaluation Service
P.O. Box 24040
Los Angeles, CA 90024 (213) 475-2133

Educational Credential Evaluators, Inc.
P.O. Box 17499
Milwaukee, WI 53217 (414) 964-0477

Education Evaluators International, Inc.
P. O. Box 5397
Los Alamitos, CA 90721 (213) 431-2187

International Consultants of Delaware, Inc.
109 Barksdale Professional Center
Newark, DE 19711 (302) 737-8715

or
P.O. Box 5399
Los Alamitos, CA 90721 (213) 430-2405

Educational International
50 Morningside Drive
New York, NY 10025 (212) 662-1768

International Education Research Foundation
P. O. Box 66940
Los Angeles, CA 90066 (213) 390-6276

World Education Services
P. O. Box 745
Old Chelsea Station
New York, NY 10011 (212) 460-5644

For those interested in educational equivalents for one particular country, there is a series of books or monographs published by the American Association of Collegiate Registrars and Admissions Officers (One Dupont Circle NW, Suite 330, Washington, DC 20036). Each publication in their World Education Series describes the higher education system in a given country, and offers advice and recommendations on how to deal with their credits.

15. The Credit Bank Service

We give no credit to a liar,
even when he speaks the truth.
—Cicero

A lot of people have very complicated educational histories. They may have taken classes at several different universities and colleges, taken some evening or summer school classes, perhaps some company-sponsored seminars, some military training classes, and possibly a whole raft of other, informal learning experiences. They may have credits or degrees from schools that have gone out of business, or whose records were destroyed in some war or fire. When it comes time to present their educational past, it may mean assembling dozens of diverse transcripts, certificates, diplomas, job descriptions, and the like, often into a rather large and unwieldy package.

There is, happily, an ideal solution to these problems: the Regents Credit Bank, operated by the enlightened Department of Education of the state of New York, and available to people anywhere in the world.

The Regents Credit Bank is an evaluation and transcript service for people who wish to consolidate their academic records, perhaps adding credit for non-academic career and learning experiences (primarily through equivalency examinations). The Credit Bank issues a single widely-accepted transcript on which all credit is listed in a simple, straightforward, and comprehensible form.

The Credit Bank works like a money bank, except you deposit academic credits, as they are earned, whether through local courses, correspondence courses, equivalency exams, and so forth. There are seven basic categories of learning experiences that can qualify to be "deposited" in a Credit Bank account, and of course various elements of these seven can be combined as well:

1. College courses taken either in residence or by correspondence from regionally accredited schools in the U.S., or their equivalent in other countries.
2. Scores earned on a wide range of equivalency tests, either civilian or military.
3. Military service schools and military occupational specialties that have been evaluated for credit by the American Council on Education, as described earlier.
4. Non-college learning experiences, offered as company courses, seminars, or in-house training from many large and smaller corporations, and evaluated by the American Council on Education or the New York National Program on Noncollegiate Sponsored Instruction.
5. Pilot training licenses and certificates issued by the Federal Aviation Administration.
6. Approved nursing performance examinations.
7. Special assessment of knowledge gained from experience or independent study.

The first six of these have predetermined amounts of credit. The CLEP basic science exam will always be worth 6 semester units. Fluency in Spanish will always be worth 24 semester units. Xerox Corporation's course in repair of the 9400 copier will always be worth 2 semester units. The Army course in becoming a bandleader will always be worth 12 semester units. And so forth, for thousands of already-evaluated non-school learning experiences.

The seventh category can be extremely flexible and variable. Special assessment is a means of earning credit for things learned in the course of ordinary living or job experience. The Credit Bank assesses this learning by appointing a panel of two or more experts in the field. Except in rare cases, it is necessary to go to Albany, New York, to meet with this panel.

The panel may wish to conduct an oral, a written, or, in the case of performers, a performance examination. They may wish to inspect a portfolio of writing, art, or documentation. Following the evaluation, whatever form it may take, the panel makes its recommendations for the amount of credit to be given. This has, in practice, ranged from zero to more than 80 semester units, although the typical range for each separate assessment is probably from 15 to 30 credits.

The Credit Bank has, for example, conducted special assessments in journalism, ceramics, Hebrew language, electronics engineering, aircraft repair and maintenance, and Japanese culture studies, among many others.

There is a $250 fee to set up a Credit Bank account, which includes evaluation of prior work (except special assessments), and one year of update service. After the first year, there is a $50 fee each time a new "deposit" of credits is made.

Work that is, for whatever reason, deemed not credit-worthy may still be listed on the transcript as "non-credit work." Further, the Credit Bank will only list those traditional courses from other schools that the depositor wishes included. Thus any previous academic failures, low grades, or other embarrassments may be omitted from the Credit Bank report.

Students who enroll in the Regents College of the University of the State of New York automatically get Credit Bank service, and do not need to enroll separately.

The address is Regents Credit Bank, Regents College, University of the State of New York, Cultural Education Center, Albany, NY 12230, (518) 474-8957.

16. Schools Offering the Bachelor's, Master's, and Doctorate Non-Traditionally

A log cabin in the woods, with a pine bench in it, with Mark Hopkins at one end and me at the other, is a good enough college for me.
—President James A. Garfield

The schools that follow offer Bachelor's, Master's and/or Doctorate degree programs which are, in one way or another, non-traditional. Chapter 31 is an index of those programs that are either entirely non-residential or have a very short residential component.

The basic format of each listing is as follows:

NAME OF SCHOOL
Address
City, State, Zip, Country
Telephone number
Name, title of key person
Fields of study offered
Year established

Degrees offered: Bachelor's, Master's, and/or Doctorate, Law (B, M, D, L)
Accreditation status (schools claiming accreditation from unrecognized agencies are listed as unaccredited)
Residential, Non-Resident, or Short Residency
Legal status: non-profit or proprietary; independent, state, or church-run
Tuition:
$ (free to very inexpensive: under $2,000 a year for a residential program; under $2,000 for an entire degree program non-residentially);
$$ (inexpensive: $2,000 to $5,000 a year residential; $2,000 to $3,000 a program non-residential);
$$$ (average: $5,000 to $7,000 a year residential; $3,000 to $4,000 a program non-residential)
$$$$ (high: $7,000 to $10,000 a year residential; $4,000 to $5,000 a program non-residential)
$$$$$ (very high: over $10,000 a year residential; over $5,000 a program non-residential).
Bear in mind that
- these are approximations; costs regularly change
- books, fees, travel, postage, etc. may add to the cost
- scholarships may subtract from the cost
- at state schools, out of state students often pay more
- while many non-residential schools have a fixed fee for the entire degree program, some charge per unit or per year.

✪ = One of the schools that readers write to me about the most. This does not imply that they are necessarily either good or bad, just, perhaps, more in the public eye.

See page 70 for explanation of abbreviations and symbols

AALBORG UNIVERSITY CENTRE
Langagerveje 2
Aalborg, DK-91000, Denmark
Peter Plenge, Chief Administrator
Economics, engineering, business, social work
1971
B,M,D, Equivalent of accreditation
Residency
Non-profit, state
(08) 159111
$

After one year of residential study, students at this experimental Danish university combine work experience with independent study projects, reading, small group meetings, and fieldwork. The degrees in economics, engineering, business administration, and social work are based on passing examinations.

ACADIA UNIVERSITY
Wolfville, Nova Scotia B0P 1X0 Canada
David Green
Many fields
B, Equivalent of accreditation
Residency
Non-profit, state
(902) 542–2201

Although it is not possible to complete all the degree requirements at Acadia, persons who have done work elsewhere can complete their degree non-residentially here. Work can be done by correspondence, work at other schools, Canadian armed forces classes, and examinations, which can be taken at remote locations. Credit prior learning is assessed and awarded on the basis of a Challenge for Credit examinations. Many courses on audio or videotape.

ADELPHI UNIVERSITY
University College ABLE Program
Garden City, NY 11530 USA
Ellen Hartigan, Dean University Admissions
Many fields
1896
B, M, D, Accredited
Residency
Non-profit, independent
(516) 294–8700
$$$

B.A. and B.S. available through the ABLE program which requires one meeting a week, either day, evening or weekend at any of four different centers. Also available are two types of Extended Learning courses, one is self-paced study, the other is listening to a weekly radio broadcast; both require only four class meetings. Credit for prior learning and by examination. Certificate programs at the post-Bachelor's level are available, with 4 credits instead of "usual" 3 so students can earn degrees more quickly.

ALABAMA STATE UNIVERSITY
Continuing Education, 915 S. Jackson St.,
Montgomery, AL 36195 USA
Arthur D. Barnett, Director of Admissions
Many fields
1874
B, Accredited
Residency
Non-profit, state
(205) 293–4291
$$

Bachelor's degree can be earned through weekend, evening, and summer program. Credit for independent study, non-academic prior learning, and by examination.

ALASKA PACIFIC UNIVERSITY
4101 University Dr.
Anchorage, AK 99508 USA
John Schafer, Director of Admissions
Many fields
1957
B, M, Accredited
Residency
Non-profit, church
(907) 561–1266
$$$

Credit for independent study, non-academic prior learning, and by examination. Thirty-six credits in residency required. Only private university in Alaska. Programs in liberal arts, elementary education, human resources, communications, natural resources, values and service, and management.

ALVERNIA COLLEGE
Reading, PA 19607 USA
Beth Calabria
Many fields
1958
B, Accredited
Residency
Non-profit, independent
(215) 777–5411
$$$

Bachelor's may be earned through weekend, evening, and summer programs. Credit for independent study, non-academic prior learning, and by examination.

ALVERNO COLLEGE
Weekend College, 3401 S. 39th St.
Milwaukee, WI 53215 USA
Mary Lou Koch, Assistant Director of Admissions
Nursing, professional communications, business and management
1887
B, Accredited
Residency
Non-profit, independent
(414) 382-6100
$$$
Credit for independent study, non-academic prior learning, and by examination. Classes involve intensive study, close working relationships with faculty, and maximum opportunity for self-directed study. The weekend program enrolls both recent high school graduates and women who have been out of school for some time.

AMBASSADOR COLLEGE
300 W. Green St.
Pasadena, CA 91129 USA
Joseph W. Tkach, Chancellor and President
Many fields
1947
B, Unaccredited, state authorized
Residency, Non-profit, church
(818) 304-6000
$$
Established by Herbert Armstrong and the Worldwide Church of God. Ambassador College places primary emphasis on the education of the whole person, not on the intellect alone. Authorized to grant degrees by the state of California.

AMERICAN COASTLINE UNIVERSITY
5000 A W. Esplanade, #197
Metairie, LA 70006
Dr. Raymond Chasse, President
Science, technology, business areas, others
1986
B, M, D, Unaccredited, state registered
Non-resident
(504) 830-2525
$$
All work may be done over home computers, through participation in one of four international computer services (Compuserve, GEnie, MCI, or Delphi). The university operates its own computer bulletin board in Austria, and has resident directors in six nations.

AMERICAN COLLEGE ✪
270 Bryn Mawr Ave.,
Bryn Mawr, PA 19010 USA
William J. McCouch
Professional
1927
M, Accredited
Short residency
Non-profit, independent
(800) 441-9466
$$
Offers an external Master of Science in financial services, through a combination of correspondence study and short residency, primarily for life insurance agents. Also work leading to C.L.U. and C.F.S. certificates. Formerly known as the American College of Life Underwriters.

AMERICAN COLLEGE IN LONDON
100 Marylebone Lane
London W1M 5FP England
Business, fashion, interior design, commercial art.
1976
B, Accredited
Residency
Proprietary
(01) 486-1772
$$$
Students can transfer among campuses in London, Atlanta, and Los Angeles. There is an affiliation with the University of Wisconsin-Stout. Atlanta location is at 3330 Peachtree Rd. NE, Atlanta, GA 30326, (404) 231-9000.

AMERICAN COLLEGE IN PARIS
31 Ave. Bosquet
B, Accredited

Paris, 75007 France
Johanna Stobbs, Director of Communications
Many fields
1962
Residency
Non-profit, independent
(33/1) 45559173
$$$$

Bachelor's degrees in international business administration, international affairs, art history, French studies, European cultural studies, computer science, international economics, and comparative literature are offered through year-round study in Paris. Summer sessions are also offered. All instruction is in English. The student body is about half American and half from 60 other countries. New York office is at 80 E. 11th St., Suite 434, New York, NY 10003, (212) 677–4870.

AMERICAN COLLEGE OF FINANCE
185 N. Wolfe Rd.
Sunnyvale, CA 94088 USA
Elbert H. Stutts, President
Financial development for non-profit organizations
1982
M, Unaccredited, state authorized
Short residency
Non-profit, independent
(408) 735–1201
$$$

Master's degree program to prepare staff and management for financial development responsibilities in non-profit organizations. Authorized to grant degrees by the state of California.

AMERICAN COLLEGE OF OXFORD
Warnborough College, Boars Hill
Oxford, OX1 5ED England
Humanities, science, social science, business
B, Unaccredited
Residency
(0865) 730901

Study offered through Warnborough College, Oxford. The college was the subject of an unfavorable half-hour program on the BBC.

AMERICAN GRADUATE UNIVERSITY
733 N. Dodsworth Ave.
Covina, CA 91724 USA
Paul R. McDonald, Sr., President
Contracting with federal government; acquisition management
1975
M, Unaccredited, state authorized
Non-resident, proprietary
(818) 966–4576
$$$

M.B.A. in the specific area of contracting with the federal government, and a Master of Acquisition Management. Courses may be taken entirely by correspondence, or by attending seminars given at various locations around the U.S. The university is accredited by the National Association of Private Non-traditional Schools and Colleges, a legitimate but unrecognized accreditor. A Bachelor's degree is required for admission. The 24-person faculty is comprised of accountants, lawyers, and business and government executives. Authorized to grant degrees by the state of California.

AMERICAN INSTITUTE FOR COMPUTER SCIENCES
1704 11th Ave. South
Birmingham, AL 35205
Lloyd Clayton, Jr., President
1989
B, Unaccredited
Non-resident
(800) 872-2427
$$

Completion of seven home study courses results in the B.S. in computer programming. No faculty are mentioned in the ten-page catalogue. AICS, like all too many other schools, devotes much attention to a misrepresentation of the notorious Sosdian & Sharp study (see page 17). Same location and management as three other schools, including Dr. Clayton's School of Natural Healing and Chadwick University.

AMERICAN INTERNATIONAL COLLEGE
1000 State St.
Springfield, MA 01109 USA
Dr. Elizabeth Ayres, Dean, School of Continuing Education
Business, human services
1885
B, Accredited
Residency
Non-Profit, independent
(413) 737–7000
$$$

The degree is available through evening and weekend study through the College of Continuing and Graduate Studies. A REACH program offers special support for older students who have never been in college.

AMERICAN INTERNATIONAL COLLEGE OF LONDON
see: Richmond College

AMERICAN INTERNATIONAL OPEN UNIVERSITY
see: Clayton University

AMERICAN NATIONAL UNIVERSITY (CA)
7002 Moody, #205
La Palma, CA 92041 USA
1987
Unaccredited, state authorized
(213) 865–1161

Authorized by the state of California to grant degrees. Did not respond to three requests for information on their programs. (Unrelated to a diploma mill of this name, operated from southern California until the mid-1980s.)

AMERICAN OPEN UNIVERSITY ✪
New York Institute of Technology
Central Islip, NY 11722 USA
Angela Richards, Director, Academic Studies
Business administration, general studies, behavioral science
1955
B, Accredited
Non-Resident
Non-profit, independent
(800) 222–6948
$$

The American Open University is the distance learning arm of New York Institute of Technology. The B.S. or B.A. can be completed by correspondence study or through computer interaction. No prior computer experience is necessary. The business administration degree has a management option. The behavioral science degree has options in community mental health, criminal justice, psychology, and sociology. All academic instruction is in the distance learning/independent study mode. No on-campus study is required. Students have 24 weeks to complete each course which has 8 assignments, a midterm, and final examination. A minimum of 30 credits must be taken with A.O.U./N.Y.I.T. The cost is $85 per unit. Transfer of credit, nationally normed exams, challenge exams, and life experience demonstrated by portfolio may be used as prior learning credit if approved. New York phone is (516) 348–3306.

AMERICAN PACIFIC UNIVERSITY
3001 Redhill Ave., Bldg 4, #220
Costa Mesa, CA 92626 USA
Mehdi Vazirnia, President
Business, criminal justice, education, general engineering
1983
B, M, D, Unaccredited, state authorized
Non-Resident , Proprietary
(714) 957–3322
$$

All study is by correspondence. Bachelor's, Master's and Doctorates in business administration, education, criminal justice administration, and a Bachelor's in engineering. Concurrent Bachelor's/Master's and Master's/Doctorates are offered. Four to six courses plus a dissertation are required for the Ph.D. All but two courses may be waived for prior experience. Many of the students are from Africa and Asia. Authorized to grant degrees by the state of California.

AMERICAN TECHNOLOGICAL UNIVERSITY
P.O. Box 1416 Hwy. 190 West
Killeen, TX 76540 USA
Laura Henderson, Admissions Advisor
Technological fields
1973
M, Accredited
Short residency
Non-profit, independent
(817) 526–1150

Correspondents report substantial credit was given them toward a degree for prior learning and careeer experience. They do not wish to appear in this book, but when I leave them out, people write and say "Why didn't you put them in," so this brief notice is a compromise.

See page 70 for explanation of abbreviations and symbols

AMERICAN UNIVERSITY
4400 Massachusetts Ave., NW
Washington, DC 20016 USA
Maurice O'Connell, Dean Admissions
Many fields
1893

B, M, D, Accredited
Residency
Non-profit, church
(202) 885–6000
$$$$

Degrees in a variety of fields can be earned through evening classes, credit for life and job experience, examinations, study abroad, and community operated programs. The university hosts the Washington Semester program.

AMERICAN UNIVERSITY OF LONDON
Archway Central Hall, Archway Close
London, N19 3TD England
Khurshid A. Khan, Ph.D, President
Liberal arts, business, engineering, sciences
1984

B. M, D, Unaccredited, state licensed
Non-resident
Non-profit, independent
(01) 263-2986
$$

The university operates under the laws of the state of Iowa (which registers, but does not investigate schools). It was originally established as the London College of Science and Technology. The catalogue states that full-time undergraduate and graduate courses are offered in London, in addition to totally non-resident degrees at all levels through its Distance Learning Center. Credit is earned through independent study, prior work and experience, examinations, and courses offered by the armed forces. Each student works with one or more adjunct faculty through guided independent study. A thesis is required of Master's and Doctoral candidates.

AMERICAN UNIVERSITY OF ORIENTAL STUDIES
309 Saltair
Los Angeles, CA 90049 USA
1984

Unaccredited,
state authorized
(213) 225–0686

Did not respond to three requests for information, nor is information provided in California's state directory, other than the information that the school is authorized to grant degrees.

ANDREW JACKSON UNIVERSITY COLLEGE
13315 Query Mill Rd., Potomac
Gaithersburg, MD 20878 USA
Jean-Maximillien De La Croix De Lafayette
Business, management, economics,
human resources management
1980

B, M, D, Apparently unlicensed
Non-resident
Non-profit, independent
(301) 990–1426
$$

Established by Dr. Jean-Maximillien De La Croix de Lafayette, lawyer, author, and art patron. Instruction by correspondence study, or residentially in London through London International College and London College for Electronic Engineering. Many courses on cassette in English, French, Arabic, or Greek. Four years, or three years plus three summers, required for a Bachelor's degree. Master's requires two years of study, and Doctorate two years beyond Master's. Credit for life experience learning. Faculty advisor evaluates student's past work, chooses or develops courses to be taken, and works with the student on a one-to-one basis. Each course has an examination every 20 to 40 days, and a final exam. Originally in Baton Rouge, Louisiana (original name: American Community College). Not approved by the Maryland State Board for Higher Education. In a recent letter, Dr. De La Croix de Lafayette indicated he may be retiring.

ANNA MARIA COLLEGE
Paxton, MA 01612 USA
Donna Varney, Director of Admissions
Business
1946

M, Accredited
Residency
Non-profit, church
(617) 757–4586
$$$

The Master of Business Administration can be earned in from 12 to 18 months of intensive weekend study. Classes are held both in Paxton and in Boston.

ANTIOCH UNIVERSITY ✪
Antioch International
Yellow Springs, OH 45387 USA
C. Robert Friedman, Dean
Many fields
1952

M, Accredited
Short residency
Non-profit, independent
(513) 767–1031
$$$$

Non-resident Individualized Master of Arts, requiring two five-day seminars on campus. Students develop own curriculum with guidance from student-recruited mentors. Work involves independent study, research, practicums, workshops, conferences, and traditional courses. A thesis is required. Students may be anywhere in North America, many locations worldwide. Also offered is an M.A. in the psychology of therapy and counseling, based in London, England. Students there are in residence one day a week for two-and-a-half years. A clinical internship is offered the second year. Students write six essays and a thesis. The cost of this program is $6,925. Antioch has regional centers in Los Angeles, Seattle, New England, Philadelphia, and Santa Barbara. In 1989, the center in San Francisco closed, and programs were transferred to New College.

ARMSTRONG COLLEGE
2222 Harold Way
Berkeley, CA 94704
Dr. Franklin T. Burroughs, President
Business

B, M, Fate uncertain
Residency
Proprietary
(415) 848-2500
$$$

Bachelor's and M.B.A.s are offered through day or evening study. After many years on probation, Armstrong's accreditation was revoked in 1990, and at press time an appeal had yet to be heard. Formerly known as Armstrong University.

ARMSTRONG STATE COLLEGE
11935 Abercorn St.
Savannah, GA 31406 USA
Thomas P. Miller, Director of Admissions
Business, education
1935

B, M, Accredited
Residency
Non-profit, state
(912) 925–4200
$$

Bachelor of Arts, Bachelor of Science, Bachelor of Business Administration, Master of Business Administration, and Master of Educational Administration are offered entirely through evening study.

ARTS AND SCIENCE UNIVERSITY
Department of University Correspondence Courses,
Rangoon, Burma
Bachelor of Arts, Science, Economics, and Law
1920

B, Equivalent of accreditation
Non-resident
Non-profit, state
Auto 31144

Degrees can be earned entirely through correspondence study, plus passing necessary examinations. Some courses are also given through radio lectures. More than 25,000 students are enrolled in Burma's only non-traditional university.

ASIAN AMERICAN UNIVERSITY
2043 El Cajon Blvd.
San Diego, CA 92104 USA
William S. H. Yeung, President
1980

D, Unaccredited,
state authorized
Proprietary
(619) 299–0030
$$

Authorized to grant degrees by the state of California. Did not respond to three requests for information about their programs.

ATHABASCA UNIVERSITY ✪
Box 10,000,
Athabasca, Alberta TOG 2RO Canada
Mr. Kerry Joyes, Information Officer

B, Equivalent of accreditation
Non-resident
Non-profit, independent

See page 70 for explanation of abbreviations and symbols

Many fields
1970

(403) 675–6148
$$

Canadian residents or foreigners resident in Canada only. Bachelor's degrees in administration, arts, general studies, nursing, social work, English, history, sociology/anthropology, psychology, Canadian studies, and French. An open distance-education institution serving more than 10,000 students across Canada. All courses are offered by correspondence through sophisticated home study packages. Students set up their own study schedules and work at their own pace. There are three degree programs: Bachelor of Administration, Bachelor of General Studies, and B.A. All students are assigned a telephone tutor to whom they have toll-free access. Some courses are supplemented by radio and television programs, audio- and videocassettes, seminars, laboratories, or teleconference sessions. Centers at more than 100 locations in western Canada.

ATLANTIC UNION COLLEGE
South Lancaster, MA 01561 USA
Sakae Kubo
Many fields
1882

B, Accredited
Short residency
Non-profit, church
(800) 282–2030
$$

Students take 1 "unit" each semester. A "unit" is a six-month study project, requiring two weeks on campus, and the balance of the time in independent study. A minimum of at least the two final units must be taken within the Adult Degree Program; hence four weeks of residency is required to earn the Bachelor's degree. Bachelor's degrees are offered in art business, behavioral science, communications, computer science, education, English, health science, history, interior design, modern languages, music, physical education, personal ministries, religion, social work, and theology. Experiential learning credit through portfolio appraisal. In Massachusetts, the toll-free number is (800) 325–0099.

AUGUST VOLLMER UNIVERSITY
217 N. Main St.
Santa Ana, CA 92701

Unaccredited,
state authorized

Authorized to grant degrees by the state of California. Did not respond to two requests for information on their programs.

AUGUSTANA COLLEGE
29th and Summit
Sioux Falls, SD 57197 USA
Dean Schueler, Director of Admissions
Many fields
1860

B, M, Accredited
Residency
Non-profit, church
(605) 336–5516
$$$

The Twilight Degree Program offers a Bachelor of Arts degree through courses given in the evening, at the noon hour, or on the weekend. Credit for independent study, non-academic prior learning, and by examination.

AURORA UNIVERSITY
347 S. Gladstone
Aurora, IL 60507 USA
Dr. Michael Sawdey, Registrar
Many fields
1893

B, M, Accredited
Residency
Non-profit, independent
(312) 892–6431
$$$

Self-designed degree programs in many fields. Bachelor of Arts in accounting, business administration, computer science, criminal justice, economic theory, engineering science, industrial management, and sociology, all offered through evening courses. Weekend College courses for B.A. in computer science/business, business administration, management, and marketing. Master of Science degree programs in management areas of business, criminal justice, and information systems. All graduate classes are held during the evening on campus, or at various off-campus sites. Nineteen majors are offered through the evening program, and four at Weekend College. Credit for life experience, military credits, etc.

AUSTRALIAN COLLEGE OF APPLIED PSYCHOLOGY
245 Broadway

Diplomas, licensing unclear

Sydney, N.S.W. 2007 Australia
Dr. John Castles, Principal
Counseling and psychotherapy
Non-resident or residency
(02) 692–0632

The diploma (not degree) course is offered in classes, or by home study. The principal is a pharmacist and clinical psychologist who has conducted courses in clinical hypnosis, counseling, psychology, and self-awareness.

BALDWIN-WALLACE COLLEGE
275 Eastland Rd.
Berea, OH 44017 USA
Linda L. Young, Associate Registrar
Many fields
1845
B, M, Accredited
Residency
Non-profit, church
(216) 826–2900
$$$

Bachelor of Arts, Bachelor of Science, Bachelor of Science in education, Bachelor of Music, Bachelor of Music Education through evening study or the Weekend College which meets on alternate weekends. Credit for prior learning and CLEP examinations. Master of Business Administration in a Saturday program. Master of Business Administration executive program meets on alternate weekends. Also there is an international M.B.A. program.

BALL STATE UNIVERSITY
Muncie, IN 47306 USA
Thomas Bilger, Registrar
Education
1918
M, Accredited
Residency
Non-profit, State
(317) 289–1241
$$

Master of Education program, including a program in psychometrics, can be completed entirely through evening study.

BARAT COLLEGE
Lake Forest, IL 60045 USA
Loretta Brickman, Director of Admissions
Many fields
1858
B, Accredited
Residency
Non-profit, independent
(312) 234–3000
$$$

Bachelor of Arts through a combination of coursework and credit for prior learning experiences. Evening students may complete majors in management and business, human resource emphasis, computing and information systems. Barat offers a Degree Completion Program for nurses, awarding up to 60 credit hours for nurse's training plus additional credit for CLEP scores and work achievement.

BARD COLLEGE ✪
Continuing Studies Program
Annandale-on-Hudson, NY 12504 USA
Mary Backlund, Director of Admissions
Liberal arts, fine arts, sciences, applied fields
1860
B, Accredited
Short residency
Non-Profit, independent
(914) 758–6822
$$$$

Bachelor of Arts, Bachelor of Science, and Bachelor of Professional Studies, designed "to meet the special needs of adults who have left college without completing their studies." Credit for prior learning experience and for achievement measured on standard proficiency tests. Students attend evening seminars and classes which meet two hours each week; they may also meet with tutors for advanced study twice a month over the course of a 15-week term, or enroll in the regular undergraduate classes held during the day. To graduate, a student must earn 124 credits, 30 of them while enrolled in the program. Minimum time to complete the degree is one academic year (10 months).

BARRY UNIVERSITY
11300 NE 2nd Ave.
Miami, FL 33161 USA
Mr. Robin R. Roberts, Dean of Admissions
Many fields
B, M, D, Accredited
Residency
Non-profit, church
(305) 758–3392

See page 70 for explanation of abbreviations and symbols

1940
$$$$

Degrees offered in accounting, management, marketing, computer science, economics, finance, sociology, philosophy, and psychology. Credit for prior professional and work experience. Classes held in various locations in south Florida.

BARUCH COLLEGE

17 Lexington Ave.
New York, NY 10010 USA
Dr. John Fisher, Director of Admissions
Business administration, public administration
1919

B, M, Accredited
Residency
Non-profit, state
(212) 725–3000

This college of the City University of New York offers the Bachelor of Business Administration, Master of Business Administration, and Master of Public Administration entirely through evening study.

BEIJING BROADCASTING AND TELEVISION UNIVERSITY

Beijing, China
Science, technology, mathematics, English
1960

Equivalent of accredited
Non-resident
Non-profit, state

Established in 1960 as the Beijing Television College, offering instruction primarily by written correspondence studies, rather than by television. More than 420,000 students are enrolled, from all over China. Students are divided into three categories: full-time (four days of study or more per week; they receive full pay for their time), half-time and spare-time. A typical student spends four hours each day watching television courses and eight hours doing homework. Weekly assignments are mailed to a local tutor. Two examinations are given each year. Most courses are in science, technology, mathematics, and English.

BELLARMINE COLLEGE

Newburg Rd.
Louisville, KY 40205 USA
Maria Poschinger
Business, education, nursing
1950

B, M, Accredited
Residency
Non-profit, independent
(502) 452–8211
$$

Bachelor of Arts in accounting, business administration and commercial science and Bachelor of Science in commerce, available entirely through evening study. Also M.B.A. and M.S.N. and M.A. in education through evening programs.

BEMIDJI STATE UNIVERSITY

Center for Extended Learning, Deputy Hall 110,
Bemidji, MN 56601 USA
Lorraine F. Cecil
English, history, sociology, community service, vocational education, and criminal justice
1913

B, Accredited
Non-resident or residency
(218) 755–3924
$$

Credit for life experience and prior learning experiences may be allowed toward the requirements. New credit is earned through on-campus classes, extension classes in other cities, and through independent guided home study. Learning packages (a syllabus, books, and sometimes audio- or videocassettes) are provided. Continued contact with B.S.U. is maintained in a variety of ways: by mail, telephone, exchange of cassettes, and conferences with academic advisors. As the Coordinator of External Studies puts it,"unique solutions exist for unique situations." Although the program was originally designed for students in northern Minnesota, there is no specific regulation governing residence, and there are some out-of-state students.

BEREAN COLLEGE

1445 Boonville
Springfield, MO 65802 USA
Zenas J. Bicket, Ph.D.
1985
Bible and theology studies

B, Accredited
Non-resident
Non-profit, independent
(417) 862–2781
$$

Accredited by the National Home Study Council, a recognized agency. Studies by correspondence. Credit by examination and for life experience. Primarily for religious workers (clergy, missionaries). Many courses available in Spanish.

BERNADEAN UNIVERSITY
13615 Victory Blvd., Suite 114 — D, Law, No apparent licensing
Van Nuys, CA 91401 USA — Non-resident
Joseph Kadans, Ph.D. — Non-profit
Theology, law, reflexology, iridology, naturopathy, etc. — (818) 988–5710

A division of the Church of Universology, they have offered correspondence degrees in everything from theology to astronutrition to law. The two-room headquarters is in a Los Angeles suburb. Bernadean used to be in Nevada, but lost permission to operate in that state. Founder and president Joseph Kadans, Ps.D., N.D., Th.D., Ph.D., J.D. is licensed to practice law. At times, Bernadean has been recognized by the Committee of Bar Examiners in California. Also offered have been Doctor of Naturopathy, Doctor of Iridology, Doctor of Preventative Medicine, and Doctor of Reflexology. At one point, Bernadean offered a certificate good for absolution of all sins to its graduates.

BETA INTERNATIONAL UNIVERSITY — B, M, D, Law, unlicensed
204 E. High St., — Non-resident
Jefferson City, MO 65101 USA — Non-profit, independent
Dr. Ellis — (314) 636–6709
Many, including law — $$

New evangelical Christian school (part of the ministry of the brotherhood of Beta Phi Epsilon) offering non-religious degrees of all kinds, including law, by correspondence. The law program (four years of correspondence study) qualifies students to take the first year and main bar exam in California. Accreditation is claimed from "Af Sep" which is identified in the eight-page newsprint (complete with advertising) catalogue as "a private not-for-profit accrediting association for Directed-study and Correspondence institutions of higher education... Af Sep is currently in the process of preparing a petition (sic) for recognition before the U.S. Department of Education to be recognized as a National Accrediting body." I am unfamiliar with Af Sep. No names are given in the catalogue other than "Dr. Ellis."

BETHEL COLLEGE — B, Accredited
McKenzie, TN 38201 USA — Residency
James R. Shannon, Director of Admissions — Non-profit, church
Business — (901) 352–5321
1842 — $$

Bachelor of Science in business adminstration, entirely through evening study. Credit is given for life experience learning and for internships. Student-initiated majors are available.

BISCAYNE COLLEGE
see: Saint Thomas University

BLOOMSBURG UNIVERSITY
College of Extended Programs and Graduate Study, — B, Accredited
Bloomsburg, PA 17815 USA — Residency
John H. Abell, Dean of Extended Programs — Non-profit, state
Many fields — (717) 389–4004
1839 — $$

Degrees in natural and physical sciences, social sciences, humanities and arts, business administration, health science, and education. A maximum of 60 credits for the degree can be earned through assessment of prior learning, or a combination of this and equivalency exams and departmental challenge exams prepared by the college. The program requires 128 semester units. Thirty-two of the last 64 units must be earned in residence. Credit is offered for evening classes, television courses, and experiential learning assessments.

BLUEFIELD STATE COLLEGE
see: West Virginia Board of Regents B.A. Program

See page 70 for explanation of abbreviations and symbols

BORICUA COLLEGE
3755 Broadway
New York, NY 10032 USA
Francia Castro, Director of Admissions
Liberal arts, natural and social sciences, business, education
1974

B, Accredited
Short residency
Non-profit, independent
(212) 694–1000
$$

Bilingual (Spanish-English) college, offering the B.S. through individualized instruction, independent study, and field internships.

BOSTON COLLEGE
Chestnut Hill, MA 02167 USA
Dr. Louise M. Lonabocker, Registrar
Many fields
1963

B, M, D , Accredited
Residency
Non-profit, church
(617) 552–8000
$$$$$

All of the courses required for the Bachelor of Arts degree in American studies, business, economics, English, history, political science, psychology, and sociology can be earned entirely through evening study. Most courses are taught for two-and-a-half hours, one evening per week.

BOSTON UNIVERSITY
Metropolitan College, 755 Commonwealth Ave.
Boston, MA 02215 USA
Arlene F. Becella, Registrar
Many fields
1839

B, M, D , Accredited
Residency
Non-profit, independent
(617) 353–2000
$$$$$

Bachelor of Liberal Studies, Bachelor of Science, Master of Criminal Justice, Master of Liberal Arts, Master of Science in Computer Information Systems, Master of Urban Affairs, Master of City Planning may be earned through evening or weekend study with the university's Metropolitan College. The Overseas Program, primarily for military and Department of Defense employees, offers Master of Science in Business Administration, Master of Science in management, Master of Science in computer information systems, Master of Education, Master of Arts in international relations, Master of Science in mechanical engineering. Locations include Belgium, England, Italy, the Netherlands and West Germany. Credit for prior learning, independent study, and by examination.

BOULDER GRADUATE SCHOOL
2880 Folson, Suite 104
Boulder, CO 80304
Antonio Núñez, Academic Dean
1979

M, Unaccredited, state authorized
Residency
Non-profit, independent
(303) 449-4676
$$$

Master's degrees in psychology and counseling and in health and wellness, emphasizing a balance between traditional academic training and experiential learning. Formerly the Colorado Institute of Transpersonal Psychology.

BOWLING GREEN STATE UNIVERSITY
Office of Continuing Education, 300 McFall Center,
Bowling Green, OH 43403 USA
Joan Bissland, Director of Adult Learners Services
Many fields
1910

B, M, D, Accredited
Residency
Non-profit, state
(419) 372–8181
$$

B.A. degrees in arts and science, business administration, health and human services, technology, musical arts education, art, mass communication, nursing, health and physical education, and recreation available through evening study. Master's degree program in organizational development, through an external degree plan involving a combination of on-campus study and independent study. Other evening Master's programs, including an M.B.A. Credit for prior learning, by exam, and portfolio assessment.

BRADLEY UNIVERSITY
118 Bradley Hall

B, M, Accredited

Peoria, IL 61625 USA
Gary R. Bergman, Director of Enrollment Management
Many fields
1897

Residency
Non-profit, independent
(309) 677–1000
$$$

Bachelor's and Master's may be earned through evening, weekend, and summer programs; also courses on site at business and industrial locations. Special programs in nursing, engineering, education, business, manufacturing, construction, international studies, radio and television, and international business.

BRANDON UNIVERSITY
270 18th St.
Brandon, Manitoba R7A 6A9 Canada
T. Mitchell, Dean of Students
Education, general studies, arts, science, music, nursing, mental health
1880

B, M, Accredited
Residency
Non-profit, independent
(204) 728–9520
$$

Brandon offers its Bachelor of Education and General Studies, B.A., B.S., Bachelor of Music, Master of Music, as well as the Professional Year for teachers, in remote locations in northern Manitoba. The Northern Teacher Education Programme is offered in seven residential centers, and also makes use of "traveling professors" who regularly fly in to remote communities to offer courses and advice. Many of the students are of native ancestry. Evening, spring, and summer programs.

BRIAR CLIFF COLLEGE
3303 Rebecca St.
Sioux City, IA 51104 USA
James J. Hoffman, Dean of Admissions
Many fields
1930

B, Accredited
Residency
Non-profit, church
(712) 279–5321
$$$

B.S.N. weekend programs for nurses. Evening and weekend college courses offered in nursing, business administration, accounting, mass communications, and pastoral ministry. "Project Access" provides credit for life experience. Extensive internship program.

BRIGHAM YOUNG UNIVERSITY ✪
237 HCEB
Provo, UT 84602 USA
Dr. Robert W. Spencer, Dean of Admissions
Independent studies
1875

A, B, Accredited
Short residency
Non-profit, church
(801) 378–1211
$$

Bachelor of Independent Studies program offered through independent study and a short period of on-campus study. The Bachelor's degree requires a maximum of attendance at five seminars on campus—one of each of five units of the program. Students having 32 or more semester hours of accepted college credit may transfer them into the program to help fill course requirements. A score of 610 or higher on CLEP exams is necessary for a student to have the corresponding B.I.S. study area considered for waiver, and then only after having successfully completed the seminar associated with the study area. Only one study area can be waived by CLEP exams. The total elapsed time can range from 16 months to 8 years. There is also a non-resident Associate's degree in English or geneaology.

BRITISH COLUMBIA OPEN UNIVERSITY
Box 94000
Richmond, BC Y6Y 2A2 Canada
Ian Mugridge, Dean, Open University
1978

B, Equivalent of accreditation
Non-resident
Non-profit, independent
(604) 270–8021
$$

Bachelor of Arts with specialization in biology, economics, English, geography, history, mathematics, psychology or sociology or Bachelor of Arts in Administration Studies may be earned entirely by home study through the Learning at a Distance Program. Many courses have a television component. Credit based on experience is possible in the Bachelor of Arts in Administration Studies program. Formerly called the Open Learning Institute.

See page 70 for explanation of abbreviations and symbols

BRYANT COLLEGE
Evening Division
Smithfield, RI 02917 USA
Nancy G. Parchesky, Dean of Admissions
Business administration, criminal justice
1863

B, M, Accredited
Residency
Non-profit, independent
(401) 232–6000
$$$

Bachelor of Science in business administration and criminal justice; Master of Business Administration, offered entirely through evening and weekend study.

BURLINGTON COLLEGE
95 North Ave.
Burlington, VT 05401 USA
Dennis McBee, Director of Admissions
Transpersonal psychology, many fields.
1972

B, Accredited
Short residency
Non-profit, independent
(802) 862–9616
$$$

Bachelor of Arts, primarily through non-resident study. All students must attend a one-week workshop in Burlington, and are encouraged but not required to attend a one-week residential session twice a year. The minimum time for completion of a degree is six months. Because of the need to meet from time to time with advisors, students living far from Vermont are not encouraged to apply. Students are encouraged to develop their own majors, through the "BAIM" (B.A. Individualized Major) program.

CALDWELL COLLEGE
External Degree Program
Caldwell, NJ 07006 USA
Marilyn S. Goodson, Director, External Degree Program
Many fields
1979

B, Accredited
Short residency
Non-profit, church
(201) 228–4424
$$$

Degrees in business administration, English, foreign languages, history, psychology, religious studies, and sociology. This is primarily an off-campus, independent study program which utilizes tutorial relationships with professors. Students spend one weekend per semester on campus. Credit is given for life experience assessment and by examination.

CALIFORNIA AMERICAN UNIVERSITY
230 W. 3rd Ave.,
Escondido, CA 92025 USA
Dr. Paul Hersey, President
Management
1976

M, Unaccredited, state authorized
Short residency
Non-profit, independent
(619) 741-6595
$$$

Master of Science in Management involving one five-week summer session and four tutorials directed by senior professors. There is a specialization in organizational behavior. A discount in tuition is offered for a spouse attending at the same time. The faculty of 10 all have earned traditional Doctorates.

CALIFORNIA COAST UNIVERSITY ✪
700 N. Main St.
Santa Ana, CA 92701 USA
Thomas M. Neal, Jr., President
Engineering, education, behavioral science, business
1974

B, M, D, Unaccredited, State approved
Non-resident
Proprietary
(714) 547–9625
$$

California Coast University was one of the first of California's non-resident universities. Non-resident degrees are offered at all academic levels in the above-mentioned fields of study. Credit is given for prior in-school learning experiences, or for equivalency challenge examinations prepared and administered by the university. All department heads and adjunct faculty hold degrees from traditional schools. The university operates from its own building in a Los Angeles suburb, and maintains a lending library to ensure availability of textbooks for all students throughout the world. Combined programs are offered for earning the Bachelor's and Master's or the Master's and Doctorate simultaneously. Accreditation is from the National

Association of Private Non-traditional Schools and Colleges, an unrecognized accrediting agency. Former name: California Western University.

CALIFORNIA COLLEGE FOR HEALTH SCIENCES ✪
222 West 24th St.
National City, CA 92050
Judith Eberhart, Dean
1979

M, Accredited
Non-resident
(619) 477-4800
Appx. $$$

Master of Science in Community Health Administration and Wellness Promotion available entirely through home study courses. Any of the fifteen courses may be challenged by taking the final exam without taking the course. The degree prepares professionals to become specialists in health promotion in private industry and education. Non-degree programs are offered in wellness management, wellness program development, and wellness counseling. The school is accredited by the National Home Study Council.

CALIFORNIA COLLEGE OF COMMERCE
940 Pine Ave.
Long Beach, CA 90813 USA
James H. Miller, Administrator
1921

B, M, Unaccredited, state authorized
Proprietary
(213) 436–9767

Authorized by the state of California to grant degrees. College did not respond to three requests for information about their programs.

CALIFORNIA GRADUATE INSTITUTE
1100 Glendon Ave.
Los Angeles, CA 90024 USA
Marvin Koven
Psychology and psychotherapy
1968

M, D, Unaccredited, State approved, Residency
Non-profit, independent
(213) 208–4240
$$

Established to expand the scope of traditional graduate study in psychology and psychotherapy. Faculty are practicing professionals in the field of mental health. Curriculum includes clinical psychology, behavioral medicine, psychoanalysis, and marriage, family and child counseling.

CALIFORNIA GRADUATE SCHOOL OF MARITAL AND FAMILY THERAPY
4340 Redwood Hwy., Bldg. F #220
San Rafael, CA 94903 USA
Dr. Martin Kirschenbaum
Marital and family therapy, clinical psychology
1976

D, Unaccredited,
State authorized, Residency
Non-profit, independent
(415) 472–5511
$$$

The Psy.D. in marital and family therapy and the D.M.F.C. (Doctor of Marital, Family and Child Therapy) are approved by the state of California, so graduates can take state licensing examinations. A Psy.D. in clinical psychology is also available. Classes offered evenings and weekends.

CALIFORNIA INSTITUTE OF INTEGRAL STUDIES
765 Ashbury
San Francisco, CA 94117 USA
Jeff Aitken, Admissions Officer
Many fields
1968

M, D, Accredited
Residency
Non-profit, independent
(415) 753–6100
$$$

Master's degrees are offered in East-West psychology, integral counseling psychology, philosophy and religion, and social and cultural anthropology. The Ph.D. is available in clinical or counseling psychology, East-West psychology, and philosophy and religion. Most programs involve a combination of intellectual study, personal experience of psycho-spiritual growth processes, and practical fieldwork in counseling, community service, teaching, or creative independent study. Formerly called the California Institute of Asian Studies.

CALIFORNIA INTERNATIONAL UNIVERSITY

1649 Wilshire Blvd.
Los Angeles, CA 90017 USA
Mitsugu Honda, President
Business management, international business, accounting
1973

B, M, Unaccredited,
State authorized, Residency
Non-profit, independent
(213) 381–3719
$$

Specializes in education for international students for whom English is the second language. Evening classes. Authorized to grant degrees by the state of California.

CALIFORNIA NATIONAL OPEN UNIVERSITY
see: Open University of America

CALIFORNIA PACIFIC UNIVERSITY ✪
10721 Treena St., Rm. 114, P.O. Box 261387
San Diego, CA 92126 USA
N. C. Dalton, Ph.D., President
Management and human behavior, business
1976

B, M, Unaccredited
State approved, Non-resident
Non-profit, independent
(619) 695–3292
$$

M.A. in human behavior, the M.B.A., and the Bachelor's in Business Administration degree programs may be completed entirely by correspondence study. Highly structured programs utilize home study delivery systems. Limited experiential credit is given at undergraduate level only. Students are supplied with study guides written by university faculty, to accompany recognized textbooks in the field. The school is "committed to the training and education of business managers and leaders in the technical, quantitative and theoretical areas of business management (as well as in) interpersonal skills and human resource management."

CALIFORNIA SCHOOL OF PROFESSIONAL PSYCHOLOGY
2152 Union St.
San Francisco, CA 94123 USA
Timothy Gallagher, Director of Admissions
Psychology, organizational behavior
1969

M, D, Accredited
Residency
Non-profit, independent
(415) 346–4507
$$$$$

Ph.D. and Psy.D. programs in clinical psychology; Ph.D. programs in industrial and organizational psychology; and a part-time M.S. program in organizational behavior, offered at campuses in Berkeley, Fresno, Los Angeles, and San Diego. Some evening and weekend courses are scheduled. Clinical Ph.D. programs at all campuses are accredited by the American Psychological Association.

CALIFORNIA STATE UNIVERSITY, CHICO
Chico, CA 95929 USA
Dr. Kenneth C. Edson, Director of Admissions
Mr. Bruce Rowen, Registrar
Environmental planning, public administration,
social science, California studies
1887

B, M, Accredited
Residency
Non-profit, state
(916) 895–6321
$

A part of California's "Thousand Mile Campus," Chico State offers the Bachelor of Arts in environmental planning, public administration and social science; Master of Arts in California studies, environmental planning and social science; and the Master of Public Administration, with elements of independent study and credit for prior learning.

CALIFORNIA STATE UNIVERSITY, DOMINGUEZ HILLS ✪
1000 E. Victoria St.,
Dominguez Hills, CA 90747 USA
Dr. Donald Lewis
Humanities, quality assurance
1960

M, Accredited
Non-resident or residency
Non-profit, state
(213) 516–3743
$$

The External Degree Program in Humanities offers a non-resident M.A. in history, literature, philosophy, music, and/or art. The program is offered by "parallel instruction." Students do all the work that residential students do, in the same general time frame, but do not attend classes. Total of 30 semester hours for the degree. Eighty percent must be earned after enrolling. Credit for independent study projects, correspondence courses, and a thesis or a creative project. Communication with faculty by mail and telephone. A full-time student can finish in one academic year. (This is a rare opportunity to earn an accredited Master's degree non-residentially. I am biased. My wife completed her M.A. here in 1985, and is a testimonial to the program.) The M.S. in quality assurance requires 36 semester hours, with attendance at various business locations in southern California. Total cost: $4,400. Contact person for quality assurance: Paul Davis, Program Administrator.

CALIFORNIA STATE UNIVERSITY, NORTHRIDGE

18111 Nordhoff St.	M, Accredited
Northridge, CA 91330 USA	Residency
Lorraine Newlon, Director of Admissions	Non-profit, state
Engineering	(818) 885–1200
1958	$$

Master of Science in engineering in a non-traditional mode, with elements of independent study, and credit for prior experience. This program is for employees of the Naval Weapons Center or for local residents.

CALIFORNIA STATE UNIVERSITY, SACRAMENTO

6000 J St.,	B, M, Accredited
Sacramento, CA 95819 USA	Residency
Larry D. Galsmire, Director of Admissions	Non-profit, state
Many fields	(916) 278–6111
1947	$$

The degree programs have various non-traditional elements, including independent study and internships. They include: Bachelor of Arts, Bachelor of Science, Bachelor of Music, Master of Arts, Master of Science, M.B.A., Master of Social Work.

CALIFORNIA UNIVERSITY FOR ADVANCED STUDIES

see: Goodbye Index, Chapter 30

CALUMET COLLEGE

2400 New York Ave.	B, Accredited
Whiting, IN 46394 USA	Residency
Sharon Sweeney, Director of Admissions	Non-profit, church
Many fields	(219) 473–7770
1951	$$

Bachelor's degrees in general studies, social sciences, humanities and arts, business administration, and other individualized programs. Up to 75% of the units required can come from an assessment of prior learning experience. A course is offered in the preparation of life experience portfolios.

CAMBRIDGE COLLEGE

Institute of Open Education, 15 Mifflin Place	M, Accredited
Cambridge, MA 02138 USA	Residency
Bruce Grigsby, Director of Enrollment Services	Non-profit, independent
Education	(617) 492–5108
1970	$$$

The Master of Education is offered through an intensive 12-month program for working professionals. Each student must complete seven courses, participate in 12 one-day weekend workshops, participate in a year-long professional seminar, and produce a Master's project (research paper, media presentation, community project, etc.). Courses are given one weekday evening per week. Some interest-free loans are available.

CAMBRIDGE GRADUATE SCHOOL OF PSYCHOLOGY

3456 W. Olympic Blvd.	M, D, Unaccredited
Los Angeles, CA 90019 USA	State approved, Residency
Michael A. Callahan, Administrative Director	Proprietary
Psychology	(800) 472–1932

1982 $$
Weekend and evening classes for professionals already working in psychological service areas. The programs are approved by the state of California, enabling graduates to sit for state licensing exams in clinical psychology and in marriage, family, and child counseling.

CAMPBELL UNIVERSITY
P.O. Box 546 B, M, Accredited
Buies Creek, NC 27506 USA Residency
Herbert V. Kerner, Dean of Admissions Non-profit, church
Many fields (919) 436–3242
1887 $$$
The Bachelor's and Master's can be earned entirely through evening and weekend study, and are open to active military personnel, veterans, and civilians. Special degree program in business and juris doctrine of law.

CANADIAN SCHOOL OF MANAGEMENT ✪
150 Bloor St. West, Suite 715 B, M , Accredited
Toronto, Ontario M5S 2X9 Canada Non-resident
Dr. George Korey Non-profit, independent
Business, management (416) 960–3805
1976 $$
The Canadian School of Management is a college of advanced management studies offering non-resident self-directed study in business administration, health services administration, nursing administration, management, diplomatic and consular studies, and facilities management. There is emphasis on learning through practical experience. Credit is given for prior learning experience as documented in a portfolio. C.S.M. is a member of the International University Without Walls Council. Accredited by the National Home Study Council.

CANISIUS COLLEGE
2001 Main St. B, M, Accredited
Buffalo, NY 14208 USA Residency
Penelope H. Lips, Director of Admissions Non-profit, independent
Technical and liberal studies (716) 883–7000
1870 $$$
Bachelor of Arts and Bachelor of Science in technical and liberal studies may be earned through evening and summer programs. Credit for independent study, non-academic prior learning, and by examination. Part-time students pay $153 per credit. Up to 50% of the credit can come from work done at other approved institutions.

CAPITAL UNIVERSITY
Adult Degree Program, 330 Renner Hall B, Accredited
Columbus, OH 43209 USA Residency
Dr. Daina McGary, Associate Dean, Adult Education Non-profit, church
Many fields (614) 236–6696
1976 $$$
A University Without Walls program begun in 1976 by the Union for Experimenting Colleges and Universities and taken over in 1979 by the venerable Capital University. Beginning students must complete the equivalent of 124 semester credit hours, largely through guided independent study. A Bachelor of Arts, with various majors, or a Bachelor of General Studies, with no major, can be earned. All students must complete a senior project, showing Bachelor's-level abilities and serving as a learning experience. The university maintains Adult Degree Program offices in Cleveland and Dayton as well. Evening and weekend courses; credit for experiential learning available through portfolio assessment/competency statement development.

CARDINAL STRITCH COLLEGE
Office of Adult Education, 6801 N. Yates Rd. B, M, Accredited

Milwaukee, WI 53217 USA | Residency
Kenneth L. Steidle, Director of Admissions | Non-profit, church
Many fields | (414) 352–5400
1937 | $$$

Bachelor's degree programs are offered in many fields. Credit for experiential learning. The business/economics degree can be earned entirely through evening study. Programs in Management for Adults offers Bachelor's and Master's degrees in management and a Master's in health services administration which can be obtained by attending one evening a week. In addition, a certificate in sales productivity and management is offered through Programs in Management for Adults.

CARIBBEAN CENTER FOR ADVANCED STUDIES
see: Miami Institute of Psychology

CARSON-NEWMAN COLLEGE
Extension Division, Russell Ave. | B, M, Accredited
Jefferson City, TN 37760 USA | Residency
Jack W. Shannon, Director of Admissions | Non-profit, church
40 majors available | (615) 475–9061
1851 | $$$

Bachelor of Arts and Bachelor of Science in many fields, available entirely through evening study. Credit by examination, independent study, and for military experience. Self-designed majors are available. Master's degrees are offered in education, nursing, and teaching.

CASTLETON STATE COLLEGE | B, M, Accredited
Castleton, VT 05735 USA | Residency
Dr. Lyle Gray | Non-profit, state
Teacher education, business, liberal arts | (802) 468–5611
1787 | $$

Bachelor's and Master's may be earned through weekend, summer, and evening classes. Special programs in nursing education. Credit for independent study, non-academic prior learning, and by examination.

CEDAR CREST COLLEGE | B, Accredited
Allentown, PA 18104 USA | Residency
Curtis D. Bauman, Registrar | Non-profit, church
30 majors available | (215) 437–4471
1867 | $$$$

Bachelor's degree may be earned through weekend, evening, and summer classes (minimum of 30 credits to be earned after enrolling). Special programs include nursing, accounting, legal assistant, nuclear medical technology, genetic engineering technology. Credit for life experience and by proficiency exam.

CENTENARY COLLEGE (LA)
P.O. Box 41188 | B, Accredited
Shreveport, LA 71134-1188 USA | Residency
Caroline Kelsey, Director of Admissions | Non-profit, church
Various fields | (318) 869–5131
1825 | $$$

Bachelor of Arts, Bachelor of Science and Bachelor of Music degrees may be earned entirely through evening study.

CENTENARY COLLEGE (NJ)
400 Jefferson St. | B, Accredited
Hackettstown, NJ 07840 USA | Residency
James Pegg, Director of Admissions | Non-profit, independent
Many fields | (201) 852–1400, ext. 215
1867 | $$$

Bachelor's may be earned in fields including equine studies, fashion, interior design, communication, educa-

See page 70 for explanation of abbreviations and symbols

tion, business, liberal arts, psychology, and English, through weekend, evening, and summer programs. Credit for independent study, non-academic prior learning, and by examination.

CENTER FOR BUSINESS STUDIES
see: Clayton University

CENTER FOR PSYCHOLOGICAL STUDIES
1398 Solano Ave.
Albany, CA 94706 USA
Margaret S. Alafi, Ph.D., President
Clinical and developmental psychology
1979
D, Unaccredited, State approved
Residency
Non-profit, independent
(415) 524–0291
$$$
The Center serves mature professionals who have completed a Master's degree or its equivalent. Ph.D. degrees are offered in clinical and developmental psychology. Both Doctorates are approved by the California State Department of Education and meet educational requirements for the psychology license. Students are encouraged to pursue their own research interests for their dissertations and receive ample faculty support. Students may concentrate their studies in organizational psychology. Part-time study is available; the academic calendar is geared to the needs of working students. Former name: the Graduate School of Human Behavior.

CENTER GRADUATE COLLEGE
19225 Vineyard Ln.
Saratoga, CA 95070 USA
Robert Baratta-Lorton
Mathematics
1980
M, Unaccredited
State approved, Residency
Non-profit, independent
(408) 867–3167
$
The sole offering is a Master of Arts in education with a specialization in elementary mathematics. The course-work is designed for current or prospective mathematics resource teachers at the elementary school level.

CENTRAL MICHIGAN UNIVERSITY ✪
Institute for Personal Growth and Development,
Rowe Hall 131
Mt. Pleasant, MI 48859 USA
Robert Trullinger, Director, Extended Degree Programs
Administration, management and supervision
1892
B, M, Accredited
Non-resident
Non-profit, state
(517) 774–7136
$$
The M.S. in Administration program offers graduate degrees through intensive classes given at various locations nationwide. One can earn a general administration and management degree or specialize in health services administration or public administration. All programs are operated under the sponsorship of companies, military bases, or professional organizations. In most cases, anyone may enroll, whether or not they have an association with the sponsor. Classes are offered in Michigan; Washington, DC; Hawaii; and at locations throughout the Southeast and Midwest. Twenty-one semester hours (of 36 required) must be completed through Central Michigan. Up to 10 units can come from prior learning assessment. C.M.U. also offers programs in community college administration in Canada. For Michigan residents there is a program leading to a Bachelor of Individualized Studies or a B.A./B.S. in Liberal Studies. Thirty units must be earned from Central Michigan.

CENTRE DE TELE-ENSEIGNEMENT UNIVERSITAIRE
6, Ave. H. Maringer, B.P. 33.97
Nancy, F-54015 France
Prof. Jean-Marie Bonnet
Many fields
B, M, Equivalent of accredited
Non-resident
Non-profit, state
83-40-02-45
The Centre is a confederation of seven universities, offering degree studies by correspondence, based primarily on taped lectures (in French, of course), with supplementary written materials. The tapes are available by mail, and are also broadcast on the radio and available at various regional centers. Students must enroll

first in one of the participating universities (Besançon, Dijon, Metz, Mulhouse, Nancy, Reims, Strasbourg), and then in the Centre. Even though all coursework is done through the Centre, the degree is awarded by a participating university. Bachelor's (license) studies are offered in many fields, and the Master's in only a few.

CENTRE NATIONAL DE TELE-ENSEIGNEMENT
12, Place du Pantheon — B, Equivalent of accredited
Paris, 75005 France — Non-resident
M. Masclet — Non-profit, state
Many fields — (1) 46-34-9700
1987

Programs available nationwide through the Centre Audiovisuel des Université de Paris. The degrees are awarded solely on the basis of examinations, which must be taken in France. Instruction in French language, using radio programs, tapes, and a method conference held on a Saturday once a month. In the U.S., information is also available from the Embassy of France, Cultural Attaché, 972 5th Ave., New York, NY 10021.

CENTRO SUPERIOR DE ESTUDIOS EMPRESARIALES — M, Situation unclear to me
Castellana, 91 — Non-resident
Madrid 16, Spain — 456 00 05
Business — $$

(P.O. Box 010113, Miami, FL 33101), Mexico City, and Bogota. The literature (all in Spanish) states that they have been authorized by the Ministry of Education to grant degrees. The Master's requires two semesters. The cost is $1,600 if done with textbooks alone, or $2,400 if you are also sent cassette tapes of lectures. A thesis of 80 to 150 pages is required. I am concerned that the U.S. address is given as "CESEM (the school's acronym) USA & Intern. University." If this refers to "International University" it may mean an affiliation with one of the existing International Universities (some okay, some less than wonderful), but my letters have not been answered.

CENTURY UNIVERSITY
2155 Louisiana Blvd. N.E., #8600 — B, M, D., Unaccredited, state authorized
Albuquerque, NM 87110 — Non-resident
Donald Breslow, President — Proprietary
Many fields — (213) 645-3636
1978 — $$$

Organized primarily for professional administrators with extensive experience. Tuition is by guided independent study, which involves no classes, one-on-one faculty counseling, and credit for life experience learning. Degrees take a minimum of nine months to complete. The university was authorized to grant degrees by the state of California. The program is viewed by Century as the final year of traditional study for each degree, so candidates are expected to have substantial experience in their field. Century claims accreditation from an unrecognized accrediting agency. Like many other schools, Century misrepresents the findings of a study on the acceptance of non-traditional degrees (see page 17). In 1990, Century moved its offices from Los Angeles to Albuquerque. 12 of the 32 faculty have their own doctorates from Century.

CHADWICK UNIVERSITY — B, M, Unaccredited
1704 11th Avenue South — Non-resident
Birmingham, AL 35205 — Proprietary
Jean Berman, Director of Admissions — (205) 933-5680 or (800) 729-2423
Business — $$
1989

One of four schools established by Dr. Lloyd Clayton, Jr. (see also: Dr. Clayton's School of Natural Healing, American Institute of Computer Science). The ten-page catalogue lists no faculty, and misrepresents the Sosdian-Sharp study on the value of non-traditional degrees (see page 17). Completion of six home study courses is required for the Bachelor's and five for the M.B.A.

CHAMINADE UNIVERSITY
3140 Waialae Ave. — B, Accredited

See page 70 for explanation of abbreviations and symbols

Honolulu, HI 96816-1578 USA
Dr. William Murray, Director of Admissions
Many fields
1955

Residency
Non-profit, independent
(808) 735–4711
$$

Bachelor of Arts, Science, Business Administration, Fine Arts, and General Studies offered through accelerated evening programs on military bases primarily for military personnel and their dependents. Weekend and summer programs are also available. Credit for military training, independent study, examinations, and non-academic prior learning.

CHAPMAN COLLEGE
333 Glassell St.
Orange, CA 92666 USA
Anthony Garcia, Dean of Admissions
Many fields
1861

B, M, Accredited
Residency
Non-profit, independent
(714) 997–6611
$$$$$

Regional education centers are located at over 50 military installations and civilian locations, nationally. Six-, eight-, nine- and ten-week semesters are available. T.A.P.E. is a telecommunication-assisted program of education.

CHARTER OAK COLLEGE ✪
270 Farmington Ave.
Farmington, CT 06032 USA
Mrs. Patricia C. Frazier, Director of Administration
1973

B, Accredited
Non-resident
Non-profit, state
(203) 677-0076
$$

This program is available only to residents of Connecticut, Massachusetts, Rhode Island, New Hampshire, Vermont, and Maine. The college is operated by the Connecticut Board for State Academic Awards, and offers the Bachelor of Arts and Bachelor of Science degrees. The student is responsible for amassing 120 semester units, which may come from courses taken elsewhere, equivalency examinations, military study, correspondence courses, or special in-person examinations of one's knowledge level. As soon as the 120 units are earned, with at least half in the arts and sciences, and 36 in a single subject or major area, the degree is awarded. (Charter Oak used to accept enrollments from people anywhere in the world, but it just didn't work out satisfactorily.) Original name: Connecticut Board for State Academic Awards.

CHICAGO CITY-WIDE COLLEGE
Center for Open Learning
226 W. Jackson Blvd.
Chicago, IL 60606
Patrick McPhilimy, Director of Project Operations

Courses, Accredited
Non-resident
Non-profit, state
(312) 855-8213 or (800) 433-4733
$

This center is one of the city colleges of Chicago, which has been offering courses via television for more than thirty years. Many of the courses are also available on viceocassettes. All work can be completed at home, but one must take a proctored examination. These accredited units can be applied to degree programs at other schools.

CHICAGO STATE UNIVERSITY
University Without Walls, 95th St. at King Dr.
Chicago, IL 60628 USA
Dr. Michelle Howard-Vital, Dean, Continuing Education
Many fields
1867

B, Accredited
Short residency
Non-profit, state
(312) 995–2400
$$

A multi-ethnic, "commuter" institution in the city's far South Side oriented to the problems of the urban environment and the educational needs of older learners. A student, with the assistance of the learning coordinator and faculty advisor, enters into trimesterly learning agreements, ordinarily with a field advisor, a practitioner in the student's area of interest, often drawn from within his or her employing agency. The past academic and other relevant experience of the student is assessed after one trimester in the program, at which time an estimate is made of how long the degree program will take. A culminating project demonstrating competence, knowledge, and critical perspectives on one's field of study serves as the focal point for graduation assessment. Chicago State is one of five schools offering the Board of Governor's Bachelor's Degree program, in which much of the work can be done at a distance.

CINCINNATI BIBLE COLLEGE AND SEMINARY
2700 Glenway Ave., P.O. Box 043200 — B, M, Accredited
Cincinnati, OH 45204 USA — Residency
Steve Price, Assistant Director of Admissions — Non-profit, church
Religious fields — (513) 244–8100
1824 — $$
The Bachelor of Arts, Science, or Music is offered in many fields, ranging from Christian education to journalism to ministry to the deaf. Master's degrees are in 11 areas of concentration. The Master of Arts can be earned by taking courses in module form. More than half the units can be earned at extension locations in Maryland, Ohio, Iowa, Nebraska, Missouri, and Florida. Courses on the main campus are available days or evenings. Up to 25% of the units for a Bachelor's degree may be earned by the college's own correspondence courses. The schools are accredited by the American Association of Bible Colleges (a recognized accreditor) and have candidacy status with North Central Association, their regional accreditor.

CITY UNIVERSITY
16661 Northup Way — B, M, Accredited
Bellevue, WA 98008 USA — Non-resident
C. Florence Hagen, Registrar — Non-profit, independent
Many fields — (800) 426–5596
1973 — $$
Distance learning is offered entirely through the use of a home computer, or by more traditional (old-fashioned) means. Degrees offered in business, health care administration, computer science, nursing, accounting, and finance. City University offers programs in 26 areas of the state of Washington; Portland, Oregon; Santa Clara, California; several British Columbia locations, and Zurich, Switzerland. The university offers a Bachelor's in Business Administration, Health Care Administration, an M.B.A. or M.P.A. (public administration) and an M.A. in applied behavioral sciences via "distance learning" or independent study anywhere in the world. The M.B.A. may also be completed entirely by home computer. Also, a nursing B.S.N. program is offered through evening study, and programs in computer science either by evening or weekend study. Toll-free phone in Washington (800) 542–7845.

CITY UNIVERSITY LOS ANGELES ✪
3960 Wilshire Blvd — B, M, D, Law, Unaccredited,
Los Angeles, CA 90010 USA — State authorized, Non-resident
Henry L. N. Anderson, Chancellor — Non-profit, independent
Arts & Sciences, Law, Life Science/Natural Hygiene, — (213) 382–3801 or (800) 262-8388
Electromedical Sciences — $$
C.U.L.A. regards itself as "a finishing school" for students whose studies were interrupted earlier in life. Students should have at least two years of college credits before applying. Little credit for experiential learning. There is a three-day "Bachelor Challenge" Exam for those who have elsewhere completed 75% of the work for a Bachelor's. A typical student takes 7 to 10 months to complete a degree. Law students qualify to take the California bar exams. In a catalogue mailed in May, 1990, C.U.L.A. still claimed accreditation by the International Accrediting Commission for Schools, Colleges and Theological Seminaries, an unrecognized agency which was closed by Missouri authorities in early 1989. The catalogue reports that Johnny Carson, Muhammad Ali, Ethel Kennedy, and Coretta King are alumni. (This school is not mentioned in the Who's Who listings for these people.)

CITY UNIVERSITY OF NEW YORK—CITY COLLEGE
138th St. at Convent Ave. — B, M, Accredited
New York, NY 10031 USA — Residency
Susan Weingartner, Director of Admissions — Non-profit, state
Many fields — (212) 690–6741
1847 — $1,333
Bachelor's degree may be earned through weekend, evening, and summer programs. Fields include engi-

neering, architecture, medicine, liberal arts, science, and performing arts. Credit for tutorial, independent study, and by examination. Up to 30 credits may be earned for the life experience thesis program. Programs of the Center for Work Education are designed primarily for working adult members of labor unions. It offers flexible scheduling, weekend classes, and life experience credit. Phone: 690–5300. The Center for Vocational Teacher Education program leads to state certification and a B.S. in vocational education. Its phone: 690–5420.

CLARK UNIVERSITY
College of Professional and Continuing Education,
950 Main St.
Worcester, MA 01610 USA
Laura Myers, Director of Continuing Education
Many fields
1953

B, M, Accredited
Residency
Non-profit, independent
(617) 793–7408
$$

Bachelor of Arts in liberal arts or Bachelor of Science in business administration, Master of Public Administration and Master of Arts in liberal arts offered entirely by evening study or summer programs. Life experience programs for academic credit.

CLAYTON UNIVERSITY✪
P. O. Box 16150
Clayton, MO 63105 USA
Eugene Stone, President
Business, behavioral science, engineering, education
1972

B, M, D, Unaccredited (state has no licensing), Non-resident
Non-profit, independent
(314) 727–6100
$$$

Clayton offers degrees at all levels through their Interdisciplinary Program Institute (art, business, chemistry, music, and many other fields); the Behavioral Sciences Institute; and the Nutritional Science Institute. The catalogue lists about 200 part-time faculty advisors, most with traditional Doctorates. Credit is given for certified life experience learning. Originally called Open University, and later American International Open University. In England, Clayton degrees are offered through the Centre for Business Studies, Greenwich.

CLEVELAND STATE UNIVERSITY
E. 24th and Euclid
Cleveland, OH 44115 USA
Dr. Richard C. Dickerman, Director of Admissions
Many fields
1964

B, M, D, Law, Accredited
Residency
Non-profit, state
(216) 687–2000
$$

Degrees offered are the Bachelor of Arts, Science, Business Administration, Education, and Engineering; and the M.A., M.S., Master of Urban Affairs, and M.B.A. Most of these are available entirely through evening study and/or Saturday classes.

CLINICAL PSYCHOTHERAPY INSTITUTE
671 Barberry Ln.
San Rafael, CA 94903 USA
Thomas E. McCormick, President
Clinical psychotherapy
1981

M, D, Unaccredited, State authorized
(415) 479–3243

Authorized to grant degrees by the state of California. Did not respond to three requests for information on their programs.

COLLEGE FOR HUMAN SERVICES
345 Hudson St.
New York, NY 10014 USA
Alida Mesrop, Dean
Human service, business
1964

B (M?), Accredited
Short residency
Non-profit, independent
(212) 989–2002
$$$

Bachelor of Professional Studies in human service professions or business, for persons over 21 whose family incomes fall below the poverty line. Over 90% of the students are either black or Hispanic. The two-and-a-half year program is divided into eight 16-week "crystals" (terms) in which "dimensions" (courses) are taught by "co-ordinator-teachers." The school locates jobs for all students in one of 285 city agencies. Students work three days a week and take classes two days. An M.S. in administration has been under development. Campuses have been established in Florida, and in Oakland, California.

COLLEGE MISERICORDIA

Lake St.	B, Accredited
Dallas, PA 18612 USA	Residency
David M. Payne, Dean of Admissions	Non-profit, church
Many fields	(717) 675–2181
1924	$$$

Bachelor of Arts through weekend study; Bachelor of Science in Nursing, B.A. in business, and Bachelor of Music through evening study. Master's degrees in nursing, occupational therapy, education, and human services administration. Evening and weekend courses. A Bachelor's degree can be earned in four years of evening study.

COLLEGE OF MOUNT SAINT JOSEPH

Division of Continuing Education	B, Accredited
Mount Saint Joseph, OH 45051 USA	Residency
Mary Kay Meyer, Director of Continuing Education	Non-profit, church
Many fields	(513) 244–4805
1920	$$

The PM College offers Bachelor's degree programs in paralegal studies, liberal arts, business, and accounting, in classes that meet one evening a week in this west Cincinnati suburb. The Weekend College offers the Bachelor of Arts in business (management or marketing), communication arts, human services, gerontology, accounting, or liberal arts and Bachelor of Science in nursing and in management of nursing services. Classes meet five weekends out of each 13-week term. Each class is three-and-a-half hours long, and up to three can be taken between Friday evening and Sunday evening. Credit is available for experiential learning.

COLLEGE OF MOUNT SAINT VINCENT

263rd St. and Riverdale Ave.	B, Accredited
Riverdale, NY 10471 USA	Residency
Lenore M. Mott, Director of Admissions	Non-profit, independent
More than 30 fields	(212) 549–8000
1847	$$$

B.A. and B.S. programs in more than 30 fields through evening, summer, and weekend programs (every other weekend), both on and off campus. Also Bachelor of Science for R.N.'s. Up to 30 credits may be granted for experiential learning. Also credit by examination. More than 250 established internships are available for students. There is a College Emeritus, for those who have not studied since high school, or have limited college experience, and are age 55 or older. College Emeritus has substantially reduced tuition.

COLLEGE OF NEW ROCHELLE

School of New Resources	B, Accredited
New Rochelle, NY 10801 USA	Short residency
Patricia Furman, Associate Dean for Administrative Services	Non-profit, independent
Liberal studies, liberal arts	(914) 632–5300
1972	$$

The School of New Resources has six campus sites in the greater New York area: one in New Rochelle and one in each of the five boroughs of New York City. Degrees can be earned through evening and weekend study. Credit is given for life experience learning.

COLLEGE OF NOTRE DAME OF MARYLAND

4701 N. Charles St.	B, Accredited
Baltimore, MD 21210 USA	Residency

Jacqueline L. Strzelczyk, Director of Admissions
Many fields
1873

Non-profit, church
(301) 435-0100
$$$

Bachelor of Arts and Bachelor of Science in Nursing through weekend and summer programs. Several Master's programs as well. Credit for non-academic prior learning, independent study, and by examination. A dual-degree (B.A./B.S.) program in engineering with the University of Maryland. The literature reminds us, several times, that this Notre Dame is neither in Paris nor South Bend, but in Baltimore.

COLLEGE OF SAINT CATHERINE
2004 Randolph Ave.
St. Paul , MN 55105 USA
Jennifer Hentho, Dean of Admissions
Many fields
1905

B, Accredited
Residency
Non-profit, church
(612) 690-6000
$$$

College degree programs for adult women. Bachelor of Arts in business administration, communication, information management, nursing, occupational therapy, social work, and theology through Weekend College. Some evening classes are available. Credit for CLEP exams, and through CARL, a Credit for Academic Relevant Learning program.

COLLEGE OF SAINT FRANCIS ✪
500 Wilcox St.
Joliet, IL 60435 USA
Charles Beutel, Director of Admissions
Health Arts
1925

B, M, Accredited
Residency
Non-profit, church
(815) 740-3360
$$$

Bachelor of Science program with a major in health arts for registered nurses and other health professionals. Students are required to complete at least eight courses and may do so at any of 100 locations in 25 states, from California to New York. New locations are added regularly. Classes meet one evening a week. Full-time students may complete the degree in less than a year, while those taking one course at a time will normally take two-and-a-half years. 128 semester units are required for the degree, of which 32 must be earned after enrollment. Through the Prior Learning Assessment Program, the college recognizes the health professional's previous education and experience for college credit. Up to three years of college credit may be earned through an assessment of prior learning. A Master's degree program in health services administration is also available off campus at 25 locations in 11 states.

COLLEGE OF SAINT MARY
1901 S. 72nd St.
Omaha, NE 68124 USA
Dr. Patricia Snipp
Many fields
1923

B, Accredited
Residency
Non-profit, church
(402) 399-2400
$$$

The Weekend College offers a Bachelor of Science degree in business administration, computer information management, marketing, management, human resources management, and human services. Summer and evening study programs are also available; B.S.N. programs for nurses. Credit by examination and portfolio assessment.

COLLEGE OF SAINT ROSE
432 Western Ave.
Albany, NY 12203 USA
Mary O'Donnell, Director of Admissions
Many fields
1920

B, Accredited
Residency
Non-profit, independent
(518) 454-5111
$$$

Bachelor of Arts or Bachelor of Science in which up to 75% of the required credits may be earned through an assessment of prior learning experiences. The assessment may take six months or more. Only students matriculated at the College of Saint Rose are considered for assessment.

COLLEGE OF SAINT SCHOLASTICA
1200 Kenwood Ave.
Duluth, MN 55811 USA
Nancy Ferreira, Dean of Admission
Nursing, physical therapy, medical technology
1912
B, M, Accredited
Residency
Non-profit, church
(218) 723–6000
$$$
Bachelor's and some Master's may be earned through summer and evening classes. Credit for independent study, non-academic prior learning, and by examination. There is a requirement of 48 credits.

COLLEGE OF STATEN ISLAND
130 Stuyvesant Place
Staten Island, NY 10301 USA
Elaine Bowden, Registrar
Many fields
1955
B, Accredited
Residency
Non-profit, state/local
(718) 390–7733
$
The college is part of the City University of New York. Bachelor's degrees in many fields, through a totally individualized course of study. Credit is earned for classes held on-campus, off-campus, and at work sites, independent study projects, work experience, and prior learning experience, credit by examination, departmental challenge exams, and internships. Non-credit courses offered to prepare adult students returning to college.

COLORADO CHRISTIAN UNIVERSITY
School of Professional Studies
180 S. Garrison St.
Lakewood, CO 80226
Dr. Gene R. Marlatt, Dean
1914
B, Accredited
Residency
Non-profit, non-denominational
(303) 238-5386, ext. 152
$$$
The B.A. in Management of Human Resources can be earned in 12 months through evening or weekend programs, if the participant has an A.A. or 56 hours of transferable credit, is over 25, and prepares a life experience portfolio (which can be worth up to 40 units). Formerly Rockmont College. No connection whatever with a defunct diploma mill called Colorado Christian University.

COLORADO STATE UNIVERSITY✪
SURGE Program, Division of Continuing Education,
Fort Collins, CO 80523 USA
Marcia Bankirer, Director, Division of Continuing Education
Business, engineering, chemistry, computer science
1870
M, Accredited
Non-resident or Residency
Non-profit, state
(800) 525–4950
$$
Master of Business Administration and Master of Science in Engineering in an external program, involving a combination of coursework and independent study. The engineering degrees are in civil, electrical, mechanical, agricultural, and chemical engineering. Some offerings via videotape. The program is designed for certain industries that subscribe to the SURGE program, and agree to guarantee a certain number of enrollments. The program is then open to employees of those industries, but not readily to the general public. Programs have been offered in California, Colorado, Montana, North Dakota, Washington, and Wyoming. The university "specializes" in offering programs to meet educational needs not met by local institutions. It is possible to acquire viedotapes directly from the university, for persons who are not able to view them through their company or employer.

COLUMBIA PACIFIC UNIVERSITY✪
1415 3rd St.
San Rafael, CA 94901 USA
Richard L. Crews, M.D., President
Many fields
1978
B, M, D, Law, Unaccredited
State approved, Non-resident
Proprietary
(800) 227–0119
$$$$
Non-resident degrees in many fields through schools of Arts and Sciences, Health and Human Services, International Law and Business, and Administration and Management. The university is approved by the

state of California. More than 5,000 students enrolled. 15% of faculty have their own Doctorate from Columbia Pacific. Degrees are based on credit for prior learning, completion of a core curriculum normally requiring 9 to 12 months, and a major project, thesis, or dissertation. A quarterly surcharge is added for persons who do not finish within one year. There is a graduation fee of $25 to $235. The university has two locations: its own building in San Rafael and a retreat center in Petaluma. I served as a consultant to Columbia Pacific in its early years, but not since 1984. Toll-free phone number within California (800) 552–5522.

COLUMBIA STATE UNIVERSITY

3925 N. I-10 Service Rd., #117
Metairie, LA 70002 USA
Dr. Ronald Pellar
Many fields
1976

B, M, D, Unaccredited,
State registered, Non-resident
Proprietary
(504) 889–8831
$$

Offers Bachelor's, Master's, and Doctorates in many fields, including business, computer science, political science, public health, communication, agriculture, engineering, and theology. Registration with the Louisiana Board of Regents is an automatic, non-evaluative process. They claim to be accredited by the International Accreditation Association. I have not heard of this organization, and the school has not responded to my letters.

COLUMBIA UNION COLLEGE ✪

7600 Flower Ave.
Takoma Park, MD 20912 USA
Charlotte Conway, Director of Admissions
Various fields
1904

B, Accredited
Non-resident
Non-profit, church
(301) 270–9200
$$$

The Bachelor of Arts can be earned entirely through correspondence study. Credit for standard equivalency examinations or work experience after the student has earned at least 24 semester hours in the program. At least 30 units must be earned after enrolling at Columbia Union (between 8 and 12 courses). Students may select any of the following areas of concentration: business administration, education, English, history, psychology, or religion. (The psychology degree cannot be done entirely through home study.) All students must write a major paper, related to literature, science, religion, or arts or pass a comprehensive examination to qualify for graduation. The school is owned by the Seventh-Day Adventist Church, but non-church-members are welcome. Students may live anywhere in the world, but all work must be done in English.

COLUMBIA UNIVERSITY

Teachers College, 525 W. 121st St.
New York, NY 10027 USA
Roland Hence, Director of Admissions
Education
1887

D, Accredited
Short residency
Non-profit, independent
(212) 678–3000
$$$$$

The Doctor of Education degree is offered through an innovative program called AEGIS: Adult Education Guided Independent Study. The program requires two years to complete, largely through guided independent study, with advisement available by correspondence, telephone, or optional campus visits. Participants must attend a seminar on campus one Saturday each month, plus a three-week intensive summer session for both summers of enrollment. The program is designed for experienced self-directed professionals with at least five years of experience in program development or administration of adult education or training. Admission is highly competitive; about 20 students per year are admitted.

CONCORD COLLEGE

see: West Virginia Board of Regents B.A. Program

CONCORDIA UNIVERSITY

12800 North Lake Shore Drive
Mequon, WI 53092
Dr. David Zersen, Dean, School of Adult and Continuing Ed.
Management and communication, liberal arts, health care,

B, Accredited
Residency
Non-profit, church
(414) 243-4341
$$$

nursing
1881
Concordia offers Bachelor's degrees in an accelerated modular format, for full-time working adults. Credit is awarded following portfolio assessment, as well as by telecourses, correspondence courses, challenge exams, and through independent study. The school operates adult learning centers in Appleton, Green Bay, Madison and Kenosha, Wisconsin; Fort Wayne, Indiana; and St. Louis, Missouri. The B.S. in nursing is for RNs, and meets one night a week for 73 weeks.

CONNECTICUT BOARD FOR STATE ACADEMIC AWARDS
see: Charter Oak College

COOK'S INSTITUTE OF ELECTRONICS ENGINEERING
Hwy. 18, P.O. Box 20345
Jackson, MS 39029 USA
Wallace L. Cook, Director
Electronics engineering
1945
B, Unaccredited, state authorized
Non-resident
Proprietary
(601) 371–1351
$$$$
Bachelor of Science in Electronics Engineering, entirely by correspondence study, involving completion of 36 courses. Advanced placement is available for experienced electronic technicians having satisfactory prior schooling. The tuition is as low as $3410 in such cases. At least 15 of the 36 courses must be completed after enrolling. The school literature explains in great detail why they are not accredited (no home study engineering program is), and makes clear the distinction between their B.S.E.E. and the correspondence B.S. in Engineering Technology offered by their chief competitor, Grantham. Wallace Cook, the owner, established this school more than 40 years ago.

COVENANT COLLEGE
Quest Program,
Lookout Mountain, TN 37350 USA
Donovan Graham, Dean of Extended Programs
Organizational behavior
1955
B, Accredited
Residency
Non-profit, church
(404) 820–1560
$$$
The Bachelor of Arts in organizational behavior is offered in an innovative program in which a group of 16 to 20 students meets one evening a week for 52 weeks. Nine courses are offered during this period, consecutively, for one to five weeks each. All students complete a major research project, applying management and organizational behavior to a problem or need in his or her occupational field or place of service. All work is done in "a biblical framework; "Covenant is affiliated with the Presbyterian Church of America. A degree program can begin whenever and wherever 16 to 20 students are ready. Applicants must have 60 semester units of credit and five years of work experience to qualify. CLEP and military credit are accepted. Students can earn up to 32 units toward graduation (not admission) from life experience. The program is offered in the Chattanooga, Tennessee area.

CREIGHTON UNIVERSITY
California St. at 24th
Omaha, NE 68178 USA
Dr. Shirley L. Dooling, Dean of Nursing
Nursing
1878
B, M, Accredited
Residency
Non-profit, independent
(800) 228–7212, ext. 2027
$$$
The Accelerated Nursing Curriculum program offers persons with a B.A. or B.S. in another field the opportunity to earn a professional degree (B.S.N.) in nursing in one year. There is also a three-year Bachelor's/Master's option.

DALLAS BAPTIST UNIVERSITY
7777 W. Kiest Blvd.
Dallas, TX 75211 USA
Dr. Gary R. Young, Registrar
Many fields
B, Accredited
Residency
Non-profit, church
(214) 331–8311

1898 $$

Most courses are offered through evening study, and some on Saturdays. The Bachelor of Career Arts program will award up to 30 hours of the necessary credits for the degree for prior learning experiences. The degree is offered in aviation, management, business administration, computer science, criminal justice, engineering management, fire protection management, pastoral ministries, real estate, secretarial science, and other areas. Credit is generously, but realistically, awarded for government, military, aviation and other career experience. (For instance, their brochure indicates a C.P.A. or C.L.U. certificate is worth the portfolio maximum of 30 credit hours.)

DARLING DOWNS INSTITUTE OF ADVANCED EDUCATION

P.O. Box Darling Heights — B, M, Equivalent of accredited
Toowoomba, Australia 4350 — Non-resident
G. Edmondson, Senior Administration Officer — Non-profit, state
Applied science, arts, business, education, engineering — (61 7) 6 312100

Degree programs make extensive use of audio-and videotapes as well as written materials. Evening courses, and external study programs are offered.

DARTMOUTH COLLEGE

MALS Admissions, 301 Wentworth Hall — M, Accredited
Hanover, NH 03775 USA — Residency
Dr. J. Laurie Snell, Chair, MALS Program — Non-profit, independent
Liberal Studies — (603) 646–3592
1769 — $$$$$

Dartmouth College's Master of Arts in Liberal Studies program is designed for adults to continue their liberal education. Students typically attend three summers, or, for those who do continuous work, five consecutive terms. (About 40% of the 200 active students are from out of the area). The program combines classes, a weekly colloquium, student-led seminars, independent study, and a final project assignment. Meals and housing are available on the Dartmouth campus, if desired. Seventy-five percent of the MALS students receive some form of financial assistance. Students plan their own course of study. There are no core courses and no majors.

DE LA SALLE UNIVERSITY

Career Development Department, P.O. Box 3819 — M, D, Accredited
Manila, Philippines — Residency
Dr. Carmelita Quebengco, Dean — Non-profit, church
Business, management, economics — 59–48–06
1911

The university offers a Master's and Doctorate degree in management and a M.S. in economics in a part-time program, with evening study. It is designed for working students in public services, education, commerce and industry, and private agencies.

DE PAUL UNIVERSITY (Illinois)

25 E. Jackson Blvd. — B, M, Accredited
Chicago, IL 60604 USA — Residency
Brian Spittle, Director of Adult Admissions — Non-profit, church
Many fields — (312) 341–8000
1898 — $$$

The School for New Learning offers a B.A. and M.A. that may be earned through weekend and evening programs. Each degree is individually designed. Credit for learning from life or work experience is given. The MALS, or Master of Arts in Liberal Studies, program offers a multidisciplinary liberal arts curriculum for adult learners, involving a self-designed program emphasizing team-taught courses and colloquia. All classes are offered in the evening, generally once a week, at two Chicago locations. All students take the same four core courses, two colloquia, and six elective courses, and then complete an "integrating project."

DEAKIN UNIVERSITY

Off-Campus Studies — B, Equivalent of accredited

Victoria, 3217 Australia
Humanities, social sciences, education,
1975
Non-resident
Non-profit

Deakin operates as an open university, for Australians only, with voluntary attendance at tutorials and weekend schools. The Bachelor of Arts is offered in humanities, social sciences, and education. Also offered are Bachelor of Education, Graduate Diploma of education administration, Master's in education, education administration, and business administration, and a Graduate Diploma in computing. Special entry offers the opportunity for adults who haven't completed secondary level education to enroll in the Bachelor of Arts.

DEFIANCE COLLEGE
701 N. Clinton St.
Defiance, OH 43512 USA
Terry L. Taylor, Director of Admissions
Many fields
1850
B, Accredited
Residency
Non-profit, church
(419) 784-4010
$$$

Bachelor of Art and Bachelor of Science in a wide variety of fields, through weekend, evening, and summer programs. Credit for prior learning, independent study, and by examination. A two-semester interdisciplinary core course is required. In addition to many traditional majors, there are unusual majors in municipal and industrial recreation, natural systems, and therapeutic recreation.

DELAWARE VALLEY COLLEGE
Doylestown, PA 18901 USA
Stephen W. Zenko, Director of Admission
Business, biology, computer systems, management
1896
B, Accredited
Residency
Non-profit, independent
(215) 345-1500
$$$

The Bachelor of Science in these fields is available entirely through evening study.

DRAKE UNIVERSITY
25th St. and University Ave.
Des Moines, IA 50311 USA
Jennifer G. Hantho, Director of Admissions
Many fields
1881
B, M, Accredited
Residency
Non-profit, independent
(515) 271-3181
$$$$

A wide range of both undergraduate and graduate degrees is available through evening classes. Evening students may earn the Master's degree in 12 areas. In the Bachelor of General Studies program, 75% of the required 124 semester units can be earned by alternative means, including credit for prior learning experiences and equivalency examinations. The remaining 30 units can be taken by attending weekend, evening, or summer courses on the Drake campus. The Master of General Studies degree provides individualized study in broad areas for the mature adult at the Master's degree level. The program requires a Bachelor's degree from a regionally accredited institution and permits entrance into graduate courses under the advice of assigned counselors, usually without an admissions test. A broad focus on study must be indicated. Less than one-half of the coursework can be taken in one department or field (not more than 40% in the College of Business Administration).

DREXEL UNIVERSITY
32nd and Chestnut
Philadelphia, PA 19104 USA
Keith Brooks, Associate Dean, Admissions
Various fields
1891
B, M, Accredited
Residency
Non-profit, independent
(215) 895-2000
$$$$

Bachelor of Science in architecture, business administration, engineering, general studies; Master's in business administration, home economics, and library science, all available through evening study. The M.L.S. in library science can be earned through evening and weekend classes in two years or less.

DRURY EVENING COLLEGE

900 N. Benton Ave.,
Springfield, MO 65802 USA
Michael Thomas, Director of Admissions
Many fields
1873

B, Accredited
Residency
Non-profit, independent
(417) 865–8731 ext. 207
$$$

The Bachelor of Science in many fields may be earned entirely through evening study. Advanced placement possible by CLEP or credit by proficiency examination. The Drury degree can also be earned in London, England, through Lansdowne College.

DURHAM UNIVERSITY

Tuition House, 27/37 St. George's Road,
London, SW19 4DS England
Business administration
1988

MBA, Equivalent of accredited
Short residency
Non-profit, state
$$

In mid-1988, Durham introduced a distance learning M.B.A., administrated by non-degree-granting Rapid Results College, which specializes in coursework preparing students for various university examinations. The plan sounds comparable to that offered by the University of Warwick through Rapid Results College's rival; Wolsey Hall.

DYKE COLLEGE

112 Prospect Ave.
Cleveland, OH 44115 USA
Laura T. Darvas, Director of Admissions
Business areas
1848

B, Accredited
Non-resident or short residency
Non-profit, independent
(216) 696–9000
$$

Bachelor of Science in business areas (management, marketing, accounting, health services management, among others) in which an adult student proceeds at his or her own pace through completion of 126 semester hours under guidance of professional mentors. All work may be done non-residentially, but occasional meetings with mentors on campus are suggested, so only students living within 50 miles are accepted. Options (which may be mixed) for earning credit are: homestudy through learning contracts, group study at various locations, life/work experience and/or proficiency exams (both at 1/3 tuition), previous credit transfer. Tuition can be greatly reduced by life/work experience credit and proficiency exams. This is the first such program approved by the Ohio Board of Regents, and is the oldest and largest external degree program in Ohio.

EAST CENTRAL COLLEGE CONSORTIUM

Hiram College
Hiram, OH 44234 USA
Gary G. Craig, Dean of Admissions
1850

B, Accredited
Residency
Non-profit, independent
(216) 569–5278
$$$$

The consortium of seven liberal arts colleges cooperates in offering a Bachelor of Arts degree in general studies, sciences, humanities and arts, business administration, and health sciences. Substantial credit may be granted for prior learning experience after completion of a well-documented portfolio written under the guidance of a faculty advisor. Registration at one of the colleges and fulfillment of some residency requirements are mandatory. The participating schools are Bethany College (West Virginia); Heidelberg College, Hiram College, Marietta College, Mount Union College and Muskingum College (all in Ohio); and Westminster College (Pennsylvania).

EAST TENNESSEE STATE UNIVERSITY

P.O. Box 24429
Johnson City, TN 37614 USA
Richard Yount, Registrar
Many fields
1911

B, M, Accredited
Residency
Non-profit, state
(615) 929–4112
$$

Twenty two different credit programs are available entirely through on-campus evening classes.

EASTERN CONNECTICUT STATE COLLEGE
83 Windham St.
Willimantic, CT 06226 USA
Dr. Arthur C. Forst, Director of Admissions
Many fields
1889

B, M, Accredited
Residency
Non-profit, state
(203) 456–5286
$

Bachelor's may be earned through weekend, evening, and summer programs. Credit by examination and for non-academic and military prior learning. Up to 60 credits can be earned through CLEP exams. Higher tuition for out-of-state students.

EASTERN ILLINOIS UNIVERSITY
Charleston, IL 61920 USA
Wolf, Director of Admissions
Many fields
1895

B, Accredited
Non-resident or short residency Dale W.
Non-profit, state
(217) 581–2223
$$

Bachelor of Arts, with a minimum of 15 units to be earned on campus. Eastern Illinois is one of five members of the Board of Governors Bachelor of Arts program, a non-traditional program designed for working adults, in which most of the work can be completed off-campus, through independent study, equivalency examinations, and credit for life experience. A major is not required. Skills and knowledge acquired by non-academic means can be evaluated for academic credit.

EASTERN MICHIGAN UNIVERSITY
Division of Continuing Education
Ypsilanti, MI 48197 USA
Paul T. McKelvey, Dean of Continuing Education
Educational administration
1849

M, Accredited
Residency
Non-profit,state
(313) 487–1081
$$

Master of Arts in educational administration, with much of the work possible through independent or off-campus study, combined with on-campus meetings and seminars. Several on-campus courses are available on weekends. The Master of Liberal Studies offers the opportunity to design an individualized interdisciplinary program. An M.L.S. in woman's studies promotes feminist scholarship.

EASTERN OREGON STATE COLLEGE
Division of Continuing Education
La Grande, OR 97850 USA
James C. Lundy
1929

B, Accredited
Residency
Non-profit, state
(503) 963–2171
$$

Bachelor's may be earned through weekend, evening, and summer programs. Credit for independent study, cooperative work experience, non-academic learning, and by examination.

EASTERN WASHINGTON UNIVERSITY
Cheney, WA 99004 USA
Roger Pugh, Admissions officer
General studies
1882

B, Accredited
Residency
Non-profit, state
(509) 359–2397
$$

Bachelor of Arts in general studies, specifically for persons with professional or paraprofessional experience. This includes, for instance, mechanics, computer programmers, police officers, nurses, secretaries, firefighters, draftspeople (look how hard I'm trying to be non-sexist) and others. Twenty-five percent of the work must be done after enrollment, which would normally require one academic year (9 months). A main advantage here is the school's willingness to give life experience credit to people in fields that other schools might not agree are credit-worthy. I have heard from a few people who enrolled in Eastern Washington long enough to get credit for, say, their secretarial experience, then transferred this credit to another, faster school.

ECKERD COLLEGE ✪
Program for Experienced Learners, P.O. Box 12560

B, Accredited

St. Petersburg, FL 33733 USA
Dr. Gerald Dreller, Director,
Many fields
1959

Non-resident
Non-profit, independent
(813) 867–1166
$$

External Bachelor's degree programs available through weekend, evening, and summer programs. Credit by examination, independent study, and for prior learning. Directed independent study. No physical residency is required, but students must complete at least nine courses through Eckerd College. Two correspondents report that Eckerd encouraged them to enroll in the evening program instead, saying that "most external students end up there anyway."

EDINBORO UNIVERSITY OF PENNSYLVANIA
Edinboro, PA 16444 USA
Terrence Carlin, Director of Admissions
Many fields
1857

B, Accredited
Residency
Non-profit, state
(814) 732–2000
$$

Bachelor of Arts in English, speech communication, geography, sociology, psychology; Bachelor of Science in education, industrial and trade leadership; and Bachelor of General Business through evening, weekend, and summer programs. Credit for non-academic prior learning, independent study, and by examination. The assessment of prior learning is done in Edinboro's Life Experience Center and can take a month or less. For a small fee, they will conduct a brief inspection of one's resume or credentials and advise whether or not they think it is worthwhile to go ahead with the more expensive complete assessment. Edinboro's Opportunity College is designed to help adult students earn credit while continuing employment and family responsibilities.

ELECTRONIC UNIVERSITY NETWORK ✪
385 8th St.
San Francisco, CA 94103 USA
R. Timothy Leister, President
Many fields

B, M, Accredited
Non-resident
Proprietary
(800) 22–LEARN
Cost varies widely

TeleLearning Systems' Electronic University offers courses that can be taken from home, using IBM, Apple II or Commodore home computers. Students are linked directly over telephone lines to universities. The list of participating schools changes frequently, but have included, for instance, Boston University, Ohio University, Penn State University, University of Illinois, and University of San Francisco. Most schools do not offer entire degree programs over the computer, but there is an M.B.A. that can be so earned from Saginaw Valley State University, and Bachelor's degrees from Thomas A. Edison State College and the University of the State of New York. There is access to more than 80 computer data base systems, permitting students to tap into some large libraries while doing their coursework. The cost is from 14¢ to 65¢ per minute. Undergraduate courses average about $400 each. M.B.A. courses a good deal more.

ELIZABETHTOWN COLLEGE ✪
Elizabethtown, PA 17022 USA
Dr. Gloria Hay, Director of Continuing Education
Liberal studies and professional studies
1899

B, Accredited
Short residency
Non-profit, church
(717) 367–1151
$$$

Bachelor of Liberal Studies and Bachelor of Professional Studies, which may be earned with only three all-day seminars on campus to plan and discuss the independent study program. Credit is given for prior learning experiences, both traditional and non-traditional. The independent study program includes completion of core and major subject requirements, which can be met by transfer of credits, life experience credits, and traditional study.

ELMHURST COLLEGE
Office of the Evening Session, 190 Prospect
Elmhurst, IL 60126 USA
Michael C. Dessimoz, Director of Admissions
23 majors
1871

B, Accredited
Residency
Non-profit, independent
(312) 279–4100 ext. 486
$$$

Bachelor's degree program through weekend, evening, and summer study. Elmhurst also offers a degree completion program for working registered nurses, with courses offered in hospitals in the Chicago area. Also, special accelerated program in business administration. Credit for independent study, prior learning experience, and by examination.

ELMIRA COLLEGE
Park Place — B, Accredited
Elmira, NY 14901 USA — Residency
Robert C. French, Director of Admissions — Non-profit, independent
Many fields — (607) 734–3911
1855 — $$$$

Bachelor of Science and Master of Science, both in education, available entirely through evening study. Fields available include accounting, business, chemistry, computer information systems, education, general studies, human services, mathematics, nursing, psychology, and social studies.

ELON COLLEGE — B, M, Accredited
Elon College, NC 27244 USA — Residency
R. Albertson, Registrar — Non-profit, church
Business, education — (919) 584–9711

All Bachelor's degrees and an M.B.A. and a Master of Education are available through evening study.

EMBRY-RIDDLE AERONAUTICAL UNIVERSITY✪
Center for Independent Studies — B, Accredited
Daytona Beach, FL 32014 USA — Non-resident
Thomas W. Pettit, Director, Center for Independent Studies — Non-profit, independent
Aeronautics — (904) 239–6392
1926 — $$$

Bachelor of Professional Aeronautics with no classroom attendance through self-paced, independent study. To qualify, one must have certified civilian or military training and professional experience in any of the following specialties: air traffic control, airways facilities, airline command pilot, aviation safety, air carrier pilot, corporate pilot, flight technology, aircraft maintenance, aircraft dispatcher, commuter airline pilot, aviation weather, electronic operations and maintenance, flight operations administration, flight simulation, navigations systems, or certified flight instructor. From 18 to 60 semester credit hours of advanced standing are given for professional aeronautical experience. Credit is also given for CLEP, USAFI, DANTES, E-RAU examinations, military service schools, aviation licenses and credentials, and transfer credit from accredited colleges. Tuition includes study guides and audiocassette fees but not textbooks.

EMPIRE STATE COLLEGE✪
2 Union Ave. — B, M, Accredited
Saratoga Springs, NY 12866 USA — Non-resident and residency
Lora Montague, Director of Admissions — Non-profit, state
Liberal arts and sciences — (518) 587–2100
1971 — $$

A part of the State University of New York, Empire State College provides programs in 40 locations across New York state. The primary mode of study is independent study guided by faculty mentors. Together, students and mentors develop a degree program within the college's 11 broad areas of undergraduate study. Credit is given for college-level learning gained from work and other life experience. The Bachelor's degrees can be completed entirely at a distance. The Master of Arts requires four days on campus at the beginning and end of each semester, and is offered in business and policy studies, labor and policy studies, and culture and policy studies. They combine independent study with three three-or-four-day weekends on campus each year. In addition, the Center for Distance Learning offers structured courses and degree programs in business administration, human services and interdisciplinary studies for students seeking more structured learning, but without classroom attendance or travel. Faculty guidance is by mail and telephone.

EUBANKS CONSERVATORY OF MUSIC AND ARTS
4928 S. Crenshaw Blvd. — B, M, Unaccredited, state

See page 70 for explanation of abbreviations and symbols

Los Angeles, CA 90043 USA
Rachel A. Eubanks, President
Music and arts
1951
authorized, Residency
Non-profit, independent
(213) 291–7821
$$

The Bachelor's and Master's degrees are offered in performance (classical or jazz), theory and composition, accompanying, and church music. Courses are offered evenings and on weekends. There are a few correspondence courses, and limited credit is given for life experience learning. The conservatory is authorized to grant degrees by the state of California.

EULA WESLEY UNIVERSITY
900 E. Cornell
Ruston, LA 71270 USA
Dr. Samuel Wesley, President
Business, sociology, religious studies
B, M, D, Unaccredited, state registered, Non-resident
(318) 255–4396
$$

Established in Phoenix, in founder Samuel Wesley's home. Wesley told an Arizona Republic reporter his Doctorate was earned from Eula Wesley "after his thesis...was reviewed by members of the...board of directors," whom he identified as two local educators. Both denied they were on the board, or had conferred the degree. "They're lying," Wesley told the reporter. The article says "Wesley later admitted...his degree was an honorary one, and had been awarded by... James Jenkins, an umployed janitor and Eula Wesley, Wesley's mother..." In Arizona, E.W.U. was accredited by the International Accrediting Commission for Schools, Colleges and Theological Seminaries, an unrecognized agency, whose founder, George Reuter, according to the *Republic*, came to Phoenix but never visited the "campus." Wesley said Reuter also arranged for five Nigerians to become correspondence students. Now registered with the board of regents in Louisiana (a non-evaluative automatic procedure).

EUROPEAN UNIVERSITY
Amerikalei 131
Antwerp, 2000 Belgium
Various fields
B, I am confused by status
Residency
(021) 631167
$$

The literature is impressive looking and in full color. But I remain confused, and letters to President Nieberdine have not been answered. To their credit, they reproduce "affiliation agreements" between Troy State and Central State University (both accredited), in which those schools agree to accept E.U.'s students into their M.B.A. program. Membership is claimed in the American Association of Collegiate Schools of Business. I cannot locate such an organization. There is an American Assembly of Collegiate Schools of Business, but E.U. is not a member. The literature states that more than 1,500 students are enrolled in the residential Bachelor's program in language, business, information systems, hotel administration, or public relations, and that the university operates its own radio station in Antwerp. Courses also given in Brussels and in Montreux, Switzerland.

EUROPEAN UNIVERSITY INSTITUTE
Via dei Roccettini, 5
San Domenico di Fiesole, Italy
Werner Maihofer, Principal
Various fields
1976
D, Equivalent of accreditation
Residency
Non-profit, state
(055) 477–931

The institute was established in 1976 by the nine member nations of the European Economic Community. Students plan independent study projects, under the guidance of faculty tutors and research supervisors. About 10% of the students come from countries outside the Common Market. The degree of Ph.D. is awarded on completion and publication of the dissertation. Fields of study include economics, history and civilization, law, political science, and social science.

EUROPEAN UNIVERSITY OF AMERICA
2130 Fulton St.
San Francisco, CA 94117 USA
Business administration
M, Unaccredited, state approved
Residency
Non-profit, independent
(415) 668–0964
$$

The focus is on international business. Students take courses in theory and method, and then work on a personal/professional project that serves as a framework for in-depth research and the development of practical skills. The program requires 10 to 14 months of full-time attendance to complete.

EUROTECHNICAL RESEARCH UNIVERSITY
P.O. Box 516
Hilo, HI 96721 USA
James G. Holbrook, President
Mainly scientific and engineering fields
1983

D, Unaccredited, state registered
Non-resident
Proprietary
(808) 935-6424
$$$

The university was established in California in 1983 and moved permanently to Hawaii in 1989. It offers doctorates based on research performed by the student in non-academic settings—normally an industrial or government laboratory or other institution. The program is based on the European model, where a doctorate requires original scientific research, but does not involve any classroom coursework. Eurotech's program is based on and follows exactly the pattern at the University of Southampton, with whom a formal link has been established. Eurotech's president prefers to discuss intended work, goals and problems personally with each prospective student, thus inquirers are asked to provide a resume or detailed letter with telephone number on requesting the catalogue. Substantial scholarship assistance is available for students who show evidence of creative work or achievements at the time of application. The university is appropriately registered with the state of Hawaii.

EVERGREEN STATE COLLEGE
Olympia, WA 98505 USA
Christine Kerlin, Director of Admissions
Many fields
1967

B, M, Accredited
Short residency
Non-profit, state
(206) 866–6000
$$

Students have the option of creating "independent contract" courses of study for supervised research under a faculty mentor. Groups of two or more students may work under a "group contract." Credit is given for internship programs, involving, for instance, work in local hospitals, clinics, or businesses. Full-time interdisciplinary programs, in which the majority of Evergreen's students are enrolled, are available on campus as well. Students involved in independent study are still expected to visit the campus and meet with their faculty mentors at least once a month. All students must be enrolled for at least nine months before earning the degree. During the presidency of former governor (then senator) Dan Evans, Evergreen developed a national reputation for its innovative approaches to undergraduate non-traditional education. (My daughter enjoyed Evergreen for the year she was there...but she now prefers the traditional programs at University of California, Berkeley.)

EVERYMAN'S UNIVERSITY
16 Klausner St.
Ramat Aviv, Tel Aviv, Israel
Prof. Nehemia Levtzion, President
Many
1974

B, Equivalent of accreditation
Non-resident
Non-profit, , independent
(03) 422–511
$$

Israel's first open university (Ha'universita Ha'petuha in Hebrew) offers the Bachelor's degree on completion of 18 home study courses, given only in Hebrew. Each course consists of a home study kit, which may include written materials, laboratory equipment, simulation games, etc. Many courses are supplemented by radio and television programs. Each course requires 16 to 18 weeks to complete, working 15 to 18 hours a week. Courses are available in natural sciences, social sciences, mathematics, life sciences, business administration, computer studies, and humanities. Non-credit courses are available in Arabic, computers, and ecology. The university was established by the Rothschild Foundation. The Israeli government is gradually assuming financial responsibility. There are also group study programs with regular weekly study sessions, particularly in commercial firms, labor unions, disadvantaged neighborhoods, and banks. More than 12,000 are enrolled.

FAIRFAX UNIVERSITY ✪
2900 Energy Centre

B, M, D, Unaccredited, state registered

New Orleans, LA 70163 USA
Malcolm Large, The Administrator
Many fields
1986

Non-resident
Non-profit, independent
(504) 585–7303
$$

"Programme Participants" (students) work at their own pace, assisted by a "Programme Supervisor" (faculty), to complete work required by a "Study Plan" (learning contract). On completion of this work plus a paper, thesis, or dissertation, and the approval of an external assessor, degree is awarded. My wife and I were two of the four founders of Fairfax; we resigned three months after the first enrollment in 1986. Fairfax is registered with the Board of Regents in Louisiana, an automatic, non-evaluative procedure. When I visited the address in 1990, I found a no Fairfax office, but a "Headquarters Company" service, that apparently forwards mail and messages to The Administrator in England. The academic aspects of Fairfax appear sound, but I have had complaints about difficulty in communicating with the principals, which may be due to this geographic arrangement. Finally, I must say that I am mightily annoyed that the president of Fairfax has attempted (unsuccessfully) to get authorities in California to prevent me from selling this book, because, among various other reasons, he alleges I give an improperly good write-up to a school with which Fairfax is involved in a lawsuit. See also: Cornerstone Theological Seminary.

FAIRLEIGH DICKINSON UNIVERSITY

285 Madison St.
Madison, NJ 07940 USA
Rita Bennett, Director of Admissions
Many fields
1958

B, M, D, Accredited
Residency
Non-profit, independent
(201) 593–8900
$$$

Bachelor of Arts, Bachelor of Science, Master of Arts, Master of Science, and Doctor of Education programs, offered through centers at Madison, Rutherford, and Teaneck, primarily through evening study. The Doctorate, in educational leadership, consists of formal courses, seminars, internships, plus independent study and research. There is a "Success Program" for persons over 25 who have never attended (or have never finished) college. Some special classes are available for these students. Fairleigh Dickinson offers a number of "Accelerated" programs, in which two degrees can be completed together in less time than they would normally take separately. There are five-year B.A./M.P.A. (public administration), B.A./M.B.A., B.A./M.A. in psychology, and B.A./M.A. in Teaching programs, and one of the rare six-year B.S./M.D. or B.S./D.M.D. programs in medicine or dentistry. Degree completion program for professional athletes over 22.

FAIRMONT STATE COLLEGE

see: West Virginia Board of Regents B.A. Program

FAYETTEVILLE STATE UNIVERSITY

Murchison Rd.
Fayetteville, NC 28301 USA
Denise F. Mahone, Director, Administrative Services
Many fields
1867

B, M, Accredited
Residency
Non-profit, state
(919) 486–1111
$

Bachelor of Arts and Bachelor of Science for military personnel, their dependents, and local residents. All work can be completed through evening and weekend study. Some credit is given for prior learning experiences and for equivalency examinations. There are 24 majors available at the Bachelor's level, and 4 Master's programs: business administration, administration and supervision, special education, and elementary education.

FERNUNIVERSITÄT ✪

Feithstrasse 152
Hagen, D-5800 West Germany
Dr. G. R. Broehl, Chief, Information Division
Many fields
1974

M, D, Equivalent of
accreditation, Non-resident
(02331) 8041
$

West Germany's open university offers the Master's, Doctorate, and Diplom-Degree through completion of correspondence study units, plus examinations (which must be taken in Germany). Instruction is through a combination of written materials and audio cassettes. All courses are self-paced. Tuition is offered in the fields of mathematics, electrical engineering, information science and computers, business administration, and education. The university operates about 30 study centers in Germany for the assistance and guidance of students. All instruction in German, although a nice color brochure is available in English. More than 1,450 of Fernuniversität's over-25,000 students live outside of Germany.

FERRIS STATE COLLEGE

Gerholz Institute for Lifelong Learning
Big Rapids, MI 49307 USA
Jeffrey Cross, Director
Environmental health
1884

B, Accredited
Short residency
Non-profit, state
(616) 796–0461, ext. 3545
$$

Bachelor of Science in environmental health offered through the School of Allied Health and the Gerholz Institute for Lifelong Learning. External degree programs for people living anywhere in the United States. All of the requirements for the degree can be met through an assessment of prior learning experience, or a combination of that plus equivalency examinations, independent study, faculty-directed study, home study courses, and special projects. All students must attend a three-week summer session on campus. One year of work experience in the field of environmental health is required for admission to the program. The assessment of prior learning can take as long as nine months, and is done for a flat fee of around $250. A Bachelor of Science in health systems management, business administration, accountancy, maritime management, and vocational education is available at selected off-campus sites, but only to Michigan residents.

FIELDING INSTITUTE ✪

2112 Santa Barbara St.
Santa Barbara, CA 93105 USA
Donna Lucci, Director of Admissions
Psychology, human and organization development
1974

M, D, Accredited
Short residency
Non-profit, independent
(805) 687–1099
$$$$

Fielding offers the shortest residency of any accredited Doctoral program in the U.S. Five days are required on campus. The degrees are neither fast nor easy. The M.A. takes at least two years; the various Doctorates, three to five years. Applicants' participation in a five-day admissions workshop is mandatory. It is here that the learning contract is developed. Workshops are held three times each year. The Human and Organization Development Program offers a Master's in organization development, human development, or human services; a Ph.D. in human and organizational systems or human development; an Ed.D.; and a Doctor of Human Services. The psychology degrees (M.A., Ph.D., Psy.D.) emphasize clinical or counseling. The M.A. in psychology is not a separate program but rather a part of the Doctorate. An electronic network offers electronic mail, bulletin board service, and electronic seminars. All students and faculty must have access to a computer with communication capability.

FINDLAY COLLEGE

1000 N. Main St.
Findlay, OH 45840 USA
Dr. Edward Erner, Dean of Community Education
58 majors
1882

B, Accredited
Residency
Non-profit, church
(419) 424–4600
$$$

Bachelor of Arts or Bachelor of Science in business administration, accounting, computer science, social work, systems analysis, and other areas may be earned through summer, weekend, or evening study. Unusual majors include equestrian studies, nuclear medicine technology, and hazardous waste studies.

FLAMING RAINBOW UNIVERSITY

419 N. 2nd
Tahlequah, OK 74960 USA
Barbara Jones, Data Department
Many fields
1972

B, Accredited
Non-resident
Non-profit, independent
(918) 696–3644
$$

See page 70 for explanation of abbreviations and symbols

Bachelor of Arts in behavioral science, arts and humanities, social science, and liberal studies largely for Native Americans, or Indians, who comprise about 60% of the student body. Credit is given for prior learning experiences. After enrolling, learning comes from independent study, internships, group experiences, classes at other schools, travel, etc. Organized classes meet evenings or weekends. "Traditional testing for academic achievement is not used in Flaming Rainbow, nor are grades assigned for work completed. A portfolio is kept on each student, that contains all forms and reports made by the student for the purpose of documentation and evaluation." The minimum period of enrollment is 12 months, but the average is considerably longer. Most students are on scholarships, covering from half to three-fourths of the tuition.

FLORIDA INSTITUTE OF TECHNOLOGY
Graduate Admissions Office
150 W. University Blvd.
Melbourne, FL 32901
Director of Admissions
1958

M, Accredited
Many off-campus locations
Independent
$$$

MBA in ten fields and Master of Science in computer science, electrical engineering, management, space technology, and many other fields, offered to military and civilians at fifteen locations in Florida, New Jersey, Alabama, New Mexico, Virginia, Louisiana, and Maryland. A few years ago, the chairman of FIT's Board of Trustees resigned after newspaper reports that he had purchased his own degrees from a notorious degree mill. The newspapers failed to notice that FIT was also accepting transfer credits from said degree mill, which was soon after closed down and its owner sent to prison. FIT seems to have survived this episode quite well.

FORDHAM UNIVERSITY
School of General Studies
Bronx, NY 10458 USA
John J. Houston, Associate Director of Admissions
Liberal arts, business, pre-medical
1841

B, Accredited
Residency
Non-profit, independent
(212) 579–2000
$$$$

Bachelor of Arts, Bachelor of Science, and Bachelor of Business Administration available entirely through evening study or Saturday classes. Credit is given for life experience learning. There is an Esperanza Center for adult Hispanic students, and a separate adult admissions office.

FRAMINGHAM STATE COLLEGE
100 State St., P.O. Box 2000
Framingham, MA 01701 USA
Dr. Paul F. Weller
Liberal studies
1839

B, Accredited
Short residency
Non-profit, state
(617) 626–4550
$$

Bachelor of Arts in liberal studies in which units may be earned through equivalency exams, independent study, correspondence study, prior learning experiences, and "non-credit educational experiences." The remaining units must be earned by taking courses on campus, taking a series of weekend or summer seminars, or making other arrangements satisfactory to the advisory committee.

FRANKLIN PIERCE COLLEGE
Ringe, NH 03461 USA
Walter Antoniotti, Dean, Continuing Education
Management, accounting, computer science
1962

B, Accredited
Residency
Non-profit, independent
(603) 889–6146
$$$$

Bachelor of Science with majors in management, accounting, and computer science through weekend, evening and summer programs offered at satellite campus locations only. Credit for independent study, non-academic prior learning, and by examination. Special one-year Bachelor's program for students with 80 or more semester hours of life experience and/or transfer credit.

FRANKLIN UNIVERSITY
201 S. Grant Ave.

B, Accredited
Residency

Columbus, OH 43215
Nancy Nikiforow, Assistant Director of Admissions
Many fields
Non-profit, independent
(614) 224-6237

Degrees offered through evening courses, with credit for experiential learning through proficiency testing and portfolio assessment.

FREIE UND PRIVATE UNIVERSITÄT
Degersheimerstrasse 29
Herisau AR, 9100 Switzerland
L. Mattei, President
Various fields
D, Unaccredited
Non-resident
(071) 52 35 25

The university is legitimate, but not recognized by the Swiss Central Office for Higher Education, and the degrees are not recognized in Germany. Degrees offered in behavioral science, arts and humanities, social science, and liberal studies. They also use the French (Université Libre et Privé) and Italian (Universita Libera e Privata) versions of their name.

FRIENDS WORLD COLLEGE
Plover Lane
Huntington, NY 11743 USA
Arthur Meyer, Director of Admissions
Many fields
1965
B, Accredited
Residency
Non-profit, independent
(516) 549–1102
$$$

Bachelor of Arts degree is earned by combining academic study with individually designed independent field research and internships around the world. Faculty at campuses and program centers in the U.S., Costa Rica, England, Israel, Kenya, India, China, and Japan offer 4- to 12-week residential programs for cultural orientation, language immersion and learning plan design prior to independent field study, which may be carried out in these and other countries in the regions. (Since 1965, F.W.C. students have studied in over 70 different countries.) Students may elect traditional liberal arts majors, as well as such fields as third world development, peace and conflict resolution, UN studies, holistic and traditional healing, appropriate technology, animal behavior, women's studies, international business, and many interdisciplinary majors.

GEORGE MASON UNIVERSITY ✪
Office of Extended Studies, 4400 University Dr.
Fairfax, VA 22030 USA
Patricia M. Riordan, Director of Admissions
Individualized studies
1957
B, M, Accredited
Residency
Non-profit, state
(703) 323–2342
$$

Bachelor of Individulized Studies degree in which 85% of the necessary units may be earned by alternative means: equivalency exams or credit for life experience learning. Applicants must have at least eight years of post-high-school experience. In conjunction with an academic advisor, the student designs and completes a program of study. A total of 30 units must be completed either at George Mason or at certain other northern Virginia colleges. A Master of Arts in interdisciplinary studies is available for adult students with at least two years of work in the area of proposed study. At least 6 hours of graduate-level work must be completed before enrolling. A course of study is worked out with a member of the George Mason faculty, who supervises the performance of the work. A special project is required. Evening study is available for the residential programs.

GEORGE WASHINGTON UNIVERSITY
706 20th St., NW
Washington, DC 20052 USA
George W. Stoner, Director of Admissions
Many fields
1821
B, M, Accredited
Residency
Non-profit, independent
(202) 994–1000
$$$$

The catalogues people have sent me make it clear that they have some interesting programs in the fields of education, humanities, the social sciences, criminal justice, urban learning, forensics, telecommunication op-

See page 70 for explanation of abbreviations and symbols

eration, and administration, but for reasons they do not choose to reveal, they don't want them described in this book. You'll have to find out from Mr. George W. Stoner, director of admissions. Tell him John Bear sent you.

GEORGIA SOUTHWESTERN COLLEGE
Wheatley
Americus, GA 31709 USA
Dr. James Altman, Admissions Officer
Social science, business administration
1906
B, Accredited
Residency
Non-profit, state
(912) 928–1279
$$
Bachelor of Arts, Bachelor of Science in social science and business administration, available entirely through evening study.

GESTALT INSTITUTE OF NEW ORLEANS
3500 St. Charles Ave., Suite 208
New Orleans, LA 70115 USA
Ann Teachworth, Director
Gestalt therapy, neurolinguistic programming
1976
Diplomas, Unaccredited, state registered, Non-resident
Proprietary
(504) 891–1212
$$
Registered with the Louisiana Board of Regents, an automatic, non-evaluative process. Evening and week-end courses leading to two levels of diploma.

GLASSBORO STATE COLLEGE
Center for Experiential Education
Glassboro, NJ 08028 USA
John G. Davies, Director of Admissions
Many fields
1923
B, M, Accredited
Residency
Non-profit, state
(609) 863–5000
$$
Bachelor's degrees in many fields, in which some credit can come through an assessment of prior learning experiences, equivalency exams, and transfer credit. There is no fee for the assessment, once one has enrolled. They regard themselves as "very traditional" and do not want to hear from anyone looking for a non-traditional program, please.

GLENVILLE STATE COLLEGE
see: West Virginia Board of Regents B.A. Program

GODDARD COLLEGE ✪
Plainfield, VT 05667 USA
Gregory Dunkling, Director of Admissions
Many fields
1938
B, M, Accredited
Non-resident or residency
Non-profit, independent
(802) 454–8311
$$$
Goddard has been a pioneer in non-traditional, progressive education for more than 50 years. They offer non-traditional options for studies in business and organizational leadership, education, psychology and counseling, natural and physical sciences, feminist studies, the visual and performing arts, literature and writing, and social and cultural studies (history, philosophy, religious studies). The first nine days of each semester are spent in an All College Meeting, where the work of the coming semester is planned. In addition to the undergraduate residential program, students may choose to be "Off Campus Students" where the majority of work is done off-campus while maintaining contact by mail every three weeks. Both Bachelor's and Master's programs require a minimum of one year's enrollment at Goddard; prior learning credit is available. Life experience credit is only given at the Bachelor's level. There is a non-residential student-designed M.A. in Europe, as well.

GOLDEN GATE UNIVERSITY
536 Mission St.
San Francisco, CA 94105 USA
Archibald Porter, Dean of Admissions
B, M, D, Law, Accredited
Residency
Non-profit, independent

Many fields
1901

(415) 442–7272
$$$

Bachelor of Arts in many management-related fields; Bachelor of Science in accounting, insurance management and transportation; M.B.A.; Master of Public Administration; Master of Science in accounting and taxation; and a combined M.B.A. and law degree; D.P.A. or D.B.A. in business or public administration all available entirely through evening and/or weekend study. An executive M.B.A. program for experienced managers meets every other weekend for 20 months. Courses leading to degrees are offered through centers in various locations all over California (Los Angeles, Sacramento, San Diego, etc.). Off-campus degree programs are given at military bases in Arizona, Florida, Idaho, Nevada, New Hampshire, New Mexico, North Carolina, South Carolina, Virginia, Washington, and Guantanamo Bay, Cuba. (Two of my daughters went here for a while, happily, before moving on to other schools with broader liberal arts offerings.)

GOLDEN STATE UNIVERSITY (CA)
see Honolulu University

GOVERNORS STATE UNIVERSITY✪
University Park, IL 60466 USA
Dr. Otis O. Lawrence, Director of Assessment, BOG program
Many fields
1969

B, Accredited
Short residency
Non-profit, state
(312) 534–5000 ext.2515
$$

Bachelor of Arts may be earned through weekend, evening, summer programs, and telecourses completed through the Board of Governors Bachelor of Arts Degree Program. Fifteen credit hours must be completed at Governor's State or one of the other Board of Governors institutions (Chicago State University, Eastern Illinois University, Northeastern Illinois University, and Western Illinois University). These may be taken through independent study courses, telecourses, on-campus or off-campus courses, so that it is possible to earn this degree without ever setting foot on campus. There are evening and weekend classes. Credit for independent study, non-academic prior learning, and by examination.

GRADUATE SCHOOL FOR COMMUNITY DEVELOPMENT
431 Market St.
San Diego, CA 92101 USA
Wilhelmina Perry, President
1976

M, D, Unaccredited, state authorized
Non-profit, independent
(619) 232–0975

Authorized to grant degrees by the state of California. Did not respond to three requests for information on their programs.

GRADUATE SCHOOL OF HUMAN BEHAVIOR
see: Center for Psychological Studies

GRANTHAM COLLEGE OF ENGINEERING ✪
250 Frontage Road
Slidell, LA 70460
Arnold E. Akers, Dean of Students
Engineering technology
1951

B, Accredited
Non-resident
Proprietary
(800) 955-2527
$$

Bachelor of Science in Engineering Technology through correspondence study. Course consists of 31 courses and 4 examinations. The exams must be supervised, but can be taken anywhere. In addition, student must earn 21 semester units in English, social science, science, and elective subjects at other schools (by correspondence, in person or by equivalency exam). Catalogue indicates that a part-time student will take between four and eight years to complete the B.S.E.T. degree. All work is self-paced, so the highly motivated student can finish faster. Up to 18 semester units can be earned for prior laboratory or work experience, for work work done while enrolled in the program. Grantham is accredited by the National Home Study Council, a recognized agency. The degree can be earned with a specialization either in electronics or in computers. In 1990, the school moved from California to Louisiana.

See page 70 for explanation of abbreviations and symbols

GREENWICH UNIVERSITY ✪
100 Kamehameha Avenue
Hilo, HI 96720
Dr. John B. Bear , President
Most academic fields, plus law, theology
1972
B, M, D, Law
Unaccredited; state-registered
Non-resident
(800) FOR HILO (US and Canada)
(808) 935-9934 (elsewhere)
$$
This is "my" school (I am the full-time president), so of *course* I'm biased. Greenwich, which evolved from the International Institute for Advanced Studies, the oldest non-traditional graduate school in the U.S., and the degrees have been widely accepted by Fortune 500 companies, international organizations, and major universities. The model is one of "filling in gaps." A student's learning (however it occurred) is matched against our standards for what a degree-holder should know. Any gaps are filled in through guided independent study, based on a learning contract developed by student and faculty mentors. A major paper, thesis or dissertation is required, but it may be based on work previously completed. The adjunct faculty of 150 include many well known scholars and authors. The Greenwich University School of Theology operates from offices in England and Scotland; the School of Computer Science is in Hong Kong; and short residential programs are offered in Australia. The university (and yours truly) operate from our own ocean-front office building in Hawaii's second largest city.

HAMLINE UNIVERSITY
Snelling and Hewitt Ave.
St. Paul, MN 55104 USA
Jack K. Johnson, Dean, Continuing Studies
Public administration
1854
M, Accredited
Residency
Non-profit, church
(612) 641–2800
$$$$
Master's in public administration through an evening program, for public administrators, corporate managers, and lawyers.

HAMPSHIRE COLLEGE
Amherst, MA 01002
Olga E. Euben, Director of Admissions
Many fields
1970
B, Accredited
Residency
Non-profit, independent
(413) 549-4600
$$$$$
The B.A. is earned by completing three levels of study. In Division I, basic studies, students spend three or four semesters in residence taking courses and pursuing research. In Division II, concentration, they gain mastery of a chosen field through independent study, foreign study, internships, and/or more courses. In Division II, advanced studies, a major project is completed

HARVARD UNIVERSITY
Extension School, 20 Garden St.
Cambridge, MA 02138 USA
Michael Shinagel, Dean
Many fields
1636
B, M, Accredited
Residency
Non-profit, independent
(617) 495–4024
$$
Six hundred courses in over 65 fields of study on an open-enrollment basis. Bachelor of Liberal Arts in extension studies, Master of Liberal Arts (A.L.M.) in extension studies, certificate of special studies in administration and management, certificate of advanced study in applied sciences, certificate in public health. English as a Second Language program. Half the units for the Bachelor's degree must be earned at Harvard (either Extension School, Summer School, or the regular university). The Master's degree work must be completed in its entirety at Harvard. There is a foreign language requirement, and a thesis must be submitted.

HAWAII PACIFIC UNIVERSITY
1166 Fort Street Mall, #203
Honolulu, HI 96818
Director of Admissions
B, M, Accredited
Residency
Non-profit, independent
(808) 544-0249
Various Bachelor's degrees and the MBA are offered through Adult Continuing Education, for adults who wish to remain fully employed. Credit is given for work experience, military training, and equivalency

exams. The MBA offers concentrations in various specialties, and an internship option.

HAWTHORNE UNIVERSITY
Cotati, CA 94952 USA
General studies
1982

B, M, D, Unaccredited
Residency
(707) 795–7168

Hawthorne opened in the fall of 1982, offering degrees at all levels in general studies, with an emphasis at the Master's level in humanistic computer studies. In 1988, the university was still in operation, although apparently no longer authorized by the state of California. (The Bachelor's is offered as a convenience for those going on to higher degrees.) Hawthorne evolved from a formerly-state-approved school named Paideia, now apparently alive but dormant in Berkeley. Indeed, 7 of the 10 Hawthorne faculty have their highest degree from Paideia. They utilize the "Paideian process" in which interdisciplinary groups of 12 or so meet each week and the entire school meets one Saturday a month.

HEED UNIVERSITY
Alumni and Information Center, P.O. Box 311
Hollywood, FL 33022 USA
Dr. Marvin Hirsch, President
Psychology, philosophy, education, business administration, law
1970

B, M, D, Law, Unaccredited
Non-resident
Non-profit, independent
(305) 925–1600
$$$

Bachelor of Arts, Bachelor of Science, Master of Science, Master of Arts, Master of Business Administration, Ph.D., Doctor of Education, Doctor of Business Administration, Doctor of Arts, and Doctor of Psychology. The Ph.D. and S.J.D. degrees require a dissertation, the other Doctorates do not. In 1986, Heed moved from Florida, where they had been 16 years, to the U.S. Virgin Islands. The phone above is their Florida information center. Heed had been granted approval to conduct courses and confer degrees by the Department of Education of the Virgin Islands, but this may be in doubt. Heed also operates the Thomas Jefferson College of Law in California, which is recognized by the Committee of Bar Examiners, and awards law degrees through correspondence study, including a four-year J.D. whose graduates may take the California bar, an S.J.D. (juridical science), and a non-bar-qualifying J.D. that may be completed in as little as six months. There are combined M.B.A./J.D. and D.B.A./J.D. programs.

HEIDELBERG COLLEGE
310 E. Market St.
Tiffin, OH 44883 USA
Dr. Ramond A. Wise, Registrar
Many fields
1850

B, Accredited
Residency
Non-profit, church
(419) 448–2000
$$$$

Bachelor of Arts and Bachelor of Science in accounting, allied health, business administration, health services management, psychology, and public relations. Up to 75% of the necessary credits may be earned through an assessment of prior learning experiences, which is done on the basis of a portfolio prepared by the student. The assessment fee is $395. Non-traditional courses are available, based on a learning contract model. There is also a Weekend college which meets from Friday evening through Sunday morning during the fall, spring, and summer terms. See also: East Central College Consortium.

HERIOT WATT UNIVERSITY
Riccarton, Edinburgh, EH14 4AS Scotland
Dr. R. K. MacKenzie, Director of Studies
Construction management, acoustics, vibration, and noise control
1963

M, Equivalent of accreditation
Non-resident
Non-profit, state
(031) 225–8432
$$

A two-year course in the above fields offered entirely by video. The video lectures, course notes, and tutorial exercises are based on the traditional program at the university. It is designed for persons in building control and environmental health departments, or in inspection services. The course is available throughout the United Kingdom, and possibly overseas.

See page 70 for explanation of abbreviations and symbols

HERITAGE COLLEGE
Route 3, Box 3540
Toppenish, WA 98948 USA
Dr. Barbara Gfeller, Dean of Registration and Admissions
Education, business management, science, English, interdisciplinary studies
1907
B, M, Accredited
Residency
Non-profit, independent
(509) 865–2244
$$$

Master of Education degree through intensive weekend courses on both Toppenish and Omak campuses. Bachelor's degrees available entirely through evening study, with credit for prior learning experiences and for equivalency examinations. Credit for work experience available through on-campus LINK program. Formerly known as Fort Wright College.

HIRAM COLLEGE
Hiram, OH 44234 USA
David Frains, Dean of the Weekend College
Various fields
1850
B, Accredited
Residency
Non-profit, independent
(216) 569–3211
$$

Bachelor of Arts offered entirely through weekend study. The Weekend College meets from Friday evening through Sunday noon, every other weekend. Substantial credit may be gained for prior learning experience after completion of a well-documented portfolio written under the guidance of a faculty advisor. Programs available in fine arts, humanities, social sciences, communications, business management, and allied health. The degree can be completed in a minimum of one academic year. See also: East Central College Consortium.

HISPANIC UNIVERSITY
255 E. 14th St.
Oakland, CA 94606 USA
B. Roberto Cruz, President
Education, business, health care
1981
B, M, D, Unaccredited, state approved, Residency
Non-profit, independent
(415) 451–0511
$$

A multilingual, multicultural approach to higher education. There is a contract with Northrop University, Los Angeles, to enroll Hispanics in their school of engineering.

HOFSTRA UNIVERSITY
1000 Fulton Ave.
Hempstead, NY 11550 USA
Joan Isaac, Director of Admissions
Many fields
1935
B, Accredited
Residency
Non-profit, independent
(516) 560–6600
$$$

Hofstra's New College is a small interdisciplinary liberal arts college offering the B.A. in humanities, natural sciences, social sciences, creative studies, or interdisciplinary studies, based on a combination of individual study on campus, internship projects off campus, and classroom work. Within New College, there is a University Without Walls program for "able adults who can spend only limited time on campus, but whose life situations provide opportunity for full- or part-time learning." It is based on an individually-designed program, and it does not count credit or time as measures of progress toward the degree. It is, rather, based on development of abilities and competencies. New College students can earn up to 32 credits by examination. Some Master's and Doctoral credit can be earned by equivalency examinations. Many of Hofstra's traditional courses are offered in the evening as well.

HOLY NAMES COLLEGE
3599 Mountain Blvd.
Oakland, CA 94619 USA
Paul Bluemle, Director of Admissions
Various fields
1868
B, Accredited
Residency
Non-profit, independent
(415) 436–1321
$$$

Holy Names' Weekend College offers Bachelor of Arts degrees in business administration/economics, human services, humanistic studies, and nursing; Master of Business Administration; M.A. in English and education, and Master of Education. Classes meet every other weekend during three trimesters. Academic programs and support services are designed for the adult who works full time.

HONOLULU UNIVERSITY OF ARTS, SCIENCES AND HUMANITIES ✪
1600 Kapiolani Blvd., Suite 1440
Honolulu, HI 96814
Dr. Warren Walker, President
1978

B, M, D, Unaccredited, state registered
Non-resident
Independent
(808) 955-7333
$$

Degrees at all levels can be earned through correspondence courses, a great many of which are listed in the catalogue, in dozens of fields of study. Formerly Golden State University, which operated from four cities in California.

HOOD COLLEGE
Rosemont Ave.
Frederick, MD 21701 USA
Katherine Joseph, Director of Admissions
Many fields
1893

B, M, Accredited
Residency
Non-profit, independent
(301) 663–3131
$$$$

Bachelor's degrees in many fields in which units may be earned through an assessment of prior learning experiences, conducted by the college's Learning Assessment and Resource Center. Master of Arts in human sciences for in-service teachers and others, through late afternoon, evening, and summer study.

HOUSTON INTERNATIONAL UNIVERSITY
2102 Austin
Houston, TX 77001
Antonio Gonzalez, President
Social work and public administration
1970

B, Unaccredited, state certified
Residency
Non-profit, independent
(713) 951-9401
$$

Specializes in education for Hispanics and other international students for whom English is a second language. Degrees can be earned through evening classes. Credit can be earned through coursework, seminars, practicums, independent study, as well as credit for prior learning experience. Original name: Hispanic International University

HOWARD UNIVERSITY
University Without Walls, 2400 6th St. NW
Washington, DC 20059 USA
William H. Sherrill, Dean of Admissions
Many fields
1867

B, Accredited
Residency
Non-profit, independent
(202) 636–6100
$$$

A University Without Walls program leading to the Bachelor of Arts or Bachelor of Science degree, with a course of study determined by a learning contract negotiated between student and faculty, and involving substantial elements of independent study. Credit is given for prior learning experiences and for equivalency examinations. A bimonthly seminar on campus is the main time for contacting advisors and faculty. Students are required to keep a daily log.

HUMAN RELATIONS INSTITUTE
5200 Hollister Ave.
Santa Barbara, CA 93111 USA
Counseling psychology

M, Unaccredited, state approved, Residency
Non-profit, independent
(805) 967–4557
$$$

The degree is available through weekend courses held once a month. The institute is approved by the state of California, so graduates are eligible for the M.F.C.C. license exam.

HUMANISTIC PSYCHOLOGY INSTITUTE
see: Saybrook Institute

HUNTER COLLEGE
695 Park Ave.
New York, NY 10021 USA
Kenneth J. Kleinrock, Director of Admissions
Many fields
1870

B, M, Accredited
Residency
Non-profit, state/city
(212) 772-4490
$$

Bachelor of Arts, Bachelor of Science, and Master's degrees in many fields, available entirely through evening study and summer programs. There are combined Bachelor's/Master's programs in anthropology, economics, English, history, mathematics, music, physics, and sociology.

ILLINOIS BENEDICTINE COLLEGE
5700 College Rd.
Lisle, IL 60532 USA
Koby Loszach, Transfer Coordinator
Business, accounting, health service management, nursing, computer science
1887

B, M, Accredited
Residency
Non-profit, church
(312) 960-1500
$$$

Bachelor's degrees in the above fields, and the MBA and M.S. in management information systems, entirely through evening study. Credit is given for prior work and life experience learning. The school used to be known as Saint Procopius College.

ILLINOIS SCHOOL OF PROFESSIONAL PSYCHOLOGY
220 S. State St.
Chicago, IL 60604 USA
Shelley Probber, Director of Admissions
Psychology
1976

D, Accredited
Residency
Proprietary
(312) 341-6500
$$$$

The Doctor of Psychology (D.Psy.) degree is offered through daytime or evening classes. The D.Psy. is offered, because it is felt that the traditional Ph.D. in psychology overemphasizes research skills to the detriment of counseling or clinical skills. Graduates who have two years of supervised experience in the field can qualify to take the state licensing examination in Illinois.

INDIANA CENTRAL UNIVERSITY
see: University of Indianapolis

INDIANA INSTITUTE OF TECHNOLOGY
1600 E. Washington Blvd.
Fort Wayne, IN 46803-1297 USA
Robert K. Pfundstein, Director of Admissions
Business administration
1930

B, Accredited
Residency
Non-profit, independent
(219) 422-5561 Ext. 251
$$$

Bachelor of Science in business administration. Credit for independent study, non-academic prior learning, and by examination. Correspondence courses are available. Courses in business, computer information systems, accounting, computer science, engineering, and technical communication offered through evening study. All students must have a personal computer, and have access to the Institute's computer 24 hours a day, 7 days a week.

INDIANA UNIVERSITY ✪
External Degree Program, Division of Extended Studies
620 Union Dr.
Indianapolis, IN 46205 USA
Louis R. Holtzclaw, Associate Director, Extended Studies Division

B, Accredited
Non-resident
Non-profit, state
(317) 274-3934
$$

General studies
1975
Bachelor of General Studies available entirely through non-residential study. The degree can be done without a major, or with a major in labor studies. One hundred and twenty semester units are required, of which at least 24 must be earned from Indiana University. One quarter of the units must be upper division (junior or senior) level. The university also has evening courses, a Weekend College, and a course to assist in developing a life experience portfolio.

INDIANA UNIVERSITY OF PENNSYLVANIA ✪
Indiana , Pennsylvania 15705 USA
George E. McKinley, Director of Admissions
English and American Literature
1875
D, Accredited
Short residency
Non-profit, state
(412) 357–2100
$$
Indiana University (city of Indiana, state of Pennsylvania), offers a Ph.D. in English and American literature and in English (rhetoric and linguistics) that can be completed in two summers of study, with independent study in between. "Programs are arranged to accomodate teaching schedules of secondary, community, and four-year college teachers. With this flexibility of scheduling, graduate students can pursue their studies without interrupting their careers." Students can choose from a number of areas related to the humanistic study of literature, including psychology, history, art, and music. A dissertation is required: a book, or five or six essays on a given subject. The language requirement can be met by coursework, exams, linguistics courses, or knowledge of a computer language. The director of the program wants me to be sure to mention that this is a rigorous program for serious students who wish to be challenged intellectually. Done.

INDIANA UNIVERSITY SOUTHEAST ✪
School for Continuing Studies, 4201 Grant Line Rd.
New Albany, IN 47150 USA
Stanley H. Wheeler, Director of Admissions
General studies
1941
B, Accredited
Non-resident
Non-profit, state
(812) 945–2731 ext. 3212
$$
Bachelor's in general studies may be earned through a combination of weekend, evening, television, and correspondence study. Intensive summer courses are also available. Credit for independent study, self-acquired competencies, military training, and by examination. All coursework may be completed through the university's Correspondence Division.

INNER CITY INSTITUTE FOR PERFORMING AND VISUAL ART
1308 S. New Hampshire Ave.
Los Angeles, CA 90006 USA
C. Bernard Jackson, Director
1966
Unaccredited, state authorized
(213) 387-1161
$1,600/year
Authorized to grant degrees by the state of California. Did not respond to three requests for information on their programs.

INSTITUTE FOR INFORMATION MANAGEMENT
510 Oakmead Pkwy.
Sunnyvale, CA 94026 USA
1983
Unaccredited, state authorized
Proprietary
(408) 749-0133
Authorized to grant degrees by the state of California. Did not respond to three requests for information on their programs.

INSTITUTE FOR THE ADVANCED STUDY OF HUMAN SEXUALITY✪
1523 Franklin St.
San Francisco, CA 94109 USA
Robert T. McIlvenna, M.Div., Ph.D., President
Human sexuality
1976
M, D, Unaccredited, state approved
Short residency
Proprietary
(415) 928–1133
$$$
Master of Human Sexuality, Doctor of Philosophy, Doctor of Education, and Doctor of Human Sexuality.

Minimum of nine weeks of residency for the Master's, and 15 weeks for the Doctorates, although additional residency is encouraged. The Master's requires three trimesters of enrollment, and the Doctorate programs require 5 trimesters each, with a minimum of three weeks' residency each trimester. Founders include prominent sexologists, such as Kinsey's coauthor, Wardell Pomeroy. They believe there is a "woeful lack of professionals who are academically prepared in the study of human sexuality." The institute's intention is to rectify this lack by training professionals as sexologists. Many lectures available on videocassette. A comprehensive exam and a basic research project are required. Each Doctorate has a different emphasis: one in scientific inquiry, one in academic skills, and one in therapy and counseling. The Institute is approved by the state of California.

INSTITUTO POLITECNICO NACIONAL
Avenida Instituto Politecnico Nacional
Mexico D.F., 14 Mexico
Carlos Leon Jinojosa, Secretary
Economics, international trade
1936
B, Equivalent of accreditation
Non-resident
Non-profit, state
52-5-754-4706
$
Mexico's sistema abierto de ensenanza (open university system) offers the Bachelor's degree in economics and international trade. Study at a distance is accomplished through the use of printed materials, slides, movies, records, videocassettes, as well as group seminars held at various locations. All work in Spanish. Awarding of the degree is based primarily on passing the necessary examinations.

INTER-AMERICAN UNIVERSITY
405 Ponce De Leon
Hato Rey, Puerto Rico 00919 U.S.A.
Judith Mendez, Director of Admissions
Many fields
1960
B, Accredited
Residency
Non-profit, independent
(809) 758-8000
$
Bachelor's degrees in many fields can be earned through evening and weekend study, summer school, and through a University Without Walls program (initiated for law enforcement officers, but others are accepted) requiring one visit a week to the campus. There are nine campuses in Puerto Rico.

INTERNATIONAL ACADEMY OF MANAGEMENT AND ECONOMICS
1212 Roxas Blvd.,
Ermita, Manila, Philippines
Emmanuel T. Santos, Ph.D.
Business administration and international management
M, D, Provisionally licensed
Non-resident
57-39-81
The Master of Business Administration, Master of International Management, and Doctor of Business Administration offered residentially and by correspondence. The academy (formerly called International University) had considerable difficulties with authorities, more for political than academic reasons, during the Marcos regime. After Marcos' departure, the academy was issued a special permit by the Ministry of Education, Culture and Sports, "to offer and conduct on an experimental basis, the graduate course in business administration leading to the degree of Master of Arts in Business Administration and the Ph.D. in Management." Accreditation was claimed from an unrecognized and now defunct accrediting agency.

INTERNATIONAL COLLEGE (Santa Monica)
see: Sierra University

INTERNATIONAL INSTITUTE FOR ADVANCED STUDIES
100 Kamehameha Ave., Suite 5
Hilo, HI 96720
Dr. John B. Bear, President
Professional studies, business, management, health services management and education
1972
B, M, Unaccredited, State registered
Non-profit, independent
(808) 935-3913
$$
The International Institute was begun by a group of university faculty in St. Louis, Missouri in 1972. My colleagues and I were invited to take over its operation in 1987. Many of the programs of the Institute, includ-

ing all Doctorates, are now offered instead through Greenwich University (see page 112). Programs in the above-named fields are non-residential, but quite structured, with detailed curricula, syllabuses. and text-books. These programs will be offered for the first time during the second half of 1990. The International Institute moved from Clayton, Missouri to Hilo, Hawaii's second-largest city, in 1990. Original name: Occidental University.

INTERNATIONAL JAPAN UNIVERSITY
Unaccredited, state authorized
Chapman College R.E.C., 333 N. Glassell St.
Orange, CA 92666 USA
1982
(714) 997–6998
Authorized by the state of California to grant degrees. Did not respond to three requests for information about their programs.

INTERNATIONAL MANAGEMENT CENTRE, BUCKINGHAM
see: Northland Open University

INTERNATIONAL SCHOOL OF BUSINESS AND LEGAL STUDIES
14 Broadway
B, M, D, Unaccredited
London, SW1H 0BH England
Non-resident
A. A. Kennedy, Principal
Any field
(01) 222–5483
$
They award degrees entirely based on the credentials of the applicant. They have solicited "commission agents" in other countries, and have offered to award the degrees based on the agents' recommendation. They require that the agents have Doctorates, which they then make available for £450, and £175 more for wig and gown. They have no degree-granting authority other than that which they give themselves, but in England this sort of thing is not illegal.

INTERNATIONAL SCHOOL OF INFORMATION MANAGEMENT
18662 MacArthur Blvd., Suite 200
M, Unaccredited, state authorization in process
Irvine, CA 92715 USA
Information resources management
Proprietary
(714) 955–9224
$$$
Established in 1988 to offer the M.S. in information resources management through non-resident instruction. At presstime, I.S.I.M. was in the process of applying to the state of California for authorization to grant their degree. Instruction is by short courses used to fill "knowledge gaps" in students. Credit is given for career experience.

INTERNATIONAL UNIVERSITY (Europe)
The Avenue
B, M, Accredited
Bushey, Watford WD2 2LN England
Residency
Gordon Bennett, Director
Non-profit, independent
Business, engineering, human behavior, international relations
(0923) 49067
$$
Bachelor's and Master's degrees are offered in residence on the campus near London, in assocation with the accredited United States International University in San Diego.

INTERNATIONAL UNIVERSITY (Missouri)
1301 S. Noland Rd.,
B, M, D, Unaccredited, religious exemption, Non-resident
Independence, MO 64055 USA
Dr. John W. Johnston, Chancellor
Non-profit, independent
Many fields
(816) 461–3633
1973
$$
Degrees at all levels offered through correspondence study. Claims accreditation, but not from any recog-

nized agency. The catalogue indicates that there are campuses all over the world: Japan, Mexico, India, Australia, etc. No faculty are named in the literature, nor is the source of the degrees of the staff members given. There is, or has been, an affiliation with the Sussex College of Technology, which has been identified as a degree mill by every major British newspaper and educational authority. This affiliation is vigorously defended by International University's vice president and dean of faculties, Professor Dr. Marcel Dingli-Attard de'baroni Inguanez, Ph.D. as being "legal" and "valid" since the Sussex degrees "are definitely accepted in many countries." (I am not aware of any.) International University absorbed Mayer University in the late 1970s. See also: Marquis Guiseppe Scicluna International University Foundation.

INTERNATIONAL UNIVERSITY (New York)

485 5th Ave., Suite 1042	D, Unaccredited
New York, NY 10017 USA	Short residency
Benjamin Weisman, Ph.D., Chancellor	
Psychoanalysis, psychotherapy	(212) 687–0010
1979	$$$

The university is incorporated on the island of St. Kitts, West Indies, and derives its degree-granting powers from its own corporate charter (that is, they give themselves the right to award degrees). Twenty four credits must be earned in residence, usually during the summer on St. Kitts or another Caribbean location. The faculty include therapists and physicians, mostly with impressive traditional credentials. Five requests for a catalogue and information were not responded to; I finally received one in 1988 from a reader (who also had trouble getting it). This establishment presents mixed signals. They apparently offer a useful and legitimate program with a good faculty, but they present themselves in a curious manner. They appear to operate from New York, but they have no permission to do so, hence the St. Kitts connection, but they seem to have no offices or facility there. The New York telephone appears to be an answering service.

INTERNATIONAL UNIVERSITY (Philippines)

see: International Academy of Management and Economics

IONA COLLEGE

715 North Ave.	B, Accredited
New Rochelle, NY 10801-1890 USA	Residency
Donald Gray, Registrar	Non-profit, independent
Various fields	(914) 633–2000
1940	$$$

Bachelor of Arts and Bachelor of Science can be earned entirely through evening studies, weekend, and summer programs.

IOWA STATE UNIVERSITY

	B, M, Accredited
Ames, IA 50011 USA	Short residency
Karsten Smedal, Director of Admissions	Non-profit, state
Many fields	(515) 294–5836
1858	$$

The university offers an external degree called the Bachelor of Liberal Studies. It is primarily for residents of Iowa, who are able to attend one of the off-campus centers around the state, or occasional courses on campus in Ames. In addition, evening and weekend courses are offered leading to degrees in agriculture, business, design, education, engineering, family and consumer sciences, sciences and humanities, and veterinary medicine.

IRVINE COLLEGE OF BUSINESS

16591 Noyes Ave.	Unaccredited, state authorized
Irvine, CA 92714 USA	
Presumably business	(714) 556–8890
1985	

Authorized by the state of California to grant degrees. Despite three requests, no information was sent on their programs.

JOHN F. KENNEDY UNIVERSITY ✪

12 Altarinda Rd.
Orinda, CA 94563 USA
Ellena Bloedorn, Registrar
Career development
1964

M, Accredited
Residency
Non-profit, independent
(415) 254–0200
$$$

With the exception of the M.A. in career development, all of their splendidly innovative programs have been discontinued. What a shame. The university sees a major role for itself as assisting adults in mid-career changes (average student age is 36).

JOHN RENNIE UNIVERSITY

4 Ross
Irvine, CA 92664 USA
1984

Unaccredited, state authorized
(714) 834–9070

Authorized by the state of California to grant degrees. Did not respond to three requests for information about their programs.

JOHNS HOPKINS UNIVERSITY

School of Continuing Studies, 103 Shaffer Hall
Baltimore, MD 21218 USA
Stanley C. Gabor, Dean, School of Continuing Studies
Business, education, arts and sciences
1876

B, M, D, Accredited
Residency
Non-profit, independent
(301) 338–8490
$$

Bachelor of Science in accounting, business, literature, psychology, mathematics, and other areas; Master of Administrative Science; Master of Education, Master of Science, Master of Liberal Arts, and Doctor of Education all offered through evening study and weekend study. Credit for independent study and examinations. The School of Continuing Studies operates off-campus centers in Baltimore, Columbia, and Montgomery County, Maryland.

JOHNSON STATE COLLEGE

Johnson, VT 05656 USA
Randall Draper, Acting Director of Admissions
Many fields
1828

B, Accredited
Residency
Non-profit, state
(802) 635–2356 ext. 311
$$

Self-designed Bachelor's degree. Experiential learning credit is accepted as part of 60 credits needed for entry or 122 needed for graduation. Thirty credits needed while in the program. The program is set up to serve Vermonters with a mentor system of advisement. Credits may be earned on weekends or through independent or correspondence study.

KANSAS STATE UNIVERSITY ✪

Non-Traditional Study Program, Umberger Hall
Manhattan, KS 66506 USA
Cynthia Trent, NTS Coordinator
Interdisciplinary social science
1963

B, Accredited
Non-resident
Non-profit, state
(913) 532–5686
$$

The B.S. in interdisciplinary social science is offered through the Non-Traditional Study (NTS) program. Although no presence on campus is required, the program is limited to Kansas residents. At least 30 of the 120 units must come from Kansas State. Assessment of prior learning is available on enrollment. Credits may also be earned from military training, equivalency exams, "departmental quiz-out," outreach courses, television and TELENET courses, as well as correspondence study with other schools. In Kansas, the toll-free number is (800) 432–8222.

KANSAS WESLEYAN

100 E. Claflin
Salina, KS 67401 USA
Daniel McKinney, Registrar

B, Accredited
Residency
Non-profit, church

Many fields (913) 827–5541
1886 $$$
B.A. and B.S. available in accounting and finance, arts and communication, business administration and economics, computer science, pre-engineering, pre-law, pre-ministerial, teaching, social services, and many areas in the health sciences. Kansas Wesleyan is one of a handful of schools that do not call themselves "university" or "college" or "institute" or indeed anything.

KEAN COLLEGE
Morris Ave.
Union, NJ 07083 US
Brian Lewis, Director of Admissions
Many fields
1855
B, Accredited
Residency
Non-profit, state
(201) 527–2000
$$
Some of the degree requirements can be earned through an assessment of prior learning experiences based on a portfolio prepared by the student.

KELLER GRADUATE SCHOOL OF MANAGEMENT
10 S. Riverside Plaza
Chicago, IL 60606 USA
Tio Smith, Assistant Director of Admissions
Business administration
1973
M, Accredited
Residency
Proprietary
(312) 454–0880
$115/credit
Keller offers an accelerated, practitioner-oriented M.B.A. entirely through evening or weekend study at four Chicago locations and in Milwaukee, Wisconsin. (They purchased the DeVry Computer Schools in 1987.)

KENNEDY WESTERN UNIVERSITY ✪
23810 Roadside Dr.
Agoura Hills, CA 91301 USA
Paul Saltman, President
Business administration and management, criminal justice, education, engineering, psychology
1984
B, M, D, Law, Unaccredited, State authorized, Non-resident
Proprietary
(818) 889–8443 or (800) 635-2900
$$$
Courses based on achieving specific behavioral objectives. Credit for prior college work, work and life experience, and challenge exams. Students work with an academic support team: resident faculty advisor, adjunct faculty mentor in the student's vicinity, and work site evaluator (a senior employee at the student's place of work). Admission requires evaluation of a portfolio of work, life and educational experience, and five years of degree-related work experience. Study involves challenge exams, independent study and writing and defending a thesis or dissertation. Work may be done in any of 17 languages. An added fee of $350 for students outside the U.S. Law students may qualify to take the California bar exam. Eight-week (or longer) "Professional Executive Certificate" programs by correspondence in many fields. Like so many other schools, Kennedy-Western misrepresents the findings of the Sosdian-Sharp study on the acceptance of non-traditional degrees (see page 17).

KENSINGTON UNIVERSITY ✪
124 S. Isabel St.
Glendale, CA 91206 USA
Alfred A. Calabro, J.D., President
Business, engineering, social sciences, education, law
1976
B, M, D, Law, Unaccredited, state authorized, Non-resident
Proprietary
(818) 240–9166 or (800) 423-2495
$$
The programs are designed for the mature adult student who is capable of self-directed study. All coursework is accomplished by home study, with guidance and instruction provided by faculty advisors. Most coursework consists of guided self-paced reading of assigned texts, and completion of a final project. Non-required seminars are offered periodically in Italy, Thailand, Japan, and England (where residential programs are available at the Bachelor's and Master's level through the facilities of City Commercial College in London). The Kensington School of Law is registered with the Committee of Bar Examiners, and

its students qualify to take the California bar exam, where they have had considerable success. Toll-free number in California (800) 421–9115. Like so many other schools, Kensington misrepresents the findings of the Sosdian-Sharp study on the acceptance of non-traditional degrees (see page 17).

KENT UNIVERSITY
see: LaSalle University (Louisiana)

KINGS COLLEGE
Gateway Adult Program
Wilkes-Barre, PA 18711 USA
Sally McGuire, Part-time Studies
Wide range of fields.
1946
B, Accredited
Residency
Non-profit, independent
(717) 826–5900, ext. 8655
$$$
Up to half the required credits can come from assessment of prior learning experiences. A credit-granting course is offered to help prepare a portfolio of experiences. The cost of assessment is $30 plus tuition for the special course. Assessment may be done before entering the program.

KOH-E-NOR UNIVERSITY
see: University of Santa Monica

LAFAYETTE UNIVERSITY
10730 E. Bethany Drive, Suite 102
Aurora, CO 80014
Msgr. John Thompson, Vice President
B, M, D, Unaccredited, state authorized
Non-profit, church
(303) 368-5541
Degrees in divinity studies, religious education, pastoral wellness, psychotherapy, theology, counseling, and pastoral psychotherapy. The 1989 catalogue states that Lafayette is "the only accredited institution in the U.S." offering degree courses in nutrimedical arts and sciences. No nutrimedicine courses are offered, and Lafayette's accreditation comes from the Department of Education and Academic Affairs which "has the authority within our own church to charter and accredit..." The university is affiliated with the Mercian Rite (Orthodox) Catholic Church. No names appear in the catalogues. Father Thompson writes, "Please know that Lafayette University is state accredited." However the Colorado Commission on Higher Education does not accredit schools, and has written that Lafayette "marginally qualifies" for state authorization.

LA JOLLA UNIVERSITY
1100 Poydras St., Suite 2200
New Orleans, LA 70163 USA
Dr. Waldo Bernasconi, President
Business administration, health services administration, behavioral studies
1977
B, M, D, Unaccredited, state licensed, Short residency
Proprietary
(504) 624-8932
$$
Well, if the University of Beverly Hills can move to Iowa, why can't La Jolla University move to Louisiana. Learners participate in defining their educational needs, goals, and aspirations. Then they receive instruction on a tutorial basis, permitting them to progress at their own rate. Most work is done at a distance by guided independent study, but all students must come to the offices for oral discussions.

LA SALLE UNIVERSITY (Louisiana) ✪
639 West Causeway Approach
Mandeville, LA
Thomas McPherson, President
Many fields
1986
B., M, D., Law, Unaccredited
Non-resident
Non-profit, church
(504) 624-8932
$$
All programs offered through the education ministry of the World Christian Church, and are denominational, theocentric, and non-secular. Acceptance as a student is acceptance into the church's education ministry. Degrees entirely by correspondence study. Law program no longer qualifies students to take California bar exam. Inquirers are sent a tape explaining the programs and policies, which totally distorts the find-

ings of a survey on the acceptability of non-traditional degrees (see page 17). Accreditation claimed from an unrecognized agency. LaSalle was opened by the same people who used to run Southland University in California, shortly after Southland closed. An attempted visit to the university in Louisiana revealed what appears to be one room in a rural church. A not-too-cooperative person said the actual work goes on in another state. No connection with either La Salle Extension University (out of business) or with the traditional La Salle University in Philadelphia. Kent University is a part of this LaSalle University.

LAKE ERIE COLLEGE
391 W. Washington St. — B, Accredited
Painesville, OH 44077 USA — Residency
Jean Larson, Registrar — Non-profit, independent
Many fields — (216) 352–3361
1856 — $$$

Bachelor of Arts Bachelor of Science, Bachelor of Fine Arts may be earned through weekend and evening study. Special programs: business administration, equestrian studies. Credit for non-academic prior learning and by examination. Plan A is an alternate approach to the B.A., B.S., or Bachelor of Fine Arts for those who cannot fulfill educational objectives from the regular programs, either because of unusual subject matter, method or rate of study, or intensity of immersion. It is, in effect, a learning contract approach to the degree. There is a "3 + 3" combined program in which one earns a Bachelor's degree from Lake Erie and a Doctor of Nursing degree from the Frances Payne Bolton School of Nursing.

LAMAR UNIVERSITY — B, M, D, Accredited
4400 Pt. Arthur Rd. — Residency
Beaumont, TX 77710 USA — Non-profit, state
Elmer G. Rode, Dean of Records and Registrar — (409) 880–8969
1923 — $

Bachelor of Arts, and Bachelor of Science can be earned entirely through evening and summer programs. Some Saturday classes in graduate level education.

LANDSDOWNE COLLEGE
43 Harrington Gardens — B, Law, Accredited
London, SW7 4JU England — Residency
Gordon Bennett, Ph.D., President and Dean
Business-related fields, fine arts, interior design — (01) 373-7282

Lansdowne follows the curriculum of the accredited New Hampshire College, of Manchester, New Hampshire, and on completion of the work in London, the B.S. is awarded by New Hampshire. Comparable program with Drury College in Missouri. Lansdowne also prepares students for the Bachelor of Laws degree examinations of London University. The college's academic council is composed of five present or former administrators of excellent American non-traditional degree schools or programs. B.A. and Bachelor of Fine Arts programs are also available.

LAURENCE UNIVERSITY (California)
see: University of Santa Barbara

LEBANON VALLEY COLLEGE — B, Accredited
Annville, PA 17003 USA — Residency
Dr. Robert A. Clay, Registrar — Non-profit, church
Many fields — (717) 867–6100
1866 — $$

Bachelor of Arts and Bachelor of Science available through weekend, evening, or summer programs. Evening classes meet once a week during the academic year and twice during the summer. Weekend classes meet Friday nights or Saturdays. There is a special two-week "intensive term" in mid May in which students can complete one course. Degrees are offered in a wide variety of fields, including accounting, administration for health care professionals, computer information systems, management, and social service. Credit for experiential learning, and by examination.

LESLEY COLLEGE
29 Everett St.
Cambridge, MA 02238 USA
Elizabeth V. Little, Registrar
Many fields
1909

B, M, Accredited
Short residency
Non-profit, independent
(617) 868–9600
$$$$

Bachelor of Science in cooperation with the National Audubon Society, involving a combination of coursework and expeditions. Audubon's Expedition Institute has a two-year program, or a field component: camping, hiking, canoeing, skiing, backpacking, and cycling all over America. Students gain practical knowledge of astronomy, anthropology, ecology, etc. The balance of the time is spent in classes at Lesley. The M.S. involves a year or a year and a half on Audubon expeditions and three or four courses at Lesley. Students may switch between Lesley and Audubon. Also a short residency Bachelor's and Master's program with a variety of concentrations. Limited residency B.S. and B.A. in behavioral science programs in human services and education. Weekend and independent study are used. The M.A. and Master of Education are offered as an Independent Study Degree Program, allowing individualized curricula developed by graduate students and faculty advisory teams.

LIBERTY UNIVERSITY ✪
P.O. Box 11803
Lynchburg, VA 24506 USA
Dr. Tom Diggs, Dean, School of LifeLong Learning
Religious and business fields
1971

B, M, Accredited
Short residency
Non-profit, church
(804) 522–4700 or (800) 446-5000
$$

Liberty's School of Lifelong Learning offers accredited degrees, almost entirely through home study. Six to 12 hours (two to four courses) are normally required in residence, but "students with unique cases, such as military personnel and senior citizens will have their requirements for residency evaluated" and may need to spend as little as a week, perhaps less, on campus. Bachelor's degrees are offered in church ministries, business administration, marketing, and management. The Master's is available in counseling and biblical studies. Most courses are offered by videocassette. Faculty are regularly available by telephone. While residential students at Liberty must have taken Jesus Christ as their personal saviour, external students are not required to have done so. Liberty's chancellor is Dr. Jerry Falwell.

LINCOLN UNIVERSITY
Jefferson City, MO 65101 USA
Ronald Nelson, Coordinator, Admissions
Business, education, various fields
1866

M, Accredited
Residency
Non-profit, state
(314) 681–5000
$$

Master of Education, Master of Arts, and Master of Business Administration may be earned through evening or summer programs. Credit for independent study, non-academic prior learning, and by examination.

LINDENWOOD COLLEGE
St. Charles, MO 63301 USA
Arlene Taich, Dean of Evening College
Valuation science, other fields
1827

B, M, Accredited
Residency
Non-profit, independent
(341) 946–6912
$$$

B.A., B.S., M.A., and M.S. through the College for Individualized Education, in administration, psychology, health administration, gerontology, valuation sciences, communications, human and organizational development may be earned through evening and summer programs. The International Valuation Sciences degree program is primarily an off-campus degree program for experienced appraisers. There is a two-week on-campus session each year for at least two years. Credit for independent study, non-academic prior learning, and by examination.

LINFIELD COLLEGE
McMinnville, OR 97128 USA
Joan A. Claus, Division of Continuing Education
Management, systems analysis, liberal studies

B, Accredited
Residency
Non-profit, church
(503) 472–4121, ext. 247

See page 70 for explanation of abbreviations and symbols

1958 $$

Bachelor of Individualized Studies through evening, weekend, and summer programs. Credit for prior learning, independent study, and by examination. Evening and weekend courses in many fields of study, including business, gerontology, music, occupational therapy, and recreational therapy.

LOYOLA COLLEGE

4501 N. Charles | B, M, Accredited
Baltimore, MD 21210 USA | Residency
William J Bossemeyer III, Director of Admissions | Non-profit, church
31 majors | (301) 323–1010
1852 | $$$

Bachelor of Arts and Bachelor of Science through evening study. Master of Arts in psychology, afternoons, evenings, and weekends. Bachelor of Education, evenings and weekends. Master of Business Administration, evenings. Master's in education, afternoons, evenings, and weekends.

LOYOLA UNIVERSITY (Illinois)

820 N. Michigan Ave. | B, M, Accredited
Chicago, IL 60611 USA | Residency
John W. Christian, Director of Admissions | Non-profit, church
Mathematics, psychology, education, business, educational administration | (312) 670–3000
$$$
1870

Bachelor of Science in mathematics, psychology, education, business administration; Master of Arts in educational administration, all through evening study.

LOYOLA UNIVERSITY (Louisiana)

6363 St. Charles Ave. | B, Accredited
New Orleans, LA 70118 USA | Residency
Dr. Marjorie Dachowski, Director of Admissions | Non-profit, church
Many fields | (504) 865–2011
1912 | $$$

They have what sounds like an interesting and innovative Bachelor of Liberal Studies degree, and an interesting and innovative Master's program as well, but they don't want to be in this book, so you'll have to find out from Dr. Marjorie Dachowski, Director of Admissions. Tell her John Bear sent you.

MADONNA COLLEGE

36600 Schoolcraft Rd. | B, M, Accredited
Livonia, MI 48150 USA | Residency
Louis Brohl, Director of Admission | Non-profit, church
Many fields | (313) 591–5000
1947 | $$

Bachelor of Arts and Bachelor of Science degrees are offered in many fields. Evening courses are available. Life experience credits are awarded in many areas, such as allied health management, business, computer science, criminal justice, gerontology, home economics and nursing. Prior learning needs to be articulated, documented, evaluated by means of portfolio, challenge exam, or national tests (CLEP). Cooperative education for credit can be arranged. Thirty semester hours in residency are required for graduation.

MADURAI UNIVERSITY

Palkalai Nagar | B, M, Equivalent of accreditation, Non-resident
Madurai, 625 021 India
Dr. T. B. Siddalingaiah, Director | Non-profit, state
Commerce, various fields | $

Bachelor of Arts, Bachelor of Commerce, Master of Arts and Master of Commerce through a combination of correspondence study and examinations. Indian universities generally award their degrees entirely by examination. Madurai offers a wide range of correspondence courses designed to prepare students for its own examination, which must be taken in India. It is necessary to take the courses in order to be allowed to take the examinations. They are primarily designed for Indian nationals and others resident in India, and may be taken overseas by special permission.

MAINE MARITIME ACADEMY
Castine, ME 04420 USA
Dr. Verge Forbes, Academic Dean
Maritime management
1941
M, Accredited
Short residency
Non-profit, state
(207) 326-4311
$$
Master of Science in maritime management through a modular graduate degree program that can be completed "without career interruption." Courses are scheduled in compact modules that allow participants to remain fully employed while studying. A total of six four-week modules is required for the Master's. The tuition fee includes books and materials. This is a business degree, with emphasis on marine aspects.

MANCHESTER COLLEGE
North Manchester, IN 46962 USA
Bette Yap, Director of Admissions
Education
1889
M, Accredited
Residency
Non-profit, church
(219) 982-2141
$$$
The Master of Arts in education can be earned entirely through evening study.

MANHATTAN COLLEGE
School of General Studies
Bronx, NY 10471 USA
John J. Brennan, Director of Admissions
General studies
1853
B, Accredited
Residency
Non-profit, independent
(212) 920-0100
$$$
Bachelor of Science in general studies may be earned through evening and summer programs. Cooperative nursing program with E. McConnell Clarke School of Nursing.

MARIETTA COLLEGE
5th and Putnam
Marietta, OH 45750 USA
Dan Meyer, Director of Admissions
Liberal Learning
1834
B, M, Accredited
Residency
Non-profit, independent
(614) 324-4600
$$$$
Bachelor of Arts and Master of Arts in liberal learning through evening and weekend study. Credit for life experience. Also, Marietta has a non-traditional home study program where course credit is applicable to its degree program. See also: East Central College Consortium.

MARION COLLEGE
211 E. 45th St.
Marion, IN 46953
Cheryl Enyart, LEAP Program
1920
M, Accredited
Residential
Non-profit, independent
(317) 674-3317 or (800) 255-3594
$$
An M.B.A. and an M.S. in Management are offered through intensive classes that meet once a week for 16 (MSM) or 22 (MBA) months. The program is offered through LEAP, Leadership Education for Adult Professionals.

MARQUETTE UNIVERSITY
Milwaukee, WI 53233 USA
Leo B. Flynn, Director of Admissions
Engineering and many other fields
1964
B, Accredited
Residency
Non-profit, church
(414) 224-7499
$$$
The Part-Time Studies Division offers day and evening courses leading to the Bachelor's degree in engineering, criminology and law, political science, advertising, journalism, public relations, and interpersonal com-

munications.

MARS HILL COLLEGE
Center for Continuing Education — B, Accredited
Mars Hill, NC 28754 USA — Residency
Dr. L. Smith Goodrum, Dean of Admissions — Non-profit, church
Many fields — (704) 689–1166
1856 — $$$
Bachelor of Science, Bachelor of Arts, Bachelor of Social Work available through summer and evening classes. Special programs include allied health, social work, and elementary education. Credit for non-academic prior learning, independent study, and by examination must be completed as part of a regular program at Mars Hill or one of the six off-campus centers in Asheville, Brevard, Burnsville, Hendersonville, Marion, Murphy, or Waynesville.

MARSHALL UNIVERSITY
see: West Virginia Board of Regents B.A. Program

MARTIN CENTER COLLEGE
3553 N. College Ave. — B, Accredited
Indianapolis, IN 46205 USA — Residency
Jane Schilling, CSJ, Academic Dean — Non-profit, independent
Many fields — (317) 927–5150
1977 — $$
Martin Center was established in 1977 by the Rev. Boniface Hardin as an extension of his programs to develop and conduct training in the area of race relations. They offer the Bachelor's degree in many fields, including accounting, allied health education, health care management, human services, Afro-American studies, genetic counseling, substance abuse, social services, and music. Many courses through evening and weekend study. Assessment of prior learning for life learning credit.

MARY BALDWIN COLLEGE ✪
Adult Degree Program — B, Accredited
Staunton, VA 24401 USA — Short residency
Dr. James Harrington, Director, Adult Degree Program — Non-profit, church
Many fields — (703) 885–0811
1842 — $$$$
Bachelor of Arts program in which virtually all of the work can be done independently, or at a distance. The program is entirely non-residential. Students need to come to the campus only once for a day of orientation. Advanced standing is given for work done at other schools, equivalency examinations, and the assessment of prior learning. The degree program has regional offices in Richmond, Keysville, and Roanoke, Virginia, in addition to the main office in Staunton. The degree requires a minimum of nine months to complete.

MARY WASHINGTON COLLEGE — B, Accredited
1301 College Ave. — Residency
Fredericksburg, VA 22401 USA — Non-profit, state
Dr. H. C. Warlick, Vice President, Admissions — (703) 899–4100
Liberal studies — $$$$
Bachelor of Liberal Studies is available through weekend, evening, and summer programs. Thirty hours of residential credit is required. Credit for independent study, non-academic prior learning by portfolio assessment, and by examination.

MARYCREST COLLEGE
Weekend College, 1607 W. 12th St., — B, Accredited
Davenport, IA 52804 USA — Residency
Mrs. Elizabeth Shore, Registrar — Non-profit, church
Many fields — (319) 326–9226

1939 $$$

Degrees in accounting, business administration, professional communication, computer science, pre-law, social work and special studies. Credit for experiential learning and by examination.

MARYLHURST COLLEGE FOR LIFELONG LEARNING
Marylhurst, OR 97036 USA
Keith W. Protonentis, Registrar
Many fields
1893
B, M, Accredited
Residency
Non-profit, independent
(503) 636-8141
$$$

Bachelor of Arts in communication, humanities, human studies, social science, science/math, arts, crafts, and interdisciplinary studies; Bachelor of Fine Arts; Bachelor of Science in management; Bachelor of Music; Master of Science in management; and M.A. in art therapy. Baccalaureate graduation requirements include a minimum of 40 quarter hours of credit through Marylhurst (22% of the degree). Credit is earned by taking Marylhurst courses, courses at other schools, or by correspondence, and through independent studies. Fifty percent of the graduates utilize the credit for Prior Learning Experience Program to complete their degrees. The average student is 38 years old and enters with about two years of college.

MARYMOUNT COLLEGE
Tarrytown, NY 10591 USA
Mary Ellen Greenawalt, Director of Admissions
Psychology, English, history, economics and business
1907
B, Accredited
Residency
Non-profit, independent
(914) 631-3451
$$$

Bachelor of Arts, earned by spending every second or third weekend on campus to complete as many as 12 credits per term. Weekend courses run from Friday evening through Sunday afternoon. Credit for prior experiential learning.

MARYVILLE COLLEGE
13550 Conway Rd.
St. Louis, MO 63141 USA
Dr. Robert L. Adams, Registrar
Many fields
1872
B, Accredited
Residency
Non-profit, independent
(314) 576-9300
$$$

Bachelor's degree courses in management, information systems, psychology, sociology, nursing, and communications are offered through evening and weekend courses. Credit for experiential learning.

MARYWOOD COLLEGE✪
2300 Adams Ave.
Scranton, PA 18509 USA
Patrick J. Manley, Director of Admissions
Business administration, accounting
1915
B, Accredited
Short residency
Non-profit, church
(717) 348-6235
$$

The Bachelor of Science in business administration or accounting is earned through a combination of off-campus correspondence study and two two-week seminars held on the campus: one midway through the program, and one at the end. Sixty of the required 126 semester credits must be earned after enrolling at Marywood. Credit is available by independent study projects, correspondence courses, equivalency exams, and credit for life experience. The cost per credit includes textbooks. The Off-Campus Degree Program offers a free "Dial-a-Question" service. Deferred payment plans are available.

MASSEY UNIVERSITY
Centre for University Extra-Mural Studies
Palmerston North, New Zealand
Dr. T. K. Prebble, Director, Centre for University Extramural Studies
1960
B, M, Accredited
Residency
Non-profit, state
Many fields
69099
$

Massey offers an external degree program, in which the majority of work can be completed by correspondence study, utilizing books, audio- and videocassettes, regional courses, and on-campus short courses.

Degrees are offered in humanities, social sciences, science, business studies, agricultural science education and technology.

MEMPHIS STATE UNIVERSITY
University College — B, Accredited
Memphis, TN 38152 USA — Residency
Dr. John Y. Eubank, Dean of Admissions — Non-profit, state
Many fields — (901) 454-2000
1912 — $$

University College, as a regional center for the Open Learning Fire Service Program, offers the B.P.S. in fire administration and fire prevention technology to firefighters in Tennessee, Mississippi, Alabama, Kentucky, Arkansas, Georgia, and South Carolina. University College administers directed study television-assisted courses within a radius of 60 miles of Memphis. Through the Division of Engineering Technology, students may earn a Bachelor's degree in vocational/technical education. They may include up to 30 semester hours of experiential learning credit toward this degree. The College of Education offers a Bachelor's degree in educational services—a degree program designed for persons who wish to teach, but not in schools. A certain amount of experiential learning credit is applicable toward this degree. Contract degrees through University College include credit for non-traditional learning and internship experiences.

MERCY COLLEGE
555 Broadway — B, M, Accredited
Dobbs Ferry, NY 10522 USA — Short residency
Dr. Ralph W. Conant — Non-profit, independent
Many fields — (914) 693-7600
1950 — $$$

Bachelor's degree through a wide variety of methods which are designed to accommodate the adult student. Evening classes held two nights a week for eight weeks; weekend classes are once a week, either Friday evening or daytime Saturday for 16 weeks. There is a Home Study Program for students who prefer to work independently with an orientation session, mid-term and final exam required on campus. Also summer and January intersession programs. Parallel scheduling is designed to accommodate students who work rotating shifts, such as police and nurses, with the same class taught both day and evening so that the student may attend either one. Credit is awarded for life achievement and by examination. In addition, the college offers a four-year bilingual program for Spanish speaking students, and an extensive support program for learning disabled college students.

METROPOLITAN STATE COLLEGE
1006 11th St. — B, Accredited
Denver, CO 80204 USA — Residency
Dr. Kenneth C. Curtis, Dean of Admissions — Non-profit, state
Many fields — (303) 556-8514
1963 — $$

Up to half the units required for the Bachelor's degree can come from assessment of prior learning experiences. The assessment is based on a student-prepared portfolio, and the cost is based on the number of units awarded.

METROPOLITAN STATE UNIVERSITY
121 Metro Sqare Bldg. — B, Accredited
St. Paul, MN 55101 USA — Short residency
Judy C. Knudson, Vice President, Marketing — Non-profit, state
Many fields — (612) 296-3875
1971 — $$

Metropolitan State University is a pioneer in non-traditional programs. Its Bachelor of Arts degree requires one planning course and offers learning options which include: prior learning assessment, traditional coursework, internships, independent studies, and coursework from other institutions. Metropolitan also offers a Bachelor of Arts degree in nursing. All credit is offered at the upper division level. The minimum time for completing a degree is nine months. Most students are residents of the Minneapolis-St. Paul area.

MIAMI INSTITUTE OF PSYCHOLOGY
1401 S.W. 1st St. — D, Accredited
Miami, FL 33135 USA — Residency
Dr. Jorge A. Herrera, Assistant Vice President — Non-profit, independent
Psychology — (305) 541-8970
1966 — $$$

The accreditation is for the main campus, the Caribbean Center for Advanced Studies, in Puerto Rico. Ph.D. and Psy.D. degrees are offered in general clinical psychology, clinical psychology and criminal justice, clinical gerontological psychology, and clinical neuropsychology. Some courses available through evening or weekend study.

MICHIGAN STATE UNIVERSITY — M, Accredited
East Lansing, MI 48824 USA — Residency
Dr. William H. Turner, Director of Admissions — Non-profit, state
Many fields — (517) 355-1855
1855 — $$$

My alma mater offers the Master of Business Administration through evening study at Troy. M.A. in advertising, journalism, and counseling in Birmingham. M.A. in teacher education in Saginaw, Flint, Grand Rapids, and Kalamazoo. Master of Science in nursing in Benton Harbor. Master of Social Work in Sault Ste. Marie and Traverse City. Also, Michigan State offers the M.A. in education through part-time and independent study centers in Japan, England, Thailand, and the Philippines.

MILLERSVILLE UNIVERSITY OF PENNSYLVANIA — B, Accredited
Millersville, PA 17551 USA — Residency
Blair E. Treasure, Dean of Admissions — Non-profit, state
Many fields — (717) 872-3024
1852 — $$

Bachelor of Arts, in English, business administration, economics, history, mathematics, computer science, political science, psychology, social work, and physics may be earned through evening classes or summer sessions. Special program for registered nurses leads to B.A. in nursing.

MILWAUKEE SCHOOL OF ENGINEERING
P.O. Box 644 — B, M, Accredited
Milwaukee, WI 53201 USA — Residency
Ronald T. Gandes, Director, Evening College — Non-profit, independent
Engineering, engineering technology, industrial management — (414) 277-7300
$$$
1903

Bachelor of Arts; Bachelor of Science in engineering technology and industrial management; Master of Science in engineering management, entirely through evening study. Extension programs are offered in factories, plants, and other off-campus locations.

MIND EXTENSION UNIVERSITY — B, M, Accredited
9697 E. Mineral Ave. — Non-resident
Englewood, CO 80112 — Independent
(800) 777-6463
Many fields available — $$$$

Courses are offered over the university's own cable television channel, nationwide. A dozen or more major and smaller universities offer courses on the channel, in a very wide range of subjects. Only one university, Colorado State, offers a complete degree program: an MBA, comprising 63 semester units at $300 per unit plus at least $1,000 for textbooks. Courses from other universities (U. of Minnesota, U. of New Mexico, :U. of South Carolina, etc.) may be applied to degree programs at those and many other schools. The programs are prepared by each individual university and, just like on-campus education, range from lively and engaging to dry and tedious. The channel is on the air 24 hours a day.

MITCHELL COLLEGE OF ADVANCED EDUCATION
Private Bag 2
Bathurst, N.S.W. 2795 Australia
Education
B, Equivalent of accreditation
Short residency
Non-profit
The degree can be earned through the Division of External Studies by a combination of external study and short residency, which can be as short as one week per year.

MOORHEAD STATE UNIVERSITY
External Studies Degree Program
Moorhead, MN 56560 USA
Dr. Lois Fisher, Director, Continuing Education
Many fields
1885
B, Accredited
Residency
Non-profit, state
(218) 236–2181
$$
Bachelor's degrees in many fields available to students within a 100- to 150-mile radius of the university. Assessment of prior learning experience is an important part of the program and is based on evaluation of student-prepared portfolios and interviews with faculty from appropriate departments. Testing, either through oral interviews, or in written form, is required in most areas. The assessment fees, which are quite low, are based on the number of units awarded. This program is not open to students outside of the region. Many classes are offered on weekends.

MORAVIAN COLLEGE
Division of Continuing Studies
Bethlehem, PA 18018 USA
Bernard J. Story
Many fields
1742
B, Accredited
Residency
Non-profit, church
(215) 861–1400
$$$$
Bachelor of Arts and Bachelor of Science in accounting, art, computer science, criminal justice, information systems, business, and the social sciences entirely through evening study. Credit is available for independent study projects and field studies, as well as equivalency examinations.

MORE UNIVERSITY
3237 Deerhill Rd.
Lafayette, CA 94549 USA
Carol Bussen, Registrar and professor of basic sensuality
1978
Unaccredited,
state authorized
(415) 930–6972
In a Playboy interview, founder Victor Baranco said, "We have 21 acres...we have the best sex information in the world...we have jealousy handled. We have the 72-hour orgasm handled. We have the how to have children and still be happy problem solved...and we have just applied to be a university." They did, and they are authorized to grant degrees by the state of California, but they have not responded to three requests for information on their programs.

MOUNT SAINT MARY COLLEGE
Powell Ave.
Newburgh, NY 12550 USA
J. Randall Ognibene, Director of Admissions
Business, social sciences, interdisciplinary studies
1954
B, Accredited
Residency
Non-profit, independent
(914) 561–0800
$$$
Bachelor's degree programs in business management and administration, psychology, sociology, social science, and interdisciplinary studies available through evening and weekend classes.

MOUNT UNION COLLEGE
1972 Clark Ave.
Alliance, OH 44601 USA
Harold L. Hall, Director of Admissions
Many fields
1954
B, Accredited
Residency
Non-profit, church
(216) 821–5320 ext. 242
$$$$

Bachelor's degree in many fields, in which 75% of the units can come from an assessment of prior learning experiences. The assessment, which is based on a portfolio prepared by the student, can be done before enrolling, at a fixed rate of around $250. See also: East Central College Consortium.

MUNDELEIN COLLEGE
6363 N. Sheridan Rd. — B, M, Accredited
Chicago, IL 60660 USA — Residency
Martha Morris, Director of Admissions — Non-profit, independent
Many fields — (312) 989–5406
1929 — $$$

Bachelor's degrees in many fields, in which up to 75% of the required units can come from an assessment of prior learning experiences in a program called CARE: Credit for Academically Relevant Experience. The assessment is based on a portfolio, examinations, and/or faculty interviews. The assessment fee is based on the number of units awarded, and costs about a third the regular cost of earned units. Courses are also offered through a Weekend College program.

MURRAY STATE UNIVERSITY
Center for Continuing Education — B, Accredited
Murray, KY 42071 USA — Short residency
Larry Moore, Director, External Degree Program — Non-profit, state
Independent studies — (502) 762–4150
1922 — $

Bachelor of Independent Studies through correspondence study, television, and contract learning courses, as well as experiential credits. Many weekend and evening classes are available. Twenty four of the 128 semester hours must be taken with Murray State. Departmental challenge exams are available in some fields. If the exam is passed, credit is awarded. All students must attend a two-day seminar, held on a Friday and Saturday in April, August, and December. Admission to the program is based on satisfactory completion of the seminar. All students must earn credit in basic skills, humanities, science, social sciences, electives, and a study project. Murray State charges $50 for portfolio assessment, plus $5 for each credit hour awarded.

MUSKINGUM COLLEGE
see: East Central College Consortium

NAROPA INSTITUTE
2130 Arapahoe Ave. — B, M, Accredited
Boulder, CO 80302 USA — Residency
Cynthia Cunningham, Director of Admissions — Non-profit, independent
Many fields — (303) 444–0202
1974 — $$$

Founded by Tibetan master, Trungpa Rimpoche. As the local newspaper put it when accreditation came in 1986, "It's official, brothers and sisters. The Naropa Institute, Boulder's bastion of alternative education, was informed yesterday that it has received formal accreditation." Programs are offered in Buddhist studies, horticulture, martial arts, psychology, dance therapy, and movement studies. But there was no response to three requests for information on their programs.

NATIONAL COLLEGE OF EDUCATION
2840 Sheridan Rd. — B, M, Accredited
Evanston, IL 60201 USA — Residency
Gail Straus, Director of Admissions — Non-profit, independent
Behavioral sciences, management, education, health education, other fields — (312) 256–5150
1886 — $$$

Bachelor of Arts in applied behavioral sciences, in which up to 75% of the required units can be earned from an assessment of prior learning and college transfer credit. Portfolio credit costs $15 per quarter hour. The college utilizes what they call the Field-Experience Model, in which the student follows an intense program of classes (one four-hour session per week) and individual study, while remaining fully employed. The Master of Science in management requires 59 four-hour meetings (once a week for 15 months). Master of Science in adult and continuing education requires 52 weeks of class (one night a week) for 13 months. National also has a Bachelor's completion program in management and education designed for registered, licensed, certified allied health professionals. This program lasts 13 months and requires 49 class meetings—one night a week. Programs are offered in various Illinois locations; St. Louis, Missouri; McLean, Virginia; Milwaukee, and Beloit, Wisconsin.

NATIONAL INSTITUTE FOR HIGHER EDUCATION
Plassey Technical Park
Limerick, Ireland
Many fields
B, M, D, Accredited
Residency
Non-profit

N.I.H.E., Limerick, is a university-level body, established under statute by the Irish government and undertakes programs of education and research to the Doctorate level in the three constituent colleges. The rapid expansion of the Irish economy and membership in the European Community has provided many new career opportunities and generated the need for expansion of the range of programs and facilities within the higher education sector. N.I.H.E., Limerick, was established to help meet these special needs.

NATIONAL OPEN UNIVERSITY
see: Open University of America

NATIONAL SCHOOLS
292 S. La Cienega Blvd., Suite 100
Beverly Hills, CA 90211 USA
Len Nelson, President
1984
M, State authorized
Proprietary
(213) 854–0380

Authorized to grant degrees by the state of California. Did not respond to three requests for information on their programs.

NATIONAL TECHNOLOGICAL UNIVERSITY✪
P.O. Box 700, 601 S. Howes St.
Fort Collins, CO 80522 USA
Dr. Lionel Baldwin, President
Technological
1984
M, Accredited
Variable residency
Non-profit, independent
(303) 484–6050
$$$$

N.T.U. has developed a wide range of courses in technological subjects. These are transmitted by satellite television to 33 university campuses from Alaska to Florida, as well as participating businesses, where students take the classes, often in "real time" (as they are being taught in Colorado), with telephone links to the Colorado classroom. While schools may integrate the courses into their own curricula, N.T.U. offers its own Master of Science degree, available in computer engineering, computer science, electrical engineering, engineering management, and manufacturing systems engineering.

NATIONAL UNIVERSITY
University Park
San Diego, CA 92108 USA
Louise Clark, Registrar
Business, behavioral science, criminal justice, education, law, many other fields
1971
B, M, Law, Accredited
Residency
Non-profit, independent
(619) 563–7100
$$$

Each course is offered in intensive one-month modules, meeting in the evenings and selected Saturdays. Some daytime classes are offered. More than 600 courses begin each month, 12 times a year. Courses are offered in San Diego, Fresno, Irvine, Los Angeles, Oakland, Palm Springs, Sacramento, San Jose, Stockton, and Vista, California, and in San Jose, Costa Rica. Students may freely transfer from one center to another. Degrees include a Bachelor of Business Administration, B.A. in behavioral science, Bachelor of Public Administration, B.A. in interdisciplinary studies, Bachelor of Technical Education, B.S. in computer science or airway science, M.B.A., M.B.A. in health care administration, M.A. in business with emphasis in human services management or real estate management, and Master of Public Administration.

NAZARETH COLLEGE
Continuing Education Program
Rochester, NY 14610 USA
Paul W. Kenyon, Director of Admissions
Liberal arts
1924

B, Accredited
Residency
Non-profit, independent
(716) 586–2525
$$$

Bachelor of Arts in liberal arts and Master's in education offered entirely through evening study, for persons over 21.

NEW COLLEGE OF CALIFORNIA
50 Fell St.
San Francisco, CA 94102 USA
Ms. Donna Waloman, Director of Admissions
Humanities (many fields), psychology, poetics
1971

B, M, Accredited
Residency
Non-profit, independent
(415) 626–1694
$$$

This innovative school has offered its Bachelor of Arts and Master of Arts degrees in a variety of different approaches, including evening courses, weekend courses, and a series of long weekend seminars with independent study sessions in between, on-the-job practicums, tutorials, a Weekend College program for working adults, and credit for prior learning experience. In 1989, New College took over the non-traditional programs of Antioch University West. The B.A. is offered in humanities (including art, writing, psychology, mathematics, chemistry, biology, and much more). There is an M.A. in psychology and in poetics (a unique non-literature approach to the subject). The Science Institute offers science courses designed for people planning to attend chiropractic or podiatric schools. New College was started by Father John Leary, former president of Gonzaga University. Traditional courses are offered, generally in three-hour sessions. (The name "New College" comes from Oxford University where their New College was established in the 13th century!)

NEW EXPERIMENTAL COLLEGE
see: Nordenfjord World University

NEW HAMPSHIRE COLLEGE
2500 North River Rd.
Manchester, NH 03104 USA
Deborah Reid, Coordinator of Marketing
Human services, social work
1932

B, M, Accredited
Short residency
Non-profit, independent
(603) 668–2211
$$$

Bachelor's and Master's can be earned entirely through weekend study. Classes offered weekends only, once a month for four months, all day. The human services undergraduate program is designed to allow people to pursue career goals developed from their prior experience. One can enter as a freshman, sophomore, or junior. Concentrations in counseling, administration, labor studies, and criminal justice. The M.S. in human services has concentrations in administration, gerontology, and community service. There is also a Master of Social Work. A full-time student taking three courses would be at the college for one long weekend a month (Friday-Sunday) or two adjacent weekends (two Saturdays and a Sunday or two Sundays and a Saturday) each month. The New Hampshire degree is also offered in London through Lansdowne College.

NEW SCHOOL FOR SOCIAL RESEARCH
Media Studies Program, 66 W. 12th St.
New York, NY 10011 USA
Elizabeth Ross, University Registrar
Media studies
1919

M, Accredited
Residency
Non-profit, independent
(212) 741–5600
$$$

Master of Arts in media studies through the media studies program is designed for working professionals from the fields of broadcasting, cable, telecommunications, advertising, corporate communications, and education. Evening study and independent study.

NEW YORK UNIVERSITY
Gallatin Division, 715 Broadway, 6th Floor
New York, NY 10003 USA
David Finney, Director of Admissions
Over 150 majors
1831

B, M, Accredited
Residency
Non-profit, independent
(212) 598–7077
$$$$

Bachelor of Arts program requiring no specific courses (however, students are expected to be "thoroughly conversant" with a formidable list of great books as a graduation requirement). Internships, independent study and credit for life experience are available. A cooperative education program offers the B.A. largely based on internships in education, arts administration, media, business, and public/social service. The Master of Arts in individualized study involves coursework, internships, and independent study under the supervision of a faculty advisor. A scholarly, creative, or performance thesis is required. Credit is given for career experience learning. Created in 1972, the Gallatin Division offers mature, self-directed students the opportunity to plan an individualized program of study in a wide range of fields.

NEW WORLD CENTER FOR ADVANCED STUDIES
3154B College Drive, # 546
Baton Rouge, LA 70808 USA
Dr. Robert F. Kephart, President
Fire science, safety and health services
1988

B, M, D, Unaccredited, state registered
Proprietary
No listed phone

Purpose is to offer non-residential degree programs to fire and life safety professionals.

NEWPORT UNIVERSITY ✪
3720 Campus Dr.
Newport Beach, CA 92660 USA
Dr. Ted Dalton, President
Business, education, psychology, human behavior, law, engineering and religion
1976

B, M, D, Law, Unaccredited, state approved, Non-resident
Proprietary
(714) 756–8297
$$

Students are offered a variety of methods to obtain their degrees: directed independent study, classroom lectures, practicums, seminars, and workshops. Life and experiential credit is given at the undergraduate level only. An educational facilitator is assigned to each student for each course. Branch offices are maintained in England, Holland, Switzerland, India, and Japan. Newport's 15 programs are approved by the state of California. They are offered through the schools of business administration, education, professional psychology, human behavior, religion, and law. Originally known as Newport International University.

NIAGARA UNIVERSITY
Niagara, NY 14109 USA
George C. Pachter, Dean of Admissions
Many fields
1856

B, Accredited
Residency
Non-profit, independent
(716) 285–1212
$$$

Credit for non-academic prior learning and by examination. Bachelor's in business, nursing, education, arts, and sciences may be earned through evening and summer programs. Special programs in nursing, pre-engineering, pre-med, and pre-dental studies.

NOMAD UNIVERSITY
P. O. Box 2128
Seattle, WA 98111

No degrees, unaccredited
Residency
Non-profit, independent

Nomad University presents public classes for groups of 500 or more in cities worldwide. The lovely little catalogue says, "Not all that we call education is to found within the ivy-covered walls of Academic. Nomad University pitches its all-encompassing tent under the open sky wherever the conditions for learning are good. . . . There are great teachers all around us. Nomad University has assembled in our movable camp the best guides, storytellers, wizards, bards, enchantresses, seers, adventurers, old ones, healers, clowns, warriors, and adepts. . . . Because we learn from our colleagues, we are a true college. Because the walls move with the wind, we remember where the true university is." The first three courses are $25 each, and you are not told what they will be; you simply pay and then go. It is all rather charming.

NORDENFJORD WORLD UNIVERSITY
Skyum Bjerge, Snedsted
Thy, DK-7752 Denmark
Many fields
1962
B, M, D, Equivalent of accredited, Residency
45–7–936234
$$$
Six separate schools, where students come from all over the world to study for a semester to an entire degree program. New Experimental College is one of the six units, with the goal of developing a self-perpetuating community of scholars who will have a worldwide effect on technology, economics, and social planning. Not officially recognized by the Danish government. Many students arrange with schools in their home countries to award degrees based on work done at Nordenfjord. Education largely through teacher-directed independent study; some classes and seminars. Rules and plans made in the "ting"—a group meeting with elements of group dynamics, sensitivity training, and the Synanon Game. Students nearing the end of their work may call for a "high ting"—a combined examination/celebration, in which work is presented and discussion invited. Other units of Nordenfjord specialize in communications, arts and crafts, language, and philosophy.

NORTH ADAMS STATE COLLEGE
Office of Continuing Education
North Adams, MA 01247 USA
Gerald F. Desmarais, Director of Admissions
Many fields
1894
B, Accredited
Residency
Non-profit, state
(413) 664–4511
$$
Bachelor of Science in Business Administration, Bachelor of Science in computer science, and Bachelor of Arts in sociology offered through evening degree programs.

NORTH CAROLINA STATE UNIVERSITY
P.O. Box 7103
Raleigh, NC 27695 USA
Anna P. Keller, Dean of Admissions
Many fields
1887
B, M, D, Accredited
Residency
Non-profit, state
(919) 737–2011
$880
Bachelor's degrees in many fields, including design, forest resources, and textiles. Evening study available. No credit for work or life experience, but credit by exam available. Master of Public Affairs and Master of Industrial Engineering programs are offered through evening study at various centers around the state (Charlotte, Fayetteville, Greensboro, Marion, and Raleigh).

NORTH CAROLINA WESLEYAN COLLEGE
Rocky Mount, NC 27801
Carl A. Pagles, Dean of Admissions
Business, criminal justice, computer information systems
1956
B, Accredited
Residency
Non-profit, church
(919) 977–7171
$$$
Bachelor's degree in business administration, criminal justice, and computer information systems may be earned through evening and summer programs. For North Carolina residents only.

NORTH CENTRAL COLLEGE
30 N. Brainard St.
Naperville, IL 60566 USA
Mrs. Shirley R. Haines, Registrar
Many fields
1861
B, M, Accredited
Residency
Non-profit, church
(312) 420–3000
$$$
Bachelor of Arts in accounting, communications, computer science, management, marketing, and management information systems may be earned through weekend or evening programs, offered in Naperville and

See page 70 for explanation of abbreviations and symbols

Schaumburg/Rolling Meadows. Bachelor of Science in Computer Science through evening studies. Weekend College meets Friday evening and Saturday, normally every other weekend; six meetings per term.

NORTH DAKOTA STATE UNIVERSITY

State University Station — B, M, Accredited
Fargo, ND 58105 USA — Residency
George H. Wallman, Director of Admissions — Non-profit, state
Many fields — (701) 237–8011
1890 — $$

Bachelor of University Studies degrees, individually tailored programs in many fields. There is a residency requirement of one year or 45 quarter credits. Students may earn credit for prior work, educational and military experiences. The assessment must be done after enrollment and is part of a degree proposal prepared by the student in consultation with an advisor. There is no fee for the assessment. Students usually have a major emphasis or thrust to their proposed course of study but they do not have a major. They may combine previous academic credit, credit for life experience and non-traditional education, and courses offered by any department on campus.

NORTHEASTERN ILLINOIS UNIVERSITY ✪

5500 N. St. Louis Ave. — B, M, Accredited
Chicago, IL 60625 USA — Short residency
Dr. Eric B. Moch, Director of Admissions and Records — Non-profit, state
Liberal arts, education, business — (312) 583–4050
1961 — $$

Bachelor of Arts with a minimum residency requirement of 15 units, which can be completed in four months on campus. One of the five Illinois universities participating in the Board of Governors Bachelor of Arts program. Credit is given for life experience and all prior learning experiences. New credit may be earned through regular courses at any of the five schools in the program, or by correspondence study and independent study. (The five Board of Governors schools started out with almost identical programs, but now two, Western Illinois and Governors State, offer totally non-resident programs.)

NORTHEASTERN UNIVERSITY

360 Huntington Ave. — B, M, D, Law, Accredited
Boston, MA 02115 USA — Residency
Philip R. McCabe, Dean of Admissions — Non-profit, independent
Many fields — (617) 437–2000
1898 — $$

Northeastern offers what UNESCO calls "the world's leading program in Cooperative Education." They have also asked me to omit their listing from this book, but I have chosen not to. Most of Northeastern's more-than-50,000 students are employed half-time by companies all over the United States. The academic year is divided into four equal quarters. While half the students are attending full-time (including evening study), the other half are working full-time. Every three to six months, they switch. The average student earns about $30,000 during the five years of a Bachelor's program. There are many situations in which two students combine to hold a full-time job in business or industry. Bachelor's, Master's, Doctorates (Ph.D. and Doctor of Engineering) and Law degrees are offered in this manner, in a wide variety of subjects, from social science to engineering to pharmacy, nursing, and criminal justice.

NORTHLAND OPEN UNIVERSITY

7475 Sherbrooke Ave. West, Dept. 1111 — B, M, Licensed in Canada
Montreal, Quebec H4B 1S4 Canada — Short residency
Dr. Donald Gyallay, President
Management, health services administration, business administration — (514) 482–6951
$
1976

Programs can be completed at a distance with only one or two full weeks of residence required. Each learner communicates directly with faculty members and works closely with a specially appointed local faculty advisor. Northland Open University is a member of the International University Without Walls Council and International Council on Distance Education. Management programs combine theory and practice in an "action learning" self-directed approach. Professional training, management experience, and formal study at other colleges and universities are evaluated and assessed for credits. Northland was started by the founder of the Canadian School of Management, and was affiliated with them until 1984. Doctoral programs have been offered in the past. Originally established in Yellowknife, Northwest Territories (school laws are different in the territories than in the provinces). Degrees offered in England through International Management Centre in Buckingham.

NORTHWESTERN COLLEGE
Orange City, IA 51041 USA
Ronald K. De Jong, Director of Admissions
Many fields
1882
B, Accredited
Residency
Non-profit, church
(712) 737-4821, ext. 19
$$$
Bachelor's degree in many fields, in which units may be earned by assessment of prior learning experience. Only full-time students can be so assessed, on the basis of a portfolio they prepare. There is no additional fee for the assessment, which can take three to five months.

NORTHWESTERN POLYTECHNIC UNIVERSITY
4378 Enterprise St.
Fremont, CA 94539 USA
Barbara Brown, President
Electrical engineering, computer systems engineering
1984
B, M, Unaccredited, state authorized, Residency
Non-profit, independent
(415) 657-5911
$$$
The program offers the last two years of a four-year course of studies. All accepted students must have completed 50-60 semester hours of general studies before enrolling. Credit for documented life work experience, military, and equivalency exams. Students may request a "challenging exam" in any course, given during the first two weeks. If passed, credit for that course is given. The degrees can be earned in 15 to 19 months of evening study.

NORTHWESTERN UNIVERSITY
University College, 633 Clark St.
Evanston, IL 60201-3851 USA
Louise Love, Associate Dean
Many fields
1851
B, M, Accredited
Residency
Non-profit, independent
(312) 908-6950
$$$$$
Bachelor's and Master's may be earned through evening and summer programs. Bachelor's degrees offered in anthropology, economics, English, fine arts, history, math, philosophy, political science, psychology, and sociology. The Master's are in liberal arts and English.

NORTHWOOD INSTITUTE
3225 Cook Rd.
Midland, MI 48640 USA
Donald A. King, Associate Director, External Plan of Study
Management, accounting, computer science, marketing, economics
1959
B, Accredited
Short residency
Non-profit, independent
(517) 631-1600
$$
Bachelor of Business Administration degree, in either business or accounting, requiring a total of six days on the campus. Credit is given for prior learning experience and study, and for equivalency examinations. The external plan of study has many courses which can be passed by taking an open book examination. All students must attend two three-day seminars on campus, write a thesis, and pass a final oral examination "which will last for several hours and be based on questions provided to the student in advance." Fees are quite variable, depending on the approach the student takes. Northwood has offered this program at other locations around the U.S., including Florida, Michigan, Louisiana, Indiana, Texas, and California.

NORWICH UNIVERSITY ✪
Vermont College
B, M, Accredited

College Street, Montpelier, VT 05663 USA
Kelley Hunter, Assistant Director of Admissions
Art therapy, writing, liberal arts
1834
Short residency
Non-profit, independent
(802) 229–0522 or (800) 332-1987
$$$

The Alternative Education Division includes the undergraduate level Adult Degree Program (ADP) and the Graduate Program, offering the M.A. in art therapy, the Master of Fine Arts in writing, and a self-designed M.A. available in counseling, education, and other fields. The programs are designed to allow students great latitude in designing their study projects in consultation with members of the faculty. All ADP faculty are based at Vermont College and students attend nine-day residencies twice a year or one weekend meeting per month. Graduate Program faculty are based in major cities around the country and convene their students for area meetings regularly. Norwich entered the non-traditional field in 1981 by acquiring programs from the then financially strapped Goddard College.

NOVA COLLEGE
P.O. Box 492, Station G
Calgary, Alberta T3A 2G4 Canada
Reg. P. Farley, President
Any field
1977
B,M,D, Unaccredited, unlicensed, Non-resident
Non-profit, independent
No listed phone
$

In 1987, publicly Nova stopped operations in Canada, but continues operations from Europe, where degrees are granted entirely based on an assessment of present achievements. No classes are offered, either in person or by correspondence. Prospective students must sign a form stating that they understand that Nova awards are "largely 'recognition' awards." Nova warns prospective students to ask any questions in advance, since "we will not enter into any correspondence concerning Nova subsequent to registration." Their British address in London is a mail forwarding service, and incorporation is on the Isle of Man. Other previously-announced connections in Utah and on the Seychelles Islands haveapparently been discontinued. Nova has complained about my remarks on them. I might have called to discuss this, if they had a telephone. Also operates as Nova International College. Not to be confused with the accredited Nova University (which actually as a component unit called Nova College).

NOVA UNIVERSITY ✪
3301 College Ave.
Fort Lauderdale, FL 33314 USA
Stanly E. Cross, University Regustrar
Education, Administration, business, computer systems
1964
B,M,D, Accredited
Short residency
Non-profit, independent
(305) 475-7300
$$$$

Nova University has one of the more non-traditional Master's and Doctoral programs ever to achieve regional accreditation. The typical student attends one group meeting a month (generally two or three days), plus two one-week residential sessions, and from three to six practicums which emphasize direct application of research to the work place. Total time about three-and-a-half years. The university also offers a Doctor of Arts in information science in which students use interactive computers. A major part of instruction in this program is through teleconferencing, TELNET, and TYME. Residential work offered in 23 states. Nova will consider offering the program in the continental United States where a cluster of 20–25 students can be formed. Degrees are offered in educational administration, teacher education, business administration, including international management, public administration, computer studies and information science.

NYINGMA INSTITUTE
1815 Highland Place
Berkeley, CA 94707 USA
Tarthang Tulku Rinpoche, President
Human development based on Tibetan Buddhism
1973
Certificate, Unaccredited
state authorized, Residency
Non-profit, independent
(415) 843-6812
Varies

Curriculum includes philosophy, psychology, language study, meditation practice, history, culture and comparative studies.

OCCIDENTAL UNIVERSITY
Original name of International Institute for Advanced Studies; see: Greenwich University

OHIO STATE UNIVERSITY
Division of Continuing Education, 2400 Oletangy River Rd. B.M, Accredited
Columbus, OH 43210
Residency
Dr. James J. Mager, Director of Admissions
Non-profit, state
Many fields
(614) 292-3980
1870
$$
Evening and weekend courses are offered. Bachelor of Arts in English, history; Bachelor of Science; Bachelor of Business Administration; Master of Arts in education, English, history, and journalism, all available through evening study. Credit for life experience learning. Telephone-assisted language program in eastern European languages. Counseling, trouble-shooting, and workshops are available from the Department of Continuing Education.

OHIO UNIVERSITY ✪
External Student Program, 301 Tupper Hall
B, Accredited
Athens, OH 45701 USA
Non-resident
Dr. James C. Walters, Director of Amissions
Non-profit, state
General Studies
(800) 342-4791
1804
$$
The Bachelor of General Studies degree can be earned entirely through non-resident study. The External Student Program provides a counseling and advising service, and also acts as a liason in dealing with other university offices. Credit for the degree can come from assessment of prior learning experiences, correspondence courses, independent study projects, and courses on radio or television. In many correspondence courses, one can take the examination only. If passed, credit for the course is given. These exams can be administered anywhere in the world and must be supervised. Forty eight quarter hours of credit must be completed after enrolling at Ohio. Other Bachelor's degrees of Ohio University can be completed largely through external means, but some time on campus will almost certainly be required. The university also offers a College Program for the Incarcerated, at unusually low cost.

OKLAHOMA CITY UNIVERSITY ✪
B, Accredited
Competency-Based Degree Program
Non-profit, state
N.W. 23rd at N. Blackwelder
(405) 521-5265
Oklahoma City, OK 73106
Karen Powers, Director, Competency-Based Degree Program
So here's the problem. This university has a splendid and innovative degree program, with truly outstanding materials, that are a model of clarity and completeness. However, on numerous occasions, Karen Powers, Director of the Competency-Based Degree Program, has demanded that the program be deleted from this book. I did that for one edition, and got a whole bunch of letters from people saying, in effect, "Why didn't you list OCU?" My compromise is to let you know it exists, but tell you nothing about it. Why does OCU not want to be described here? "For various reasons," writes Ms. Powers, none specified.

OKLAHOMA STATE UNIVERSITY
Stillwater, OK 74078 USA
M, Residency
Dr. Robin H. Lacy, Director of Admissions
Non-profit, state
Engineering
(405) 624–5000
1890
$
Master of Engineering programs are offered through the Cooperative Extension Service at various locations statewide, combining residential and independent study.

ONE INSTITUTE OF HOMOPHILE STUDIES
3340 Country Club Dr.
M, D, Unaccredited, state authorized, Residency
Los Angeles, CA 90019 USA
David G. Cameron, President
Non-profit, independent
Homophile studies
(213) 735–5252

1956
$100/unit
Interdisciplinary curricula in anthropology, biology, sociology, history, literature, psychology, etc., of male and female homosexuality. Some credit for life experience learning. Some courses by evening and weekend study. Authorized to grant degrees by the state of California.

OPEN LEARNING INSTITUTE
see: British Columbia Open University

OPEN UNIVERSITY (England) ✪
Walton Hall
Milton Keynes, Buckinghamshire MK7 6AA England
C. R. Batten, Academic Registrar
Arts, education, mathematics, social science, science, and technology
1971
B, M, D, Equivalent of accredited
Non-resident
Non-profit, state74066
74066
$$$
England's largest non-traditional university has become the model for similar ventures worldwide. Degrees at all levels are offered through a combination of home study texts, radio and television programs, audio- and video-cassettes, week-long seminars during the summer, and home laboratory kits for science students. A Bachelor's degree can take anywhere from three to six years of part-time study; a Doctorate from three to nine years. About 30 hours of broadcast material are transmitted each week on BBC radio and television. The Open University is increasing its use of cassette material. There are currently about 67,000 undergraduate students and 1,200 graduate students registered. Started as an experiment in 1971, Open University has grown into the most elaborate correspondence school in the world. As at other British universities, credit is earned only by passing examinations.

OPEN UNIVERSITY (Missouri)
see: Clayton University

OPEN UNIVERSITY OF AMERICA
3916 Commander Dr
Hyattsville, MD 20782 USA
Many fields
(301) 779–0220
B, M, D, Unaccreded, unlicensed
Non-resident
Non-profit, independent
$$
Established in 1968 by Dr's. Daniel and Mary Rodgers. Degrees can be awarded entirely on the basis of prior achievements. The catalogue is large and, at first glance, impressive. The Open University of America System included California National Open University and Nevada National Open University. In response to my routine request for information, Chancellor Mary Rodgers, who apparently runs the university from the basement of her home, wrote to me as follows: "Your attempt to extort data from me by blackmail method [sic] is reprehensible... Be advised that you are not at liberty to criticize, extol, describe, interpret or represent knowledge about the Open University of America in any way." I can't determine if they are still operating, but there is a listed phone. Not approved by the Maryland Board for Higher Education. I shall say no more, then.

OPEN UNIVERSITY OF THE NETHERLANDS
P.O.Box 2960
Heerlen, 6401 DL Netherlands
Dr. C. W. Van Seventer
Many fields
1984
B,D, Equivalent of accreditation
Non-resident
Non-profit, state
(045) 713334
$
The Netherland's first non-traditional university. The main teaching method is self-study, supported by printed course materials, audio- or videotapes, computerized instructions, and radio and television programs. Courses are offered in management and administration, engineering, natural science, sociology, political science, law, economics, and liberal arts. The model is based on Britain's Open University. Credit is earned solely by passing examinations. Tutoring is available in study centers around the country, and by telephone. It is, in principle, possible for people from all over the world to enroll in the Open University. Some readers have been annoyed to discover that courses are in Dutch . . . but there is a plan afoot to devel-

op and offer courses in English as well.

ORAL ROBERTS UNIVERSITY
Center for Lifelong Learning
7777 South Lewis Ave.
Tulsa, OK 74171
David W. Owen, Director of Admissions
Church ministries

B, Accredited
Short residency
Non-profit, church
(918) 495-6518 or (800) 678-8876
$$

The B.S. in church ministries is offered largely through home study and independent study (audio cassettes, compter presentation), with one week per semester on campus. Credit is given for experiential learning, independent study, and equivalency exams. More degree programs are under development. Applicants must sign a pledge not to use tobacco or alcohol, not to lie, cheat, curse or steal, to participate in an aerobics program, attend church, to avoid homosexual behavior, and to commit ones life to Jesus. 40 of the 43 pages sent in response to an inquiry related to financial aid.

OREGON INSTITUTE OF TECHNOLOGY
Oretech Branch Post Office
Klamath Falls, OR 97601 USA
Dr. Russell Lyon, Registrar
Technology
1946

B, Accredited
Residency
Non-profit, state
(503) 882–6321
$$

The Bachelor of Technology degree can be earned entirely through evening study. Some credit is given for prior learning experience. The fields of study are health technologies, engineering technologies, business technologies, and laser electro-optics technology.

OTTAWA UNIVERSITY✪
10th at Cedar
Ottawa, KS 66067 USA
Richard Marck, Director of Admissions
Many fields
1865

B, Accredited
Short residency
Non-profit, church
(913) 242–5200
$$

I believe that Ottawa offers excellent programs at centers in Kansas City and Phoenix. But Director of Admissions Richard Marck won't tell me about them, so I am unable to tell you about them. Maybe you'll have better luck. Or maybe they have all the students they could possibly want.

OUR LADY OF THE LAKE UNIVERSITY
411 S.W. 24th St.
San Antonio, TX 78285 USA
Loretta Schlegel, Registrar
Computer science, management, human resources, liberal studies
1922

B, Accredited
Residency
Non-profit, church
(512) 434-6711
$$$

Bachelor's and Master's in computer information systems, management, human resources and organization, and liberal studies, through weekend study. All classes are scheduled for Friday evening, Saturday or Sunday, every other week. Eighteen weekends a year equals a full-time academic load. Credit may be earned through several testing programs and a portfolio process for evaluation of life/work experience at a cost of $50 plus one third the usual tuition for credit awarded. A 36 semester hour M.B.A. can be earned in two years. It utilizes the Decision Theater, a teaching laboratory using computer simulations and models to present real life business situations, enabling students to apply managerial theories to everyday situations.

OXFORD GRADUATE SCHOOL
American Institute of Ministry, P. O. Box 515
Dayton, TN 37321
Hollis L. Green, President
1982

M, D, Unaccredited, state authorized
Residency
Non-profit, non-sectarian
(615) 775-6597
$$$

I had better let the catalogue speak for itself: "Flexible residency through the concept of reading for a de-

See page 70 for explanation of abbreviations and symbols

gree. Qualifying examinations make Oxford available to worthy students and exit examinations validate the quality of education.... The...program accepts only experienced Christian scholars who are qualified by academic stand and practical experience. The program requires an evident balance between orthodoxy and orthopraxis (and is) primarily an andragogic educational model with synergogic learning designs." The D.Phil. program is structured "to develop distinct patterns of expectations regarding the understandings, knowledge, skills and competencies expected of D.Phil. candidates...(and) develop and implement a basic strategy for translating programmatically projected expectations into actual patterns of student progress."

PACIFIC INSTITUTE FOR ADVANCED STUDIES
12750 W. Hortense St.
Studio City, CA 91604 USA
Mason Rose, Chancellor
1940
Unaccredited, state authorized
Non-profit, independent
(818) 761-4506
No listed phone
Authorized by the state of California to grant degrees. No response to three requests for information on their programs.

PACIFIC INTERNATIONAL UNIVERSITY
5318 Middleton Dr.
San Diego, CA 92109 USA
Abbas Aryanpur Kashani, President
1984
Unaccredited, state authorized
(619) 272–6605
Authorized to grant degrees by the state of California. Did not respond to three requests for information about their programs. Almost certainly unrelated to the Pacific International University that operated from Hollywood, California, at least through 1964, offering correspondence and residential degrees in science and engineering.

PACIFIC OAKS COLLEGE
5 Westmoreland Place
Pasadena, CA 91103
Lisa Bourgeault, Director of Admissions
1945
Human development
B, M, Accredited
Residency
Non-profit, independent
(818) 795-9161
$$$
The Outreach and Extension Services offers a B.A. or M.A. program designed for part-time students who are working professionals. The evening and weekend courses are offered in southern California as well as in the San Francisco area, Portland, and Seattle.

PACIFIC SOUTHERN UNIVERSITY
9581 N. Pico Blvd.
Los Angeles, CA 90035 USA
Javad J. Khazrai, President
Business, education, engineering, human behavior
1978
B, M, D, Unaccredited, state authorized
Non-resident
Proprietary
(213) 276–3425
$$
Degrees by correspondence study in a wide range of subjects through their schools of business and management, education, engineering, and human behavior.

PACIFIC STATES UNIVERSITY
1516 S. Western Ave.
Los Angeles, CA 90006 USA
Steven Kase, President
Many fields
1928
M, D, Unaccredited, state approved, Short residency
Non-profit, independent
(213) 731–2383
$$
Master of Arts, Doctor of Education, Doctor of Product Development, and Ph.D. programs, primarily through non-residential independent study. A six-week summer session, either in Los Angeles or in London, England, is required. The university was founded in 1928 as an engineering school, and still offers residential programs in various fields. The graduate degrees are offered with a specialty in administration, general education, or psychology and counseling. They can be completed in less then a year.

PACIFIC WESTERN UNIVERSITY ✪
600 N. Sepulveda Blvd.
Los Angeles, CA 90049 USA
Philip Forte, President
Many fields
1977
B, M, D, Unaccredited, state authorized
Non-resident
Proprietary
(213) 471-0306 or (800) 423-3244
$$

The degrees can be completed either through correspondence study . Professional and career-oriented off-campus independent study programs leading to degrees in business, management science, engineering, physical and natural science, social science, education, and the helping professions. Through its Career Training Institute, Pacific Western offers vocational training leading to certificates in various fields. Doctoral programs are handled through Pacific Western's office at 7 Waterfront Plaza, 500 Ala Moana Blvd., Honolulu, Hawaii 96813.

PALO ALTO SCHOOL OF PROFESSIONAL PSYCHOLOGY
see: Western Graduate School of Psychology

PARK COLLEGE
Parkville, MO 64152
V. Peter Pitts, Vice President, Enrollment Management
Many fields
1875
B, M, Accredited
Residency
Non-profit, church
(816) 741-2000
$$$

The Portfolio Plan is an individualized degree completion program for adults, based on a learning contract which specifies credit for prior experience and new work to be done in classrooms and through independent study. Evening classes are offered in the Kansas City area, and degree completion centers are operated on or near military bases in a dozen states. There is a Master of Public Affairs and graduate study in religion for clergy and lay leaders of the Reorganized Church of Jesus Christ of Latter Day Saints.

PENNSYLVANIA STATE UNIVERSITY
Academic Information Center, 138 Sparks Bldg.
University Park, PA 16802 USA
Scott F. Healy, Deanof Admissions
Arts and sciences
1855
Asssociate's, M, D, Accredited
Non-resident; residency
Non-profit, state
(814) 865–2547
$$

The Extended Letters, Arts and Sciences Associates's degree is offered entirely through correspondence study, mostly through correspondence courses offered by Penn State. Although few Associate's degrees are listed in this book, this one is, as one of the few non-resident degrees available from a major state university. Master's and Doctorates can be earned through evening study at the Harrisburg campus in Middletown.

PEPPERDINE UNIVERSITY
24255 Pacific Coast Hwy.
Malibu, CA 90265· USA
Robert L. Fraley, Dean of Admissions
Many fields
1937
B, M, D, Accredited
Residency
Non-profit, independent
(213) 456–4000
$$$$$

Bachelor of Science; Master of Arts in education, general psychology; Master of Science in educational computing, educational therapy, school management and administration; Doctor of Education in institutional management; Doctor of Education in community college administration—all available through a combination of weekend and evening classes at four locations in the Los Angeles area. No credit is given for life experience learning. Pepperdine offers an innovative M.B.A. program for business leaders.

PHILADELPHIA COLLEGE OF TEXTILES AND SCIENCE
Evening Division, School House Ln. and Henry Ave.,
Philadelphia, PA 19144 USA
John T. Pierantozzi, Director of Admissions
Business, computers, design, science, textiles
1884
B,M, Accredited
Residency
Non-profit, independent
(215) 951–2700
$$$

See page 70 for explanation of abbreviations and symbols

Most Bachelor of Science degrees can be earned entirely through evening study. There is a special B.S. for registered nurses (the R.N. counts for half the needed credits), and another for health care professionals. M.B.A. classes meet one evening a week in Bucks and Montgomery Counties. Credit given for prior learning through examination.

PITTSBURG STATE UNIVERSITY
Pittsburg, KS 66762
James E. Parker, Director, Enrollment Services
Many fields
1903
M, Accredited
Residency
Non-profit, state
(316) 231-7000
$$

Master's degrees in many fields can be earned on a part time basis while remaining fully employed. The university serves students from Kansas, Missouri and Oklahoma.

PLYMOUTH STATE COLLEGE
Plymouth, NH 03264 USA
Clarence W. Bailey, Director of Admissions
Education
1871
M, Accredited
Residency
Non-profit, state
(603) 536–5000
$$

Master of Arts for classroom teachers, based on two eight-week summer sessions, with independent study during the nine months in between them.

POLYTECHNIC UNIVERSITY
333 Jay St.
Brooklyn, NY 11201 USA
James W. Reilly, Dean
Engineering
1854
B, Accredited
Residency
Non-profit, independent
(718) 643–5000
$$$$$

Bachelor of Science in aerospace/mechanical engineering, electrical engineering, and civil engineering available entirely through evening study.

PRATT INSTITUTE
200 Willoughby Ave.
Brooklyn, NY 11205 USA
Amanda Haigood, Director of Admissions
Many fields
1887
B, Accredited
Residency
Non-profit, independent
(718) 636–3600
$$$$

More than 80% of the units needed for the Bachelor's degree (available in many fields) can be earned through an assessment of prior learning experiences. The assessment cannot be done until the student has spent one semester in the Integrative Studies Program. Assessment is done by an analysis of a portfolio prepared by the student, and through oral interviews.

PRESCOTT COLLEGE
Adult Degree Program, 220 Grove
Prescott, AZ 86301 USA
Sue Pauli, Coordinator Student Services, ADP
Management, counseling, education, human services, individually-designed courses
1966
B, Accredited
Short residency
Non-profit, independent
(602) 778–2090
$$

Prescott's Adult Degree Program is a self-paced independent study format, using instructors from student's home community. Students normally take two courses every three months, meeting weekly with local instructors wherever they live. (Prescott helps to find them.) Small classes are offered in the late afternoon and evening on campus. Students must come to the college for a weekend orientation at the beginning of their program, and for an additional liberal arts Seminar, also on a weekend. Degree programs can be individually designed to meet students' goals. Entering students normally have a minimum of 30 semester hours of college work. One year enrollment at Prescott required to earn the degree. Credit for prior college-level learning through writing a life experience portfolio.

PROVIDENCE COLLEGE
Providence, RI 02918 USA
Michael G. Backes, Director of Admissions
Many fields
1917
B,M
Residency
Non-profit, church
(401) 865–1000
$$$$

Bachelor of Arts, Bachelor of Science in business administration and law enforcement, and Master of Business Administration, all available entirely through evening study.

PURDUE UNIVE;RSITY
West Lafayette, IN 47907 USA
William J. Murray, Director of Admissions
Engineering, education, technology, management
1869
M, Accredited
Residency
Non-profit, state
(317) 494–1776
$$

Master of Science in engineering for fully-employed engineers and Master of Science in education for persons already working in the field. Bachelor of Science in technology. All courses are offered to accommodate work schedules of adult students, evenings and weekends, and are offered in various Indiana cities. Master of Science in management, available over a Macintosh home computer, plus a total of 12 weeks on campus. The cost of this program is in excess of $22,000.

QUAD CITIES GRADUATE CENTER
639 38th Ave.
Rock Island, IL 61201
Janet Lessner, Ph.D.
Many fields
1969
M, Accredited
Residency
Non-profit, independent
(309) 794–7376
$$$

The center is sponsored by the University of Illinois, Northern Illinois University, the University of Iowa, Marycrest College, Augustana College, Iowa State University, University of Northern Iowa, Western Illinois University, and Bradley University. The degree is issued by one of these nine, depending on the program selected. Degrees offered include the Master of Arts, Master of Science, M.S. in education, M.S. in engineering, and Master of Business Administration, all available entirely through evening study.

QUEENS COLLEGE
Adult Collegiate Education, 65–30 Kissena Blvd.,
Flushing, NY 11367 USA
Betty W. Mason, DIrector of Admissions
Many fields
1937
B, Accredited
Residency
Non-profit, state-local
(212) 520–7000
$$

Bachelor of Arts degrees for persons over 30, consisting of short, long, and weekend seminars; tutorials; exemption exams; work credit; and supervised independent study. Classes are scheduled to fit the needs of students. One year of residency is usually required. Queens is a unit of the City University of New York.

QUEENS UNIVERSITY
Kingston, Ontario K7L 2N6 Canada
German, political studies, psychology
1841
B, Equivalent of accredited
Non-resident
Non-profit, state
(613)547-3283

All work for the Bachelor of Arts in German, political studies, or psychology is done at a distance, by guided study from instructors. Books and cassettes are used. There can be telephone contact with instructors. Final examinations in courses are taken under supervision at various centers, worldwide.

RAMAPO COLLEGE OF NEW JERSEY
505 Ramapo Valley Rd.
Mahwah, NJ 07430 USA
Stephen Arianas, Dean, Enrollment Management
Many fields
1969
B, Accredited
Residency
Non-profit, state
(201) 529–7500
$$

See page 70 for explanation of abbreviations and symbols

The Weekend Program offers a Bachelor's degree program with majors in American and international studies, business administration, and psychology. The evening degree program offers the same majors plus chemistry, biology, computer science, economics, environmental studies, and sociology. Up to 75 credits can be earned by equivalency tests, and through PLEX, the Prior Learning Experience program.

RAMKHAMHAENG UNIVERSITY
Huamark,
Bangkapi, Bangkok 10240 Thailand
Business, humanities, education, science, political science, economics and law
1971
B, Equivalent of accredited
Short residency
Non-profit, state
314-2045
$

With over 700,000 students, Ramkhamhaeng, on the open admission basis, is one of the world's largest universities. Degrees are offered through a combination of on-campus lectures, lectures on videotape at centers around the country, and courses broadcast nationally on 44 radio stations. It normally takes four years to earn a Bachelor's degree. Cooperative arrangements with the University of Pittsburgh, City University of New York, Southern Illinois University, and University of Surrey.

REGENTS COLLEGE
see: University of the State of New York

REGIS COLLEGE
West 50th and Lowell Blvd.
Denver, CO 80221
Business, computer information systems, management
J. Stephen Jacobs, Asst. Director, Career Education Program
1877
B, M, Accredited
Residency
Non-profit, church
(303) 458-4100
$$$$

Bachelor of Science in business administration or computer information systems through RECEP (Regis Career Education Program). Accelerated courses are offered in evenings and on weekends at several locations in the denver area. Each three-semester course is completed in five weeks; there are nine 5-week sessions a year. The Master of Science in Management is designed to be completed in 20 months, meeting one night each week.

REID COLLEGE OF DETECTION OF DECEPTION
250 S. Wacker
Chicago, IL 60606 USA
Brian C. Jayne, Dean
Polygraph techniques
1971
M, Unaccredited, state licensed
Residency
Proprietary
(800) 255–5747
$$

The college began as a school in the polygraph laboratories of John Reid, a prominent polygraph specialist. Now a Master of Science in the Detection of Deception is offered through a six-month course in Chicago, and the writing of a thesis, which may be done at a distance. Applicants must have an accredited Bachelor's degree. The program consists of lectures, laboratory work, and an internship. There is a final written exam, and each student must conduct two polygraph examinations under the scrutiny of the Degree Granting Board. Six-month programs begin each January and July. The college is authorized to grant the M.S.D.D. degree by the superintendent of public instruction.

RENSSELAER POLYTECHNIC INSTITUTE
Troy, NY 12180 USA
Residency
Conrad Sharrow, Dean of Admissions
Business
1824
D, Accredited
Non-profit, independent
(518) 266–6000
$$$$$

The Master of Science and M.B.A. are available entirely through evening study. There are accelerated programs in which a Bachelor's and either a medical, dental, or law degree can be earned in a total of six years.

RICHMOND COLLEGE
Queens Rd. — B, Accredited
Richmond, Surrey TW10 6PJ England — Residency
William Petrek, President
Many fields — (01) 940–9762

Richmond is a fully accredited American college that has no American offices or programs, but operates only in London. The degree-granting authority comes from the Educational Institution Licensing Commission of the District of Columbia, although Richmond has no offices or courses in the district. The commission assures me this is not an unusual situation. Accredited by the Middle States Association in the U.S. Advertisements also refer to them as the American International College of London.

RIDER COLLEGE
2083 Lawrenceville Rd. — B, Accredited
Lawrenceville, NJ 08648 USA — Residency
Earl L. Davis, Director of Admissions — Non-profit, independent
Commerce, chemistry, office administration, liberal studies — (609) 896–5000
1865 — $$$$

Bachelor of Arts in liberal studies, Bachelor of Science in commerce, Bachelor of Science in chemistry, Bachelor of Science in office administration, available entirely through evening study.

RIKKYO UNIVERSITY
3-chome, Nishi-Ikebukuro, Toshima-ku — D, Equivalent of accredited
Tokyo, 171 Japan — Short residency
Dr. S. Furuichi, Registrar — Non-profit, independent
Many fields — (03) 985–2204
1874

Rikkyo University offers its Doctoral degrees solely on the basis of a submitted thesis (which can be in English), plus a short series of written examinations to be taken in Tokyo. Rikkyo was established by an American bishop in 1874, and was taken over by the Japanese in 1920. Applicants are asked to secure a copy of the Regulations Governing the Awarding of Degrees at Rikkyo University before submitting any materials. Once a preliminary application (a 2,000-word summary of the dissertation and a curriculum virae) is accepted, then the full work is presented. The applicant then goes to Japan to take written exams in the topic of the dissertation, and in two languages other than his or her native one. If the applicant's level of academic achievement is commensurate with others who have earned the Doctorate at Rikkyo, then the degree is awarded: a Ph.D., Doctor of Science, Ph.D. in Economics, Ph.D. in Theology, or Ph.D. in Law. Rikkyo is also known as Saint Paul's University.

RIVERINA COLLEGE OF ADVANCED EDUCATION
P.O. Box 588 — B, Accredited
Wagga Wagga, N.S.W. 2650 Australia — Short residency
Education — Non-profit

The degree can be earned through a combination of short on-campus periods (as little as one week per year) and external study. (I have this fantasy that they will someday offer a joint program with Washington's Whitman College, thus establishing the Walla Walla-Wagga Wagga connection.

ROBERT MORRIS COLLEGE
Narrows Run Rd. — B, Accredited
Coraopolis, PA 15108 USA — Residency
Dr. Don L. Fox, Registrar — Non-profit, independent
Science — (412) 262–8200
1921 — $$

Bachelor of Science, in which all coursework can be done in the evening.

ROCHESTER INSTITUTE OF TECHNOLOGY
1 Lomb Memorial Dr. — B, M, Accredited
Rochester, NY 14623 USA — Residency

Richard Fuller, Director of Admissions
Technical fields, art, design, graphic arts, photography
1829

Non-profit, independent
(716) 475–6631
$$$$

Bachelor of Science in many technical fields, including engineering and computer science, photography and graphic arts; Master of Science in engineering technology or business technology through a combination of evening study, independent study, and some fieldwork. Master of Science in mathematical statistics requiring two short on-campus seminars plus independent study and a thesis.

ROCKFORD COLLEGE

5050 E. State St.
Rockford, IL 61108 USA
Dr. Gerald K. Wuori, Dean of Admission
Many fields
1847

B, M, Accredited
Residency
Non-profit, independent
(815) 226–4050
$$$

Bachelor of Science in general education, B.A., Bachelor of Fine Arts, Master of Arts in Teaching, and Master's in business administration, all available through evening courses.

ROCKHURST COLLEGE

5225 Troost Ave.
Kansas City, MO 64110 USA
Thomas J. Audley, Director of Admissions
Economics, industrial relations, psychology, sociology, business administration
1910

B, M, Accredited
Residency
Non-profit, church
(816) 926–4000
$$

Bachelor of Science and Bachelor of Arts, available entirely through evening study. M.B.A. through evening and weekend classes. Cooperative Education Program alternating semesters of college with full-time salaried work. Internships and practicums in communication, psychology, and politics.

ROGER WILLIAMS COLLEGE

Open Division
Bristol, RI 02809 USA
William Dunfey, Director of Admissions
Many fields
1945

B, Accredited
Residency
Non-profit, independent
(401) 255–2371
$$$

Bachelor's degrees in many fields, including engineering and industrial technology, career writing, historic preservation, marine biology, and theater in which up to 75% of the necessary units can be earned through an assessment of prior learning experiences, equivalency exams, etc. The assessment is based on a portfolio, oral interviews, and tests. Assessment takes two to five months, and there is no extra charge for it. Programs include combinations of external courses; independent studies; internships; and classroom courses, day, evening, or summer.

ROGER WILLIAMS UNIVERSITY

see: East Coast University

ROLLINS COLLEGE

Division of Continuing Education, Campus Box 2725,
Winter Park, FL 32789 USA
David G. Erdmann, Dean of Admissions
Many fields
1885

B, M, Accredited
Residency
Non-profit, independent
(305) 646-2000
$$$$$

Bachelor of Arts degree in women's studies, accounting, anthropology, sociology, business studies, communication arts, economics, environmental studies, humanities, international affairs, psychology, and public affairs offered through weekend and evening study. The Master of Liberal Studies is an interdisciplinary program for adults, offered evenings on a part-time basis. This "great books" approach meets one evening a week in spring and fall, and several evenings a week in winter and summer.

ROOSEVELT UNIVERSITY
430 S. Michigan Ave.
Chicago, IL 60605 USA
Gary K. Wolfe, Dean, College of Continuing Education
General studies
1945

B, Accredited
Residency
Non-profit, independent
(312) 341–3500
$$$

The External Degree Program offers courses leading to Bachelor of General Studies. Courses offered in a variety of programs ranging from public administration to computer science. There is an option for prior learning assessment. The degree is offered through the College of Continuing Education for persons over 25. Concentrations in the College of Continuing Education include: telecommunications and hospitality management and 30 other specialties. There are also special programs in labor education and health administration for professionals in the field. Classes are held evenings and weekends in Chicago and the suburbs, as well as off campus. Roosevelt offers a "Discovery Program," in which individuals with no Bachelor's degree can, through a year or less of testing and tutorials, enter the Master's degree program directly. A Master's degree is offered in General Studies on campus. Note: there was also a large diploma mill called Roosevelt University.

ROSKILDE UNIVERSITY CENTER
Postbox 260
Roskilde, DK-4000 Denmark
Mrs. Boel Jørgensen, Vice-Chancellor
Many fields
1972

B, M, Equivalent of accredited, Residency
Non-profit, state
(02) 75 77 11

An experimental university, specializing in interdisciplinary studies. Clusters of approximately 60 students, 5 teachers, and a secretary work together in a house for two years, during which time subgroups work together on interdisciplinary research and creative projects in humanities, social science, and natural science. Nearly 3,000 students are involved. The two years of basic studies are followed by one-and-one-half to three-and-one-half years of specialized studies, leading to the degree. Subjects include foreign language, international development, socio-technicological planning, public relations, sciences, etc.

RUDOLF STEINER COLLEGE
9200 Fair Oaks Blvd.
Fair Oaks, CA 95628 USA
Judith Blatchford, Registrar
Education and arts
1976

B,Unaccredited, state authorized, Residency
Non-profit, independent
(916) 961–8727
$$

A foundation year, an arts program, and Waldorf training based on the insights of Rudolf Steiner and others. If general education requirements have been met elsewhere, the B.A. may be earned through this study. The school is authorized by the state of California to grant degrees.

RUSSELL SAGE COLLEGE
The Evening Division, 140 New Scotland Ave.
Albany, NY 12208 USA
Dr. Robert E. Pennock, Dean of Continuing Education
Many fields
1949

B, M, Accredited
Residency
Non-profit, independent
(518) 445–1717
$$$

All degree programs are available entirely through evening study. Fields of study include elementary education, health education, business, nursing, computer science, sociology, art, etc. Up to 30 of the required 120 units in the Bachelor's program can come from credit for experiential learning.

RUTGERS UNIVERSITY
311 N. 5th St.
Camden, NJ 08102 USA
Dr. Deborah E. Bowles, Director of Admissions
Various fields
1927

B, M, Accredited
Residency
Non-profit, state
(609) 757–6104
$$

See page 70 for explanation of abbreviations and symbols

Bachelor of Arts and Bachelor of Science in accounting, computer science, management, physics, microelectronics, English, and psychology available through summer and evening classes in Camden, New Brunswick, and Newark.

RYOKAN COLLEGE
12581 Venice Blvd.
Venice, CA 90066 USA
Alvin P. Ross, President
Human behavior, counseling psychooogy, clinical psychology
1979
B, M, D, Unaccredited, state approved, Residency
Non-profit, independent
(213) 390–7560
$$
The programs are for mature career-oriented people with at least two years of undergraduate college work. Classes are held in supportive small group settings. The college is approved by the state of California.

SACRED HEART UNIVERSITY
Box 6400
Bridgeport, CT 06606 USA
Douglas J. Bohn, Associate Dean
Many fields
1963
M, Accredited
Residency
Non-profit, independent
(203) 374–7999
$$$
Master's degrees (M.A., M.S., M.B.A.) available entirely through evening study. Cooperative education and life work experience are available, as well as credit for equivalency exams.

SAINT AMBROSE COLLEGE
518 W. Locust St.
Davenport, IA 52803 USA
Patrick O'Connor, Dean of Admissions
Many fields
1882
B, Accredited
Residency
Non-profit, church
(319) 383–8765
$$$
Bachelor of Arts, Bachelor of Science, and Bachelor of Elected Studies may be earned through weekend, evening, and summer programs. Special programs: degree completion for nurses. Credit for non-academic prior learning and by examination.

SAINT EDWARDS UNIVERSITY
3001 S. Congress
Austin, TX 78704 USA
John Lambert, Director of Admissions
Many fields
1885
B, M, Accredited
Residency
Non-profit, independent
(512) 448–8500
$$$
Bachelor's degree program through New College in business, humanities, and social sciences, in which some of the degree requirements can be met through assessment of prior learning. The assessment is based on analysis of a portfolio prepared by the student in a special research course offered for that purpose. The cost is based on a fee for each credit awarded. Saint Edwards also offers a Bachelor of Arts in behavioral sciences and criminal justice. Bachelor of Business Administration, and Master of Business Administration, and human resources, through evening study.

SAINT FRANCIS COLLEGE (New York)
180 Remsen St.
Brooklyn, NY 11201 USA
George Lynes, Dean of Admissions
Special studies
1859
B, Accredited
Residency
Non-profit, independent
(718) 522–2300
$$$
Bachelor of Arts in special studies, available entirely through evening study in the School of Continuing Education. Up to 98 credits will be accepted from other schools and equivalency exams. Credit, also, for experiential learning. Up to 10 credits may be awarded to armed forces veterans for electives.

SAINT FRANCIS COLLEGE (Pennsylvania)
Loretto, PA 15940
Gerard J. Rooney, Director of Admissions
Industrial relations
1847

M, Accredited
Residency
Non-profit, church
(814) 472-3000
$$$$

M.A. in industrial relations can be earned entirely through evening study at the college's branches in Harrisburg and Pittsburgh.

SAINT FRANCIS XAVIER UNIVERSITY
Antigonish, Nova Scotia B2G 1C0 Canada
Education

M, Accredited
Residency
Non-profit
(902) 867–3952

A Master's degree in adult education is offered through a short residency and guided independent study.

SAINT GEORGE CENTER FOR TRAINING
1515 Arch St.
Berkeley, CA 94708 USA
Dorothea Romanikiw, President
1975

M, Unaccredited, state authorized, Residency
Non-profit, independent
(415) 848–2393

Authorized to grant degrees by the state of California. No response to three requests asking for information on their programs.

SAINT JOHN'S COLLEGE
Graduate Institute
Santa Fe, NM 87501 USA
Director, Graduate Institute
Liberal studies
1864

M, Accredited
Residency
Non-profit, independent
(505) 982–3691
$$

Saint John's has long been known for its full-time undergraduate programs based entirely on a study of great books of Western civilization. They also offer an innovative Master of Arts in liberal studies, also based on great books, over a period of four eight-week summer sessions in four consecutive years, and/or a fall and spring term program of two evenings a week. The program is offered on both Saint John's campuses, in New Mexico and Maryland, and students are encouraged to move from one to the other. The address in Maryland is Saint John's College, Graduate Institute, Annapolis, Maryland 21404, (301) 263–2371, Director of Admissions John Christensen.

SAINT JOHN'S UNIVERSITY
31916 Pat's Lane
Springfield, LA 70462
Many fields

B, M, D, Unaccredited, state registered
Non-resident
Non-profit, church
(504) 294-2129
Variable costs

Saint John's University of Practical Theology offers degrees in religion and theology, metaphysics, psychology, addictionology, hypnotherapy, parapsychology, business, police science, social justice, security and private investigation, social services, education, and journalism. There is also a high school equivalency programhich has been accepted by some traditional colleges. fHundreds of home study classes, ranging from foot reflexology to The Confidence Man to "Creating a Succe$$ful Hypnotherapy Center." There is free tuition for prisoners and half price for members of the AARP. Accreditation has been claimed from two unrecognized agencies. Two-part catalogue is sold for $4. The American Counselors Society and the National Society of Clinical Hypnotherapists operate from the same address. Neither has a listed telephone number. Former names: Eastern Nebraska Christian College, Midwestern University. Former locations: South Dakota, Nebraska, Missouri, and Ponchatoula, Louisiana. Unrelated to another unaccredited St. John's University that operated from New Orleans in the 1980s.

SAINT JOSEPH'S COLLEGE
North Windham, ME 04062 USA

B, M. Accredited
Short residency

See page 70 for explanation of abbreviations and symbols

Patricia M. Sparks, Dean
Professional arts, health care administration, and business
1912
Non-profit, church
(800) 343–5498
$$

Three degree completion programs are offered through directed independent study with campus-based faculty supervision: Bachelor of Science in professional arts (oriented to registered nurses), Bachelor of Science in health care administration, and Bachelor of Science in business administration. A three-week residency is required on the campus in North Windham, Maine. Master's in health care administration is offered in the same format, with a two-week residency requirement. (This Master's program is a candidate for accreditation.)

SAINT JOSEPH'S UNIVERSITY COLLEGE
5600 City Ave.
Philadelphia, PA 19131 USA
Randy H. Miller, Director of Admissions
Many fields
1851
B, M, Accredited
Residency
Non-profit, church
(215) 879–7300
$$$

Bachelor of Arts and Bachelor of Science, over 30 majors; Master's in business administration, chemistry, computer science, education, health administration, health education, public safety, criminal justice, gerontological services, American studies; all through evening study. Non-traditional students may also obtain Bachelor's degrees part time or full time in the day through the Continuing Education program. Up to 75 credits may be transferred from four-year colleges; 64 from two-year colleges; up to 60 credits from an R.N. program can be accepted toward the Bachelor's.

SAINT LEO COLLEGE
State Rd. 52
St. Leo, FL 33574 USA
Frank G. Krivo, Dean of Admissions
Psychology, business, public administration, criminology
1889
B, Accredited
Residency
Non-profit, church
(904) 588-8200
$$$

Bachelor's in psychology, business, public administration, or criminology available through weekend, evening, or summer programs. Weekend students attend classes every other weekend.

SAINT MARTIN'S COLLEGE AND SEMINARY
P. O. Box 12455
Milwaukee, WI 53212
Evelyn Pumphrey, Registrar
Business, divinity, ministry
B, M, D, Unaccredited
Residency or correspondence
Non-profit, church
(414) 264-2455
$$$

Bachelor's or Master's in business, Master of Divinity, and Doctor of Ministry offered residentially. Students unable to pursue regular classes may work through the Department of Extension Studies. Certificate programs are available in Black Theology, thanatolog y Christian education, and pastoral education.

SAINT MARY COLLEGE
4100 S. 4th St., Traffic Way
Leavenworth, KS 66048 USA
Teresa Redlingshafer, Director of Admissions
Various fields
1923
B, Accredited
Residency
Non-profit, church
(913) 682-5151
$$

Bachelor of Science in accounting, business administration, computer science, or public affairs may be earned through weekend or evening study. Also, a B.S.N. program is offered for nurses with R.N. degree. Saint Mary also offers B.S. degree programs on the Donnelly College campus in Kansas City, Kansas. This is an upper-level (junior-senior) program especially designed for community college graduates and transfer students in the Kansas City area. Saint Mary also offers classes and workshops for teachers, that apply toward certificate renewal, including computer classes through the state-approved Teacher Education Program in computer studies.

SAINT MARY'S COLLEGE (California)
Extended Education, P.O. Box 784 — B, Accredited
Moraga, CA 94575 USA — Residency
Dr. Robert Rosby, Dean of Extended Education — Non-profit, church
Management or health services administration — (415) 376-4411
1863 — $$$
The Bachelor's degree in management or health services administration based on a learning contract. All students complete a core curriculum, a fieldwork project and various other courses comprising an area requirement. To enter the program, applicants must have 60 units of previous academic credit and work experience in the degree area.

SAINT MARY'S COLLEGE (Minnesota)
2510 Park Ave. — M, Accredited
Minneapolis, MN 55404 USA — Residency
Dr. Marilyn R. Frost, Minneapolis Graduate Dean — Non-profit, church
Human development and education — (612) 874-9877
1912 — $$$
Master of Arts in human development or education, for persons living in one of the geographical areas in which Saint Mary's has regional advisors. These areas include a 150-mile radius around San Francisco, Minneapolis, St. Paul, and Winona. Under special provisions, some students are accepted from outside these areas. All students must spend some time on the graduate campus in Minnesota, but this can be as little as one weekend. Credit is given for completion of learning contracts negotiated between the student and the advisor. Most students complete the Master's in 18 to 24 months.

SAINT MARY-OF-THE-WOODS COLLEGE
Saint Mary-of-the-Woods, IN 47876 USA — B, M, Accredited
Ellen Cohen, Director of Non-Traditional Student Admissions — Short residency
Non-profit, church
Many fields — (812) 535–5151
1840 — $$
Baccalaureate majors offered are: accounting, business administration, English, history, humanities, journalism, management, marketing, paralegal studies, political science, psychology, religion, and social work. There is a special B.A. in womens studies. Credit is awarded for prior learning. Excellent student support services are provided. Students are guided by faculty via mail and phone in off-campus independent study. The M.A. in pastoral studies requires about 30 days on campus. The college admits men and women to its programs, but only women can earn degrees. Take *that*, Faith Evangelical Lutheran Seminary!

SAINT PETER'S COLLEGE
2614 Kennedy Blvd. — B, M, Accredited
Jersey City, NJ 07306 USA — Residency
Robert J. Nilan, Dean of Admissions — Non-profit, church
Many fields — (201) 333–4400
1872 — $$$
The degree programs are available through evening, weekend, and summer courses. Credit for life experience learning and equivalency exams. Courses also offered at a branch campus in Englewood Cliffs.

SAINT PROCOPIUS COLLEGE
see: Illinois Benedictine College

SAINT THOMAS UNIVERSITY — B, M, Accredited
16400 N.W. 32nd Ave. — Residency
Miami, FL 33054 USA — Non-profit, church
Kevin Shay, Director of Admissions — (305) 625–6000, ext. 119
1962 — $$$
Bachelor of Arts, Bachelor of Science, and Master's degrees may be earned through evening, weekend, and summer programs in the School of Continuing and Adult Education. Fields include accounting, business man-

See page 70 for explanation of abbreviations and symbols

agement, chemistry, sports administration, computer science, elementary education, finance, political science. Credit by examination, independent study, and non-academic prior learning. Program open to Florida residents only. Formerly called Biscayne College.

SAM HOUSTON STATE UNIVERSITY
Huntsville, TX 77431 USA
Dr. R. A. Reiner, Associate V.P. for Academic Services
Many fields
1879
B, M, D, Accredited
Residency
Non-profit, state
(409) 294–1111
$
Many subjects are offered through evening and weekend courses. Correspondence courses are available.

SAN FRANCISCO STATE UNIVERSITY
Extended Education, 1600 Holloway Ave.
San Francisco, CA 94132 USA
Peter Dewees, Dean, Continuing Education
Many fields
1899
M, Accredited
Residency
Non-profit, state
(415) 338–1373
$
Many courses leading to Bachelor's and Master's degrees are available through evening and weekend study. The Open University program offers access to 3,000 courses. Anyone may enroll, but only 24 units of work can be transferred into a regular degree program (6 units at the Master's level). The Over-60 program offers greatly reduced fees for people over 60, on a space available basis in each class.

SAN JOSE STATE UNIVERSITY
Washington Square
San Jose, CA 95192 USA
Edgar Chambers, AEVP Admissions/Records
Health care administration, community health education
1857
B, Accredited
Residency
Non-profit, state
(408) 924–1000
$
Bachelor of Science in health care administration and Bachelor of Arts in community health education. They are called "external" degrees but a fair amount of on-campus or near-campus work is required. Credit is earned through coursework (evenings, summers), examinations, directed independent study, and parallel instruction (doing all the work of a required class without attending the class meetings). There is no opportunity for self-paced accelerated work. Students must have 56 semester units earned elsewhere before admission, and the remaining units can take three to four years of part-time study to earn. (San Jose State has not responded to nine requests for information about their programs, since 1982, so this information comes from library research.)

SANGAMON STATE UNIVERSITY
Springfield, IL 62708 USA
Dr. Gerald Curl, Director of Admissions and Records
Many fields
1969
B, Accredited
Residency
Non-profit, state
(217) 786–6626
$$
The INO, or individual option program, is based partially on a University Without Walls model: a learning proposal is developed, a learning contract negotiated, and the student pursues the Bachelor's degree through selected off-campus study, internships, foreign study, independent study, or exchange with other institutions. Evening and weekend classes are offered. Credit for prior learning.

SARAH LAWRENCE COLLEGE
Bronxville, NY 10708 USA
Robin Mamlet, Director of Admissions
Liberal arts, fine arts
1926
B, M, Accredited
Residency
Non-profit, independent
(914) 793–4242
$$$$$
The Continuing Education for Women program offers the opportunity to earn the Bachelor and Master of Arts through part-time daytime study combined with independent study. Students take three seminar courses at a time with accompanying one-on-one conferences with faculty. In the individualized studies program, students present a specific plan of study appropriate to the faculty resources of the college, leading to

an M.A. degree.

SAYBROOK INSTITUTE
1550 Sutter St.
San Francisco, CA 94109 USA
Chester Gerhardt, Admissions/Records Officer
Psychology, human science
1970
M, D, Accredited
Short residency
Non-profit, independent
(415) 441–5034
$$$

Courses are offered in an independent study format: a course guide is provided, specifying the required readings and including written lecture materials prepared by the faculty. Students may design their own courses as well. Student work focuses within four areas of concentration: clinical inquiry, systems inquiry, health studies, and consciousness studies. All students must attend a five-day planning seminar in San Francisco, and two one-week national meetings each year. Degrees can take from two to four years to complete. Many well-known psychologists are associated with Saybrook (Rollo May, Stanley Krippner, Richard Farson, Nevitt Stanford, Clark Moustakas, etc.). Saybrook, until 1982, was called the Humanistic Psychology Institute.

SCHILLER INTERNATIONAL UNDERSITY
Friederich-Ebert-Anlage 4
Heidelberg, 6900 West Germany
Dr. Walter Leibrecht, President
1964
B, M, Accredited
Residency
Many fields
(0 62 21) 1 20 46

Schiller works on the the American system, through centers in Germany, France, England, and Spain. Degree-granting power used to be "under the authority of a charter granted by the state of Missouri" (in their corporate charter, they gave themselves the right to grant degrees). Now the Bachelor's degree is under authority of Delaware. Evening and summer programs are offered in various fields. Bachelor's degrees are offered in business administration, law and public administration, applied sciences, economics, European studies, foreign languages, international relations, and psychology. Master's degrees in business, hotel and tourism, international management, economics, international relations, language and literature.

SCHOOL FOR INTERNATIONAL TRAINING
Kipling Rd.
Brattleboro, VT 05301 USA
Dr. Ward Heneveld, Director
International studies and administration, English as a second language
1964
B, M, Accredited
Residency
Non-profit, independent
(800) 451–4465
$$$

Bachelor of International Studies, through either a World Issue Program or a World Studies Program, combining intensive on-campus study with an overseas internship of at least 27 weeks. Master of Arts in Teaching and Master's program in intercultural management concentrates on developing skills useful in international and intercultural professions. Both Master's may be completed in 12 to 16 months, and include an internship. Phone in Vermont is (802) 257–7751.

SEATTLE INTERNATIONAL UNIVERSITY
33919 9th Ave. South
Federal Way, WA 98003 USA
Carl A. Lindberg, Director of University Affairs
Business administration
1982
B, M, Unaccredited, state licensed, Residency
(206) 838–8431
$$

The Bachelor's and Master's in business administration are offered entirely through evening and weekend study. The M.B.A. does not require prior business experience. Core courses are required in international business and entrepreneurial studies. The university is not accredited, but is appropriately registered with the Washington State Council for Postsecondary Education.

SEATTLE UNIVERSITY
12th Ave. and E. Columbia
M, D, Accredited

Seattle, WA 98122 USA
Lee Gerig, Dean of Admissions
Many fields
1891

Residency
Non-profit, church
(206) 626–5720
$$$

Master of Arts in Education, Master of Education, Master of Business Administration, Master of Public Administration, Master of Software Engineering, Master of Transporation Engineering, Master of Religious Education, Master of Ministry, Master of Pastoral Ministry, Master of Existential Phenomenological Therapeutic Psychology, and Doctor of Education in educational leadership, all through evening study, with some weekend classes.

SHEPHERD COLLEGE
see: West Virginia Board of Regents B.A. Program

SHIMER COLLEGE ✪
438 N. Sheridan Rd., P.O. Box A500
Waukegan, IL 60079 USA
Bobbie Groth, Director of Admissions
General studies, humanities, natural sciences, social sciences
1853

B, Accredited
Non-resident
Non-profit, independent
(312) 623–8400
$$$

Shimer used to be affiliated with the University of Chicago, and still bases its curriculum on the foundation of the "Great Books of the Western World." Teaching is through the Socratic, or shared inquiry, method. Degrees may also be earned through a weekend program, meeting one weekend a month in Lake Bluff, Illinois.

SIENA HEIGHTS COLLEGE
1247 Siena Heights Dr.
Adrian, MI 49221 USA
Norman A. Bukwaz, Dean of External Programs
Health, business, general studies, trade and industrial areas
1919

B, Accredited
Residency
Non-profit, church
(517) 263–0731
$$$

The degree completion program offers the opportunity to earn the Bachelor's degree in many fields. Substantial credit is given for prior life experience. Up to 80% of the required 120 semester hours can be earned through the assessment (including courses taken elsewhere). New work is done through a combination of evening and weekend classes. The program is designed for individuals who already have at least two years of college.

SIERRA UNIVERSITY
1020 Pico Blvd.
Santa Monica, CA 90405 USA
Director of Admissions
Humanities, human sciences, and science
1975

B, M, D, Unaccredited, state approved, Short residency
Non-profit, independent
(213) 452–3993
$$

Students develop individualized degree programs with faculty, in many locations worldwide. Students may select a tutor, subject to university approval, in their geographic region. Student and tutor develop a study plan, specifying courses to be taken and other work to be done. Students meet weekly with their tutor, and monthly with a core faculty. Students attend a monthly seminar and a triannual colloquium. Bachelor's and Master's degrees can be earned in a minimum of one year. The Doctorate requires three years beyond the Bachelor's, at least two of them after enrolling at Sierra. The program emphasizes integration of theory and practice and offers academic credit for documented life experience. The university is approved by the state of California. Former name: University Without Walls.

SKIDMORE COLLEGE ✪
University Without Walls
Saratoga Springs, NY 12866 USA
Dr. Robert H. Van Meter, Director, University Without Walls

B, (M?), Accredited
Short residency
Non-profit, independent

More than 50 majors | (518) 584-5000
1911 | $$

Skidmore is one of the pioneers of the non-traditional movement, having offered a university without walls program since 1970. It is possible to earn their Bachelor of Arts or Bachelor of Science with a total of two days on campus: one for advising and planning, and the second to present a degree plan to a faculty committee. Skidmore makes it clear that they hold their graduates to "standards of knowledge, competence and intellectual attainment which are no less comprehensive and rigorous than those established by traditional...programs." After fulfilling requirements in the degree plan each student completes a final project—a project demonstrating competence in one's field. Students can major in any of the dozens of fields offered by Skidmore, or can devise their own majors. In 1990, a Master's program was rumored to be on the verge of happening.

SOMERSET UNIVERSITY
Ilminster, Somerset TA19 OBQ England
David J. Rogers, Director of Studies
Arts, sciences, business, law, music, theology
1982

B, M, D, Unaccredited, state registered, Non-resident
Proprietary
(0460) 57255
$$

Degrees at all levels are through correspondence study. Although Somerset has received much criticism from the British press, what they are doing is legal, since they registered with the Louisiana authorities (an automatic, non-evaluative process). Somerset's director of studies explains degree-granting authority this way: "The University authorises itself to award degree..." The Somerset catalogue (which is sold for $8) lists a number of officers and faculty with traditional British credentials and a duke as the chancellor. Graduate degrees are based on faculty-guided research leading to writing and presenting a thesis. Higher Doctorates (Doctor of Literature, Science, Laws or Divinity) are awarded entirely based on prior work. Louisiana address: 650 Poydras St., #2304, New Orleans, LA 70130, phone (504) 566-0141. See also:Harley Universit (see chapter 22), established by Somerset's founder, Dr. Raymond Young, an American.

SONOMA STATE UNIVERSITY
1801 E. Cotati Ave.
Rohnert Park, CA 94928 USA
Dr. Frank M. Tansey, Dean of Admissions
Psychology
1960

B, M, Accredited
Short residency
Non-profit, state
(707) 664–2778
$

The B.A. in psychology can be completed entirely through evening courses. There is a one-year external Master's degree in psychology. Although there is no requirement for taking any specific classes, students must attend occasional meetings with a faculty advisor. The program is designed jointly by student and faculty, and can include coursework, fieldwork, research, and independent study. Applicants must have a Bachelor's degree, one year of graduate-level experience in humanistic psychology, and 9 units of credit previously earned (in residence or by extension) from Sonoma State. A requirement of basic knowledge of psychology can be met through courses or by an examination. Credit for prior experience and evening courses. About 40 new applicants are admitted each fall.

SOUTHEAST ASIA INTERDISCIPLINARY DEVELOPMENT INSTITUTE
Taktak Dr.
Antipolo, Rizal Philippines
Msgr. Patricio R. Getigan, Ph.D., President
Organizational development & planning; instructional development & technology

M, D, Unaccredited
Residency
Non-profit, independent
695–4791
$$$

The M.A., M.A./Ph.D., and Ph.D. are offered by S.A.I.D.I. in organizational development and planning. Students work with a faculty committee to plan an independent study program, including Socratic and practicum conferences. The programs are offered using a modular system, offering an integrative and experiential approach to learning. Since the courses are self-paced, the student may take from 15 to 32 months to complete the modules.

SOUTHEASTERN INSTITUTE OF TECHNOLOGY
200 Sparkman Drive

B, M, D, Unaccredited, state approved
Residency

Huntsville, AL 35807
Applied science, engineering, management
Raymond C. Watson, Jr., President
1976
Non-profit, independent
$$

Residential courses for the MS., M.S. in engineering, M.S. in management, MBA, and Doctor of Engineering, Management, or Science. Bachelor's degrees are not offered separately, but may be combined with a Master's program. All faculty are professional practitioners. Students may complete their Doctorate away from Huntsville if they begin the program there, and then leave. The programs are licensed and approved by the State of Alabama.

SOUTHEASTERN MASSACHUSETTS UNIVERSITY
Old Westport Rd.
North Dartmouth, MA 02747 USA
Barrie G. Phelps, Director of Admissions
Many fields
1895
B, Accredited
Residency
Non-profit, state
(617) 999–8000
$$

Bachelor's degree in history, sociology, psychology, political science, Portuguese, humanities, management, accounting, and other fields. Up to 75% of the required number of units can be earned through an assessment of prior learning experience. The assessment is based on evaluation of a portfolio, which is prepared in a class given for that purpose. The assessment costs a flat fee of around $480, and is offered through the Division of Continuing Education.

SOUTHEASTERN UNIVERSITY
501 Eye St. SW
Washington, DC 20024 USA
William H. Sherrill, Dean, Admissions
Business, public administration, accounting, taxation
1879
M, Accredited
Residency
Non-profit, independent
(202) 488–8162
$$

On Saturdays and Sundays, Southeastern offers a Master of Business Administration, Master of Science in accounting or taxation, and Master of Business and Public Administration. Classes last all day, once a week, and the degree requires 36 credit hours for completion.

SOUTHERN CALIFORNIA UNIVERSITY FOR PROFESSIONAL STUDIES
3301 W. Lincoln Ave.
Anaheim, CA 92801 USA
Business management
(714) 952–9090
B, M, Unaccredited, state authorized, Non-resident
Non-profit, independent
$$

The degrees offered by correspondence study are the Bachelor of Business Management in either marketing or management, and the Master of Business Management. Courses are offered by mail, phone, and the use of audio- or videotape. Each course may be completed in 4 to 12 weeks. For the Master's, 50 units of work (10 courses) must be completed after enrolling. Credit is given for other college work, prior learning, and life experience assessment. Challenge exams may be taken in the various courses and if passed, credit is awarded.

SOUTHERN ILLINOIS UNIVERSITY
Carbondale, IL 62901 USA
B. Kirby Browning, Director of Admissions
Many fields
1869
M, Accredited
Residency
Non-profit, state
(618) 453–2121
$$

Master of Science in administration of justice, through coursework, independent study, and work projects. Master of Science in engineering biophysics through coursework plus a field internship. Master of Arts in rehabilitation administration, with five weeks of independent study for each week spent on campus. Weekend program in industrial technology. Programs offered at selected military bases.

SOUTHERN METHODIST UNIVERSITY
Dallas, TX 75275 USA
Dr. Robert Patterson, Director, Evening and Summer Studies
B, M, Accredited
Residency
Non-profit, church

Many fields
1911
(214) 692-2000
$$$$
Bachelor of Arts, Bachelor of Business Administration, Bachelor of Applied Sciences, and Master of Liberal Arts, all through evening study in the School of Continuing Education.

SOUTHERN OREGON STATE COLLEGE
1250 Siskiyou Blvd.
Ashland, OR 97520 USA
Larry Nollenberger, Director Program Advising
Many fields
1926
B, Accredited
Residency
Non-profit, state
(503) 482-3311
$$
"Special Academic Credit" (credit by examination, equivalency exam, prior learning experience, and correspondence credit) may be applied to degree programs. Fields include business, education, performing arts, nursing, social sciences, sciences, math, humanities. Up to 90 credits may be earned in this manner. Assessment based on a portfolio prepared by the student after taking a required course in this subject. Students must complete 45 credits at S.O.S.C., exclusive of prior learning credit.

SOUTHERN VERMONT COLLEGE
Monument Rd.
Bennington, VT 05201 USA
Kathryn True, Director of Admissions
Many fields
1926
B, Accredited
Residency
Non-profit, independent
(802) 442-5427
$$$
Bachelor's degree program for Licensed Practical Nurses offered through Evening Extension Program. Many courses through evening, weekend, and summer classes. Bachelor's degrees in accounting, business, English, environmental studies, communications, criminal justice, health services, human services, resort management, private security, and social work. Offers telecourses to fulfill some degree requirements. Independent studies and internships are an important element for degree programs. Students with special interests are encouraged to formulate their own degree programs with faculty or staff advisor.

SOUTHWEST STATE UNIVERSITY
Marshall, MN 56258 USA
Philip Coltart, Director of Admissions
Humanities, social science, education, business, science, technology
1963
B, Accredited
Residency
Non-profit, state
(507) 537-6286
$$
Bachelor's may be earned in these fields through evening classes.

SOUTHWEST UNIVERSITY ✪
4532 W. Napoleon Ave.
Metairie, LA 70001 USA
Reg Sheldrick, Ph.D., Administrator
Various fields
1982
B, M, D, Unaccredited, state registered, Non-resident
Proprietary
(504) 455-2900
$$
Southwest University was established in 1982 by its president, Dr. Grayce Lee, and Dr. Reg Sheldrick. (Sheldrick also established the school now called Newport University.) Southwest University maintains a curriculum development office in Omaha, Nebraska. Originally established in Phoenix, Arizona. Degrees at all levels in business administration, education, counseling and psychology, hospital and public administration, holistic health sciences, engineering, criminal justice, and entrepreneurship. Credit for experiential learning, and by correspondence courses, research projects, and a thesis or dissertation. Southwest is appropriately registered with the Board of Regents of Louisiana, which acknowledges schools but does not evaluate them.

SOUTHWESTERN ADVENTIST COLLEGE
Keene, TX 76059 USA
Dr. Marie Redwine, Director, Adult Degree Program
B, accredited
Short residency
Non-profit, church

See page 70 for explanation of abbreviations and symbols

Many fields (817) 645–3921
1893 $$$
B.A., B.S., and Bachelor of Business Administration through the Adult Degree Program (ADP). Virtually all work can be completed at a distance, following a two-week admission seminar, held each April, June, and October. The only residency requirement is a 3-day on-campus interim seminar once a year. Credit is earned by transfer of credit, proficiency exams, credit for prior learning, and independent study by mail and telephone. ADP students pay 80% of the tuition of on-campus students. Majors include behavioral science, business, communication, education, English, home economics, mathematics, office administration, physical education, religion, social science, social work, and Spanish. Toll-free number outside Texas: (800) 433–2240.

SPRING ARBOR COLLEGE
Continuing Studies, 106 Main St. B, Accredited
Spring Arbor, MI 49283 USA Residency
Darlene T. Mefford, Registrar Non-profit, church
Management of human resources (517) 750–1200, ext. 300
1873 $$$
Bachelor of Arts in management of human resources can be earned in 12 to 15 months through weekend, evening or summer programs if participant has Associate Arts degree, is employed full time, is 25 years old or older, and prepares a portfolio of life experiences for evaluation.

SRI LANKA INSTITUTE OF DISTANCE EDUCATION
P.O. Box 1537 B (equivalent), equivalent of
Maligawatte, Colombo, Sri Lanka accreditation, Short residency
Science, technology, management
Higher National Diplomas in mathematics, science, technology, and management through correspondence studies, with occasional face-to-face meetings at one of 12 national centers. Some fields require attending laboratory sessions. Instruction is given in English, Sinhala, and Tamil.

STATE UNIVERSITY COLLEGE
Cooper Center B, Accredited
Brockport, NY 14420 USA Short residency
Marsha R. Gottovi, Director of Admissions Non-profit, state
Science, natural science, liberal studies (716) 395–2211
1835 $$
Bachelor of Liberal Studies, with a minimum of three weeks on campus for an annual seminar. The degree is offered in science, natural science, and social science. Students may design their own concentrations or majors. Credit is given for prior learning experiences, both formal and informal, as well as for equivalency exams, independent study, and correspondence courses. The minimum time of enrollment is one academic year (nine months).

STATE UNIVERSITY OF NEW YORK (BUFFALO)
Millard Fillmore College, 3435 Main St. B, M, Accredited
Buffalo, NY 14214 USA Residency
Kevin Durkin, Director of Admissions Non-profit, state
Arts & sciences, management, nursing, engineering, architecture (716) 831–2202
1946 $$
More than 350 evening classes each semester, with credits applicable to various degree programs.

STATE UNIVERSITY OF NEW YORK (OLD WESTBURY)
College at Old Westbury, P.O. Box 210 B, Accredited
Old Westbury, NY 11568 USA Residency
Michael Sheehy, Director of Admissions Non-profit, state
Many fields (516) 876–3082
1967 $$
Bachelor of Arts, Bachelor of Science, and Bachelor of Professional Studies in which some units can be earned through a combination of assessment for prior experience and equivalency examinations.

STEPHENS COLLEGE ✪
College Without Walls, Campus Box 2083
Columbia, MO 65215 USA
LuAnna Andrews
Many fields
1833
B, Accredited
Short residency
Non-profit, independent
(314) 876-7125
$$$$

Bachelor of Arts through a program primarily of independent study. The only firm residential requirement is attendance at a liberal studies seminar.Seminars a year are given on the Stephens campus. The seminar requires eight days or two weekends on campus with a total of seven weeks of independent study before, between, and after the weekends. Forty three-unit courses are required for the degree. Ten must be completed with Stephens faculty after enrolling. Courses may be completed by guided independent study, or weekend courses at Stephens. A program called Learning Unlimited is for women over 23 who wish to earn the Bachelor of Arts, Bachelor of Science, or Bachelor of Fine Arts through on-campus weekend and residential classes.

STETSON UNIVERSITY
421 No. Blvd.
Deland, FL 32720 USA
Gary A. Meadows, Dean of Admissions
Many fields
1883
B, Accredited
Residency
Non-profit, church
(904) 734-4121
$$$

Bachelor of Arts and Bachelor of Science in many fields through evening study. Bachelor of Science in medical technology in conjunction with area hospitals. Credit for equivalency examinations.

SUFFOLK UNIVERSITY
Beacon Hill
Boston, MA 02114 USA
William F. Coughlin, Director of Admissions
Many fields
1906
B, M, Accredited
Residency
Non-profit, independent
(617) 723-4700
$$$

Bachelor of Arts, Bachelor of Science, Master of Business Administration, and Master of Public Administration, all available entirely through evening study. Cooperative program, where students work in jobs related to their majors and can graduate in four-and-a-half years (with summer sessions).

SUMMIT UNIVERSITY
5703 Read Blvd., Suite G
New Orleans, LA 70127
Mel Suhd, Administrative Director
Many fields
1988
B, M, D, Unaccredited, State registered
Non-resident
Non-profit, independent
(504) 241-0227
$$

Each learner (student) creates a learning portfolio. He or she works with an RF/AAC (Resource Faculty/Administrative Academic Counselor) to develop a study plan. Credit is earned through writing course essays/documents, and completion of a major study which adds to human knowledge. After one has paid tuition for three years (two at the Master's level), no further tuition is required. The 11-page Bulletin states that Summit University has "more educational leaders with longer tenure in alternative education than any university in the United States." (None is listed in the Bulletin, however.) No connection with the Summit University that has operated from California and Idaho, nor the seminary of that name in Indiana.

SUSAN B. ANTHONY UNIVERSITY
6890 St-Denis St.
Montreal, Quebec H2S 2S2 Canada
President
Education, environmental studies, naturopathy, and "peace and freedom"
mid-1970s
B, M, D, Unaccredited
Non-resident
Non-profit, independent
No listed telephone
$

See page 70 for explanation of abbreviations and symbols

Established in the mid-1970s by Dr. Albert Schatz, discoverer of the antibiotic, streptomycin, who was president and is now a member of the board of directors. The catalogue also mentions a College of Naturopathy in Montreal, Canada, but there is no listed telephone there. The letterhead states that the university is "chartered by the state of Missouri" which presumably refers to having incorporated there, since Missouri's Department of Education does not charter schools. The address in Canada is that of Dr. Jean-Marc Brunet, former president of the university.

SWINBURNE COLLEGE OF TECHNOLOGY
P.O. Box 218, John St.
Hawthorn, Victoria 3122 Australia
Ian McCormick
Engineering, applied science, graphic arts
1908

B, Equivalent of accreditation
Residency
Non-profit, independent
(03) 819 011
$$$$

Swinburne is a major Australian institution following the cooperative plan of education, in which students alternate periods of up to six months of work in industry with taking classes. Evening courses available.

SYRACUSE UNIVERSITY ✪
Robert Colley, Director
Independent Study Degree Programs
Many fields
1870

B, M, Accredited
Short residency
Non-profit, independent
(315) 423–3284
$$$$

B.A. in liberal studies, B.S. in business administration or food systems management, M.B.A., Master of Fine Arts (illustration or advertising design), and Master of Social Science, all with short residency on campus, and independent study in between. Social Science requires two 14-day sessions on campus, each in July (but not necessarily two consecutive sessions). It is also offered in London. The M.B.A. requires three seven-day sessions a year for an average of two-a-half years. The M.F.A., which has been taught by many of New York advertising's best-known art directors (Lubalin, Scali, Gargano, etc.), requires three two-week sessions on campus and several shorter sessions in New York City and other metropolitan areas. The Bachelor's degrees also require three seven-day sessions a year on campus. The minimum time for the Bachelor's is one year (30 credits) for people with substantial transfer credit, but in practice, most people take quite a bit longer.

TARKIO COLLEGE
Tarkio, MO 64491 USA
Richard Phillips, Director of Admissions
Business, management
1883

B, Accredited
Residency
Non-profit, church
(816) 736–4131
$$$

Bachelor of Science in business administration, management, and related fields, requiring evening classes that meet once a week for eight weeks. Evening and weekend classes throughout Missouri; centers in St. Louis, Jefferson City, and Kansas City. Life experience credit is possible.

TECHNION INSTITUTE
Faculty of Industry and Management
The Technion
Kiryat Hatechnion, Haifa 32000, Israel
Director of Industrial Management

M, Equivalent of accreditation
Short residency
Non-profit, state

Master of Science in industrial management requiring one day a week on the campus in Haifa.

TENNESSEE WESLEYAN COLLEGE
College St.
Athens, TN 37303 USA
James G. Harrison, Director of Admissions
Applied science in business management and accounting
1857

B, Accredited
Residency
Non-profit, church
(615) 745–7504
$$

The Bachelor of Applied Science program is designed to meet the needs of adult learners who have two years of business-related college studies. Evening classes are held in Knoxville, Chattanooga, Cleveland,

and Harriman, Tennessee.

TEXAS CHRISTIAN UNIVERSITY
Office of Extended Education, P.O. Box 32927 — B, Accredited
Fort Worth, TX 76129 USA — Residency
Edward G. Boehm, Director, Extended Education — Non-profit, church
General studies — (817) 921-7130
1873 — $$$

Bachelor of General Studies program, available entirely through evening study. At least 30 of the required 124 semester hours must be earned at T.C.U. Credit is given for prior academic work, and for equivalency exams, including a series of exams developed at the university. Some courses are offered on a closed-circuit television network connecting 10 colleges and universities around the state.

TEXAS TECH UNIVERSITY
Lubbock, TX 79409 USA — D, Accredited
Dr. Gene W. Medley, Director of Admissions — Residency
Education — Non-profit, state
1923 — (806) 742-2011
$

Texas Tech offers its Doctor of Education in higher education with the possibility of much shorter residency than most traditional Doctoral programs. It is necessary to earn 24 semester hours of credit in continuous enrollment during a given 12-month period. The shortest possible time frame, then, is about seven months: one semester plus one summer session. However, additional credit would have to be earned at other times, such as other summers, either in Lubbock or in external courses Tech offers in El Paso, Abilene, and other west Texas cities.

THOMAS A. EDISON STATE COLLEGE✪
101 W. State St. — B, Accredited
Trenton, NJ 08625 USA — Non-resident
Jack Phillips, Registrar — Non-profit, state/local
Many fields — (609) 984-1100
1972 — $

B.S. in business administration, applied science and technology, human services, or nursing; B.A. in any of 26 subjects, entirely by non-resident study. (Nursing degrees only for New Jersey residents.) Credit through portfolio assessment (handbook available); Edison's own exams in dozens of subjects; guided study (correspondence courses using texts and videocassettes); courses by computer (many available through Electronic University, listed separately this chapter); equivalency exams (over 400 available); military, business, and industry courses and training programs; television courses (on PBS: "The Story of English," "Cosmos," etc.); credit for licenses and certificates (C.P.A.: up to 33 credits, pilot's license: 6 or more, etc.); and transfer credit from accredited colleges. Counseling centers in various New Jersey cities (but not necessary to visit them). Foreign students are welcome with certain restrictions. There is, of course, no connection at all with a diploma mill of the same name that has operated in Florida and Arkansas.

THOMAS JEFFERSON UNIVERSITY
11th and Walnut Streets — B, M, Accredited
Philadelphia, PA 19107 USA — Residency
Susan Christian, Associate Director of Admissions — Non-profit, independent
Scientific fields, nursing — (215) 928-8850
1824 — $$$$

The College of Allied Health Sciences offers B.S. degrees in cytotechnology, dental hygiene, diagnostic imaging, medical technology, nursing, occupational therapy, and physical therapy, through evening classes. Applicants must have two years of prior college experience. The College of Graduate Studies offers the M.S. in clinical microbiology through a combination of evening classes, seminars, and a clerkship for persons with prior laboratory experience.

TOWSON STATE UNIVERSITY
College of Continuing Studies — B, Accredited

Towson, MD 21204 USA
William J. Reuling, Registrar
Many fields
1866
Residency
Non-profit, state
(301) 321–2031
$$

Bachelor of Arts and Bachelor of Science in many fields, including nursing, occupational therapy, medical technology, accounting, education, liberal arts and sciences, computer science, and business can be completed through evening study. Also weekend and summer courses. Credit for independent study, non-academic prior learning, and by examination.

TRINITY COLLEGE
PACE, 208 Colchester Ave.
Burlington, VT 05401 USA
Verna Gordon, Director of Admissions
1925
B, Accredited
Residency
Non-profit, church
(802) 658–0337, ext. 218
$$$

Trinity College offers men and women three different programs as a means to begin or resume their education at the college level. The PACE program, with a Monday through Friday schedule, offers 28 majors for a B.S./B.A. degree. Weekend College has classes every other Saturday and/or Sunday for eight weekends a semester, with five majors. Evening Degree, meeting two evenings a week for six eight-week terms, offers a Bachelor's in business administration. A minimum of 30 credits at Trinity College is required for the B.A./B.S. Applicants are eligible for advanced placement through transfer credit and credit for life/work experience or approved credits resulting from professional or military training.

TROY STATE UNIVERSITY✪
P.O.Drawer 4419
Montgomery, AL 36195 USA
Fred Stewart, Director, External Degree Program
Professional studies
1887
B, Accredited
Non-resident
Non-profit, state
(205) 834–1400
$$

Bachelor of Arts or Science in professional studies, which can be earned entirely through correspondence courses, learning contract study with Troy State, Troy State television courses (broadcast on public television on weekends), and/or credit for life and work experience. A senior project is required. Majors are available in business, criminal justice, English, history, political science, psychology, or sociology. Persons living within 200 miles of Montgomery must attend an orientation session on the campus. For those living farther away, this can be done by mail. Troy State also offers complete degree programs (Bachelor's and Master's) provided at in- and out-of-state centers, mostly military bases in Alabama, Florida, Georgia, and Europe. Minimum residency is 36 quarter hours for the Bachelor's and 35 for the Master's.

TUSCULUM COLLEGE
P.O.Box 5049
Greeneville, TN 37743 USA
Ron W. Porter, Director of Enrollment Management
Many fields
1794
B, Accredited
Residency
Non-profit, church
(615) 638–1111
$$$

Some degree programs are offered through evening classes, and at off-site locations in Memphis, Knoxville, and Chattanooga.

UNION GRADUATE SCHOOL
see: Union Institute

UNION INSTITUTE✪
440 E. McMillan St.
Cincinnati, OH 45206 USA
Dr. Jennifer King Cooper, Admissions Coordinator
Many fields
1964
B, D, Accredited
Short residency
Non-profit, independent
(513) 861-6400 or (800) 543-0366
$$$$

Established by the Union for Experimenting Colleges and Universities, a consortium including some large state universities, to be, in effect, their alternative program. The undergraduate "University Without Walls" Bachelor's degree may involve independent study, directed reading, internships, on-the-job education, classroom instruction, tutorials, etc. Credit for prior learning experiences. The required residency involves a weekend colloquium (held in various locations) and occasional seminars. At least nine months are required to earn the degree. The Ph.D. begins with a 10-day "entry colloquium" held in various locations. The Doctoral learner develops a committee of at least five, including two peers. The committee establishes a learning agreement, including an internship. All students must attend at least three five-day seminars at least six months apart, and another ten days in meetings of three or more learners. Thus a minimum of 35 days of residency is required for the Ph.D. A typical program will take two to four years. In 1990, Union moved into its own splendid old building. Former name: Union Graduate School and Union for Experimenting Colleges and Universities.

UNITED NATIONS UNIVERSITY

Toho Seimi Bldg., 15–1 Shibuya 2–Chome,
Shibuya-ku, Tokyo 150 Japan
Professor Heitor Gurgulino de Souza
1975

No degrees
Non-profit, independent
(03) 499–2811
$

Based on an idea of U Thant, as a worldwide network of advanced research and training institutions devoted to "pressing problems of human survival, development and welfare." U.N.U. has considered granting degrees of its own, but has not yet done so. Fields of special interest are human and social development, management of natural resources, and world hunger.The Japanese government pledged $100 million of the $500 million endowment goal. Other large contributions have come from Venezuela, Finland, the United Kingdom, the Federal Republic of Germany, and Ghana, with smaller amounts from many other nations. (The United States' contribution to this noble idea is, to date, $0. The Senate has twice voted down the proposal to contribute.)

UNITED STATES SPORTS ACADEMY

1 Academy Ave.
Daphne, AL 36526 USA
Paul M. McGough, Assistant Deal of Admissions
Sports management, sports medicine, coaching
1973

M, Accredited
Residency
Non-profit, independent
(205) 626–3303

The Master's degree is offered in a program that involves two summers on the campus in Alabama, and a year of home study under the supervision of a faculty mentor. About two-thirds of the faculty and staff work outside the United States, where many of them consult with foreign governments on sports matters.

UNIVERSIDAD ESTATAL A DISTANCIA

Calle 23 B 25, Av. 108
San Jose, Costa Rica
Celedonio Ramirez
Education, business, agriculture, social service, health services, administration
1977

B, M, Equivalent of accredited
Non-resident
Non-profit, state
25–8788

Costa Rica's state university for distance learning offers correspondence study consisting of written units, slides, audio- and videocassettes, leading to the Bachelor's in education and other fields after about two years of study. Evening and weekend study is offered on campus.

UNIVERSIDAD IBEROAMERICANO

Av. Cerro de las Torres No. 395,
Mexico 21, D.F., 04200 Mexico
Ernest Dominguez Quiroga, Rector
Sociology
1943

B, Equivalent of accredited
Residency
549–3500

The Bachelor's degree in sociology is based largely on individual study with study guides, required weekly group sessions on the university campus, and individualized tutorials with the faculty as requested by the student. The time involved is at least five years.

See page 70 for explanation of abbreviations and symbols

UNIVERSIDAD MEXICANA DEL NORESTE
5a Zona No. 409, Apartado Postal No. 2191 J,
Col. Caracol, Monterrey, N.L., Mexico
Banking, finance, leisure time management
1974
B, Equivalent of accredited
Non-resident
40–12–05

This open university program offers the Bachelor's degree in banking and finance, and in management of leisure time. Studies are based on learning guides and audiocassettes. About four years are required to complete the degree.

UNIVERSIDAD NACIONAL ABIERTA
Avenida Gambria 18, San Bernardino
Caracas, 101 Venezuela
Many fields
1975
B, Equivalent of accredited
Non-resident
Non-profit, state

Venezuela's open university offers the Bachelor's degree in social sciences, management, land and sea sciences, engineering, mathematics, and physics. Students work at their own pace through teaching modules consisting of printed and audio-visual materials. Some courses are offered on radio or television. Laboratory work, where required, may be done at the university or at other institutions.

UNIVERSIDAD AUTONOMA NACIONAL DE MEXICO
Circuito Exterior de la Ciudad Universitaria,
Mexico, D.F. 04510 Mexico
Jorge Carpizo McGregor, Rector
Many fields
B, Graduate, Equivalent of accredited, Non-resident
Non-profit, state
550–52–15
Very inexpensive

Mexico's national open university has prepared substantial course texts, each created by a team including academics, audio-visual specialists, and a graphic designer. A text consists of a work guide, written material, boxes of laboratory or field experiments, self-evaluation materials, and perhaps movies, tapes, and other audio-visual aids. An examination at the university must be taken after completing each course. There are courses offered in dental surgery, poultry breeding (graduate program), English literature, Hispanic literature, history, economics, philosophy, sociology, education, law, business administration, psychology, nursing, international relations, mass media, and accounting.

UNIVERSIDAD NACIONAL DE EDUCACION A DISTANCIA
Ciudad Universitaria
Madrid, 28040 Spain
Elisa Pérez Vera, Rector
Many fields
1972
B, Equivalent of accredited
Short residency
Non-profit, state
(91) 449–3600

The national open university of Spain offers degrees in a wide range of academic subjects. Each group of 150 students has a professor-tutor responsible for guidance and personal contact. More than 40 centers around the country (including 11 within large business, government, and military offices) are available for seminars, conferences, and lectures. Most work is done at a distance by use of written and audio-visual materials.

UNIVERSIDAD NACIONAL DE EDUCACION "ENRIQUE GUZMAN Y VALLE"
La Cantuta
Chosica, Peru
Literature, science, geography, mathematics and industrial technology
1905
B, Professional, Equivalent of accredited, Non-resident or short residency
Non-profit, state
91–00–52
$

Peru's open university pilot project is for working teachers, and offers them correspondence and short residency study. Most work is done at a distance by use of written materials.

UNIVERSITA LIBERA E PRIVATA
see: Freie und Private Universität

UNIVERSITE DE PARIS VII—VINCENNES
Route de la Tourelle
Paris, CEDEX 12, 75571 France
Many fields
B, M, D, Equivalent of accredited, Residency
Non-profit, state

The Vincennes campus of the University of Paris is known as the "university of second chance." The more than 30,000 students come from over 100 countries. Degrees in languages, linguistics, the social sciences, fine arts, theater, and cinematography through evening study, small group study, and student-directed study.

UNIVERSITE LIBRE ET PRIVEE
see: Freie und Private Universität

UNIVERSITI SAINS MALAYSIA
Minden
Penang, Malaysia
Many fields
B , Equivalent of accredited
Residency
Non-profit, state
(04) 883–822

For the first four years of this five-year program, students study by correspondence and independent study, using printed materials, tapes, and slides mailed to them. They must come to the campus once a year for a seminar of a few weeks. The fifth year is done entirely in residence.

UNIVERSITY ASSOCIATES GRADUATE SCHOOL
8517 Production Ave.
San Diego, CA 92121 USA
J. W. Pfeiffer, President
Human resource development
1979
M, Unaccredited, state approved, Residency
Proprietary
(619) 578–5900

The Master's program is intended for people already working in human resource development. It is a self-paced program permitting them to earn the degree while remaining fully employed.

UNIVERSITY CENTER AT HARRISBURG
2986 N. 2nd St.
Harrisburg, PA 17110 USA
A. Jane Collier, Financial Officer
Many fields
1958
B, M, Accredited
Residency
Non-profit, independent
(717) 238–9694
Varies

An educational consortium involving several Pennsylvania institutions Shippensburg University of Pennsylvania, Lebanon Valley College, and Elizabethtown College) to offer various degree programs, primarily through evening and weekend study.

UNIVERSITY DE LA ROMANDE
c/o Neil Gibson and Co., P.O. Box 3
Sudbury, Suffolk, CO10 6DW England
Many fields
B, M, D, Unaccredited
Non-resident
Proprietary
(0787) 278478
$$

Pay attention, this is complex. U.D.L.R. was established in Sudbury, England, by Neil Gibson & Company. The spokesman for Neil Gibson was John Courage. Then a book was published on non-traditional degrees, by William Ebbs, which called U.D.L.R. the best non-traditional school in the world. John Courage and William Ebbs do not exist but are, in fact, the same person, Raymond Seldis of Neil Gibson and Company. Early advertising identified U.D.L.R. as a private and fully accredited Swiss university. The accrediting agency turned out to be non-existent. Now the university advertises from a post office box on the Isle of Man, and clearly states that it is not accredited. But the mail goes to Sudbury, as it always has. This is all quite legal under British law. Degrees are earned by writing a thesis, which can be quite short. (Seldis has apparently left, and UDLR is in new hands. Neil Gibson and Company also used to sell degrees that even they admitted were fake from the University del Puerto Monico, Panama.)

UNIVERSITY FOR HUMANISTIC STUDIES
2002 Jimmy Durante Blvd.
B, M, D, Unaccredited, state

Del Mar, CA 92014 USA
Alison Brown, Director of Admissions
Many fields
1977

approved, Short residency
Proprietary
(619) 296–7204
$$

Degrees in psychology, including marriage, family, and child counseling and transpersonal studies; clinical health education; clinical nutrition; body therapy; body psychology; specialized studies (individualized studies); and corporate fitness administration. Coursework is primarily classroom based, evening and weekend. Options for out-of-town students include tutorial study and directed independent study. Dissertation required of all Doctoral students. Written comprehensive examination required of all Master's students. Some programs require an oral exam as well. Master's degrees take at least 12 to 15 months to complete; Doctoral degrees take at least two-and-a-half to three years to complete. Bachelor's degrees take 9 to 12 months for every 45 quarter units of study needed (180 units needed to graduate). Up to 70 units of documented life/work experience may be applied toward undergraduate admission. No life/work experience is accepted at the graduate level. Inka dinka doo.

UNIVERSITY OF ALABAMA, NEW COLLEGE ✪

External Degree Program, P.O. Drawer ED
University, AL 35487 USA
Dr. Harriet Cabell, Director, External Degrees
Many fields
1831

B, M, Accredited
Short residency
Non-profit, state
(205) 348–6010
$$

The degrees of Bachelor of Arts or Bachelor of Science may be earned entirely through non-resident independent study with the exception of a two-day degree planning seminar on the campus at the start of the program. At least 32 semester hours of work must be completed after enrolling at the University. This can be by out-of-class contract learning, correspondence courses, television courses, Weekend College, prior learning evaluation, or on-campus courses at the university. Degrees offered in human services, humanities, social sciences, natural sciences, applied sciences, administrative sciences, and communication. A 12-semester-hour senior project is required of all students. Academic advising and planning can be done by telephone. There often seem to be waiting lists to get into this program. There is a Master's in Criminal Justice, requiring two weeks on campus, offered through the College of Continuing Studies, Box 2967, Tuscaloosa, AL 35486.

UNIVERSITY OF AMERICA

One Canal Place, Suite 2300
New Orleans, LA 70130 USA
James W. Benton, President
Many fields
1987

B, M, D, Unaccredited, state registered, Non-resident
Proprietary
(504) 521–8658
$$

Degrees in almost any field can be earned through independent study. Students without Bachelor's or Master's but with sufficient career experience may enroll in Doctoral programs. Students with sufficient work experience may be awarded the degrees upon completion of an acceptable essay and a "strategic outline for their future career goals and projected advances." While the registered address is in New Orleans, the President lives in Arkansas. Like many other schools, the University misrepresents the findings of a study on the acceptability of non-traditional degrees (see page 17). Same management as the Theological University of America. President Benton, who lives in Arkansas, chooses not to reveal the source of his own doctorate. Accreditation has been claimed from the American Education Association for the Accreditation of Schools, Colleges and Universities, an organization with which I am not familiar. Has used addresses in Arizona, California, and Hawaii.

UNIVERSITY OF ARIZONA

Tucson, AZ 85721 USA
Dr. Jerome Lucido, Director of Admissions
Many fields
1885

B, M, Accredited
Residency
Non-profit, state
(602) 626–2751
$$

Evening programs leading to the B.A. in general studies, M.B.A., M.Ed. in reading or bilingual/bicultural education, Ph.D. in higher education or educational foundations. There is a public administration program primarily for police officers. Several programs are offered in Sierra Vista/Ft. Huachuca including an M.S.

in electrical engineering via microwave link and a B.S. in Nursing. Correspondence and independent study programs can be part of some degree programs.

UNIVERSITY OF ARKANSAS
Fayetteville, AR 72701 USA
Larry F. Matthews
Management, international relations
1871
B, M, Accredited
Residency
Non-profit, state
(501) 575-5346
$$

Programs are offered to military and civilian personnel at various military bases in Europe. The degrees include a Master of Arts in international relations and a Master of Science in management. The work has been offered at bases in England, Germany, Italy, Spain, and Turkey.

UNIVERSITY OF BALTIMORE
Charles at Mount Royal
Baltimore, MD 21201 USA
Clare MacDonald, Director of Admissions
Many fields
1925
B, M, Unaccredited
Residency
Non-profit, state
(301) 625-3348
$$

Bachelor's, Master's, M.B.A., and J.D. may be earned through evening and summer programs. Fields of study include computer science, criminal justice, corporate communication, law, political science, and others. There is an accelerated Bachelor's/Master's program in which some courses can be applied to the requirements for both degrees simultaneously.

UNIVERSITY OF BRIDGEPORT
Bridgeport, CT 06601 USA
Kenneth Best,
Director of Public Information
1927
B, M, Accredited
Residency
Non-profit, independent
(203) 576-4000
$$$$

Bachelor of Arts, Bachelor of Science, Master of Arts, and Master of Science in education, engineering, and nursing, all through evening study.

UNIVERSITY OF CALIFORNIA, BERKELEY
M.B.A. Evening Program, 333 Golden Gate Ave.
San Francisco, CA 94102 USA
Mac Jordan, Chair, Business, UC Extension
Business administration
1868
M, Accredited
Residency
Non-profit, state
(415) 0292
$$

Master of Business Administration, through the Graduate School of Business, available entirely through evening courses taught from six to nine in San Francisco.

UNIVERSITY OF CALIFORNIA, DAVIS
Davis, CA 95616 USA
Dr. Gary Tudor, Director of Admissions
Various
1905
B, M, Accredited
Residency
Non-profit, state
(916) 752-1011
$$

The Academic Re-entry Program provides preadmission advising for older students who are re-entering an academic program after work and life experience. Admission by special action may be possible for persons who do not meet the formal admission requirements if they present evidence of academic potential (test scores, recent coursework, "late bloomers," etc.). Part-time status may be elected by persons who are employed, retired, have family responsibilities, or health problems.

UNIVERSITY OF CALIFORNIA, IRVINE
Campus Dr.
Irvine, CA 92717 USA
James E. Dunning, Director of Admissions
Various fields
B, M, Accredited
Residency
Non-profit, state
(714) 856-5414

1965 $$

Master of Science in educational administration and Master of Arts in social ecology and in teaching of Spanish available through evening study. There is a combined Bachelor's/Master's in business administration, in which both degrees can be completed in five years.

UNIVERSITY OF CALIFORNIA, LOS ANGELES
3371 GSM — M, Accredited
Los Angeles, CA 90024 USA — Residency
Thomas E. Lifka, Registrar — (213) 825–4316
Business administration, engineering — $$
1919

Master of Business Administration for fully employed persons with a minimum of five to eight years of work experience (two evenings per week for three to four years) and executive M.B.A. for mid-career managers with eight to ten years of experience, five of which must be as managers (alternating Fridays and Saturdays for two years), through the Graduate School of Management. Master of Engineering involves one afternoon and one evening a week, for employed engineers with at least five years' experience, through the Engineering Executive Program.

UNIVERSITY OF CALIFORNIA, SANTA BARBARA — B, M, Accredited
Santa Barbara, CA 93106 USA — Residency
Dr. Charles W. McKinney, — Non-profit, state
Dean of Admissions — (805) 961–2311
1944 — $$

Bachelor of Arts in law and society, through evening study in the College of Letters and Science; Master of Science in electrical engineering for advanced students requiring technical upgrading, and for U.S. Navy employees at Point Mugu.

UNIVERSITY OF CHICAGO
5801 Ellis Ave. — M, Accredited
Chicago, IL 60637 USA — Residency
Maxine Sullivan, Registrar — Non-profit, independent
Business administration — (312) 753–1234
1891 — $$$$$

The Master of Business Administration is offered in two non-traditional modes: entirely through evening study at a downtown Chicago location; and in an Executive Program requiring one day on campus every week for two years, plus a five-day residential seminar.

UNIVERSITY OF CINCINNATI — B, Accredited
Cincinnati, OH 45221 USA — Residency
Robert W. Neel, Director of Admissions — Non-profit, state
Many fields — (513) 475–8000
1819 — $$

Bachelor's degrees in natural science, social science, engineering, humanities, arts, and business administration, which may be earned entirely through evening study. There is an extensive cooperative education program, a Weekend University, and an innovative Learning at Large program.

UNIVERSITY OF CONNECTICUT — B, Accredited
Stamford, CT 06903 USA — Residency
Ann G. Quinley, Director of Admissions — Non-profit, state
Many fields — (203) 322–3466
1881 — $$

Bachelor of Arts and Bachelor of General Studies through evening study. Credit for independent study and by examination.

UNIVERSITY OF DELAWARE
Clayton Hall — B, M, Accredited

Newark, DE 19716 USA — Residency
Dr. N. Bruce Walker, Dean of Admissions — Non-profit, state
Many fields — (302) 451-8123
1883 — $$

Bachelor of Arts or Bachelor of Science in chemistry, computer and information services, criminal justice, engineering technology and technical management, English, history, and psychology; M.B.A.; and M.Ed. all available through evening study.

UNIVERSITY OF DELHI
School of Correspondence Courses, 5 Cavalry Lines — B, M, Accredited
Delhi, 110007 India — Non-resident
Ruddar Datt, Principal — Non-profit, state
Many fields — 251-7645
1962 — $

Bachelor of Arts, Bachelor of Commerce, and Master of Arts in Hindi, political science, history, and Sanskrit; and Master of Commerce available through correspondence study. All courses are available through correspondence, and some radio courses, for people anywhere in the world. Examinations must be taken in India (six locations), or at foreign centers in Kabul (Afghanistan), Tehran (Iran), Beijing, Moscow, Bonn, London, Jakarta (Indonesia), Sydney, Hong Kong, and Tokyo.

UNIVERSITY OF DENVER
New College, 2300 S. York St., — B, M, Accredited
Denver, CO 80208 USA — Residency
Dr. Roger Campbell, Dean of Admissions — Non-profit, independent
Many fields — (303) 871-1200
1864 — $$$$

Bachelor of General Studies in data processing, communications, or liberal arts; Master of Special Studies; Master of Liberal Arts through weekend and evening classes. There is a special Bachelor's in business, for women, given by the Weekend College, which meets every other weekend.

UNIVERSITY OF DETROIT
4001 McNichols Rd. — B, M, Accredited
Detroit, MI 48221 — Residency
Robert A. Mitchell, S.J., President — Non-profit, independent
Many fields — (313) 927-1000
1877 — $$$

Evening classes leading to a wide variety of Bachelor's and Master's degrees. The Bachelor of Business Administration is offered in accounting, economics, finance, management, marketing, and personnel. There is an evening M.B.A. as well. The College of Liberal Arts offers evening programs leading to the Bachelor and Master of Arts degrees in a wide variety of fields. The College of Engineering and Science offers the Bachelor of Science in engineering, the Master of Computer Science, Master of Engineering Management, and Master of Engineering through evening study. The School of Education and Human Services offers late afternoon and evening programs leading to the Bachelor of Arts in criminal justice and Bachelor of Science in nursing and human resource development; certification programs in elementary and secondary education; and Master's in criminal justice, education, health services administration, and health care education.

UNIVERSITY OF EAST ASIA
G.P.O.Box 3001 — B, M, Accredited
Macau — Non-resident
T. L. Tomáz, Principal, College for Lifelong Education — Private
Many fields — 27322
1981 — $$

The College for Lifelong Education offers non-residential external degree programs in the English language. In addition to printed materials, there is use of audio- and videotapes. There is an English language home study program in Chinese law. Programs have been designed with the cooperation of Britain's Open University and Massey University in New Zealand. This is the only university in Macau. Its local name is

See page 70 for explanation of abbreviations and symbols

Universidade da Asia Oriental.

UNIVERSITY OF GEORGIA
Athens, GA 30602 USA
Dr. Claire Swann, Director of Admissions
Business administration, early childhood education, public administration
1785
B, M, Accredited
Residency
Non-profit, state
(404) 542–2112
$$
Bachelor's degree program offered largely in the evening with independent study available limited to equivalent of one academic year. The M.B.A. and Master's degrees in early childhood education and public administration are also available through evening study.

UNIVERSITY OF GUAM
U.O.G. Station
Mangilao, Guam 96923
Kathleen R. Owings, Director of Admissions
Many fields
1952
B, M, Accredited
Residency
Non-profit, state
734–2177
$
Bachelor's degree may be earned through evening and summer programs. Many majors in the colleges of arts and science, education, agriculture and life sciences, and business and public administration.

UNIVERSITY OF HAWAII—MANOA
2444 Dole St.
Honolulu, HI 96822 USA
Donald R. Fukuda, Director of Admissions
Many fields
1907
B, M, Accredited
Residency
Non-profit, state
(808) 948–8111
$$
Bachelor of Arts in history, mathematics, sociology; Bachelor of Business Administration; Master of Arts in educational administration, all through evening study in the College of Continuing Education. Some classes are given at Hickham Air Force Base.

UNIVERSITY OF HAWAII—WEST OAHU
96-043 Ala Ike
Pearl City, HI 96782
Stella L. T. Asahara, Student Services Coordinator
Humanities, social science, professional studies
1976
B, Accredited
Residency
Non-profit, state
(808) 456-5921
$
Bachelor's degree programs in humanities (English, history or philosophy), social sciences (including political science and economics), or professional studies (business or public administration) are available through daytime and/or evening classes. All degrees can be earned entirely through evening study. Instead of a major in one of these areas, students may pursue study related to a major *theme*, such as American studies, Asian studies, justice administration, etc. Courses are also offered on weekends, and at three off-campus locations.

UNIVERSITY OF IDAHO
Video Outreach Program, Janssen Engineering Building
Moscow, ID 83843
Matt E. Telin, Director of Admissions
Engineering, computer science, psychology (human factors)
M, Accredited
Non-resident
Non-profit, state
(208) 885-6911
$$
Master's degrees in electrical, mechanical, civil and computer engineering, computer science, and psychology (human factors) are offered via the Video Outreach program.

UNIVERSITY OF INDIANAPOLIS
1400 E. Hanna Ave.
Indianapolis, IN 46227 USA
Dr. C. R. Stockton, Academic Dean
B, M, Accredited
Residency
Non-profit, state

Many fields
1902

(317) 788–3368
$$$

A variety of Bachelor's and Master's degrees can be earned entirely through evening study. The Executive M.B.A. program meets one Friday and three Saturdays each month. In this program, it is possible to earn the degree in two years (comprising 19 Fridays and 50 Saturdays). Formerly called Indiana Central College.

UNIVERSITY OF IOWA ✪

Center for Credit Programs, W400 Seashore Hall
Iowa City, IA 52242 USA
Susan Beadle, B.L.S. Adviser
Liberal studies
1847

B, Accredited
Non-resident
Non-profit, state
(319) 353–4963
$$

The Bachelor of Liberal Studies degree entirely by correspondence from the University of Iowa and the University of Northern Iowa. Students must earn 62 semester hours of credit (by correspondence from the University of Iowa or from any other accredited school.) At least 45 semester hours must be earned at the Iowa Regents Universities (University of Iowa, Iowa State University, University of Northern Iowa). No credit for life experience learning. There are no majors in the program, but students must earn 12 credits in three of these five areas: humanities, communication and arts, science and math, social sciences, and professional fields (business, education, etc.). Credits may be earned through correspondence, Saturday, evening, off-campus, television, or telebridge courses. "Telebridge" is a statewide system of two-way audio conferencing which permits classes to be held at remote locations. The B.L.S. program is only open to people living in the U.S.

UNIVERSITY OF KANSAS

102 Bailey Hall, School of Education Graduate Division
Lawrence, KS 66045 USA
Dr. George Woodyard, Associate Dean, Graduate School
Public administration, education
1864

M, Accredited
Residency
Non-profit, state
(913) 864–2700
$$

Master of Public Administration through evening study, and Master of Science in Education through evening study and at the Kansas City campus (K.U. Regents Center).

UNIVERSITY OF KENTUCKY

103 Frazee Hall
Lexington, KY 40506 USA
G. Kendall Rice, Director of Admissions
Business, public administration
1865

M, Accredited
Residency
Non-profit, state
(606) 258–9000
$$

Master of Business Administration and Master of Public Administration may be earned through a combination of weekend and evening classes. University of Kentucky also offers television courses and correspondence courses in many fields.

UNIVERSITY OF LAVERNE

S.C.E., 1950 3rd St.,
La Verne, CA 91750 USA
Adeline Cardenas-Clagu, Director of Admissions
Many fields
1891

B, M, Accredited
Residency
Non-profit, independent
(714) 593–3511, ext. 501
$$$$

Bachelor's or Master's may be earned through evening, weekend, and summer programs. Fields include liberal arts, graduate and professional studies, business, communications, behavioral sciences, education, child development, pre-medicine and pre-law. Residence centers in California, Alaska, Greece, and Italy.

UNIVERSITY OF LONDON ✪

Senate House, Malet St.
London, WC1E 7HU England

B, M, D, Law, Equivalent of accredited, Non-resident

See page 70 for explanation of abbreviations and symbols

Registrar
Many fields
1836

Non-profit, state
(01) 636–8000
$

London was the world's first external degree program, and after a century and a half, it is still among the best. They do have an annoying policy that only holders of their own Bachelor's could enroll in most Master's programs, but there are a few exceptions. Anyone may apply directly for the Master's in agricultural development, French studies, and classics. Exams may be taken at British embassies and consulates. Degrees are based solely on examinations and a thesis. London gave the exams, but not the coursework to prepare one. That, too is changing. Optional correspondence and audio-visual materials, study courses and informal tutorial assessment have been made available. There are new programs in accounting, banking, management and nursing, with agrarian development and computer science under development. Seventy five percent of students still take law, but only graduates of universities in the U.K. may apply for the external law degree. . Several correspondence schools offer non-degree preparation for London's exams. One is Wolsey Hall, 66 Banbury, Oxford OX2 6PR, another is Rapid Results College, Tuition House, London SW19 3BR.

UNIVERSITY OF LOUISVILLE
S. 3rd St.
Louisville, KY 40292 USA
Belinda L. Wyss, Assistant Director, Special Student Services
Many fields
1798

B, M, Accredited
Residency
Non-profit, state
(502) 588–6933
$$

Eighty degree programs at the Bachelor's and Master's level are available through part-time and/or evening studies. Evening and weekend courses on the main campus and at three other sites. Transitions Program offers counseling for adults thinking of entering or returning to college, and evening workshops on topics of relevance. The Adult Commuter Center and Evening Student Services (ACCESS) provides a place for adults to call their own for typing, studying, conversation, as well as university functions (admissions, bookstore, financial aid, etc.).

UNIVERSITY OF MAINE
Continuing Education, 122 Chadbourne Hall
Orono, ME 04469 USA
William J. Munsey, Director of Admissions
Many fields
1865

B, M, Accredited
Residency
Non-profit, state
(207) 581–6192
$$

Bachelor of University Studies, Bachelor of Science in elementary education, Master of Arts in English or speech, Master of Science in education, Master of Business Administration, Master in Liberal Studies, Master of Public Administration, Master of Science in medical technology, all of which may be earned through evening courses given at Orono and Portland.

UNIVERSITY OF MARY
7500 University Dr.
Bismarck, ND 58501 USA
Neal Kalberer, Director of Admissions
Various fields
1957

B, M, Accredited
Residency
Non-profit, church
(701) 255–7500
$$$

Business, and accounting programs available through evening study. Some weekend classes. Credit for prior learning, equivalency exams, and independent study.

UNIVERSITY OF MARYLAND ✪
University College
College Park, MD 20742 USA
Dr. Paul Hamlin, Dean, Statewide Undergraduate Programs
Technology & management, behavioral & social sciences, humanities, fire science
1856

B, Accredited
Short residency
Non-profit, state
(301) 985–7036
$$

University College, the continuing education campus of the University of Maryland, offers B.A. and B.S. degrees in a flexible format through its Open University. Attendance is optional except for the introductory session and examinations. There are learning centers throughout the Washington-Baltimore area. A primary concentration in fire science is offered by independent study in a six-state region and the District of Columbia. Credit is available for relevant college-level prior learning.

UNIVERSITY OF MASSACHUSETTS—AMHERST ✪

University Without Walls, Montague House
Amherst, MA 01003 USA
Doris Dickinson, Chair, U.W.W. Admission Committee
Humanities, sciences, social sciences, engineering, business, health sciences
1863

B, M, Accredited
Non-resident or Short residency
Non-profit, state
(413) 595–1378
5

University Without Walls program leads to either a B.A. or B.S. degree designed by the student, an advisor, and a faculty sponsor from UMass or one of the four colleges in the Amherst area. Courses involve both independent study and time spent on the main campus and/or at other centers. Students may earn much credit through a narrative prior learning portfolio: a written essay and, if relevant, video- and audiotapes, performances, presentations, photographs, etc. The assessment may be done anytime after enrollment. Late afternoon, evening, and weekend classes offered. The College of Engineering offers an M.S. in engineering management, computer engineering and electrical engineering entirely by videotape or satellite transmission from National Technological University. While occasional appearances are required on campus, the requirement is not enforced for out-of-state students. Address: Video Instruction Program, 113 Marcus Hall, UMass, Amherst 01003, (413) 545–0063, Merillee Neunder, Director.

UNIVERSITY OF MASSACHUSETTS—BOSTON

College of Public and Community Service
Boston, MA 02125 USA
Ronald E. Ancrum, Director of Admissions
Public, community, legal and human service, community development
1964

B, Accredited
Residency
Non-profit, state
(617) 929–7000
$$

Bachelor's degree program in public and community service, human service, legal service and housing, and community development. Many of the required units can come from an assessment of prior learning experience—but there is still the requirement of one year of residency at the university.

UNIVERSITY OF MIAMI

P.O. Box 248025
Coral Gables , FL 33124 USA
Deborah Triol-Perry, Dean of Enrollments
Many fields
1925

B, M, D, Accredited
Residency
Non-profit, independent
(305) 284–2211
$$

M.B.A. with classes held every other weekend, for fully-employed persons sponsored by their employers. Miami offers an intriguing Honors Program in medicine, law, international studies, and marine and atmospheric science. Well-qualified applicants (mostly high school seniors) are admitted simultaneously to the Bachelor's and the Doctoral programs. Miami also offers a two-year M.D. program for persons with substantial experience in the sciences.

UNIVERSITY OF MICHIGAN

200 Hill
Ann Arbor, MI 48109 USA
Dr. Clifford F. Sjogren, Director of Admissions
Social work, education, library science
1817

M, Accredited
Residency
Non-profit, state
(313) 764–1817
$$

The University of Michigan offers graduate courses in social work and in education and library science through the off-campus program, sponsored by the respective departments and by the Extension Service. Independent study courses at the graduate level as well as the undergraduate level are available through

See page 70 for explanation of abbreviations and symbols

the Extension Service. It is not, however, possible to earn an entire degree through either the off-campus program or the independent study program. Students anywhere in the world can take independent study courses. The School of Business Administration has an evening M.B.A. program.

UNIVERSITY OF MINDANAO
Bolton St. — M, Equivalent of accredited
Davao City, Mindanao Island Philippines — Non-resident
Paquita Gavino, Dean, College of Education — Non-profit, independent
Education — 7–54–56
1946
The university's On-the-Air Project offers the Master's degree in education entirely through radio broadcasts. Students submit term papers, prepare workbooks, and take examinations at the university.

UNIVERSITY OF MINNESOTA✪
Program for Individualized Learning, 201 Westbrook Hall, — B, Accredited
Minneapolis, MN 55455 USA — Non-resident
Kent Warren, Admissions Coordinator — Non-profit, state
Many fields — (612) 624–4020
1851 — $$
B.A. and B.S. degrees for students willing to take responsibility for designing and implementing their degree programs. The program (formerly called University Without Walls) offers no courses or exams of their own. Instead, they assist students in using resources at the university, at other institutions, and in the community. These might include local or correspondence courses, independent study projects, and assessment of prior learning. At least a year of study is required after admission. Since there are no predesigned majors or prescribed curricula, each student develops an individualized degree plan. A set of standards, called graduation criteria, provide a framework for structuring and assessing degree programs. Requirements include an area of concentration, broad learning in the liberal arts, and a command of written English. Programs are not available in general business administration, accounting, teaching, engineering, or computer science.

UNIVERSITY OF MISSOURI—COLUMBIA
2-64 Agriculture Bldg, College of Agriculture — B, Accredited
Columbia, MO 65211 USA — Short residency
Dr. Gary L. Smith, Director Admissions and Registrar — Non-profit, state
Agriculture — (314) 882–6287
1839 — $$
Bachelor of Science in agriculture. Credit is awarded for relevant prior learning documented by examination, portfolio of prior learning, or other acceptable means and for satisfactorily completing on-campus or extension-taught courses, correspondence courses, and other independent study. Only students who have not enrolled in any school full time for at least five years are accepted. Prior college-level work not required but preferred. Primarily for those interested in agricultural or agriculturally-related occupations. The program is not available to persons outside the United States.

UNIVERSITY OF MISSOURI AT ST. LOUIS
8001 Natural Bridge Rd. — B, Accredited
St. Louis, MO 63121 USA — Residency
Mimi La Marca, Director of Admissions — Non-profit, state
General studies — (314) 553–5451
1963 — $$
The Continuing Education division offers extension courses during the day and evening at various locations. There is a Bachelor of General Studies program. Some credit is given for life experience learning.

UNIVERSITY OF NATAL — M, Equivalent of accreditation
King George V Avenue
Durban 4001, South Africa — Non-profit, state
Business administration
Qualified persons can earn the MBA based entirely on a thesis in the field.

UNIVERSITY OF NEBRASKA
College of Continuing Studies — B, Accredited
Omaha, NE 68182 USA — Residency
John Flemming, Director of Admissions — Non-profit, state
General studies — (402) 554–2393
1908 — $$

Courses from many sources with credits leading to the student-planned Bachelor of General Studies degree, offered "to established adults only," with credit for life experience and "amnesty for past college failures." Twenty four semester hours of coursework must be earned in residence at University of Nebraska at Omaha.

UNIVERSITY OF NEW ENGLAND — B, M, Equivalent of accredited
Armidale, N.S.W. 2351 Australia — Short residency
Ian Small, Acting Director, Dept. of External Studies — Non-profit, state
Many fields — (067) 73–2999
1938 — $

Bachelor's degrees are offered in arts, economics, social science, and urban and regional planning. Master's degrees are awarded in economics, education, educational administration, and urban and regional planning. The Department of External Studies provides administrative support, but external teaching is the responsibility of the same full-time academic staff who teach internal students. Instruction is mostly by correspondence, including printed lecture notes, course outlines, and audiocassettes. Students must also attend residential vacation schools on campus and there are voluntary weekend schools, the majority of them held in Sydney. Enrollment in most programs is restricted to full-time residents of Australia, or Australians with resident status who are temporarily overseas.

UNIVERSITY OF NEW HAMPSHIRE
Division of Continuing Education, 6 Garrison Ave. — B, M, Accredited
Durham, NH 03824 USA — Short residency
Stanwood C. Fish, Dean, Admissions — Non-profit, state
Various fields — (603) 862–1360
1866 — $$

Bachelor of Science in child and family studies, Bachelor of Engineering Technology, Bachelor of Science in nursing, Bachelor of Science in health management and policy (external degree option), Bachelor of Science in medical technology, Bachelor of Arts in psychology, Master of Public Administration, Master of Library Science available through evening and/or external degree programs. Prior learning experiences are assessed in nursing, medical technology, and health management programs. Bachelor of General Studies and Bachelor of Professional Studies, with substantial credit for life experience, are offered at over fifty centers statewide.

UNIVERSITY OF NEW HAVEN
300 Orange Ave. — B, M, Accredited
West Haven, CT 06516 USA — Residency
Dr. Robert Caruso, Dean of Admissions Services — Non-profit, independent
Many fields — (203) 932–7000
1920 — $$$

Bachelor's degrees in all fields except applied mathematics, natural sciences, English, and world music can be earned entirely through the Division of Evening Studies. More than 50 majors are available. Among the unusual ones are arson investigation, forensic science, dietetic technology, executive housekeeping administration, music and sound recording, and tourism and travel administration.

UNIVERSITY OF NORTH AMERICA
see: listing for this "school" in Diploma Mill chapter

UNIVERSITY OF NORTHERN IOWA ✪
1222 W. 27th St. — B, Accredited
Cedar Falls, IA 50614 USA — Non-resident
Dr. Constantine Curris, President — Non-profit, state

See page 70 for explanation of abbreviations and symbols

Liberal studies
1876

(319) 273–2311
$$

See University of Iowa for description of a shared non-resident Bachelor's degree program. Instead of filling out my information questionnaire, Nancy Bramhall wrote across it "We do not wish to be included in your book." I'm sorry, Ms. Bramhall, but as long as you offer an accredited non-resident Bachelor's degree, I owe it to my readers to keep you in. This is a perfect example of how schools can vary in the way they present and market their programs. Iowa and Northern Iowa offer the identical program. Iowa cooperates with me totally, and could not be more helpful. Northern Iowa grumpily says, "Leave us out."

UNIVERSITY OF OKLAHOMA ✪

660 Parrington Oval
Norman, OK 73019 USA
Dr. Dan A. Davis, Associate Dean, College of Liberal Studies
Liberal studies
1890

B, M, Accredited
Short residency
Non-profit, state
(405) 325–1061
$

Bachelor of Liberal Studies and Master of Liberal Studies with two or three weeks each year on campus, plus directed independent study. B.L.S. students work in three areas: humanities, natural sciences, and social sciences. It is like a four-year degree, each year requiring one seminar session on campus. (Sessions are held at least twice a year.) Three of the four years may be waived, based on prior study, or by passing an equivalency exam. In the fourth year, the student completes a study in depth and attends a mandatory seminar. There is an Upper Division Option for people with two years of college, beginning with a five-day residential seminar, then completion of all three phases in about a year, with one required seminar. The final seminar is the same as in the four-year B.L.S. There are no majors; students do elective study based on their interests. The M.L.S., largely for people with a specialized Bachelor's who wish a broader education, begins with a two-week seminar on campus.

UNIVERSITY OF PENNSYLVANIA

Credit Programs, College of General Studies, 210 Logan Hall
Philadelphia, PA 19104 USA
Dr. David Burnett, Director, College of General Studies
Many fields
1740

B, M, Accredited
Residency
Non-profit, independent
(215) 898–7326
$$$$

Bachelor of Arts through College of General Studies. Penn's evening division offers the same degrees as traditional residential students receive. There is a Master of Arts in gerontology through evening study program, and other graduate courses offered in the evening. No weekend classes, and no credit for life experience learning.

UNIVERSITY OF PHOENIX

4615 E. Elwood St.,
Phoenix, AZ 85040 USA
Nina Omelchenko, Acting Admissions Director
Business, management, nursing, health services
1976

B, M. Accredited
Non-resident or Residency
Proprietary
(602) 966-7400
$$$

The M.B.A. can be earned entirely "on line" over a home computer network. Bachelor's degree in business administration, management, nursing, or health services and the Master of Business Administration or M.A. in Management entirely through evening study, in a minimum time period of 13 months for the Bachelor's, 14 months for the Master of Arts in Management, and 22 months for the M.B.A. Classes meet one night a week in Phoenix, as well as in Tucson, Salt Lake City, Denver, Albuquerque, and various cities in southern and northern California. Applicants for the Bachelor's degree must have two years of full-time related work experience and 30 semester credits of college work. Master's applicants must have a Bachelor's and three years of full-time related work experience.

UNIVERSITY OF PITTSBURGH ✪

External Studies Program, 3808 Forbes Ave.
Pittsburgh, PA 15260 USA
Joanne Ratey-Rosol, Director of Admissions

B, Accredited
Short residency
Non-profit, state

Psychology, economics, public admnistration, many other fields
1787
(412) 624–7210
$$$
Bachelor of Arts in psychology, economics, and public administration, as well as all core courses required for any degree offered in the College of General Studies. Students use textbooks and faculty-prepared self-instructional manuals, attend three three-hour Saturday workshops for each course, and take exams at off-campus testing sites. Courses, faculty, and transcript credits are the same as for Pitt's traditional classroom-based programs. The workshops are required for all but handicapped students, inmates in Pennsylvania prisons, and people who were enrolled at Pitt but have been transferred to another location.

UNIVERSITY OF PUERTO RICO
P.O. Box 5000
Mayaguez, Puerto Rico 00709 USA
Antonio Santes, Director of Admissions
Education
1911
B, Accredited
Residency
Non-profit, state
(809) 834–4040
$
Bachelor's courses in education for employed teachers, through evening, weekend, and summer classes. Offered through the Division of Academic Extension and Community Services which was created to provide educational opportunity for the adult working population, disadvantaged groups, and minorities.

UNIVERSITY OF QUEBEC
Télé-Université, 214, Avenue St.-Sacrement,
Quebec, G1N 4M6 Canada
Jean-Guy Béliveau
Many fields
1972
B, Accredited
Residency
Non-profit
(418) 657–2262
$
Télé-Université is one of the 11 units of the University of Quebec—a University Without Walls within the huge university. Programs are offered for the training of teachers of French and mathematics, and some general courses for the public. Instruction is largely by use of television, videotapes, textbooks, telephone conferences, and experimental kits, all for home study, plus, in the teacher training programs, weekly three-hour group meetings. Instruction in French.

UNIVERSITY OF REDLANDS
1200 E. Colton Ave.
Redlands, CA 92374 USA
Stephen Hankins, Dean of Admissions
Liberal arts, business, information systems
1907
B, M, Accredited
Residency
Non-profit, independent
(714) 793–2121
$$$$
Whitehead Center offers degree programs for the working adult throughout southern California: B.S. in business and management (total cost $7,907), B.S. in information systems ($10,331), and M.B.A. ($10,825). Forty units may be earned from assessment of prior learning via student-prepared portfolio. At least 40 units from another institution is required. Johnston Center offers degree programs for residential undergraduates, allowing them almost total academic freedom to create their own majors. Interdisciplinary and custom-designed traditional majors are available. Students are "graded" by narrative evaluations. Students mostly live in the same dormitory, and are expected to address issues of community and cross-cultural awareness.

UNIVERSITY OF RHODE ISLAND
Kingston, RI 02881 USA
David G. Taggart, Dean of Admissions
English, business, public administration, other fields
1892
B, M, Accredited
Residency
Non-profit, state
(401) 792–1000
$$
Bachelor of Arts in English (women only), Bachelor of Science, Master of Arts in English, Master of Business Administration, and Master of Public Administration entirely through evening study at six cities around the state.

UNIVERSITY OF RICHMOND
Richmond, VA 23173 USA
Thomas N. Pollard Jr., Dean of Admissions
Many fields
1830
B, M, Accredited
Residency
Non-profit, state
(804) 289–8640
$$$$

Bachelor of Arts, Bachelor of Commerce, Master of Commerce, and Master of Humanities, all available entirely through evening study.

UNIVERSITY OF SAN FRANCISCO
College of Professional Studies, Ignatian Heights
San Francisco, CA 94117 USA
Patrick M. Woods, Director of Admissions
Many fields
1855
B,M, Accredited
Residency
Non-profit, church
(415) 666–6886
$$$

The College of Professional Studies administers undergraduate and graduate programs for working adults. Through the Experiential Learning Center, the undergraduate programs offer students the opportunity to apply for credit for experiential learning. Classes are held in the evenings or on the weekend and meet once a week for at least four hours. In addition to class attendance, students are expected to spend 15 to 20 hours per week in class preparation. Degrees offered include Bachelor of Public Administration; B.S. in applied economics, organizational behavior, and information systems management; Master of Non-profit Administration; Master of Public Administration (also with a concentration in health services administration); Master of Human Resources and Organization Development; M.A. in writing.

UNIVERSITY OF SANTA BARBARA ✪
4050 Calle Real, #200
Santa Barbara, CA 93110 USA
John A. R. Wilson, Vice President
Education, business/finance
1973
M, D, Unaccredited, state approved, Short residency
Non-profit, independent
(805) 569–1024
$$

U.S.B. offers the M.A. and the Ph.D. in education and the Doctor of Education, with emphasis in education, counseling psychology, business and finance, or international studies, as they relate to the field of education. The programs require a minimum of three weeks of residency in Santa Barbara. The degree programs have been approved by the state of California. They require from one to three years to complete. The 12 resident faculty and more than 50 non-resident advisors all have traditional Doctorates. U.S.B. offers both independent study and correspondence study in many aspects of the field of education including counseling psychology. Candidates for the degree must complete courses and independent study work, and pass an examination in each study area. Originally established in Florida as Laurence University.

UNIVERSITY OF SANTA MONICA
2107 Wilshire Blvd.
Santa Monica, CA 90403 USA
H. Ronald Hulnick, President
Applied human relationships
1976
M, Unaccredited, state approved, Residency
Non-profit, independent
(213) 454–7559
$$

Competency-based curricula in which students earn the degree by demonstrating knowledgte, skills, and qualities of efficiently relating with themselves and others. Started by John-Roger, and based in part on the "practical applications of the Traveler's teachings." John-Roger says that "through Koh-E-Nor University, a Wisdom School will effect realization of truth beyond the verbal level. Each student and teacher will become truth... We shall bring in students...who will finally answer that inner call that shall evoke their beingness." Formerly called Koh-E-Nor University.

UNIVERSITY OF SARASOTA ✪
8060 N. Tamiami Trail
Sarasota, FL 34243 USA
Pamela A. Kline, Director of Development
Business, education
M, D, Accreditation candidate
Short residency
Non-profit, independent
(813) 355–2906

1969 $$$

Master of Business Administration, Master of Arts in education, and Doctor of Education. Some intensive coursework in Florida is required. Courses are in the summer, with one-week seminars in winter and spring. Total residency may be as short as six weeks. The university's programs consist of seminars, supervised individual research and writing, combined with the residential sessions. Master's candidates either write a thesis or complete a directed independent study project. Doctoral students must write a dissertation. Many of the students are teachers and school administrators. Toll-free number: (800) 331–5995. (Originally known as Laurence University, the predecessor of the Laurence University that opened in California and is now the University of Santa Barbara.)

UNIVERSITY OF SASKATCHEWAN
Division of Extension, 109 Kirk Hall
Saskatoon, Saskatchewan S7N 0W0 Canada
Prof. D. Bicknell, Director of Undergraduate Studies
Many fields

B, Equivalent of accredited
Residency
Non-profit, state
(306) 343–3313
$$

Wide variety of studies offered through Evening Degree Studies, Independent Degree Studies, and Off-Campus Degree Studies in agriculture, arts and sciences, commerce, education, home economics, and physical education. A Bachelor of Commerce with a major in health care administration has a large element of home study, but one full year must be spent on campus. Five of the six full-year classes and 15 of 28 half-year classes are available through home study in this program.

UNIVERSITY OF SOUTH AFRICA ✪
P.O. Box 392, Muckleneuk Ridge
Pretoria, 0001 South Africa
The Registrar (Academic)
Many fields
1960

B, M, D, Equivalent of accredited, Non-resident
Non-profit
(012) 440–3111
$

UNISA offers Bachelor's, Master's, and Doctorates entirely by correspondence (with the exception of final examinations, which may be taken at South African embassies and consulates worldwide). Degrees at all levels are offered in a many fields through a technique called "tele-tuition," using course materials, tapes, slides, etc. The cost of the programs, government subsidized, is very low. A minimum of 10 courses is required for the Bachelor's degree; minimum time: Three years. Before registering, one must obtain a Certificate of Full or Conditional Exemption from the South African Matriculation Examinations, obtained from the Matriculation Board, P.O. Box 3854, Pretoria, South Africa, 0001. Ask for a certificate to register at UNISA. People worldwide are admitted, primarily if they can show that is difficult or impossible for them to pursue the degree where they are, whether for reasons of isolation, subject matter, time, or money. NOTE: A reader who has mastered the intricacies of dealing with UNISA has written a very helpful, detailed 110-page manual on how to do it. See the Bibliography for information on this report.

UNIVERSITY OF SOUTH CAROLINA
University Campus and Continuing Education
Columbia, SC 29208 USA
Deborah Haynes, Director of Admissions
Business
1801

B, Accredited
Residency
Non-profit, state
(803) 777–7700
$$

Bachelor of Science in business administration in the areas of marketing, finance, and management through evening programs. Credit for equivalency exams and military courses. No credit for life experience.

UNIVERSITY OF SOUTH FLORIDA
4202 Fowler Ave.
Tampa, FL 33620 USA
Dr. Kevin Kearney, Director, BIS
1956

B, Accredited
Short residency
Non-profit, state
(813) 974–4058
$$

The Bachelor of Independent Studies program requires from two to six weeks on campus, spread out over anywhere from 14 to 69 months. All students must have knowledge in three broad areas of study: social sciences, natural sciences, and humanities. Each area has an extensive program of guided independent study and a two-week on-campus seminar for research, writing, peer interaction, and when relevant, laboratory experience. Up to two areas can be waived for students who have sufficient work and background and who pass an equivalency exam in the field. All students must write a thesis and defend it orally in a one-day examination on campus. The average student takes more than five years to earn the degree, but there is a wide range. Applicants with an A.A. degree and those with an A.S. in selected health related fields qualify for a two-area curriculum contract and no thesis is required.

UNIVERSITY OF SOUTHERN CALIFORNIA

University Park	B, M, D, Accredited
Los Angeles, CA 90089 USA	Residency
Joseph Merante, Dean, Admissions	Non-profit, independent
Many fields	(213) 743–2311
1880	$$$$$

Bachelor's degrees are generally offered through evening classes in the Los Angeles area. Their "Flex Ed" system is based on cassettes, workbooks, and a one-on-one tutorial system, with hours set to the students' convenience. A Master of Science in Safety is offered through weekend study in the San Francisco area. Graduate degrees in education and public administration are offered in the San Francisco and Sacramento areas. The Doctor of Education for teachers and administrators is available through summer residency plus independent study. The Doctor of Administration is offered in the District of Columbia. Two Master's degrees are given in Europe: an M.A. in international relations open to anyone in London; and an M.S. in education, an M.S. in systems management, and an M.A. in international relations for the "military community" in Germany. American citizens not in said community may obtain special permission to attend.

UNIVERSITY OF SOUTHERN MISSISSIPPI

Southern Station, P.O. Box 5167	B, M, Accredited
Hattiesburg, MS 39406 USA	Residency
Danny W. Montgomery, Director of Admissions	Non-profit, state
Education	(601) 266–5006
1910	$$

The work for several Bachelor's and Master's degrees in education can be completed by evening and weekend study, or over two summer sessions.

UNIVERSITY OF TENNESSEE

615 McCallie Ave.	B, M, Accredited
Chattanooga, TN 37402 USA	Residency
Dr. Ray P. Fox, Dean of Admissions & Records	Non-profit, state
Many fields	(615) 755–4141
1886	$$

Bachelor of Arts, Bachelor of Science, Master of Business Administration, Master of Science, and Master of Education, all available entirely through evening study. Some credit may be given for prior work and volunteer experience through the Individualized Education Program.

UNIVERSITY OF TEXAS	B, M, Accredited
Arlington, TX 76019 USA	Residency
R.Z. Prince,	Non-profit, state
Director of Admissions	(817) 273–2011
1895	$Bachelor of Arts and Master of Arts in

many fields, available through evening study.

UNIVERSITY OF THE STATE OF NEW YORK✪

Regents College, Cultural Education Center	B, Accredited
Albany, NY 12230 USA	Non-resident
C. Wayne Williams, Executive Director	Non-profit, state
Business, nursing, technology, many other fields	(518) 474–3703
1784	$

B.A. and B.S. by non-residential study. Probably the largest and, along with Thomas Edison State College, the most popular non-resident degree program in the U.S. The oldest state educational agency in America has no faculty, no campus, and no courses of its own. It evaluates work done elsewhere, and awards its own degrees to persons who have accumulated sufficient units, by whatever means. Credit for all prior college courses and many non-college learning experiences (company courses, military, etc.). The university recognizes many equivalency exams and offers its own, as well, given nationwide and, by arrangement, at foreign locations. Each degree has its own requirements with regard to areas of emphasis, however they are not restrictive. They require a minimum number of units in the arts and sciences. The program is described in a 24-page viewbook, sent free to all who request it. If non-school learning experiences cannot be assessed easily at a distance, or by exam, the student may go to New York for an oral examination. The University makes available a service called DISTANCELEARN, which is a computer database of courses offered by other schools that can be completed through home study.

UNIVERSITY OF TOLEDO

Adult Liberal Studies, University College
Toledo, OH 43606 USA
Richard J. Eastop, Dean of Admission Services
Liberal studies, many fields
1872

B, M, Accredited
Residency
Non-profit, state
(419) 537–2051
$$

Adult Liberal Studies program offers people over 25 the opportunity to earn the Bachelor's degree through a combination of independent study, evening classes, regular coursework, plus a thesis. All students begin with an introductory planning seminar. Generous credit is given for CLEP exams. Nine seminars are given in various fields of study, usually one evening a week, for a total of 54 of the required 186 quarter hours. Thirty-five hours of traditional courses must be taken, before writing a thesis in an area of special interest. Toledo also offers 2+2 programs that allow holders of Associate's degrees to complete a Bachelor's in various fields.

UNIVERSITY OF TULSA

600 S. College
Tulsa, OK 74104 USA
John C. Corso, Dean of Admissions
Education
1894

D, Accredited
Residency
Non-profit, independent
(918) 592–6000
$$$

The Doctor of Education degree may be completed in about two years of evening study, plus writing a dissertation.

UNIVERSITY OF UTAH

Salt Lake City, UT 84112 USA
John S. Landward, Director of Admissions
Business, administration, engineering
1850

M, Accredited
Residency
Non-profit, state
(801) 581–7200
$$

Master of Business Administration, Master of Engineering, and Master of Administration may be earned entirely through evening study.

UNIVERSITY OF WALES ✪

University Registry, Cathays Park
Cardiff, CF1 3NS Wales
The Registrar
Many fields

M, D, Equivalent of accredited
Short residency
Non-profit, state
(0222) 22656
$

External Ph.D.'s may be pursued at any of the campuses of the university. Each candidate works with a director of studies, who is a present or former full-time member of the academic staff. An applicant must have an approved Bachelor's degree, demonstrate that there are adequate facilities at the "home base" for pursuing research (library, laboratory, archives, etc.), and be able to pay regular visits to the university (typically three visits a year to meet with the director of studies, or one month a year in continuous work). Initial inquiries to the department head of the relevant department, or the registrar of the institution chosen. They are: University College of Wales, Aberystwyth, Dyfed SY23 2AX; University College of North

See page 70 for explanation of abbreviations and symbols

Wales, Bangor, Gwynedd LL57 2UW; University College, Cathays Park, Cardiff CF1 3NR; University College of Swansea, Singleton Park, Swansea SA2 8PP; Saint David's University College, Lampeter, Dyfed SA48 7ED.

UNIVERSITY OF WARWICK ✪
66 Banbury Rd., Wolsey Hall,
Oxford, OX2 6PR England
Business

M, Equivalent of accredited
Short residency
Non-profit, state
$$$

Students anywhere in the world may register with Warwick, and then pursue the M.B.A. from home, with the aid of a distance learning course developed by Wolsey Hall, a private school that has, for many years, offered distance learning courses for the University of London's external degrees. There is an eight-day residency each year on campus in England or in Hong Kong, Singapore, or Malaysia. The period of study is normally four years, roughly twelve hours a week, but it can be three years if the dissertation is completed during the final year of study. There is direct contact with tutors. Wolsey Hall also offers a free six-lesson course in essential study skills, for those who have been away from learning for a while. Optional weekend seminars are held three times a year in England, Hong Kong, Malaysia, and Singapore. Access to a personal computer is desirable but not essential.

UNIVERSITY OF WATERLOO ✪
Correspondence Office
Waterloo, Ontario N2L 3G1 Canada
B. A. Lumsden, Associate Director, Distance Education
Many fields
1957

B, Equivalent of accredited
Non-resident or short residency
Non-profit, state
(519) 888–4050
$

Bachelor's degrees may be earned entirely by correspondence. They include a non-major B.A., a B.A. with a major in classical civilization, economics, English, geography, history, philosophy, psychology, sociology, or social development studies; a Bachelor of Environmental Studies in geography; and a B.S in general science. Credit is given for prior academic experience, but no credit is given for experiential learning. The programs are available to people in Canada and the United States, but U.S. students pay three to four times the tuition of Canadians. All courses are offered on a rigid time schedule, in which papers and exams must be done by very specific times. As a result, there have been postal delivery problems with some U.S. students, and so, while they are admitted, the university is not overly enthusiastic about the prospect. (Suggestion: there are six assignments per course; it might well be worth the expense of sending them in via Federal Express.)

UNIVERSITY OF WEST LOS ANGELES
10811 Washington Blvd.
Culver City, CA 90230 USA
Teri Canon, Dean, School of Paralegal Studies
Paralegal
1966

B, Accredited
Residency
Non-profit, independent
(213) 313–1011
$$

Bachelor of Science in paralegal studies can be earned through two years of evening classes.

UNIVERSITY OF WISCONSIN—GREEN BAY
Individualized Learning Programs Office
Green Bay, WI 54301 USA
Myron A. Van de Ven, Director of Admissions
General studies
1965

B, Accredited
Short residency
Non-profit, state
(414) 465–2000
$$

Non-traditional program is available primarily for Wisconsin residents. (Persons in other states may enroll provided they can visit campus a minimum of two times for each course.) The Bachelor of Arts in general studies degree begins with structured independent study and becomes more individualized with time. There are self-paced learning guides, radio and television courses, internships, and research projects, based on learning contracts. An entrance seminar is required to provide a detailed overview of the program. Credit for prior learning is available.

UNIVERSITY OF WISCONSIN—MADISON ✪

College of Engineering, 432 N. Lake St.
Madison, WI 53706 USA
Cheri McKentley, P.D. Counselor
Engineering
1849

Certificate, Accredited
Non-resident
Non-profit, state
(608) 262–0133
$$

The Professional Development Degree program in engineering may be earned through correspondence and independent study or one can combine them with coursework from local accredited universities. Students select the courses, time, format, and place and may pace the study to complete the program from within one to seven years. A guided, independent study project is required. A Bachelor of Science in engineering, or comparable degree, is required for admission to the program. The average P.D.D. program costs between $2,500 and $4,500 depending on the courses selected. Correspondence courses are the least expensive but also require the most work.

UNIVERSITY OF WISCONSIN—OSHKOSH

800 Algoma Blvd.
Oshkosh, WI 54901 USA
Dr. Robert J. Chaffin, Director,
Liberal Studies
Degree program
1871

B, Accredited
Residency
Non-profit, state
Liberal Studies
(414) 424–1234
$$

A Bachelor of Liberal Studies degree may be earned through a combination of 94 credits of weekend classes and 34 elective credits. Students take one course at a time, meeting every third weekend. Credits earned through prior academic experience at accredited institutions, evening courses, independent study, experiential learning (a portfolio process), accredited television courses, CLEP examinations, and challenge examinations may be applied to this degree. An Associate's degree (Two years) is also available through this program. A prerequisite course that is offered four times a year must be completed to enter the program. Inexpensive, on-campus housing is available for weekend students. A minimum of 30 credits in residency is required.

UNIVERSITY OF WISCONSIN—PLATTEVILLE

Extended Degree Program, Pioneer Tower 513
Platteville, WI 53818 USA
Dr. John C. Adams, Director, Extended Degree Program
Business administration
1866

B, Accredited
Residency
Non-profit, state
(608) 342–1468
$$

The Extended Degree Program offering the Bachelor's degree in business administration is open to Wisconsin residents only. A minor in accounting is offered. Areas of concentration are finance, marketing, management, and personnel and labor relations. Credit can be earned through independent study and evaluation of prior learning achieved through work and life experience. Some courses are available through teleconferencing. Toll-free number in Wisconsin only: (800) 362–5460.

UNIVERSITY OF WISCONSIN—SUPERIOR

Extended Degree Program, Old Main 237
Superior, WI 54880 USA
Jon Wojciechowski, Director of Admissions
1893

B, Accredited
Short residency
Non-profit, state
(715) 394–8101
$$

The Superior campus of the University of Wisconsin system offers a Bachelor of Arts degree which can be completed entirely through off-campus independent faculty-guided study. However, on-campus conferences with faculty are required. The student designs a major program based on personal or career goals. Competency-based, self-paced courses developed by the university faculty in a wide variety of fields are the primary mode of learning in addition to learning contracts. The student has the option of requesting credit for prior learning through the development of a portfolio. The program is open to Wisconsin residents or Minnesota residents who qualify for reciprocity.

See page 70 for explanation of abbreviations and symbols

UNIVERSITY ON THE AIR

Taipei, Taiwan
Juang Huai-i, President
Many fields
1986

B, Equivalent of accredited
Non-resident
Non-profit, state
(02) 282–9355
$

Degree courses are offered entirely by radio and television. Full-time students must be over 20, with a high school diploma; anyone can study part time. Sixty of 128 credits must be in one field of study. More than 30,000 students. Instruction in Chinese.

UNIVERSITY SYSTEM OF NEW HAMPSHIRE

School for Lifelong Learning, Dunlap Center
Durham, NH 03824 USA
Alvin L. Hall, Dean
General studies, professional studies (management, behavioral sciences)
1972

B, Accredited
Residency
Non-profit, state
(603) 862–1692
$$

Bachelor of General Studies and Bachelor of Professional Studies degrees may be earned by independent study for adults with at least 60 credit hours. Courses are available evenings, weekends, and through video courses. Learning contracts, and credit for life experience learning. Self-designed degree programs are offered.

UPPER IOWA UNIVERSITY ✪

External Degree Program, P.O. Box 1861
Fayette, IA 52142 USA
Michelle Rourke, Director of External Programs
Public administration, accounting, management, marketing
1857

B, Accredited
Short residency
Non-profit, independent
(319) 425–5251
$$

Upper Iowa's External Degree Program offers the opportunity to earn a Bachelor of Science in public administration, management, marketing, or accounting with only two to four weeks of residency. The balance of the program is conducted through directed independent study, with learning modules containing assignments and other course material. Frequent interaction with the faculty is encouraged by phone or by mail. Students entering the program with 60 or more semester units must spend one two-week session on campus. Those with fewer than 60 units must attend two two-week sessions. Home study modules are available in a wide variety of fields, from accounting to chemistry, history to fine arts. Previous college work, job training, and other educational experience is evaluated for credit.

UPPSALA UNIVERSITY

External Study Programme, P.O., Box 256
Uppsala, S-751 05 Sweden
Ann-Kristin From
Many fields
1477

None, Equivalent of accredited
Non-resident
Non-profit, state
46–18–155400
$

Correspondence courses (in Swedish only) in law, business administration, development studies, international relations, political science, and English and French, for Swedes living in other countries. The courses come from the university and from Hermods, the Swedish National Correspondence Institute. Books, tapes, and assignments are mailed to Swedish nationals worldwide. Examinations may be taken at any Swedish embassy or consulate. Instruction in Swedish.

UPSALA COLLEGE

Center for Continuing Education
East Orange, NJ 07019 USA
Selma Brookman, Director of Continuing Education
Many fields
1893

B, M, Accredited
Residency
Non-profit, church
(201) 266–7000
$$$

Bachelor of Arts and Bachelor of Science degrees can be earned entirely through evening study in the Division of General Studies. Special R.N. programs. Other courses through weekend study. Credit by examination, and for life experience learning.

URBANA UNIVERSITY
College Way
Urbana, OH 43078 USA
Thomas A. Gallagher, Vice President
Business, social sciences, education, natural science, pre-professional
1850

B, Accredited
Residency
Non-profit, independent
(513) 652–1301
$$$

Bachelor of Arts and Bachelor of Science through weekend, evening, and summer programs. Credit for independent study, non-academic prior learning, and by examination. Self-designed majors.

VANDERBILT UNIVERSITY
Owen Graduate School of Management
Nashville, TN 37203 USA
Director, Executive MBA Program
Business administration
1873

M, Accredited
Residency
Non-profit, independent
(615) 322–2513
$$$$$

Designed for mid-career executives and professionals who do not wish to interrupt their career. Courses are offered through weekend study: a Friday and Saturday every other weekend. Toll-free numbers: in Tennessee, (800) 222–6936; elsewhere, (800) 238–6936.

VERMONT COLLEGE ✪
see: Norwich University

VILLANOVA UNIVERSITY
University College, Adult Services
Villanova, PA 19085 USA
Rev. Harry J. Erdlen, O.S.A., Dean of Admissions
Many fields
1842

B, Accredited
Residency
Non-profit, church
(215) 645–4500
$$$$

Bachelor's may be earned through weekend, evening, and summer programs. Fields of study include many majors in liberal arts and sciences, commerce and finance (accountancy, business administration, economics), engineering, and nursing.

VILLARREAL NATIONAL UNIVERSITY ✪
P.O. Box 2218
Lima, Peru
Dr. Teodoro Quiñones Rojas, Coordinator, International Program
Many fields
1963

M, D, Equivalent of accredited
Non-resident
Non-profit, state
28–78–82
$$$

In 1988, the largest university in Peru began offering completely non-resident Master's and Doctoral programs, in English, to people living in the U.S. After a student is accepted, he or she may select a local Mentor, or the university will assign one, living in the U.S. The mentor supervises completion of a thesis, dissertation, or "Graduate Project." When the mentor approves the completed work, it is submitted to a field coordinator, who in turn submits it to the program coordinator in Lima, who submits it to the dissertation committee. Finally, the student must present it orally to the committee in Lima. (This requirement may be waived in exceptional circumstances, and only when the student pays for the committee to come to him or her.) All communication should go to the U.S. office: International Program, V.N.U., U.S. Information Office, 4521 Campus Dr., Suite 444, Irvine, CA 92715, (714) 856–3522. Although the literature is not very impressive-looking, and the US office does not seem to respond to specific questions, causing much frustration among students, would-be students, and me, the school is a good one, the program innovative and worth the effort to deal with their U.S. representatives.

VIRGINIA COMMONWEALTH UNIVERSITY

910 W. Franklin St.
Richmond, VA 23284 USA
Horace Wooldridge, Acting Director of Admissions
General studies, interdisciplinary studies
1837

B, M, Accredited
Residency
Non-profit, state
(804) 257–1200
$$

Bachelor of General Studies for working adults. Individually developed degree requirements in the form of an individualized curriculum plan. Encouragement to utilize CLEP, military, and non-college health field education. Some use of courses taught at other institutions of the Capital Consortium for Continuing Higher Education. Program requires minimum of 30 credits to be completed at V.C.U. in regular day, evening, or weekend classes. Master of Interdisciplinary Studies Program, serving evening and part-time graduate students, enables students to combine studies in three graduate programs into a coherent, individualized, multidisciplinary program. Program is a joint venture with Virginia State University in Petersburg and requires some study at V.S.U. Thesis or final project is required.

WALDEN UNIVERSITY ✪

415 First Avenue North
Minneapolis, MN 55401 USA
Harold Abel, President
Administration/management, education, human services, health services
1970

D, Accredited
Short residency
Non-profit, independent
(800) 237–6434
$$$$

Walden serves mid-career professionals with a Master's or equivalent. Doctoral programs (Ed.D. or Ph.D.) can be completed through a combination of independent study, intensive weekend sessions held regionally, personal interaction with faculty, and a three-week summer residency in Minnesota. Admissions workshops are held in a dozen or more cities in the U.S. and Canada each year. Each student is guided by a faculty advisor, with a reader and external consultant/examiner added at the dissertation stage. Each student completes a series of knowledge area modules, in areas ranging from research methodology to social systems. Ed.D. candidates must complete a 200-hour supervised internship. Walden received its accreditation in 1990. The academic policy board is chaired by Harold Hodgkinson, former director of the National Institutes of Education.

WASHINGTON COLLEGE OF LAW

Washington Institute for Graduate Studies
2268 E. Newcastle Drive
Sandy (Salt Lake City), UT 84093 USA
Gary James Joslin, Director
Taxation
1976

M, D, Unaccredited, state registered
Non-resident
Non-profit, independent
(801) 943–2440
$$$

Lawyers and CPAs may earn the Master's degree in taxation (LL.M. Tax for lawyers, M.Tax. for CPAs). Four hundred hours of class is required, in residence or through home study video tapes. Most students take two years complete the program. The colleges uses what they identify as the most advanced integrated system of textbooks on taxation of any graduate tax program. The doctorate (J.S.D. for lawyers, Ph.D. for CPAs) requires the Master's in taxation, and a book-length dissertation of publishable quality, which must be defended before a specialist panel. The school is accepted for CPE credit by the Treasury, Internal Revenue Service for Enrolled Agents, and by the state boards of accountancy of virtually all states requiring such approval. The college is registered with the Utah Board of Regents. The college is a division of Washington Institute for Graduate Studies, a Utah educational corporation. Accreditation is from an unrecognized agency, which the catalogue does not mention is unrecognized.

WASHINGTON UNIVERSITY

University College
St. Louis, MO 63130 USA
Venita Lake
Many fields
1853

B, M, Accredited
Residency
Non-profit, independent
(314) 889–6700
$$$$

Bachelor of Science and Master of Liberal Arts, available through evening and weekend study, in the School of Continuing Education of University College.

WAYLAND BAPTIST UNIVERSITY
1900 W. 7th
Plainview, TX 79072 USA
Lorraine Nance, Director of Academic Services
Occupational education, occupational technology, business, religion
1908

B, M, Accredited
Residency
Non-profit, church
(806) 296–5521
$$

Bachelor of Science in occupational education in which more than 75% of the necessary units can be earned through an assessment of prior learning experience. Wayland centers are located in Amarillo, Lubbock, Wichita Falls, San Antonio, and Honolulu, Hawaii, as well as on the main campus in Plainview. A degree plan is prepared upon request either prior to or after enrollment, based on documentation submitted by the student. The assessment generally takes less than one month and is completed without cost to the student.

WAYNE STATE UNIVERSITY
University Studies and Weekend College, 6001 Cass
Detroit, MI 48202 USA
Ronald C. Hughes, Director of Admissions
General studies
1868

B, Accredited
Residency
Non-profit, state
(313) 577–2424
$$

The Bachelor of General Studies and Bachelor of Technical and General Studies degrees are offered through a combination of television courses broadcast in the early morning or late evening, four-hour evening workshops, and a weekend conference every few months. Students must complete the equivalent of a year of studies in social science, natural science, and humanities, and a final year of interdisciplinary advanced studies. The residential sessions are held at a variety of locations, such as public libraries, union halls, and in the Jackson State Prison. The Weekend College is a non-traditional, adult-oriented program leading to Bachelor of General Studies or Technical and General Studies degrees. A minimum of 40 semester hours of residency in Detroit is required.

WEBSTER UNIVERSITY ✪
470 E. Lockwood
St. Louis, MO 63119 USA
Dr. Leigh Gerdine, President
Business, computers, health
1915

M, Accredited
Residency
Non-profit, independent
(314) 968–6900
$$$$$

Now, here's the problem. Their innovative Master's programs, offered in dozens of locations around the U.S., used to be described in glowing terms in this book. I received more than 20 letters from people who enrolled as a result of my report and were happy. Then the coordinator of Experiental and Individual Learning wrote and demanded that I stop providing information on their programs. So I left them out of the last edition. Then, needless to say, I got a bunch of letters from people saying, in effect, "How come you didn't put anything in on Webster." That is a question that might be well posed to Webster's president, Dr. Leigh Gerdine.

WEIMAR COLLEGE
20601 W. Paoli Ln.
Weimar, CA 95736 USA
Herbert E. Douglass, President
1978

B, Unaccredited, state authorized
Non-profit, independent
(916) 637–4111
$$

Authorized to grant degrees by the state of California. Did not respond to three requests for information on their programs.

WENTWORTH INSTITUTE OF TECHNOLOGY
550 Huntington Ave.

B, Accredited

Boston, MA 02115 USA
Robert A Schuiteman, Dean of Admissions
Technical, design
1904
Residency
Non-profit, independent
(617) 442–9010, ext. 264
$$$

Weekend College offers Bachelor's degrees in architectural building construction, computer science, construction management, electronics, interior design, and mechanical technical management.

WEST COAST UNIVERSITY
440 S. Shatto Place
Los Angeles, CA 90020 USA
Roger Miller, Director of Admissions
Engineering, computers, business, other fields
1909
B, M, Accredited
Residency
Non-profit, independent
(213) 487–4433
$$$

Bachelor of Science in engineering (mechanical, electrical, electromechanical, industrial), computer science, industrial technology, business administration; Master of Science in engineering (aerospace, electrical, mechanical, systems), computer science, management information systems, acquisition and contract management, engineering and technical management, business administration, and international business administration. All courses available through evening study at locations in Los Angeles, Orange, San Diego, Ventura, and Santa Barbara counties. Credit for non-degree courses (business, military). Credit for life experience by challenge examination.

WEST LIBERTY STATE COLLEGE
see: West Virginia Board of Regents B.A. Program

WEST LONDON UNIVERSITY
16 Gloucester Place
London, W1H 3AW England
Dr. George Prior, Director
Many fields
B, M, D, Unaccredited
Non-resident
(01) 486–0390

The university first came to my attention in 1988. Accreditation is claimed from the European Accreditation Association, an organization I have been unable to locate. Although the well-designed catalogue discusses certain work that may be required, it also states that in certain cases, the Ph.D. may be awarded based entirely on prior experience. The main office appears to be in Dublin, Ireland (120–121 Lower Baggot St.), with the London address used for the College of Distance Learning. The only name given in the literature is that of George Prior, director.

WEST VIRGINIA BOARD OF REGENTS B.A. PROGRAM
203 Student Services Bldg., West Virginia University
Morgantown, WV 26506 USA
Dr. Alan W. Jenks, Coordinator, Regents B.A. Program
Many fields
1867
B, Accredited
Short residency
Non-profit, state
(304) 293–0111
$$

Bachelor of Arts program, requiring a minimum of 15 semester hours in residence at any of the member schools in the state. "As long as the student can provide evidence that he/she possesses college equivalent knowledge or skills, his/her achievements will be credited and recognized as applicable toward this degree program." The evaluation of life experience costs a modest $50, regardless of the amount of credit granted. The member schools are: Bluefield State College, West Virginia State College, Concord College, West Virginia Tech, Fairmont State College, West Virginia University, Shepherd College, West Liberty State College, Marshall University, and Glenville State College.

WEST VIRGINIA COLLEGE OF GRADUATE STUDIES
Sullivan Hall
Institute, WV 25112 USA
Kenneth O'Neal, Director of Admissions
Many fields
1972
M, Accredited
Residency
Non-profit, independent
(304) 768–9711
$$

Uses the classrooms of other institutions to offer Master's degrees in counseling, humanistic studies, school psychology, business and management, engineering (chemical, civil, industrial, management), environmental studies, and information systems. Classes are offered by late afternoon and evening study at many locations in the 16-county area served, including Institute, Charleston, Bluefield, Beckley, and Lewisburg. There are also intensive short courses throughout the year, and summer sessions. Toll-free number in West Virginia only: (800) 642–2647.

WEST VIRGINIA STATE COLLEGE
see: West Virginia Board of Regents B.A. Program

WEST VIRGINIA TECH
see: West Virginia Board of Regents B.A. Program

WEST VIRGINIA UNIVERSITY
203 Student Services Center
Morgantown, WV 26506 USA
Dr. Glenn Carter, Director of Admissions
Education, business administration
1867

B, M, Accredited
Residency
Non-profit, state
(304) 293–0111
$$

Master of Arts in education and M.B.A. available through evening study. "Academic forgiveness" of any less-than-wonderful grades more than five years old. See also: West Virginia Board of Regents B.A. Program.

WESTERN GRADUATE SCHOOL OF PSYCHOLOGY
575 Middlefield Rd.
Palo Alto, CA 94301 USA
John Emanuele, President
Clinical psychology
1978

M, D, Unaccredited, state approved, Residency
Non-profit, independent
(415) 493–6433
$$$

The Ph.D. in clinical psychology is offered to working professionals, through classes offered in the late afternoon and evening. Normally, two years of classes plus a lengthy period of supervised fieldwork are required. Students who have knowledge in a specific subject area may take challenge examinations, rather than the entire course. The program is approved by the state of California, and thus graduates can take the state licensing exams without further qualification. Former name: Palo Alto School of Professional Psychology.

WESTERN ILLINOIS UNIVERSITY ✪
Non-Traditional Programs, 309 Sherman Hall
Macomb, IL 61455 USA
Dr. Hans Moll, Director, Non-Traditional Programs
Many fields
1899

B, Accredited
Non-resident
Non-profit, state
(309) 298–1929
$$

The Board of Governors B.A. can be earned entirely by correspondence study. Fifteen of 120 semester hours must be earned at a B.O.G. university, and 40 must be upper division. The 15 units that must be earned after enrolling can be done by correspondence, on campus in Macomb, or through extension courses at locations around the state. Students who did not graduate from an Illinois high school must pass an exam on the U.S. and Illinois state constitution, or take an equivalent course in political science. All students must pass a University Writing Exam. Western Illinois provides a helpful guide to the preparation of a prior learning portfolio. Credit for learning experiences and many equivalency exams. The total cost of the program depends on the number and type of courses taken. The cost of assessing a life experience portfolio is only $30. Students from other countries are admitted, but they must have a U.S. address to which materials can be sent.

WESTERN INSTITUTE FOR SOCIAL RESEARCH
3220 Sacramento St.
Berkeley, CA 94702 USA

B, M, D, Unaccredited, state approved, Residency

Dr. John Bilorusky
Psychology, education, social sciences, human services/community development
1975

Non-profit, independent
(415) 655–2830
$$

Degrees at all levels, primarily for people concerned with educational innovation and/or community and social change, through a combination of residential and independent study. The typical student is enrolled for two to three years, which must include two months per year residency or several days every couple of months. The approach involves intensive study with a faculty advisor and in small seminars, and projects combining practical and intellectual approaches to community and educational problems. The school has been approved by the state of California. Former name: Western Regional Learning Center.

WESTERN INTERNATIONAL UNIVERSITY
10202 N. 19th Ave.
Phoenix, AZ 85021 USA
Elena Pattison, Director of Admissions
Business, accounting, computers, management, general studies
1978

B, M, Accredited
Residency
Non-profit, independent
(602) 943–2311
$$

B.S. in accounting, management, or computer information science; B.A. in general studies; M.B.A.; M.S. in accounting and computer information science, offered by evening study on campuses in Arizona and in London, England. Subject areas include management, accounting, and computer information science. Courses are given in an "accelerated semester" format. Each course takes one month, two evenings a week. The undergraduate programs may be completed in 29 months. The Master's degree is a 12-month program. Advanced standing may be awarded if the student proves to be competent in and can demonstrate knowledge of course content. Assessment by portfolio and COMP/ACT Composite Examination are two ways of demonstrating this knowledge.

WESTERN MARYLAND COLLEGE
Westminster, MD 21157 USA
Joseph S. Rigell, Director of Admissions
Education of the deaf and sensory impairment
1867

M, Accredited
Residency
Non-profit, independent
(301) 848–7000
$$$$

Master of Education and Master of Science in sensory impairment, two programs to prepare professionals to teach the hearing impaired and to work with the hearing and visually impaired. Courses are conducted during late afternoon and evening hours except in the summer. Programs can also be completed in three consecutive nine-week summer sessions, with provision for independent study at home in between.

WESTERN MICHIGAN UNIVERSITY
Kalamazoo, MI 49008 USA
Robert M. Hedrick, Dean of Admissions
Many fields
1903

B, M, D, Accredited
Residency
Non-profit, state
(616) 383–1600
$$

The following degrees are available through the Office of Evening and Weekend Programs: Bachelor of Business Administration, Bachelor of Arts, Bachelor of Science, Master of Arts in Education, Master of Social Work, Master of Arts, and Education Specialist. The following degrees are available entirely through off-campus regional centers: Bachelor of Science in general university studies, mechanical engineering and manufacturing; Master of Arts in many fields; Master of Social Work; Master of Science; and Master and Doctor of Public Administration. Residency requirements can be satisfied through work completed at a W.M.U. regional center.

WESTERN NEW ENGLAND COLLEGE
School of Continuing Higher Education, 1215 Wilbraham Rd.
Springfield, MA 01119 USA
Lori-Anne Reidy, Director Admissions
1919

B, Accredited
Residency
Non-profit, independent
(413) 782-3111
$$$

Bachelor of Arts in liberal studies and Bachelor of Science in law enforcement are offered entirely through part-time evening study.

WESTERN STATES UNIVERSITY
P.O. Box 430
Doniphan, MO 63935 USA
Dr. Zdena Hudson-Zajickova, President
Many fields

B, M, D, Unaccredited
Non-resident
(314) 996–7388
$$

Founded by Dr. Glenn E. Hudson, whose Doctorate is from the University of England at Oxford, a diploma mill whose proprietors were sentenced to federal prison in 1987 for selling degrees for $200 each. Dr. Hudson's Bachelor's and Master's are from Metropolitan Collegiate Institute, a non-existent school that sells degrees for $100. Western States has used addresses in Yuma, Arizona, and Salt Lake City. A recent publication refers to the headquarters in the Philippines. They claim to be "licensed in the state of Missouri." Missouri does not license schools. Their materials include information photocopied (without credit) from another school's catalogue. Degrees based entirely on life experience plus a project, which can be an account of how one planned and started a business. They were accredited by the International Accrediting Commission for Schools, Colleges and Theological Seminaries, which was shut down by Missouri authorities in 1989.

WESTFIELD STATE COLLEGE
Western Ave.
Westfield, MA 01086 USA
William M. Crean, Director of Admissions
Many fields
1838

B, M, Accredited
Residency
Non-profit, state
(413) 568–3311
$

Weekend, evening, and summer classes leading to a Bachelor of Arts, Bachelor of Science, Master of Arts, Master of Science, and Master of Education.

WESTMINSTER COLLEGE (Pennsylvania)
New Wilmington, PA 16172 USA
Robert A. Latta, Acting Dean of Admissions
Many fields
1852

B, Accredited
Residency
Non-profit, church
(412) 946–8761
$$$$

Up to 75% of the necessary units may be earned by an assessment of prior learning experiences. Assessment is limited to students admitted to degree program, and is combined with minimum of nine course units completed in residence. Cost of assessment is $395, regardless of amount of credit awarded. Completion of assessment portfolio typically requires at least six months. Evening courses and assessment offered through Lifelong Learning Program. See also: East Central College Consortium.

WESTMINSTER COLLEGE (Utah)
Office of Adult and Extended Education, 1840 S. 13th East
Salt Lake City, UT 84105 USA
Brad Ericson, Association Director of Admissions
Many fields
1875

B, Accredited
Residency
Non-profit, independent
(801) 488–4200
$$$

Bachelor's degrees in 25 fields. Up to one third of the necessary units may be earned by an assessment of prior learning experiences. Some degrees in business and the social sciences may be earned through evening programs. Assessment is limited to students admitted to a degree program and is done after enrollment, at a cost of $173 for the class and a $300 assessment fee.

WHITWORTH COLLEGE
Spokane, WA 99251 USA
Dr. Dale E. Soden,
Coordinator of Continuing Studies
1890

B, M, Accredited
Residency
Non-profit, church
(509) 466–3222
$$

Bachelor of Arts in accounting, Bachelor of Arts in business management, Bachelor of Science in health management, M.S. in health education/promotion or health administration through evening and summer programs and independent study. The tuition for degrees earned in the evening is one quarter of that for daytime programs.

See page 70 for explanation of abbreviations and symbols

WILLIAM CAREY INTERNATIONAL UNIVERSITY
1539 E. Howard St.
Pasadena, CA 91104 USA
(818) 797–1200

M, D, Unaccredited, state approved
Non-profit, independent

$$

Approved by the state of California to grant degrees. Did not respond to two requests for information on their programs.

WILLIAM LYON UNIVERSITY
814 Morena Blvd.
San Diego, CA 92110 USA
Dr. Henry W. Gaylor, Jr., President
Business, computer science, education, engineering, human behavior, psychology
1986

B, M, D, Unaccredited, state approved, Non-resident
Proprietary
(619) 298–9040
$$$

No traditional residency required, but students must meet in person with faculty mentors in their area, for a total of at least 90 hours. Work for the degree involves a learning contract (called "Matriculant's Semester Registration Agreement"), covering method of study (innovative, involving computers, videotapes and videodiscs; or traditional), number of sessions, locations, etc. Faculty consist of academic advisors and learning resource specialists. Learning sessions must be preplanned, prescheduled, and done in person with the faculty. No instruction is offered by correspondence. Credit is given for prior learning experiences. The university is approved by the state of California. Original name: Lyon International University.

WINONA STATE UNIVERSITY
Regional Campus
Winona, MN 55987 USA
Pauline Christensen, Chair, Adult Division
Many fields
1858

B, M, Accredited
Residency
Non-profit, church
(507) 457–5000
$$

Bachelor's degrees in arts, sciences, business, education, nursing, and paralegal; Master of Science degrees in education, counseling and educational administration; and M.B.A. Adult students in undergraduate degrees, except teaching or nursing, may qualify for credit for life experience. Many courses available evenings. Minimum of 48 credits required from W.S.U.

WITTENBERG UNIVERSITY
School of Continuing Education, P.O. Box 720
Springfield, OH 45501 USA
Kenneth G. Benne, Director of Admissions
Liberal studies, business administration
1845

B, Accredited
Residency
Non-profit, church
(513) 327–6231
$$$$

The degrees of B.A. in Liberal Studies, B.A. in Business Administration, and a B.A. degree completion program for registered nurses can be done entirely through evening study. Credit is given for standard equivalency exams, and special exams will be devised in areas not covered by standard tests.

WORLD COLLEGE WEST
101 S. San Antonio Rd.
Petaluma, CA 94952 USA
Dr. Elden Jacobson, Program Director
Values, meaning and culture
1971

B, Accredited
Residency
Non-profit, independent
(707) 765–4500
$$

The B.A. is available through a weekend program for adults. The degree program consists of 18 weekend seminars (2 units each), some electives (faculty-guided independent study, or local courses), an internship, a brief intercultural experience, and an individual "senior invention" (a senior project).

WORLD OPEN UNIVERSITY
P.O. Box 8286

M, D, Unaccredited

Rapid City, SD 57709 USA
Dr. Shu-Tien Li, President
Many fields
1972

Non-resident
Non-profit, independent
(605) 343–3334
$$$

World Open University is part of the Li Institution of Science and Technology, established by Dr. Shu-Tien Li, who earned his Doctorate at Cornell University in 1926, and who, according to the school's literature, served as president of nine colleges and universities in China. The university offers Master's and Doctorates through four graduate faculties: letters and humanities, engineering and technology, administration and management, and mathematics and science. There is an adjunct (part-time) faculty of more than 120 in 15 countries. A major requirement of earning the Doctorate is having two major papers published in regular journals of recognized learned or professional societies. They incorporated in South Dakota, and operated for a time from Orange, California, before returning to Rapid City, "because it is the geographic center of [the] North American continent." Dr. Li established the university in 1972 at age 72 and, in 1990, he and it were apparently still going strong.

WORLD UNIVERSITY
P. O. Box 2470
Benson, Arizona 85602
H. John Zitko, President

D, Unaccredited
(602) 586-2985

I have read through a good deal of typewritten literature issued by the World Headquarters of the Secretariat in Tucson and the Desert Sanctuary Regional Campus in Benson, and I'm afraid I am still quite uncertain about what they do, other than award 'cultural doctorates,' and hold conferences. There has been an affiliation with Columbia Pacific University which is alternately referred to as 'California Pacific University' (unless there is also an affiliation with California Pacific University). One newsletter reports that their trustee in Los Angeles, Countess Pauline de Farrell de Milos has "recently been decorated with the Grand Star of Stanislaus, the highest honor ever given to a world citizen."

WORLD UNIVERSITY OF AMERICA
107 N. Ventura St.
Ojai, CA 93023 USA
Dr. Benito F. Reyes, President
Many fields
1974

B, M, D, Unaccredited, state approved, residency
Non-profit, independent
(805) 646–1444
$$

Degrees and certificates offered in many fields of study, including thanatology, astrology, out-of-body experience, seven kinds of yoga, avasthology, astronomy, and spiritual ministry. Their goal is to establish a World University in every state in the union and to promote spiritual growth within the framework of an academic curriculum. The literature asks, "With all the modern appliances, why are we not happy?" Indeed. Not affiliated with the formerly accredited World University (Puerto Rico). Several other unaccredited schools have mentioned an affiliation with World University, but not yet one in every state, as best I can tell.

XAVIER EVENING COLLEGE
College of Continuing Education
Cincinnati, OH 45207 USA
Rene A. Durand Jr., Director of Admissions
Various fields
1831

B, M, Accredited
Residency
Non-profit, church
(513) 745–3000
$$$

Xavier offers a Bachelor of General Studies, a Bachelor of Science in business administration, and other Bachelor's degrees in nuclear medical technology, modern foreign languages, computer science, and communication arts, either through weekend study or evening study. Extremely low tuition is available for people over 60.

YUIN UNIVERSITY
14409 E. Ramona Blvd.
Baldwin Park, CA 91706

B, M, D, Unaccredited
Residency
Proprietary
(818) 960-667

See page 70 for explanation of abbreviations and symbols

Acupuncture $$

Authorized to grant degrees by the state of California. Did not respond to two requests for information on their programs.

17. Weekend Colleges

Sunday should be different from another day.
People may walk, but not throw stones at birds.
—Dr. Samuel Johnson

Happily, this chapter is probably on the way out, and may not appear in the next edition of this book. The simple reason is that weekend colleges have become so commonplace, they can hardly be considered non-traditional for much longer.

As one answer to ever-increasing expenses, more and more colleges have been paying attention to making more efficient use of their facilities. A typical college or university might use its classrooms and lecture halls for about six hours a day, 200 days a year. That's a total of 1,200 hours a year out of the 8,760 possible, or a feeble .140 batting average.

One of the innovative solutions that arose in the 1970s was the idea of weekend college: a degree program in which all the courses are taught intensively on Friday evening, Saturday, and/or Sunday. In some cases, the students actually move onto campus on Friday afternoon, and remain until Sunday evening, living the life of a student for 48 hours each week.

Some weekend colleges operate every weekend, others every other weekend, and some just one weekend per month.

The 7th edition of this book listed 5 pioneer institutions that were offering weekend programs. The 8th edition listed 14, and the 9th edition 50. Now weekend colleges have become so commonplace, there is really no point in listing the hundreds of programs that exist. Many of the schools are described in chapter 16. If no school near you is listed there, the best solution is to check with the community colleges, colleges, and universities in your vicinity. The odds are improving that if they do not already have a weekend program, one is on the drawing board.

18. High School Diplomas and Associate Degrees

Education is what remains when you have forgotten everything you learned in school.
—Albert Einstein

HIGH SCHOOL DIPLOMAS BY CORRESPONDENCE STUDY

The first thing to say is that, even if you have not completed high school, you probably will not need to do so in order to enroll in a non-traditional college degree program.

The high school diploma is the usual "ticket of admission" to a traditional university. However, many universities, both traditional and non-traditional, believe that anywhere from two to seven years of life or job experience is at least the equivalent of a high school diploma. So if you are over the age of 25, you should have no trouble finding schools that do not require a high school diploma. If you are between 18 and 25, you may have to shop around a little, or may find it necessary to complete high school (or its equivalent) first.

Here are the four ways to complete high school (or its equivalent) by non-traditional means:

1. The High School Division of a University

While many of the universities with correspondence programs (listed in chapter 12) offer high-school-level correspondence study as well as college-level, only three major universities actually award high school diplomas based on correspondence study. These diplomas are the exact equivalent of a traditional high school diploma, and are accepted everywhere.

Brigham Young University offers its high school diploma in association with a local school district, while the University of Arkansas and the University of Nebraska award their own high school diplomas.

Brigham Young University
Adult High School Diploma Program, Provo, UT 84602

University of Arkansas
External High School Diploma Program, Division of Continuing Education, Fayetteville, AR 72701

University of Nebraska
High School Completion Program, Division of Continuing Studies, Lincoln, NE 68583

2. State Equivalency Examinations

Each of the 50 states offers a high school equivalency examination, sometimes called the G.E.D., which is the equivalent of a high school diploma for virtually all purposes, including admission to college. Although each state's procedures differ, in general the examination takes from three to five hours, and covers the full range of high school subjects: mathematics, science, language, history, social studies, etc. It must be taken in person, not by mail. For the details in any given state, contact that state's Department of Education in the state capital.

(My twin daughters each took the equivalency exam when they were 15, part way through the 10th grade. As soon as they learned they had passed, they left high school forever. One immediately enrolled in college; the other worked for three years, and then entered a university. Neither had any problem with college admission as a result of their equivalency diploma. And both ended up as straight-A students, despite the lack of whatever they might have learned in three years of high school.)

3. Private Correspondence Schools

There are quite a few private, usually proprietary (profit-making) schools or institutes that award high school diplomas or equivalency certificates through correspondence study. They tend to be more expensive and not quite as widely accepted as the university programs or the state equivalency exams. On the other hand, they may be faster and more generous in the credit given for prior experience. Here are three accredited schools offering this program:

American School
850 E. 58th St., Chicago, IL 60637

Home Study International
6940 Carroll Ave., Takoma Park, MD 20912

International Correspondence Schools
Scranton, PA 18515

4. Home Education

There is a large and growing movement toward educating children at home. It isn't easy, but it can be richly rewarding, and much help and support is available, largely through the auspices of John Holt's organization. Holt is the author of *How Children Fail* and other books on educational reform, and founder of a magazine called *Growing Without Schooling.* Information is available from John Holt's Book and Music Store, 729 Boylston St., Boston, MA 02116.

ASSOCIATE'S DEGREES

The Associate's degree, a relatively recent innovation, is awarded at the conclusion of two fulltime years of successful study by community and junior colleges, as well as being given halfway through the Bachelor's degree program by some (but not too many) Bachelor's-granting colleges.

The standard degrees are the A.A. (Associate of Arts) and A.S. (Associate of Science), but many other titles are used.

Thousands of different Associate's programs exist, and many of them are available by part-time, evening, or correspondence study. Many take into account life experience, previous courses, or credit by examination.

To describe or even list them all would have doubled the size of this book, and a reader survey a few years ago convinced me that only a tiny percentage of readers have interest in this degree. Fortunately, for those who are interested, there does exist a directory of such programs. It is called *A Directory of U.S. College and University Degrees for Part-Time Students,* and it is sold at bookstores and by the National University Extension Association, One Dupont Circle NW, Suite 360, Washington, DC 20036.

It is arranged alphabetically by states and cities, and lists more than 2,000 Associate's degree programs in all 50 states.

19. Law Schools

Why does a hearse horse snicker
Hauling a lawyer away?
—Carl Sandburg

The law is a curiosity of the academic world. On one hand, it is possible to graduate from a world-famous law school and not be able to practice law. And on the other hand, it is possible to practice law without ever having seen the inside of a law school.

What makes this unusual set of circumstances possible is, of course, the Bar exam. In all fifty states of this union, the way most people are "admitted to the Bar" is by taking and passing the Bar exam. Each state administers its own exam, and there is the Multi-State Bar exam, which is accepted by most states for some or all Bar exam credit.

Until the twentieth century, most lawyers learned the law as Abraham Lincoln did—by apprenticing themselves to a lawyer or a judge, or studying on their own, and when they had learned enough, taking the Bar. Although a few states theoretically still permit this practice, for all intents and purposes, it survives only in California, where the study of law is, in many aspects, different from the rest of the U.S., which is why California is considered separately in this chapter.

In a few states, if one graduates from a law school in that state, it is not necessary to take that state's Bar exam in order to practice law. In a few states, graduates of unaccredited law schools may be permitted to take the Bar exam. There are two problems I have in reporting this: one is that the situation keeps changing; states seem regularly to revise or reinterpret their regulations; the other is that rules and regulations seem often to be rather flexible or at least inconsistent in the way they are interpreted (see the chapter on Bending the Rules).

THE BAR EXAM

The Bar exam has come under increasing criticism in recent years, on a number of grounds.

- There often seems to be little correlation between performance on the Bar and performance as a lawyer. Most Bar exams, for instance, do not test ability to do legal research, conduct interviews, or argue in court.
- A test score that will pass in one state will fail in another. Consider the score required to pass, in several states, in one recent year:

California: 145	Pennsylvania: 129
New York: 135	Texas: 128
Florida: 130	Wisconsin: 125

One critic has pointed out that if California test takers had gone en masse to New York, their pass rate would have been 74% instead of California's rather dismal 42% that year.

- In recent years, the Bar exam has undergone frequent and major changes. Gordon Schaber, former chairman of the ABA's section on legal education, points out that the California exam underwent "10 serious structural changes" between 1974 and 1983, during which time the pass rate dropped 12%. Following significant changes in 1983, the pass rate dropped another 9%. The failure rate would probably be even greater, but nearly half the minority graduates at UCLA (which has the largest minority law student population in the state) chose not even to take the California Bar exam. The pass rate for Blacks has been less than 25%, although the majority of Blacks who failed in California would have passed the New York or Pennsylvania exam with the same scores.
- Although the quality of law education is generally felt to continue to improve, the percentage of people passing the Bar has steadily declined in recent years. As one example, Schaber cites the entering Stanford class of 1981, which had the highest LSAT (Law School Admissions Test) scores ever, and a grade point average of 3.79 on a scale of 4. Yet when this class graduated and took the Bar exam, only 75% passed—down 17% from a few years earlier.

Can it be, people are asking more and more, that there may be too many lawyers in the world, and the already-established ones are trying to limit the new competition? In recent years, the number of lawyers has increased at more than double the rate of the population as a whole. There are more lawyers in Chicago than in all of Japan; more in New York than in all of England.

THE LAW DEGREE

Until the early 1960s, the law degree earned in America was the LL.B., or Bachelor of Laws. An LL.D., or Doctor of Laws, was available at some schools as an advanced law degree, earned after several years of study beyond the LL.B. Many lawyers didn't like the idea that lots of other professionals (optometrists, podiatrists, civil engineers, etc.) put in three years of study after college and got a Doctorate, while lawyers put in the same time and got just another Bachelor's. Law schools took heed, and almost universally converted the title of the law degree to a J.D., which can stand for Doctor of Jurisprudence or Juris Doctor. Most schools offered their alumni the opportunity to convert their old LL.B.'s into nice shiny J.D.'s. One survey reported that a large percentage accepted, but another report suggests that very few of these actually *use* the J.D. professionally, still listing the LL.B. in legal directories.

THE SITUATION IN CALIFORNIA

California is the only state that permits study of law by correspondence, or with private tutors (normally lawyers or judges), and it is one of three states (Georgia and Alabama are the others) that regularly allows graduates of unaccredited law schools to take the Bar exam. (I say "regularly" because, as indicated earlier, there are apparently special case exceptions in other states, from time to time.)

There are two kinds of unaccredited law schools: approximately 20 that offer regular residential courses in California, often through evening and/or weekend study; and about a dozen that offer study entirely by correspondence. There used to be no requirement that the correspondence schools be located in California, but from 1990, only California schools are permitted.

The California procedure works like this: after completing one year of law study, which must include a documented 864 hours of study (about 17 hours a week), the student must take the First Year Law Students' Qualifying Exam, known as the "Baby Bar." This is a consumer protection measure, to help students studying law non-traditionally determine whether or not they are making progress.

Once the Baby Bar is passed, the student then continues for three additional years of study, 864 hours a year. When at least four years have passed and at least 3,456 hours have been logged, the regular Bar exam may be taken.

Copies of past years' versions of the Baby Bar, with answers, may be purchased from the State Bar of California, P.O. Box 7908, San Francisco, CA 94129.

The Baby Bar is required of all students studying either with correspondence law schools, or with unaccredited residential law schools. In the last three years, students from 11 correspondence schools and 21 residential unaccredited schools have taken the regular Bar exam.

CALIFORNIA EXAM PERFORMANCE

One could spend days studying and analyzing the huge amounts of data made available by the State Bar of California, giving pass rates by school, by date, by kind of school, by ethnic background, by number of previous exam attempts, and so forth. In an earlier edition of this book, I erred by basing calculations on the number of exam passes rather than the number of *people* who passed. If, for instance, one person failed the Bar ten times, this should be counted as one person failing, and not ten, in calculating a school's pass-fail percentages.

Rather than fill this chapter with endless charts and tables, I have elected to present only the following data:

- Complete summary of statistics for a recent Bar exam.
- For unaccredited residential schools, first time exam takers' pass rates, cumulative for six consecutive Bar exams (three years).
- For correspondence law schools, just the last results.

Unfortunately, the California Bar does not make available results of the Baby Bar by individual schools, or even by the sub-categories of "residential" and "correspondence." It would be most helpful if they did.

Please bear in mind that these statistics will vary considerably from year to year and school to school.

ALL CALIFORNIA BAR EXAM TAKERS

	Took Exam	Passed	Percent
All students	7,515	3,780	50.3%
First timers	4,913	3,212	65.4
Second timers	637	178	27.9
California accredited schools that are ABA-approved			
First timers	2,968	2,164	72.9
Repeaters	976	278	28.5
California accredited schools not ABA-approved			
First timers	520	202	38.8
Repeaters	855	132	15.4
California schools neither accredited nor approved			
First timers	92	26	28.3
Repeaters	175	13	7.5
Out of State law schools			
First timers	784	539	68.8
Repeaters	189	59	31.2
Correspondence law schools			
First timers	10	1	10.0
Repeaters	47	4	8.5
Private study with lawyer or judge			
First timers	1	0	0.0
Repeaters	16	1	6.2
Lawyers from other states			
First timers	433	244	56.4
Repeaters	229	64	27.9
Stanford University			
First timers	79	67	84.8
All applicants	86	70	81.4
Harvard University			
First timers	73	66	90.4
All applicants	77	67	87.0

UNACCREDITED RESIDENTIAL LAW SCHOOLS FIRST TIME TAKERS ONLY, 6 CONSECUTIVE BAR EXAMS

	Took Exam	Passed	Percent
American College	51	1	1.9%
California College of Law	1	0	0.0
California Northern U.	7	5	71.4
Central California U.	6	0	0.0
Charles Dederich School of Law	11	9	81.8
Citrus Belt Law School	45	13	28.9
Lincoln U.	56	22	39.3
Pacific Coast U.	17	7	41.2
Peninsula U.	21	6	28.6
People's College	14	3	21.4
Simon Greenleaf School of Law	10	4	40.0
U. of Northern California	49	9	18.4
Western Sierra Law School	19	0	0.0

CORRESPONDENCE LAW SCHOOLS, MOST RECENT AVAILABLE RESULTS

	Took Exam	Passed	Percent
Bernadean University	5	0	0%
City U. Los Angeles	6	0	0%
Kensington U.	5	3	60%
Kenmar	1	0	0%
LaSalle U./Southland U.	8	0	0%
Newport U.	1	0	0%
North American College	5	0	0%
Thomas Jefferson U.	8	0	0%
U. of Honolulu	3	0	0%
William H. Taft U.	3	1	33%

To summarize three key numbers: the percent of first-time passers for

Traditional accredited law schools:	65%
Unaccredited residential law schools:	28%
Unaccredited correspondence law schools:	7%

Of course it is clear, at least at this sitting, that the rate for Kensington and Taft combined is 50%, while the rate for everyone else is zero. Since these numbers are very small, it is probably wise to look both at results over a longer period of time (e.g., Thomas Jefferson has had no passes in more than 80 attempts since 1985), and trends (Kensington had a poor record in 1986-87, but an excellent one later on).

Bear in mind, also, that the unaccredited school results reflect only those students who passed the Baby Bar and went on to take the regular Bar. Since the Baby Bar pass rate was around 13%, at the last sitting, it is not unreasonable to suggest that the percent of people who start an unaccredited program and eventually pass the Bar is considerably less than those figures of 28% and 7%.

Opponents of the non-traditional approach argue that the lower pass rates "prove" that the approach cannot work. Supporters point out that truly dedicated and highly motivated students *do* pass, and that many of these people would never have been able to pursue the degree by traditional means. They also suggest that many people take the Bar exams as a matter of curiosity, with little expectation of passing.

It is clearly the case that for the would-be lawyer who cannot afford either the time or the money for traditional law study, or who cannot gain admission to an accredited law school, California approaches offer the best hope.

In addition to qualifying students for the California Bar, completion of unaccredited law programs may also qualify graduates to take the exams required for practice before U.S. tax and patent courts, workers compensation boards, the Interstate Commerce Commission, and various other federal courts and agencies. As with any degree program, potential students should satisfy themselves in advance that the degree will meet their personal needs.

THE CORRESPONDENCE LAW SCHOOLS

Many of these schools are described in more detail in chapter 16.

BERNADEAN UNIVERSITY

13615 Victory Blvd., Room 114, Van Nuys, CA 914401

The school is not authorized to operate by the State of California even though it has been recognized by the Committee of Bar Examiners, an unusual situation. A part of the Church of Universology, which in the past has offered absolution from all sins to its graduates. Total tuition, without books, about $3,000.

CALIFORNIA COLLEGE OF LAW

P. O. Box 449, Beverly Hills, CA 90213

CITY UNIVERSITY LOS ANGELES

3960 Wilshire Blvd., 5th Floor, Los Angeles, CA 90010

Offers both a three-year non-Bar-qualifying and a four-year qualifying degree.

COLUMBIA PACIFIC UNIVERSITY
1415 Third St., San Rafael, CA 94901
Offers only a three-year non-Bar-qualifying degree in international law.

GREENWICH UNIVERSITY
100 Kamehameha Ave., P.O. Box 1717, Hilo, HI 96721
The school I run begins offering law degrees in late 1990. The non-bar-qualifying degrees will be in various specialties: law for physicians; for accountants; for educational administrators; for engineers; and for clergy; etc.

KENSINGTON UNIVERSITY
124 S. Isabel St., Glendale, CA 91206
Tuition is approximately $10,000 for the full program, not including books.

LA SALLE UNIVERSITY
Mandeville, Louisiana
If students can find a lower tuition within 30 days of enrolling, La Salle will refund the difference. Does not qualify students to take the California bar.

NEWPORT UNIVERSITY SCHOOL OF LAW
3720 Campus Dr., Newport Beach, CA 92660
Tuition is approximately $9,000 for the full program, not including books.

NORTH AMERICAN COLLEGE OF LAW
254 S. Euclid St., Anaheim, CA 92802
Tuition is approximately $6,000 for the full program, not including books.

SOUTHLAND UNIVERSITY
Closed in California in the mid 1980s. La Salle University, Missouri, subsequently opened under the same management, and using many of the same materials.

THOMAS JEFFERSON COLLEGE OF LAW
A part of Heed University, with its main office in the Virgin Islands. Tuition is about $7,200 for the full program, not including books. See in Chapter 16.

UNIVERSITY OF HONOLULU
P. O. Box 387, Kapaa, Kauai, HI 96746
Tuition is about $6,600 for the full program, not including books.

WILLIAM H. TAFT UNIVERSITY
10061 Talbert Ave., Suite 200, Fountain Valley, CA 92708
Tuition is about $7,800 for the full program, not including books.

UNACCREDITED RESIDENTIAL LAW SCHOOLS

Only listed are those schools who have had at least one graduate take the Bar in the last three years.

AMERICAN COLLEGE OF LAW
135 S. Lemon St., Anaheim, CA 92805

CAL NORTHERN SCHOOL OF LAW
101 Salem St., Suite One, Chico, CA 95926
Five of seven (70%) passed the Bar at a recent sitting.

CENTRAL CALIFORNIA COLLEGE OF LAW
2135 Fresno St., Room 317, Fresno, CA 93721

CHARLES DEDERICH SCHOOL OF LAW
P. O. Box 24, Badger, CA 93603
The only time graduates of the Synanon-operated law school have taken the Bar, in Fall 1986, 9 of 11 (82%) passed.

CITRUS BELT LAW SCHOOL
6370 Magnolia Ave., Riverside, CA 92506
Six of 15 (40%) passed at a recent sitting.

LINCOLN UNIVERSITY LAW SCHOOL
281 Masonic Ave., San Francisco, CA 94118
1050 Park Ave., San Jose, CA 95126
Six of 18 (33%) passed the Bar at a recent sitting.

NORTHERN SCHOOL OF LAW
101 Salem St., Suite One, Chico, CA 95926
Five of seven candidates (70%) passed the Bar at a recent sitting.

NORTHERN VIRGINIA SCHOOL OF LAW
P. O. Box 1343, Alexandria, VA 22313
The degree requires four and a half years of weekend study, but it is no longer approved to enroll new students. Founded by Alfred Avins, who was instrumental in establishing what is now called the Widener University School of Law..

PACIFIC COAST UNIVERSITY COLLEGE OF LAW
440 Redondo Ave., Room 203, Long Beach, CA 90814

PENINSULA UNIVERSITY COLLEGE OF LAW
436 Dell Ave., Mountain View, CA 94043

PEOPLE'S COLLEGE OF LAW
660 S. Bonnie Brae St., Los Angeles, CA 90057

SIMON GREENLEAF SCHOOL OF LAW
2530 Shadow Ridge Lane, Orange, CA 92667
Two of three passed at a recent sitting.

UNIVERSITY OF NORTHERN CALIFORNIA
816 H St., Sacramento, CA 95814
Seven of 26 (27%) passed at a recent sitting.

WESTERN SIERRA LAW SCHOOL
6035 University Ave., Suite 2, San Diego, CA 92115

INTERSTATE LEGAL STRATEGIES

Since the rules for becoming a lawyer vary so much from state to state, the question often arises: what about qualifying to practice law in one state (an "easier" one), and then moving to another state to practice.

It is possible, but quite impractical. Twenty-seven of the 50 states permit lawyers from another state to take the Bar in their state, but, in all but two cases, only after they have practiced in their "home" state for a minimum number of years, and only if their degree is from an ABA-approved, accredited school. The minimum waiting time ranges from 3 years in Maine and Wisconsin to 20 years in Connecticut, but is 4 or 5 years in most states. Indiana and Iowa will, under certain conditions, permit lawyers admitted in other states to take their Bar with no waiting period.

STUDYING LAW NIGHTS OR WEEKENDS

In previous editions, I included a list of law schools that offered the law degree entirely through evening and/or weekend study. This practice, once relatively rare, has grown so rapidly that there are now a great many schools doing it. One might simply check any standard school directory or the yellow pages of the telephone book for this information now.

PARALEGAL DEGREES

Many people who are intrigued by the law, and wish to be involved with the law, are unwilling or unable to pursue a law degree or to be admitted to the Bar. A fairly satisfactory solution for some of these people is to pursue an alternative degree, entirely by correspondence, or with short residency, in a law-related subject.

For instance, many people have earned non-resident Master's or Doctorate degrees in business law, law and society, import-export law, consumer law, and so forth. The titles of such degrees are things like M.A. in legal studies or Ph.D. in corporate law. Of course such degrees do not permit one to practice law. Many schools offering non-resident non-traditional degrees will consider such degree programs.

There are also many people with law degrees (both traditional and non-traditional, residential and correspondence) who have never passed the Bar, but who are still working in the law. They have jobs with law firms, primarily doing research, preparing briefs, etc. They cannot meet with clients or appear in court, but they are most definitely lawyers working in the law.

Two of the schools offering paralegal studies (but not degrees) by correspondence are:

BLACKSTONE SCHOOL OF LAW
P. O. Box 790906, Dallas, TX 75379 (214) 418-5141
For many years, they did offer law degrees which qualified for bar exams. Now the son of the founder is operating it as a paralegal school only.

SCHOOL OF PARALEGAL STUDIES
6065 Roswell Road N.E., #3118, Atlanta, GA 30328

20. Medical and Health-Related Schools

Géronte: It seems to me you are locating them wrongly. The heart is on the left and the liver is on the right.
Sganarelle: Yes, in the old days that was so, but we have changed all that, and teach medicine by an entirely new method.
—Molière

Note: In previous editions, I restricted this chapter to schools offering only the M.D. degree. Now, in response to many letters, it seems appropriate to expand it to include other schools which offer only degrees related to the health sciences, nutrition, healing, and so forth. The emphasis is on the "only," for there are many schools that offer programs in health sciences, nursing, etc., as just a small part of a much broader curriculum. Such schools are listed in chapter 16. (There will probably still be many letters. The biggest wave of angry complaint letters I've ever received was after one edition in which I referred to osteopathy as an "alternative" medical therapy.)

MEDICAL SCHOOLS

There are, of course, no legitimate correspondence medical schools, but there are some non-traditional approaches to earning a traditional medical degree.

The traditional approach in the U.S. consists of attending a regular college or university for four or more years to earn a Bachelor's degree (in any field; it need not be scientific), and then going on to medical school for another four years, after which the Doctor of Medicine (M.D.) is awarded. Then one spends anywhere from two to eight years of internships, residency, and training in clinical specialities (surgery, psychiatry, etc.).

The problems caused by this huge expenditure of time and money (tuition of $20,000 a year is not uncommon) are compounded by the even greater problem of admission to a traditional medical school. The simple fact is that the great majority of applicants are not admitted. Many schools have anywhere from 10 to a 100 applicants for each opening. Although schools are not allowed, by law, to have quotas by race or by sex, as they once did, they definitely have quotas based on age. Applicants over 30 have a much harder time getting in, and those over 40 have almost no chance at all. The schools argue that their precious facilities should not be taken up by persons who will have fewer years to practice and to serve humanity.

Is there a shortage of doctors?

The reason it is so hard to get into medical school is that there are not enough openings available. And the reason there are not enough openings available is the subject of bitter debate between and among medical and political people.

The American Medical Association and the Association of American Medical Colleges have both said, throughout the 1980s, that we would have too many doctors by the 1990s. But in 1988, a major study conducted by the RAND Corporation and the Tufts University School of Medicine suggested that there may be some significant shortages by the year 2000, especially in major areas of specialty such as heart, chest, blood, kidney, gastrointestinal, blood disease, cancer, and infectious disease.

The A.M.A. suggests that too many doctors, whether from medical schools or from other countries, may mean that U.S. doctors' skills could deteriorate because the physician "may not perform certain procedures frequently enough to maintain a high level of skill." But RAND/Tufts suggest that by 2000, cities with populations of 200,000 may not have anywhere near the specialists they need.

Andy Rooney writes that "the A.M.A. sounds like a bricklayers' union. The bricklayers want to limit membership in the union so that there will always be more bricks that need to be laid than there are bricklayers to lay them. Doctors don't want a lot of young doctors offering their services for less so they can pay back the money they borrowed to get through medical school."

ACCELERATED MEDICAL PROGRAMS

One slightly non-traditional approach to the M.D. is that of compressing the total elapsed time between high school and receiving the M.D. by two or three years. Many schools now offer a "3-4" program in which you enter medical school after the third year of college, and receive the Bachelor's degree after the first year of medical school. While most accelerated programs take seven years, some take six (Boston University, Lehigh University, Wilkes College, for instance), and one (Wofford College in South Carolina) takes five. The U.S. is, apparently, moving very slowly toward the British system, in which one enters medical school right after high school, and earns the Bachelor of Medicine in four or five years. (In England, the Doctor of Medicine is a less common advanced degree.)

Ph.D. INTO M.D.

The first two years of medical school are usually spent learning the relevant academic subjects (anatomy, physiology, biology, etc.). On the assumption that a person who has already earned a Ph.D. in certain fields will have this knowledge, two schools—one in the U.S. and one in Mexico—offer a two-year M.D. to such people. Applicants must have a Ph.D. in the biological, physical, or engineering sciences, or in mathematics.

UNIVERSITY OF MIAMI

P.O. Box 520875, Miami, FL 33152
There is theoretically no age limit to this program, but applicants under 40 have preference. The program consists of eight and a half months of preclinical study, twelve and a half months of intensive medical study, and 10 weeks of elective clinical work. The total cost exceeds $25,000. Only 36 students are admitted each year, and competition is fierce. A few non-U.S. citizens are permitted in each class.

UNIVERSIDAD AUTONOMA DE CIUDAD JUAREZ

Apardado Postal 231, Ciudad Juarez, Chihuahua, Mexico
Juarez offers a special program for non-Mexicans. Since Juarez is right on the border with the U.S., some Americans choose to live in El Paso, Texas and cross the border to their classes each day.

FOREIGN MEDICAL SCHOOLS

In previous editions of this book, I spent several pages discussing the history, philosophy, and present practice of dealing with foreign medical schools: those in Mexico that cater to English-speaking students from the U.S. and elsewhere, and those throughout the Caribbean established to provide a medical education for Americans unable to get into an American medical school.

The situation is immensely complex, and almost impossible to evaluate for a non-medical layman. Thankfully, there is a book that tells the prospective student at a foreign medical school just about everything one needs to know. In his delightfully written, and heavily opinionated book, Carlos Pestana, M.D., Ph.D., a professor at the University of Texas medical school provides a helpful historical perspective, analyzes the avenues of re entry into the American system for the graduate of a foreign school, and then evaluates dozens of medical schools from Grenada to the Philippines to Poland that deal with students from other countries.

Before spending a dollar with any school or advisory service, spend $13 to buy Dr. Pestana's book, Foreign Medical Schools for U.S. Citizens. Information on ordering appears in the Bibliography section.

USING EXAM PASS RATES TO JUDGE SCHOOLS

People who attend a medical school outside the U.S. and wish to be licensed in the U.S. must pass a qualifying exam, administered by the Educational Commission for Foreign Medical Graduates (3624 Market St., Philadelphia, PA 19104). One valuable measure used to evaluate foreign schools is the percentage of its graduates who take and pass the exam. In past years, the range is literally from 0% to 100%. Unfortunately, however, ECFMG no longer publishes data on exam pass rates, claiming that too many schools were misusing them in their marketing.

Here is an old set of numbers, from when ECFMG was releasing them, for all schools with 25 or more Americans taking the exam.

School, Country	Americans who took exam	passed exam	Percent
Sackler School of Medicine, Israel	33	33	100
St. George's U., Grenada	218	173	79
U. of the East, Philippines	27	12	44
Far Eastern U., Philippines	44	19	43
Universidad de Monterrey, Mexico	47	20	43
Universidad de Montemorelos, Mexico	26	11	42
University of Santa Tomas, Philippines	45	19	42
Universita degli Studi di Roma, Italy	107	45	42
American U. of the Caribbean, Montserrat	363	146	40
Institut de Medicin, Romania	35	14	40
Ross U., Dominica	118	46	39
Universidad Autónoma de Nuevo Leon, Mexico	37	14	38
Universidad Autónoma de Guadalajara, Mexico	861	294	34
Universidad Autónoma de Ciudad Juarez, Mexico	255	66	26
Universidad de Guadalajara, Mexico	35	9	26
National University of Athens, Greece	32	8	25
Universita degli Studi di Bologna, Italy	62	14	23
Universidad Nacional Autónoma, Mexico	34	7	21
Universidad de Sevilla, Spain	25	5	20
Católica Madre y Maestra, Dominican Republic	68	11	16
Universidad Nordestana, Dominican Republic	63	10	16
Universidad de Zaragoza, Spain	49	7	18
U. Autónoma de Santo Domingo, Dominican Rep.	90	12	13
Universidad Central del Este, Dominican Republic	1139	167	13
Universidad Autónoma de Guerrero, Mexico	32	4	12
Aristotelian University of Thessalonika, Greece	32	3	9
Universidad de Santiago, Spain	37	2	5

ILLEGAL MEDICAL DEGREES

Very few fake school operators take the higher risk of offering fake medical degrees, although there are a handful of them sprinkled throughout the Diploma Mill chapter. Two of the largest operations were closed down in 1984 as a result of the F.B.I. Dip Scam operation: the Johann Keppler School of Medicine (which had operated from various addresses in Canada, Switzerland, the U.S., and Mexico), and the United American Medical College (operating from Louisiana and Florida). In both cases, the perpetrators went to prison.

In the mid 1980s, it was discovered that two medical schools in the Dominican Republic, known as CETEC and CIFAS, were involved in selling M.D. credentials at a cost of $5,000 to $50,000. It has never been fully determined how many of the more-than-5,000 M.D. degrees awarded by these two schools were genuinely earned and how many were sold to people who never attended the school.

One man arrested and jailed as a medical degree broker, earned $1,500,000 in fees from his 165 clients, 44 of whom actually passed the foreign medical students exam and were practicing medicine in the U.S.

MEDICAL SCHOOL REFERRAL SERVICES

There are several services that claim they can smooth the way for Americans and others to deal with medical schools in other countries. Some also deal with dental and veterinary schools. Some apparently have a working arrangement with one particular school while others deal with a variety of schools. Here are some that have advertised regularly in the Sunday New York Times and elsewhere. The fees seem to range from $50 to $500 or more:

FOREIGN MEDICAL EDUCATION CONSULTANTS
P. O. Box 9932, Berkeley, CA 94709

MEDICAL EDUCATIONAL CORPORATION
1655 Palm Beach Lakes Blvd., West Palm Beach, FL 33401, (305) 683-6222

76 Orange Dr., Jericho, NY 11753, (516) 933-7448

PROVEN STUDENT SERVICE

P. O. Box 130094, Sunrise, FL 33313, (305) 748-5172

WORLDWIDE MEDICAL EDUCATION INSTITUTE

318 4th St., Union City, NJ 07087, (201) 867-2864

THE MEDICAL SCHOOLS

Complete details on the 60-odd foreign schools that welcome students from the U.S. and other countries can be found in Dr. Pestana's book, described earlier. Here are some of the larger ones:

AMERICAN UNIVERSITY OF THE CARIBBEAN
Monserrat, British West Indies. U.S. office at 1000 Northwest 37th Ave., Miami, FL 33125, (305) 643-1150.

FACULTÉ LIBRE DE MÉDICINE
Catholic University of Lille, Lille, France. U.S. representative: Committee for International Medical Exchange, 1014 E. Willow Grove Ave., Wyndmoor, PA 19118, (215) 233-1602. Their specialty is offering the first two years of medical school, after which the student transfers to a school in his or her own country. (It is generally easier to transfer into the third year than to enter into the first year.)

GRACE UNIVERSITY
Nevis, West Indies. U.S. representative, Atlantic Admissions Services, Inc., 169-12 Hillside Ave., Jamaica, NY 11432, (212) 884-7832.

ROSS UNIVERSITY
Dominica, West Indies. U.S. office c/o Caribbean Admissions, Inc., 16 W. 32nd St., 6th Floor, New York, NY 10001, (212) 279-5500.

SACKLER SCHOOL OF MEDICINE
University of Tel Aviv, Tel Aviv, Israel. U.S. office at 17 E. 62nd St., New York, NY 10021, (212) 688-8811.

SAINT GEORGE'S UNIVERSITY
Grenada, West Indies. U.S. office at One E. Main St., Bay Shore, NY 11706, (516) 665-8500.

SEMMELWEIS UNIVERSITY OF MEDICINE
Budapest, Hungary. U.S. office at P.O. Box 654, Bronxville, NY 10708, (904) 684-0650.

SPARTAN HEALTH SCIENCES UNIVERSITY
Vieuxfort, St. Lucia, West Indies. U.S. office at 7618 Boeing Dr., Suite C, El Paso, TX 79925, (915) 778-5309.

UNIVERSIDAD AUTONOMA DE GUADALAJARA
Guadalajara, Jalisco, Mexico. U.S. office at 10999 I-10 West, Suite 355, San Antonio, TX 78230, (512) 692-9192.

UNIVERSITY OF HEALTH SCIENCES
St. John's, Antigua, West Indies. U.S. representative: M.S.C.S., 505 N. Lakeshore Dr., Suite 2208, Chicago, IL 60611, (312) 467-0081.
Also known as Antigua School of Medicine.

OTHER HEALTH-RELATED SCHOOLS

AIROLA COLLEGE
see: North American Colleges of Natural Health Sciences

AMERICAN ACADEMY OF TROPICAL MEDICINE Diploma, Unaccredited
16126 E. Warren Non-resident
Detroit, MI 48224 USA Non-profit, independent
Ben Allie, M.D. (313) 882–0641

Tropical medicine $662

Offers diplomas and certificates, not degrees. The Academy is incorporated in Ohio, but since their literature indicates the work is not transferable as college credit, they are not regulated by the Ohio Board of Regents. Awards the designations of FAATH (Fellow of American Academy of Tropical Medicine) or FICTN (Fellow of International College of Tropical Medicine). Application fee: $662 or $672.

AMERICAN COLLEGE OF HEALTH SCIENCE

see: College of Life Science

AMERICAN COLLEGE OF NUTRIPATHY

6821 E. Thomas Rd. B, M, D, Unaccredited
Scottsdale, AZ 85251 USA Non-resident
Dr. Steven Calrow, Dean (602) 946–5515
Nutripathy, nutritional philosophy $700
1976

Offers a practical (as contrasted with theoretical) approach to the healing of body, mind, and spirit. The catalogue states that "nutripathy is the condensation of most all natural healing and counseling techniques available today [having] discarded the 'foo-foo' and kept the basic 'what works.'" Also offered: Doctor of Nutripathic Theology. The catalogue is sold for $13. Accreditation from the International Accrediting Commission for Schools, Colleges and Theological Seminaries, an unrecognized accreditor. Students "must have, or desire, an active relationship with God."

AMERICAN HOLISTIC COLLEGE OF NUTRITION

1704 11th Avenue South B, M, D, Unaccredited
Birmingham, AL 35205 USA Non-resident
Dr. Lloyd Clayton Jr., President Proprietary
Nutrition (205) 933–2155
1980s $1,585-$4,995

The Bachelor's degree requires six correspondence courses. The Master's requires three additional courses and a 25-page thesis. The Ph.D. requires three more courses, and a 60-page dissertation. It is possible to earn all three degrees at the same time by taking all the courses and writing a combined thesis-dissertation. The college no longer claims to be fully accredited, No faculty are listed. The seven-man advisory board includes two M.D.s. The president, Dr. Clayton, also purveys Dr. Clayton's herbs and homeopathics, and operates the Clayton School of Natural Healing (offering a Doctor of Naturopathy degree by correspondence) as well as Chadwick University and a computer school from the same address.

AMERICAN INSTITUTE OF HYPNOTHERAPY

1805 E. Garry, #100 B, D, Unaccredited, State
Santa Ana, CA 92705 USA authorized,Non-resident
Caroline Miller, Ph.D., Dean of Academic Studies Proprietary
Hypnotherapy (714) 953–6857
1982 $2,500

Offers Bachelor's and Doctorates in hypnotherapy, entirely through correspondence study. Doctoral work involves either completion of courses and a practicum, or courses plus a final evaluation project. Students are encouraged to finish their Ph.D. in less than one year. Students and faculty are involved in hypnotherapy applications ranging from the clinical to the esoteric. The school will provide prospective students with a list of students and graduates who may be contacted. The faculty includes doctors of medicine, dentistry, and osteopathy. Authorized to grant degrees by the state of California.

AMERICAN INSTITUTE OF TRADITIONAL CHINESE MEDICINE

2400 Geary Blvd. M, Unaccredited, state
San Francisco, CA 94115 USA authorized, Residency
Chung San Cieung, M.D., President Non-profit, independent
Traditional Chinese medicine, acupuncture (415) 346–7600
1980

Three years of full-time study, preparing practitioners for entry into the field of acupuncture and traditional Chinese medicine. Authorized to grant degrees by the state of California.

ANGLO-AMERICAN INSTITUTE OF DRUGLESS THERAPY

30 Kinloch Rd., | D, Unaccredited
Renfrew, Scotland | Non-resident
Naturopathy, osteopathy | Non-profit, independent
1911 | (041) 886–3137

Doctor of Naturopathy (N.D.) and Diploma in Osteopathy offered entirely through correspondence study. Established in Indiana in 1911 by a medical doctor. Moved to Scotland in 1939, to England in 1948, and back to Scotland in 1977. The degree involves completing about 50 lessons, ranging from anatomy and physiology to chiropractic and spondylotherapy (which appears to involve emptying the stomach and appendix by means of concussion, thus having effect, according to the catalogue, on heart trouble, bust development, syphilis, and impotence). The Institute claims more than 7,000 graduates. Holders of the degree in the United States could not be licensed to practice medicine, and perhaps not even spondylotherapy.

ARNOULD-TAYLOR EDUCATION LTD.

James House, Oakelbrook Mill, Newent, | B, M, Unaccredited
Gloucestershire, GL18 1HD England | Non-resident
Mrs. K. Aldridge, Managing Director | Physiatrics
1947 | (0531) 821875

Bachelor of Physiatrics and Master of Physiatrics, entirely through correspondence study. The course consists of seven lessons for each degree, with a paper to be written at the end of each lesson. Physiatrics is the study of body weight and its effects on psychological well-being. The senior tutor is W. E. Arnould-Taylor. Since they are not officially empowered to grant degrees, they have apparently given themselves that right through their corporate charter. (This is legal in England.) They emphasize that the degrees are professional, not academic degrees, offered to persons already qualified in the field of physical therapy.

CALIFORNIA ACUPUNCTURE COLLEGE

711 S. Vermont Ave., #212 | D, Unaccredited, state
Los Angeles, CA 90025 USA | authorized, Residency
Steven Rosenblatt, President | Non-profit, independent
Chinese medicine, herbal study, homeopathy | (213) 470–9009
1978 | $3,500/year

Campuses in Santa Barbara and San Diego. A three-year program preparing students to become practitioners of acupuncture and Oriental medicine. Courses are also offered in western sciences, herbology, and homeopathy. Authorized to grant degrees by the state of California.

CALIFORNIA COLLEGE OF HEALTH SCIENCES | A, M, Accredited

See description in Chapter 16

CLAYTON SCHOOL OF NATURAL HEALING

see: American Holistic College of Nutrition

COLLEGE OF LIFE SCIENCE

see: Life Science Institute

DOCTOR CLAYTON'S SCHOOL OF NATURAL HEALING

see: American Holistic College of Nutrition

DOMINION HERBAL COLLEGE | Diplomas, Unaccredited

7527 Kingsway | Non-resident
Burnaby, British Columbia V3N 3C1 Canada | Proprietary
Judy Nelson, D.C., president | (604) 521–5822
Traditional herbalism | $725 (Can.)

The title of "Chartered Herbalist" is awarded to students who complete the 58 lessons of the correspondence course in herbalism. A Master Herbalist program is also offered. Summer seminars are not required but are recommended. The school seems to be well-regarded in the profession.

DONSBACH UNIVERSITY
see: International University for Nutrition Education

EMERSON COLLEGE OF HERBOLOGY — M, Unaccredited
582 Cummer Ave. — Non-resident
Willowdale, Ontario M2K 2M4 Canada — (416) 733–2512
Herbology — $265/year
Master of Herbology title is awarded on successful completion of 33 correspondence lessons (a total of 550 pages), covering botanic medicine, phytotherapy, pharmabotanics and herbalism. Lessons are mailed in three at a time, graded, and returned with the next set of lessons.

GALIEN COLLEGE OF NATURAL HEALING
78-79 Pinfold St. — Diplomas, Unaccredited
Darlaston, Wednesbury, WS10 9TB England — Non-resident
Munawar A. Kanday, principal
Biochemistry, healing — About $175/course
Correspondence courses, requiring about three months each, in Dr. Schuessler's biochemistry, homeopathic healing, naturopathic healing, and herbal healing. There is opportunity for misinterpretation of the credentials given. For instance, on completion of the "diploma in naturopathic healing" course, the bulletin says "successful students may use the letters 'N.D.' after their name." The name of the school is spelled "Galen" three times in the literature, but "Galien" more often.

HEARTWOOD: CALIFORNIA COLLEGE OF THE NATURAL HEALING ARTS
220 Harmony Lane — Certificates, Unaccredited
Garberville, CA 95440 USA — Residency
Robert Fasic, president — Proprietary
Massage therapy, hypnotherapy, polarity therapy, clinical nutrition — (707) 923–2021
$5,500/year
1977
Three-and nine-month residential programs for comprehensive career training. Students study "with a sensitive, talented faculty in the warmth and support of a nurturing community." Formerly known as California College of the Natural Healing Arts, which awarded Bachelor's and Master's in health-related fields, but no longer.

INTERNATIONAL COLLEGE OF NATURAL HEALTH SCIENCES
100 Wigmore Street — B, M, D, Unaccredited
London, W1H 0AE England — Non-resident
Melvyn S. Davis, Director of Education — (01) 486–0431
Nutrition, homeopathy, reflexology — $700-$2,000 (appx.)
Students are supplied with texts, and must pass proctored examinations. A thesis (unspecified length) is required for graduate degrees which many students will complete in less than a year. The combined B.S.-M.S.-Ph.D. program might take longer. The literature refers to the College "having the authority to confer degrees." The only possible "authority" could come from their own corporate charter, in which they give themselves the right to grant degrees. (They are "part of The Wigmore Organisation Ltd.")This sort of thing is legal in England.

INTERNATIONAL UNIVERSITY FOR NUTRITION EDUCATION
2336 Stanwell Circle — B, M, D, Unaccredited, state
Concord, CA 94520 USA — authorized, Non-resident
Dr. Jacob Swilling, President — Non-profit, independent
Holistic nutrition — (415) 680-8981
1978 — $2,500
Formerly Donsbach University. The staff believes that the trend of medicine is away from dangerous drugs and indiscriminate surgery. It teaches the concepts of self care through holistic principles with an emphasis on nutrition. The university has its own large building, offering residential classes and conducting nutritional research. The founder, Kurt Donsbach, has his own product line of vitamins and nutritional aids. The University is authorized to grant degrees by the state of California.

LIFE SCIENCE INSTITUTE
6600 Burleson Rd.
Austin, TX 78744 USA
T. C. Fry, President
Nutritional science
1982

Diploma, Unaccredited
Non-resident
Non-profit, independent
(512) 385–2781
$1,250

The College awards a diploma in nutritional science on completion of 105 lessons, which will take a minimum of 48 weeks to complete. The lessons are detailed and comprehensive presentations of the viewpoint and methodologies of Administrator T. C. Fry and his associates. They see conventional medicine as "untrue in philosophy, absurd in science, in opposition to natural principles, contrary to common sense, disastrous in results, and a curse to humanity." In the course of the 105 lessons, the student learns about nutrition, physiology, diet, mental and emotional well-being, and much more.

PACIFIC NATIONAL UNIVERSITY
4652 Hollywood Blvd.
Los Angeles, CA 90027 USA
Dr. David C. Chu, President
Chinese and western medicine
1980

B, M, D, Unaccredited, State authorized, Residency
Non-profit, independent
(213) 663–2130
$1,200/quarter

The curriculum integrates traditional Chinese medicine with western medical sciences. Affiliated clinic offers clinical practice. Faculty includes U.S. and Chinese medical practitioners. Three-month clinical internship in Beijing is available. Intensive instructional courses. Evening and weekend classes available. The catalogue says they were the first institution in the U.S. to grant a Ph.D. in integrated Chinese medicine.

PACIFIC SCHOOL OF NUTRITION
1257-12 Siskiyou Blvd.
Ashland, OR 97520 USA
Dr. Michael Megarit, Dean
Nutrition, business, herbology

Certificate, Unaccredited
Non-resident
(503) 770–4373
$695-$2,195

Correspondence programs leading to certification as a nutritionist or nutritionist and herbologist, through written tutorials. Those who have completed the certified nutritionist program may take a course in business and financial programs for the health professional.

SAMRA UNIVERSITY OF ORIENTAL MEDICINE
615 S. Westlake Ave.
Los Angeles, CA 90057 USA
Norman Bleicher, President
Oriental medicine, acupuncture, herbology
1975

B, M, D, Unaccredited, state
Residency
Non-profit, independent
(213) 413–4446
$4,200/year

Clinical facilities to serve the needs of local residents. Many of the faculty hold advanced degrees from Chinese institutions. Classes are taught day, evening, and weekends in both English and Chinese. The time required to earn a degree is reduced for health professionals. The university is authorized to grant degrees by the state of California.

SAN FRANCISCO COLLEGE OF ACUPUNCTURE
2051 Market St.
San Francisco, CA 94114 USA
Jay Tobin, Ph.D.
Acupuncture
1980

M, Unaccredited, state authorized
Residency
Non-profit, independent
(415) 863–3500
$4,700/year

The first acupuncture college in the western world (their literature says) offers intensive study in that field as well as clinical sciences, holistic medical studies, and traditional Oriental medicine. Authorized to grant degrees by the state of California.

SCHOOL OF NATURAL HEALING
P.O. Box 412
Springville, UT 84663 USA

D, Unaccredited, state authorized
Short residency

Dr. John Christopher, President (801) 489–4254
Herbology $395 and up
A program offering the Doctor of Herbology degree, largely through home study courses, with seven to nine day seminars by the school's founder, Dr. John R. Christopher.

SOUTH BAYLO UNIERSITY
12012 S. Magnolia St.
Garden Grove, CA 92641 USA
David Park, President
Acupuncture, Oriental medicine
1978
B, M, D, Unaccredited, state authorized, Residency
Non-profit, independent
(714) 534–5411
$3,000
Authorized to grant degrees by the state of California. Did not respond to three requests for information on their programs.

SOUTHWEST ACUPUNCTURE COLLEGE
1544 Cerrillos Rd.
Santa Fe, NM 87501 USA
Acupuncture, Oriental medicine
D, Unaccredited
Residency
(505) 988–3538
Three-year program leading to the O.M.D. degree.

UNIVERSIDAD INTERAMERICANA
see: Escuela de Medicina Dr. Evaristo Cruz Escobedo

UNIVERSIDAD MEDICO-NATURALISTA HISPANO-AMERICA
see: Cyberam University

UNIVERSITY OF DOMINICA
see: Ross University

UNIVERSITY OF PHILOSOPHY
see: University of Healing

WESTERN UNIVERSITY
see: Western Scientific University

WILD ROSE COLLEGE OF NATURAL HEALING
1220 Kensington Rd. N.W., Suite 302
Calgary, Alberta T2N 3P3 Canada
Terry L. Willard, Director
Wholistic healing, herbalism
Certificate, Unaccredited
Non-resident
(403) 270–0936
Correspondence programs leading to a Wholistic Healing Degree (WHD), or Master Herbalist certificate. Each program requires a thesis of publishable quality.

21. Religious Schools

A young theologian named Fiddle, Refused to accept his degree,
For said he "Tis enough being Fiddle, Without being Fiddle, D.D."
—Edward Lear

NOTICE REGARDING THIS CHAPTER

All right, you win. I give up. This is the last edition in which this chapter will appear. From a survey of my readers, it is of interest to perhaps 3% of you, yet it accounts for nearly a third of all my mail, two-thirds of my complaint letters and hate mail, and about 99% of my anonymous letters. It seems that whatever I say, it annoys, angers, or infuriates some people. And the problem is compounded because either I seem to have an especially hard time getting my facts straight, or the facts are elusive, or both. So I have gratefully accepted the offer of a minister from Washington to create a separate book, just of religious schools. With this in the offing (Are you ready, Josh? Let's get going!), I have cut back on the text in this section, in the feeble hope of angering fewer people and perhaps making fewer errors.

The First Amendment to the Constitution of the United States proclaims that "Congress shall make no law respecting an establishment of religion, or prohibiting the free exercise thereof."

The various states and law enforcement agencies have generally taken this to mean that churches (and the schools they establish) may grant any degrees they wish, with little or no regulation from any public agency.

To be sure, there are a great many church-run or church-affiliated universities that offer excellent educations and well-regarded degrees. But at the other end of the scale, there are more than a few church-affiliated institutions that will award any degree, including the Doctorate, on payment of their fees, no questions asked. These latter schools may well be legal, but the legality pertains to the institution and not to the holder of a degree. More than a few people have gotten into considerable trouble using these degrees. In one such highly-publicized instance, a few years ago in New York, a man with a $100 Ph.D. from a perfectly legal California church school was found to be running a family and sex therapy clinic.

There are essentially four different kinds of colleges and universities that could logically be called "religious" or "religiously affiliated:"

•Major universities that happen to be church-affiliated
Schools like Notre Dame, Texas Christian, or Southern Methodist are major universities offering primarily non-religious degree programs. Such schools would be listed in Chapter 16, if at all, but not here.

•Religious schools that also have secular degrees
These are schools where religion is an important part of work at the school, and often a statement of faith is required, but degrees in business, education, etc. can be earned. These schools are also listed in Chapter 16.

•Bible schools, that offer primarily religious degrees
These schools are listed in this chapter.

•Spiritual schools
Schools emphasizing the study of spiritual or metaphysical matters, such as the School of Metaphysics or the University of Healing are included in this chapter.

•Schools whose church connection may be pragmatic
These are schools whose founders first established churches which in turn operate their schools, sometimes out of religious belief, sometimes to avoid the necessity for state regulation, sometimes maybe even both. These schools are listed in chapter 16.

Many religious schools, especially Bible schools, report accreditation from one of a dozen or more unrecognized accrediting agencies, in more than a few instances claiming that recognized accreditors don't understand or appreciate them. Some schools, and some unrecognized religious accrediting agencies, maintain that accreditation somehow impinges on their freedom of religion, or is a violation of the constitutional separation of church and state. However, the American Association of Bible Colleges and the Transnational Association of Christian Schools (recognized accreditors in this field) seem to have no problems of this sort, nor do the many Bible colleges they have accredited.

There really are only two reasons to deal with the schools in this chapter: either because you are associated with or have interest in the church or religious discipline that runs the schools; or because they offer a faster, cheaper, and/or easier route to a degree.

Finally, I apologize in advance for any errors of doctrine or affiliation that I may have made. I have learned, from more than a few angry letters, that it may, for instance, be better to confuse the Presbyterian Church in the U.S.A. with the Church of Satan than with the Presbyterian Church in America, or the Missouri Synod Lutherans with the Wisconsin Synod. I must assume that people already affiliated with a church will be aware of what their own church schools are doing, and those who are not will surely find something to suit their needs from among the following array. Thank you.

Please note, also, that a great many well-known schools of theology offer an array of advanced degrees, especially designed for the working clergy. As an example, the Princeton Theological Seminary (Princeton, New Jersey 08542) offers the Doctor of Ministry for practicing clergy, which can be earned in two summers of residency plus completion of a doctoral project. At least sixty other schools do something comparable. They are not listed here, because of the assumption that full time clergy will probably be familiar with what is going on in their church and/or neighborhood.

AMERICAN BIBLE COLLEGE — B, M, Unaccredited
Pineland, FL — Non-resident
D. G. W. Hyatt, President — Non-profit, church
Theology, religious education — (813) 283-0519
$250-$300
Affiliated with American Evangelical Christian Churches for training Christian workers.

AMERICAN FELLOWSHIP CHURCH — D, Unaccredited
225 Crossroads Blvd., Suite 345 — Non-resident
Carmel, CA 93923 — No listed phone
$25
Established in the 1970s by Bishop T. H. Swenson, formerly an administrator at the University of California, in the model of the Universal Life Church. An honorary Doctor of Divinity degree is $15, and ordination in the church is$8 more. Also available are home study courses, information on marriage laws in all states, sample ceremonies, window stickers, and a book on tax exemption and church laws called *Non-Profit Can Be Profitable* ($18). Bishop Swenson clearly enjoys what he is doing. The church used to have the alternate name Mother Earth Church, which is being phased out.

AMERICAN NATIONAL INSTITUTE FOR PSYCHICAL RESEARCH
26560 Agoura Rd. — B, M, D, Unaccredited
Calabasas, CA 91302 — Residency
Dr. Antonia Rodriguez, President — Proprietary
Licensed vocational nursing, metaphysical sciences — (818) 880-4323
Holistic health — $1,600/program
1975
Students are trained to discover and develop their psychic gifts and to use them in a beneficial healing manner. Ph.D. requires courses in astrology, palmistry, herbology, and metaphysics. Each course meets one evening a week for 16 weeks. Accredited non-degree course for nurses is offered evenings and weekends for one year for $6,000. Founder-president Dr. Rodriguez was named one of the top ten psychics in the U.S. by the *National Star*.

She lists Doctorates in philosophy, theology, divinity and herbology. Authorized to grant degrees by the state of California.

AQUARIAN CHURCH OF THE BROTHERS AND SISTERS OF JESUS CHRIST
432 Pacific Coast Hwy. — D, Unaccredited
Hermosa Beach, CA 90254 — Non-resident
Gary W. Claussen, President — No listed phone.
Naprapathy — $45
Offers ordination as high priest, bishop, archbishop or cardinal (people can call you "His (or "Her) Eminence"), for $35 to $100. Doctor of Naprapathy, with which, it is claimed, "you are legally entitled to own and operate your own nutritional clinic," is $45. The book *The Master Game* by Robert DeRopp is "our Bible and gives us our life pathway," but "you don't have to abide by our tenets unless you want to."

BAY CITIES BIBLE INSTITUTE — B, M, Unaccredited, state-authorized
2831 Telegraph Ave. — Non-resident courses
Oakland, CA 94609 — Non-profit, independent
Robert Nellis, President — (415) 893-5717
Bible study — $675/year
Authorized to grant degrees by state of California. Courses by correspondence study, or through evening and weekend classes. Degrees may not be earned entirely through correspondence.

BETHANY BIBLE COLLEGE — B, M, D, Unaccredited
2311 Hodgesville Rd., P.O. Box 1944 — Non-resident
Dothan, AL 36302 — Non-profit
Dr. H. D. Shuemake, President — (205) 793-3189
Religious studies — $380-$500
Credit for life experience learning. Accreditation claimed from an unrecognized accreditor. Doctorates include those in Religious Education, Ministry, Sacred Theology.

CALIFORNIA BAPTIST COLLEGE — B, Unaccredited
8432 Magnolia Ave. — Residency
Riverside, CA 92504 — Non-profit, church
John E. Potter, Director of Admissions — (714) 689-5771
Business administration — $5,070
Accredited Bachelor's in business for the working manager or business owner available through weekend or evening classes.

CALIFORNIA GRADUATE SCHOOL OF THEOLOGY — M, D, Unaccredited, state approved
213 S. Kenwood — Non-resident
Glendale, CA 91205 — Non-profit, independent
Robert S. McBirnie, President — (818) 240-1650
Religious studies — $45/unit
1969
At least 48 quarter hours must be completed in after enrolling, but all courses are available on videocassettes for home study. Some credit for experiential learning in field of ministry. Offers M.A., D.Min., Ph.D. in theology, Doctor of Theology.

CALVARY GRACE CHURCH OF FAITH
Honorary degrees in divinity and psychology in exchange for a donation of $10. Ordination in the church is free; an "embellished elaborate ordination certificate on fine paper bearing our embossed corporate gold seal...encased in a pliable clear polished vinyl easily removable for framing" case. Applicants must sign a statement of their "desire to enroll by my call to work for the Lord Jesus Christ." However, International General Superintendent Spern has written me that "we want you to take out whatever you have about us in catalog out," which I am reluctant to do, because of all that wonderful prose, so I shall simply delete their address, and you'll have to find them for yourself.

CHRISTIAN INTERNATIONAL UNIVERSITY B, M, D, Unaccredited
Route 2, Box 351 Non-resident
Port Washington, FL 32454 Non-profit, church
Bill S. Hamon (901) 231-5308
Religious studies $2,000 and up
Established in Texas in 1967, they moved to Arizona in 1977 when "the Lord provided a central home," and again to Florida a few years later. They state that their credits have been accepted by "secular colleges and universities" but have not responded to my requests to learn which ones. The only staff member listed as having a Doctorate is the president, whose degree is from a school I have listed in the diploma mills chapter.

CHRISTIAN LIFE COLLEGE B, Accredited
1981 Cherokee Road Non-resident or residency
Stockton, CA 95205 Non-profit, church
Kenneth F. Haney, President Haney (209) 464-4827
Ministry $3,650
1953
Preparation for United Pentecostal ministry and other denominations with similar doctrinal positions. Four-year full-time on-campus degree, plus external Bachelor of Theology through correspondence study, for those preparing for the ministry.

CHURCH OF GOD SCHOOL OF THEOLOGY M, Accredited
900 Walker St., P. O. Box 3330 Short residency
Cleveland, TN 37320 Non-profit, church
Dr. Robert B. Thomas, Director of Admissions (615) 478-1131
Divinity $3,313/year
1975
A reader set out to discover how he could earn a regionally accredited Master of Divinity with the least possible time on campus. Following several hundred hours of research, he determined the "winner" was clearly the Church of God School of Theology. A`t COGSOT, one can theoretically spent only ten weeks on campus, taking three condensed courses, with the rest of the work done by "directed study." Following the first on-campus course, he petitioned the dean for permission to do the majority of the remaining work independently.

COLUMBIA BIBLE COLLEGE and COLUMBIA GRADUATE SCHOOL B, Accredited
P. O. Box 3122 Short residency
Columbia, SC 29230 Non-profit, church
Frank J. Bedell, Director, Undergraduate Admissions (803) 754-4100
Religious studies $3,669
The accredited Bachelor's degree is available largely but not entirely through correspondence study. Accredited by the Southern Association and others. Many courses available via taped lectures. School is "committed to the authority of the inerrant Scriptures...but hold our convictions in a pluralism of grace that respects those in the evangelical mainstream with whom we may differ."

CORNERSTONE THEOLOGICAL SEMINARY B, M, D, Unaccredited
P. O. Box 913 Non-resident
Baytown, TX 77552 Non-profit, church
Dr. William M. McKnight, President (713) 421-2349
Ministry, theology, etc. $898 and up
Cornerstone appears to be in the business of franchising religious schools. They encourage churches to establish their own college (which can have a different name), using the materials of Cornerstone. Cornerstone claims to be accredited by the State of Israel, the Washington State Department of Education, and the Louisiana State Department of Education, none of which accredit schools. They also claim accreditation from the International Accrediting Commission, which was closed by Missouri authorities. President McKnight did not respond to my several letters questioning the accreditation claims, and asking for the source of his own five doctorates, or Mrs. McKnight's three. The catalogue misrepresents the findings of a study on the acceptability of non-traditional degrees (see page 17). The catalogue states that all credits are transferable to Fairfax University and to Kent College of Louisiana (both unaccredited). The application form is one of the few I have ever seen that asks for the race of the applicant and requires that a photo be sent.

EVANGELICAL INSTITUTE FOR HIGHER EDUCATION B, Unaccredited
Stadsring 42 Non-resident
Amersfoort 3800 AZ, Holland Non-profit, church
Established in 1984 to offer programs by correspondence, many in English, to help students worldwide "arm themselves in the Christian battle." Students must sign an agreement affirming that the Bible is the absolute norm for their lives.

FAITH BAPTIST COLLEGE AND SEMINARY B, M, D, Unaccredited
P. O. Box 3005 Non-resident
Anderson, SC 29624 Non-profit, church
Dr. Michael A. Smith, President ()803) 226-5239
Ministry, theology, Christian education $18 to $28/semester hour
1969
Bachelor's in many religious fields, Master of Theology or Christian Education, and Doctor of Ministry or Theology through correspondence study. Accreditation from two unrecognized agencies, but the school has always made this distinction very clear in its literature. The aim is to offer every course in a consistently Biblical philosophy. Former name: Faith Evangelistic Christian School, of Morgantown, Kentucky.

FAITH EVANGELICAL LUTHERAN SEMINARY M, D, Accredited
P. O. Box 7186 Non-resident
Tacoma, WA 98407 Non-profit, church
Dr. Albin H. Fogelquist, Registrar (800) 228-4650
Theology, Divinity $900/program
1969
External Master of Theology, M.A., and Doctor of Ministry. Purpose is to train pastors and church workers for conservative Lutheran church and organizations. Accredited by the Association for Clinical Pastoral Education and approved for VA benefits. Only men are admitted to programs leading to or presupposing ordination, in accord, the catalogue says, with 1 Timothy 2:12: "Suffer not a woman to teach, nor to usurp authority over the man, but to be in silence."

FAITH HERITAGE COLLEGE B, M, D, Unaccredited
8419 Buena Vista Blvd. Non-resident
Lamont, CA 93241 Non-profit, church
Dearl Dawson, Pastor (805) 845-0641
Theology $250-$400/program
1981
Bachelor's degree in theology on completion of 10 courses; Master's for writing ten 10-page essays; and Doctor of Theology for researching and editing three 60-page books. The college is a ministry of First Jesus Name Church, "preserving the heritage of the apostolic church," and claims accreditation from an unrecognized agency (not identifying it as such).

FLORIDA BAPTIST COLLEGE B, M, D, Unaccredited,
P. O. Box 2758 state-authorized
Brandon, FL 33509 Residency or Non-resident
H. Larry White, Registrar Non-profit, church
Theology, religious and pastoral education (813) 684-1389
$80/3-unit course
B.A. and M.A. in pastoral studies, B.S. in religious education, and degrees at all levels in theology through an external study program. The school's "major aim is to prepare doctrinally sound, evangelistically fervent, and nationally patriotic ministers and Christian leaders." Male students "shall be clean shaven... No bushy or unisex hairstyles will be worn... Women shall wear neat, clean dresses with modest neck and hemlines. The wearing of shorts or mini-skirts is not permitted at any time.... Students shall not drink..., gamble, [or] dance" but the use of tobacco is permitted.

FREELANDIA INSTITUTE B, M, D, Unaccredited
HC81, Box 145 Non-resident

Cassville, MO 65625
C. R. Moore, President
Theology, Biblical studies, Biblical counseling, etc.
(417) 271-3627
No required fees

No tuition, but students are asked to make monthly donations of $35 to $250. No accreditation claims are made (how refreshing!); indeed, the catalogue points out that "based upon extensive professional experience and observation we conclude that the accreditation claims of current off-campus degree-granting Bible colleges and seminaries are deceptive." (Amen.) The Ph.D. requires eight years, starting from scratch, but students may begin at whatever level is appropriate for them, based on prior experience.

GOD'S BIBLE SCHOOL AND COLLEGE
1810 Young St.
Cincinnati, OH 45210
Viola E. Miller, Registrar
Religious studies
1900
Diploma, Accredited
Non-resident
Non-profit, church
(513) 721-7944

Accredited school offering residential degrees only, and a three-year non-degree home study course.

GREAT WESTERN UNIVERSITY
545 Sutter St., Suite 405
San Francisco, CA 94102
Eugene E. Whitworth, President
Many metaphysical fields
1952
B, M, D, Unaccredited
Residency
Non-profit, independent
(415) 967-1232
$70/unit

Also known as the Metaphysical University. Degree programs combine metaphysical knowledge and spiritual development with academic disciplines. Classes held evenings and weekends. No credit for life experience learning.

GREENWICH UNIVERSITY SCHOOL OF THEOLOGY
U.K. Office, 29 Howbeck Lane
Clarborough, Nr. Retford, Notts. DN22 9LW, England
The Rev. Dr. Byron Evans, Dean of Studies
Religion, theology, related areas
1958
B, M, D, Unaccredited, state-registered
Non-resident
Non-profit, independent
(0777) 703058
$1,200 and up

Established in 1958 as a part of the Geneva Theological College. In 1990, became affiliated with Greenwich University, the school that I am now running, and changed its name accordingly. Many of the students are clergy in the United Kingdom, but lay students and students living elsewhere in the world, are welcome. While meetings are occasionally held at various U.K. locations, all work may be done through correspondence study. A typical degree requires two years of part-time study. Literature is also available from the central offices of Greenwich University, 100 Kamehameha Ave., Hilo, Hawaii 96720 USA, (808) 935-9934 or (800) 367-4456 (toll-free from the US and Canada).

HOLY FAMILY INSTITUTE
Church of Good
1320 Standiford Ave. 197, Modesto, CA 95350
Rev. Paul Harney, Director
Religious family education
B, M, D., Unaccredited
Non-resident
Non-profit, church
(209) 538-6979
Low tuition donation

The Holy Family Institute "educates Mothers to *be* Mothers, and Fathers to *be* Fathers... that God's perfect design for "FAMILY" is beautiful, and includes educating children in that beautiful atmosphere of HOME." The degree is earned by taking home study courses and applying the knowledge in teaching children.

INSTITUTE FOR CREATION RESEARCH
10946 Woodside Ave. North
Santee, CA 92071
Henry Morris, President
Astrogeophysics, biology, geology, science education
1980
M, Unaccredited, status in flux, Residency
Non-profit, independent
(619) 440-2443

Degrees offered from a creationist point of view, emphasizing experiments and research that presumably have convinced the faculty that God created fossils, dinosaurs are a myth, and evolution is a hoax. The state revoked their approval, claiming that the Master of Science degree was inappropriate. The school announced its intent to appeal this decision.

INTERNATIONAL BIBLE INSTITUTE AND SEMINARY B, M, D, Unaccredited
P. O. Box 879 Non-resident or residency
Plymouth, FL 32768 (305) 886-3619
Dr. Daniel J. Tyler, Vice President
Since they threatened to sue me over what I said last edition, this time I'll just mention that they appear to be affiliated with Tyler Crusades, Inc., and appear to offer degrees and ministerial credentials by correspondence study to "all evangelical, Bible believing, God fearing, born again, spirit-filled Christians."

INTERNATIONAL COLLEGE OF SPIRITUAL AND PSYCHIC SCIENCES
1974 de Maisonneuve West B, M, D, Unaccredited
Montreal, Quebec H3H 1K5, Canada Short residency
Rev. Marilyn Zwaig Rossner, President & Dean Non-profit
Spiritual and psychic sciences, ministry, humanities (514) 937-8359
1977 $30/credit
Home study plus one to two week residential sessions leading toward degrees in the above areas, emphasizing east-west spirituality, the quest for universal human values, new paradigms for science and human culture in consciousness studies, parapsychology, paraphysics, and pastoral studies for a new age, inter-faith ministry. Affiliated with World University of America in Ojai, California.

INTERNATIONAL CORRESPONDENCE INSTITUTE B, Accredited
Chaussée de Waterloo, 45 Non-resident
1640 Rhode-Sain-Genése, Brussels, Belgium Nonprofit, church
Donald Smeeton, Associate Dean (02) 358-5946
Many religious fields Inexpensive
1967
Accredited by the National Home Study Council, Bachelor's degree can be done entirely by correspondence, in Bible, theology, missions, religious education, church administration, and church ministries. Started in Missouri. Affiliated with the Assemblies of God.

INTERNATIONAL INSTITUTE OF THEOLOGY B, M, D, Unaccredited
4901 W. Greenway Road Non-resident
Glendale, AZ 85301 Non-profit, church
Nita Marie Resler, Registrar (602) 242-8866
Religion, theology, metaphysics $25/credit hour + $400 fee
1985
Degrees from the B.A. to the Ph.D. can be earned through home study in the above areas. Accreditation is claimed from two unrecognized agencies (which are not identified as such). Ordination in New Beginnings, An Outreach Ministry, Inc., is available.

INTERNATIONAL REFORM UNIVERSITY B, M, D, Unaccredited
Benmost Bore HCR1 Box 50 Non-resident
Grandin, MO 63943 Non-profit, church
No names in Information Pacckage (314) 593-4736
Degrees at all levels offered by correspondence study by this entity of the Reform Catholic Church, Central Orthodox Synod. Fields include pastoral theology, Latin, homiletics, church law, ministry, non-profit corporate law, and soteriology. The university is the educational outreach of the Patriarch Archbishop of the Central Orthodox Synod, Inc.

KINGSWAY CHRISTIAN COLLEGE AND THEOLOGICAL SEMINARY
19th and Crocker B, M, D, Unaccredited
Des Moines, IA 50314 Non-resident or residency
Dr. Mildred A. Nation, Executive Director (515) 288-2852
Divinity, theology, Christian administration, etc. $60/course

1967
"God directed Dr. D. L. Browning to BIRTH a college that would BUILD GOD AN ARMY." The largest type in the literature states, "EARN THE TITLE AND DISTINCTION OF 'DOCTOR'" which one can do through completion of various home study courses and/or residential courses.

L.I.F.E. BIBLE COLLEGE — B, Accredited
1100 Glendale Blvd. — Non-resident
Los Angeles, CA 90026 — Non-profit, church
Dorothy O. Hammon, Registrar — (213) 413-1234
Religious studies — $2,829
1925
The Bachelor's degree may be earned through correspondence study. Accredited by the American Association of Bible Colleges.

LEE COLLEGE — B, Accredited
Continuing Education, 1161 Parker St. N.E. — Non-resident
Cleveland, TN 37311 — Non-profit, church
Dr. Ray H. Hughes, Jr., Director, Continuing Education — (615) 472-2111
Biblical study — $40/semester hour
1918
Accredited B.A. in Biblical Study or B.S. in Biblical Study through independent study. The program is designed to prepare persons for the ministry in areas of Bible, Christian education, church music, missions and evangelism, pastoral studies and theology. Forty semester credits in residence from an accredited institution are required.

LIBERTY CHRISTIAN COLLEGE — B, M, D, Unaccredited
P. O. Box 4261 — Non-resident
West Columbia, SC 29171 — Non-profit, church
Dr. Edward J. Bennett, President — No listed phone
Evangelism, divinity — No fees stated
Bachelor of Evangelism based on brief (50-word) interpretations of 200 Bible verses, seven messages, and a thesis of any length. Master of Divinity in Evangelism based on two ten-page outlines, a testimony of salvation, three book reports, and leading ten lost people to Jesus. The Doctor of Evangelism requires leading 25 lost people to Jesus and writing a 100-page thesis.

LIBERTY UNIVERSITY
See listing in Chapter 16

LOGOS BIBLE COLLEGE & GRADUATE SCHOOL — B, M, D, Unaccredited
P. O. Box 881308 — Non-resident or residential
San Diego, CA 92108 — Non-profit, church
Dr. Stan E. DeKoven, President — (619) 698-0187
Theology, Biblical studies, sacred music, etc. — $25-$50/unit
The main Logos mission is to "place" a 4-year Bible college program in local churches, where it is taught locally. More than 100 churches now offer this program. There are also external Master's and Doctorates for full time pastors and missionaries which can be earned through correspondence study. Most courses are available in English or Spanish. The catalogue misinterprets and misrepresents a government-sponsored study on the acceptance of non-traditional degrees (see page 17).

LUTHER RICE SEMINARY INTERNATIONAL — B, M, D, Accredited
1050 Hendricks — Non-resident
Jacksonville, FL 32207 — Non-profit
Divinity, ministry, theology — (904) 396-2316
Accredited by the Transnational Association of Christian Schools, a recognized accreditor, licensed by the state of Florida, and endorsed by various fundamentalist ministers, including the late Robert G. Lee, "Prince of Preachers," who believed that "this seminary has been chosen by the Lord as pivotal in training and equipping men of God to be prophets and leaders in...His kingdom."

LUTHERAN THEOLOGICAL SEMINARY AT PHILADELPHIA M, Accrecited
7301 Germantown Ave. Short residency
Philadelphia, PA 19119 Non-profit, church
Rev. George E. Keck, Director of Admissions (215) 248-4616
Divinity $2,500/year
Master of Divinity degree can be earned through weekend (Saturday and Monday) program in Philadelphia.

MID-AMERICA BIBLE COLLEGE B, Accredited
3500 S.W. 119th St. Non-resident
Oklahoma City, OK 73170 Non-profit, church
Larry Higgins, Director of Admissions (405) 691-3800
Religious fields $3,700
1953
Accredited programs are offered by correspondence study.

MOODY BIBLE INSTITUTE B, M, Accredited
820 N. LaSalle Drive Short residency
Chicago, IL 60610 Non-profit, independent
Philip Van Wynen, Dean of Enrollment Management (312) 329-4000
Religion, music, liberal arts
Some accredited Bachelor's and Master's degrees can be earned by taking courses in module form during one or two-week sessions at Christmas, summer, or spring breaks with independent study in between.

OKLAHOMA INSTITUTE OF THEOLOGICAL STUDIES B, M, D
1425 N. Rockwell Ave. Non-resident
Oklahoma City, OK 73127 Non-profit
Bible education, evangelism, religious education, theology No listed phone
Degrees offered through correspondence study. Dissertation of about ten typewritten pages required for doctorate. They are unwilling to "compromise in these days when everything seems to be turmoiling towards socialism and liberalism." Accreditation claimed from unrecognized agency at the same address. Also known as Oklahoma Institute of Theology, Herald of His Coming Good Bible College, Evangel Bible Institute, Faith Baptist Seminary, and Fundamental Bible Seminary. Regarding their legality, they say, "Did Jesus give in to the Pharisees just because they had the law on their side?" (The Pharisees are not a recognized accrediting agency.)

ORAL ROBERTS UNIVERSITY
See listing in Chapter 16.

PACIFIC COAST BIBLE COLLEGE B, M, Unaccredited
7285 25th St. Non-resident, Residency
Sacramento, CA 95822 Non-profit, church
Dr. H. Ray Stewart, President (916) 422-7915
Theology $641-$795/program
1976
The external Bachelor of Theology can be earned through coursework, Christian service practicums, credit for life experience learning, and a thesis. The Master of Theology requires completion of 24 semester hours plus a thesis of about 15 pages, with bibliography and footnotes. Seven of the nine faculty have their degrees from Pacific Coast Bible College. The school has a four-acre campus in south Sacramento. It is sponsored by the International Pentecostal Holiness Church.

PENSACOLA CHRISTIAN COLLEGE B, Unaccredited
P. O. Box 18000 Short residency
Pensacola, FL 32523 Non-profit, church
Humanities (904) 478-8496
Six-week summer session in residence, then students complete the rest of the program by correspondence with directed independent study courses. Applicants must be in full-time Christian service and have completed at least 92 semester hours.

QUEENSLAND COLLEGE OF BIBLICAL STUDIES
P. O. Box 101
Broadbeach, Queensland 4217, Australia
Harold V. Nickel, Principal
Theology, Biblical studies
1980

B, M, Unaccredited
Non-resident
Non-profit, church
(075) 386007
$25/unit

Main purpose is to train people for ministry in local churches. Operated by the Gold Coast Baptist Church. Bachelor of Theology and M.A. in Biblical studies offered by correspondence study. Affiliation claimed with "properly accredited" but not identified Bible schools in U.S.

REFORMED BIBLE COLLEGE
3333 E. Beltline NE
Grand Rapids, MI 49506
R. Joe Dieleman, Director of Admissions
Religious and other studies

B, Accredited
Residency
Non-profit, independent
(616) 363-2050
$3,665

Correspondence courses are available, but "certainly not enough to allow anyone to earn a degree."

SAINT JOSEPH THEOLOGICAL SEMINARY
P. O. Box 24832
Ft. Lauderdale, FL 33307
Theology

Unaccredited
Non-resident
Non-profit, church
(305) 772-0636

They award an "Apostolic degree in theology" by correspondence. The literature states that they "are not a degree mill . . . [T]he Orthodox Catholic Church of America has bestowed upon St. Joseph's its' [sic] approval, blessing and Apostolic Accreditation . . . "

SCHOOL OF METAPHYSICS
Windyville, MO 65783
Dr. Daniel R. Gordon, President
Metaphysics, presumably
1981

D, Unaccredited
Non-profit, church
(417) 345-8411

Although the catalogue does not mention a degree-granting program, most of the staff have Doctorates from the school. They have not responded to my letters of inquiry.

SEMINARY EXTENSION EDUCATION DIVISION
901 Commerce St., Suite 500
Nashville, TN 37203

Accredited courses
Non-resident
Non-profit, church
(615) 242-2453

This affiliate of the Southern Baptist Convention offers many home study courses in religious and theological subjects. Since the program is accredited by the National Home Study Council, a recognized accreditor, the credits are generally transferable into many degree programs at other schools.

SOUTHEASTERN COLLEGE OF THE ASSEMBLIES OF GOD
1000 Longfellow Blvd.
Lakeland, FL 33801
Dr. Thomas G. Wilson, Director, Continuing Education
Pastoral studies, Bible, Christian education, missions
1935

B, Accredited
Non-resident
Non-profit, church
(813) 665-4404
$45/credit hour

Accredited B.A. entirely by correspondence. Guided instruction by telephone or mail. Credit for prior learning by portfolio assessment. Credit by examination and by learning contract. All courses require a proctored examination, which may be taken anywhere.

SOUTHERN CALIFORNIA GRADUATE SCHOOL OF THEOLOGY
5588 N. Palm Ave.
Fresno, CA 93704
S. E. Keller, Chairman, School of MInistry
Religion, Biblical studies, theology

B, M, D, Unaccredited
Non-resident
Non-profit, church
(209) 432-8322
$800-$1,300

Education in the principles of the church. No secular subjects or degrees. All credit can come from an independent study project plus a 5-unit course in Biblical theology. Oral and written exams at the Master's and Doctoral level. Ordained ministers with more than 20 years experience will be considered for one of five honorary Doctorates awarded each year on payment of a $300 fee from the minister's church.

SOUTHWESTERN ASSEMBLIES OF GOD COLLEGE B, Accredited
1200 Sycamore Non-resident
Waxahachie, TX 75165 Non-profit, church
William Morgan, Director of Admissions (214) 937-4010
Religious and other studies $2,450
1927
Accredited Bachelor's degree through correspondence study.

SUMMIT THEOLOGICAL SEMINARY B, M, D, Unaccredited
5500 Ardmore Ave. Non-resident
Fort Wayne, IN 46809 Non-profit, church
Dr. George L. Faull, President $15-$30/credit hour
Theology, religion, Biblical counseling
Bachelor's in religion, Master's and Doctorate in religion or theology, M.A. in Biblical counseling. Summit was established to recruit and educate men for the ministry. "Our degrees are not designed to have any value in the marketplace, but only in the Church and Her educational institutions... Summit...will not knowingly accept credits from fully-accredited schools, should it be known the credits represent coursework that is humanistic."

THEOLOGICAL UNIVERSITY OF AMERICA B, M, D, Unaccredited
Canal Place One, #2300 Non-resident
New Orleans, LA 70130 Non-profit
James W. Benton, President $1,500-$2,900/program
Degrees in theological subjects through independent study, based on a learning contract developed in association with faculty members, all with traditional earned Doctorates. Same approach as the University of America (same administration; see listing in Chapter 16). The catalogue, like so many others, misrepresents the findings of a research report on the acceptance of non-traditional degrees.

TRINITY THEOLOGICAL SEMINARY B, M, D, Unaccredited
4233 Medwel Dr. Off-campus residency
Newburgh, IN 47629 Non-profit, church
Dr. G. L. Stiles, Director, Extension Study Program (812) 853-0611
Religious education, Biblical studies, divinity, theology, etc. $60-$80/credit hour
The degrees are available through home study or on campus. "Off campus residency" means that one must have a church and ministry to use as a 'laboratory' in applying the learning from the program. Forty-eight of the 56 officers, administrators and faculty have a Doctorate from Trinity (86%, an unusually high percentage). Like so many other schools, the literature misrepresents the findings of a research study on the acceptability of non-traditional degrees by failing to mention that the study only dealt with accredited Bachelor's degrees (see page 17). Former name: Toledo Bible College. Until 1990, accreditation was claimed from two unrecognized agencies (which were not identified as being unrecognized).

UNIVERSAL LIFE CHURCH/UNIVERSAL LIFE UNIVERSITY D, Law, Unaccredited
601 Third St. Non-resident
Modesto, CA 95351 Non-profit
Bishop Kirby Hensley (209) 527-8111
Many fields $12.50 and up
According to *New West* magazine, Bishop Hensley has become one of the wealthiest men in the state through offerings received for ministerial credentials and academic-sounding degrees. "Freewill" offerings of $12.50 to $100 will get the degree of your choice; a Sainthood is a mere five bucks. More than eight million have been ordained in this church. The *National Review* found Hensley to be a "genuinely religious practitioner freed from the more foolish precepts of orthodoxy by his inability to read and write." His own version of the Bible has caused more than a few of his fellow Christian to write me "hate letters," urging me not to include this "anti-Christ" in my book. Universal Life University offers a two-year program of home study leading to the Doctor of Common

Law and admission to the Universal Bar Association.

UNIVERSITY OF BIBLICAL STUDIES B, M, D, Unaccredited
7045 N.W. 16th, P.O. Box 99 State licensed
Bethany, OK 73008 Non-resident
Dr. W. R. Corvin, President (405) 789-8450
Many religious fields $439.50/module
1975
21 modules are availble for home study, covering both academic areas (history, humanities, science) and Bible studies. The credits earned are accepted by other Bible schools to apply to earning their degrees, and the University offers its own B.A. in Biblical Studies and Doctor of Ministry. Formerly known as Modular Education.

UNIVERSITY OF HEALING B, M, D, Unaccredited
1101 Far Valley Road Non-resident
Campo, CA 92006 Non-profit, church
Dr. Herbert Beierle, President (619) 478-5111
Philosophy, healing sciences, divinity $800
1975
The purpose of the university is to train practitioners who can help individuals reveal their divine nature to its greatest and highest potential and to share with others how to reveal their divinity. Correspondence programs leading to Bachelor of Philosophy, Master of Healing Sciences, Ph.D., and Doctor of Divinity. Doctorates require completion of lessons, exams, essays and a dissertation of at least ten pages. The University of Philosophy is at the same address. Accreditation is claimed from God Unlimited (not a recognized accrediting agency).

VALLEY FORGE CHRISTIAN COLLEGE B, Accredited
Charlestown Road Non-Resident
Phoenixville, PA 19460 Non-profit, church
Jerry R. Hutson, Director of Admissions (215) 935-0450
Religious studies $2,396
1938
The accredited Bachelor's degree may be earned through correspondence study.

VIRGINIA UNION UNIVERSITY SCHOOL OF THEOLOGY M, Accredited
1500 N. Lombardy St. Residency
Richmond, VA 23220 Non-profit, church
Dr. Alix B. James, Dean (804) 257-5833
Theology $5,300/year
Master of Divinity can be earned through four years of weekend classes (Fridays and Saturdays).

WESTERN CONSERVATIVE BAPTIST SEMINARY M, Accredited
5511 S.E. Hawthorne Blvd. Short residency
Portland, OR 97215 Non-profit, independent
Robert L. Garfield, Director of Admissions (503) 233-8561
Divinity, other fields $3,920
Accredited M.A. and Master of Divinity, with extensive use of videotaped courses.

22. Degree Mills

When you deal with a degree mill, it is like putting
a time bomb in your resumé.
It could go off at any time, with dire consequences.
—John Bear

In most earlier editions of this book, the degree mill section began with the following sentence: "Degree mills have been around for hundreds of years, and they are still flourishing all over the world."

Now, happily, it is possible to say that the number of currently operating phony schools has significantly diminished over the last few years, largely as a result of the "DipScam" diploma mill task force of the FBI, whose work helped secure indictments and, in most cases, convictions of a great many people who were responsible for the operation of scores of phony colleges and universities.

That doesn't mean that everything is wonderful, yet. There are still dozens of places where you can buy Bachelor's, Master's, Doctorates, even law and medical degrees, no questions asked, on payment of fees anywhere from one dollar to several thousand dollars.

One of the main reasons that such places continue to exist is that it is so very difficult to define legally exactly what is meant by the term "diploma mill" or "degree mill."

Surely any school that will send you a Ph.D. by return mail on payment of $100, no questions asked, is a fraud. What about a school that requires a five-page dissertation before awarding the Doctorate? How about 20 pages? 50? 100? 200? Who is to say? One man's degree mill is another man's alternative university. And nobody seems to want the government stepping in to evaluate doctoral dissertations before permitting schools to grant degrees. Would you want [insert the name of your least-favorite politician] grading your thesis?

Another large gray area is the one dealing with religious schools. Because of constitutional safeguards in the U.S. guaranteeing separation of church and state, most states have been reluctant to pass any laws restricting the activities of churches—including their right to grant degrees to all who make an appropriately large donation. In many states, religious schools are not regulated, but are restricted to granting religious degrees. But in some, like Missouri, if you established your own one-person church yesterday, you could start your university today, and award a Ph.D. in nuclear physics tomorrow.

How Can Diploma Mills Be Allowed to Operate?

The answer is that, as just indicated, it is almost impossible to write a law that will discriminate clearly between legitimate schools and mills. Any law that tries to define something that is subjective, whether it is obscenity, pornography, threatening behavior, or the quality of a school is bound to be controversial. There can never be a quantitative means for, in effect, holding a meter up to a school and saying, "This one scores 83; it's legitimate. That one scores 62; it is a degree mill."

Also, degree mills that do not muddy their own local waters, but sell their products only in other states or other countries, are more likely to get away with it longer. A goodly number of degree mills have operated from England, selling their product only to people in other countries (primarily the U.S., Africa, and Asia). Many British authorities seem not to care as long as the only victims are foreigners, and authorities in the U.S. find it virtually impossible to take action against foreign businesses.

After decades of debating these matters (even Prince Charles made a speech about the diploma mill problem), Britain has taken two tiny steps. Step one is to forbid unrecognized schools to call themselves a "University." However, this law had been in effect for about three minutes when England's leading diploma mill, the Sussex College of Technology found the loophole. The law declares that it pertains to everyone enrolling after April 1, 1989. Sussex immediately began offering to backdate *applications* to March 31, 1989, which appears not to be illegal. It remains to be seen how long they can get away with this.Step two is to require that unrecognized schools must say in their literature that they do not operate under a Royal Charter or an Act of Parliament (the two ways schools become legitimately recognized in Britain). This, too, is unlikely even to be noticed by degree-buyers in other lands.

Other states and jurisdictions have tried to craft laws that would permit legitimate non-traditional schools to operate while eliminating degree mills. For instance, for many years California had a law that stated that the main requirement for being authorized by the state to grant degrees was ownership of $50,000 worth of real property. That law was apparently passed to eliminate low-budget fly-by-night degree mills. But $50,000 ain't what it used to be, and from the 1960s through the early 1980s, dozens of shady operators declared that their home or their book collection was worth $50,000 and proceeded to sell degrees with wild abandon.

In 1978, I had the pleasure of advising the "60 Minutes" people from CBS on which California "universities" they might wish to send Mike Wallace in to expose. The proprietor of California Pacifica University was actually arrested while Wallace was interviewing him, and soon after, pleaded guilty to multiple counts of mail fraud, and went off to federal prison. Two years later, California Pacifica was still listed in the state's official *Directory of California Educational Institutions.*

California, thankfully, has tightened things up considerably in the last few years, with requirements that there must be elements of instruction provided by state-authorized schools. Once again, of course, we have a law trying to define subjective matters.

In 1990, I had the further pleasure of appearing on the nationally-syndicated program "Inside Edition" to help expose yet another major degree mill, North American University.

Another reason for the proliferation of degree mills in the past is that the wheels of justice ground very slowly, when they ground at all. Dallas State College was shut down by authorities in Texas in 1975. The same perpetrators almost immediately opened up as Jackson State University in California. When the post office shut off their mail there, they resurfaced with John Quincy Adams University in Oregon. It took 12 more years, and a major effort by the FBI before the Dallas State people were finally brought to justice in a federal courtroom in North Carolina in late 1987, nearly two decades after they sold their first doctorate.

It is the entry of the FBI into the arena that has changed the rules of the game.

DIPSCAM

In the late 1970s, the Federal Bureau of Investigation launched an operation called "DipScam" (for Diploma Scam), which has methodically been investigating degree-granting institutions from coast to coast and, with some cooperation from Scotland Yard and other foreign authorities, overseas as well.

I have been consulting with the FBI on matters of degree mills since 1979, and have appeared as an "expert witness" in federal court. It is most pleasing to see some of the people who have been writing me threatening letters for years departing to serve terms in federal prison.

The FBI has looked into hundreds of unaccredited schools. Some were found to be harmless, innocuous, even good, and no actions were taken. When there was evidence of chicanery, a search warrant was issued, and FBI vans hauled off tons of papers and records. In many, but not all cases, a federal grand jury handed down indictments. And when they did, in many, but not all cases, the indictees pleaded guilty to mail or wire (telephone) fraud, and received fines and sentences in federal prison. When this has happened, it is described in the listing for those schools later in this chapter.

The wording of the federal grand jury indictments is quite wonderful. Here is a sample, from one recent indictment. (This is just a small excerpt from a thick document.)

> SCHEME AND ARTIFICE: Count One: That from some unknown time prior to on or about [date] and continuing through some unknown time after [date] within the Western District of North Carolina and elsewhere in the United States, [defendants] did knowingly, intentionally, and unlawfully combine, conspire, confederate and agree with each other and with others to the Grand Jurors both known and unknown, to commit offenses against the United States, that is, having devised and intending to devise a scheme and artifice to defraud and for obtaining money by false and fraudulent pretenses, representations and promises, for the purpose of executing said scheme and artifice to defraud and attempting do so knowingly and intentionally placing and causing to be placed in a post office and an authorized depository for mail matter, and causing to be delivered by United States mail according to the direction thereon, matters and things to be sent and delivered by the United States Postal Service, in violation of Title 18, United States Code, Sections 1341 and 2, and knowingly and intentionally transmitting and causing to be transmitted by means of wire communication in interstate commerce, certain signs, signals and sounds, to wit, interstate telephone conversations, in violation of Title 18, United States Code, Section 1343.

In other words, they sent fake degrees by mail, and made interstate phone calls to their customers.

In its earlier days, DipScam went after the fake medical schools—the most dangerous fake degree-sellers of all. They were quickly able to shut down the two worst perpetrators, Johann Keppler School of Medicine and the United American Medical College, and send their respective founders to prison.

DipScam's largest case so far came to its grand finale in a federal courthouse in Charlotte, North Carolina, in October 1987. I had the pleasure to be present as an expert witness and an observer. On trial were the seven perpetrators of a long string of degree mills, most recently including Roosevelt University, Loyola University, Cromwell University, University of England at Oxford, Lafayette University, DePaul University, and Southern California University, as well as several fake accrediting agencies.

More than 100 witnesses were called over a two-and-a-half-week period, including many who established the substantial size and scope of bank deposits and investments made by the defendants. Witnesses from Europe testified to the mail forwarding services the defendants used in England, France, Belgium, Germany, Holland, and elsewhere.

The circus-like atmosphere was not helped by the fact that Jim and Tammy Faye Bakker, Jessica Hahn and company, were appearing in the courtroom right next door, and so the grounds of the courthouse were covered by photographers and reporters, none of whom took much interest in the DipScam trial.

Two of the minor players were dismissed by the judge for lack of definitive evidence, but the five main defendants were found guilty by the jury on all 27 counts of mail fraud, aiding and abetting, and conspiracy. They were sentenced to prison terms ranging from two to seven years.

The DipScam project is no longer as active, simply because there aren't that many perpetrators still in business in the U.S. But the FBI continues to be the major force active in preventing phony degrees from being sold.

WHY DEGREE MILLS PROSPER

The main reason—really the only reason—for the success of degree mills, drug dealers, and pornographers is, of course, that people keep on buying their product. They crave the degrees and somehow, despite much evidence to the contrary, they really believe that they are going to get away with it.

Unfortunately, many newspapers and magazines continue to permit them to advertise. For years, the otherwise reputable *Psychology Today* and *New York Times* regularly ran ads for phony schools, and turned a deaf ear to the please of many, self included, to stop disseminating these frauds. In 1989, when the totally fraudulent University of North America began advertising in *USA Today,* I telephoned and wrote their advertising department, suggesting that they were doing their readers a disservice by running those ads. The reply, in effect, was that no one had complained (except me), so they would keep on running the ads.

I must warn you, as emphatically as I can, that it is taking a very big risk to buy a fake degree, or to claim to have a degree that you have not earned. *It is like putting a time bomb in your resumé.* It could go off at any time, with dire consequences. The people who sold the fake degree will probably never suffer at all, but the people who buy them often suffer mightily.

In part as a result of all the publicity the FBI activities have gotten, credentials are being checked out now as never before. *Time* magazine, in an article on fake degrees (February 5, 1979), says that "with the rate at which job candidates are now fibbing on resumes and faking sheepskins, graduate schools and companies face detective work almost every time they see an application . . . . Checking up on about 12,000 inquiries a year, U.C.L.A. finds two or three frauds a week. For its part, Yale has accumulated a file of 7,000 or so bogus Old Blues."

Often people get caught when something unexpectedly good happens in their lives, and they become the focus of the news media, which love stories involving fake degrees.

DIPLOMA MILLS IN THE NEWS

Here is just a small sampling of the stories in my overflowing file on people who have gotten in trouble over degrees and credentials in recent years.

- The Chairman of the Board of a major Florida university resigned, after it became known that he had bought his degrees from an Oklahoma diploma mill.
- Two of the 1988 presidential candidates had problems over credentials claims. Joseph Biden's campaign literature "misstated" the nature of his graduate degrees, and Pat Robertson's official biography had to be changed from saying that he did "graduate study, University of London" to "studied briefly at the University of London" after the revelation he had taken only a short undergraduate seminar on art for Americans.
- In 1987, a popular columnist for *Forbes* magazine, Srully Blotnick, was dropped from the magazine when his Ph.D. credentials (as well as his research methodology) came under close scrutiny.
- In 1987, Arizona's Teacher of the Year (a major honor in that state) was found to be using a Doctorate he had

never earned.

- The biggest business scandal in Sweden in half a century, the Fermenta affair, was triggered when a former employee of a major industrialist, believed to be the richest man in Sweden, charged (correctly) that the industrialist had lied about possessing two doctorates. According to the *Economist* (November 14, 1987), "Fermenta's share price halved as this charge about bogus qualifications spread." A billion-dollar deal with Volvo was cancelled in the wake of the scandal.
- During the 1987 New York City parking meter scandals, one of the government's star witnesses, according to the *Daily News,* "admitted he has a bogus Doctorate from Philathea College . . . ."
- In 1985, Congressman Claude Pepper convened a congressional panel, which asserted that more than 500,000 Americans have obtained false credentials or diplomas. (Pepper's staff got him a Ph.D. from Union University. All "Dr. Pepper" allegedly had to do was submit four book reports, which his staff wrote for him.)
- As a result of accumulating over 7,000 "client" names from its diploma mill raids, the FBI identified more than 200 federal employees, including 75 in the Defense Department, with bogus degrees.
- Congressman Ron Wyden of Oregon said that as many as 40,000 physicians who failed their qualifying exams may nonetheless be practicing medicine.
- According to *Sports Illustrated*, the owner of the Indianapolis Colts, Robert Irsay, made the "frequent boast that he played Big Ten football at the University of Illinois, while getting a degree in electrical engineering." The magazine says he neither played football nor earned a degree.
- In 1986, a fake degree scandal rocked Indonesia, with the revelation that a war hero turned businessman was bilked of huge sums of money by an executive of his shipping line, who had been hired because of his Doctorate in economics from a U.S. degree mill, Thomas Edison College.
- And even in the Soviet Union . . . one Alexander Shavlokhov was arrested for selling at least 56 fake degrees of the Gorky Agricultural Institute, at 1,000 rubles each, to industrialists around the country. (*Note:* Russia refuses to allow me to advertise my book in that country; they say there is no need for it.)

TWO OTHER INSIDIOUS ACADEMIC FRAUDS

In addition to those who sell fake degrees, there are two other "services" that undermine the academic establishment.

One is the so-called "lost diploma replacement service." If you tell them you had a legitimate degree but lost it, they will replace it for a modest fee. That's why I have a Harvard "Doctor of Neurosurgery" diploma hanging on my wall (next to my real Michigan State one). The Harvard phony sold for $49.95. When the FBI raided one such service, in Oregon (they had been advertising in national publications), they found thousands of blank diplomas from hundreds of schools—and records showing an alarmingly large number of clients. The other is term paper and dissertation writing services. Several of them put out catalogues listing over a thousand already-written term papers they will sell, and if they don't have what you want, they will write anything from a short paper to a major dissertation for you, for a $7 to $10 a page.

HOW THIS CHAPTER HAS CHANGED

In earlier editions, I used to include all those schools that I regarded as diploma mills, religious and otherwise. The problem with this approach was that many of the schools were, in fact, operating legally, either because they were church-run, or because they were in locations with few or no laws regulating schools. Until 1985, for instance, Arizona had no laws whatsoever regulating universities and degrees, and so a good many degree mills operated from that state. Now, with the passage of a school registration law in Hawaii in 1990, every state has some form of law. A few states, such as Utah and Louisiana, have no evaluative process, but simply register any school that applies for registration.

Long ago, in this chapter, I also used to give the addresses of the degree mills. I became convinced that this served no legitimate or useful purpose, so the detailed addresses have been deleted, and I will *not* supply them if you write to me.

Finally, there are a handful of schools that I firmly believe are diploma mills, but I do not have sufficient proof to say so in print, and I do not enjoy being sued. These schools have been listed among the regular schools and Bible schools, generally with descriptions that are less than wonderful, but factual.

Some of these borderline institutions were written about in a major series of articles that appeared in the *Arizona Republic* a few years ago. The *Republic* received many threats from lawyers and aggrieved school operators, but was never sued over their series. The articles have been reprinted in a booklet, which is called *Diploma Mills: The Paper Merchants.* The booklet is available from me for $5 (includes first class postage). (John Bear,

P.O. Box 826, Benicia, CA 94510.) But don't buy this expecting to get the addresses of the mills; they aren't there either.

THE DIPLOMA MILLS

"E&T" stands for Education & Training, a British magazine that regularly reports on European and other degree mills. "COE" stands for the Council of Europe, an intergovernmental agency, based in Strasbourg, France, which keeps track of what they believe are European and other degree mills.

Academy College of Holy Studies Sheffield, England. Identified as a degree mill by E&T.
Academy of the Science of Man See: University of the Science of Man
Accademia di Studi Superiori Minerva Milan, Italy. Identified as a degree mill by COE. However the courts decided otherwise. In District Court of Fiorenzuola d'Arda in 1958, one Amorosa d'Aragona Francesco was brought to trial for using a degree from this school. The court apparently ruled that the school may not be great but it is legal. It moved from Bari to Milan a few years later, and then went out of business.
Accademia di Studi Superiori Phoenix Bari, Italy. Identified as a degree mill by COE. Very likely the same as the school just listed.
Accademia Universale de Governo Cosmo-Astrosofica-Libero de Psico-Biofisica Trieste, Yugoslavia. Identified as a degree mill by COE. Can you imagine what their school cheers sound like?
Accademia Universitaria Internazionale Rome, Italy. Identified as a degree mill by E&T.
Adams Institute of Technology See: National Certificate Company
Addison State University Ottawa, Canada. Bachelor's, Master's and Doctorates in almost any field but medical or dental are sold for about $30.
Alabama Christian College See: R/G Enterprises. No connection with a legitimate school of this name in Montgomery, Alabama.
Albany Educational Services Northampton, England. Offers to act as an agent to obtain American Bachelor's, Master's and Doctorates for a fee of $150 to $250. Letters to the director, L.W. Carroll, asking which schools he represents, have not been answered.
Albert Einstein Institut Zurich, Switzerland. Sells the phony degrees of Oxford Collegiate Institute (of the International University). One of the many fake degree operations of Karl Xavier Bleisch.
American College in Switzerland Berne, Switzerland. Totally phony Doctorates are offered by yet another of "Professor Doctor" Karl Xavier Bleisch's degree mills. Affiliations with Georgetown University and with the University of Florida are falsely claimed in the literature.
American Extension School of Law Chicago, Illinois. Identified as a degree mill by COE.
American Institute of Science Indianapolis, Indiana. Identified as a degree mill by COE.
American Institute of Technology See: Bureau for Degree Promotions.
American International Academy New York and Washington. Identified as a degree mill by COE.
American International University Established in California in the 1970s by Edward Reddeck (who was convicted of mail fraud for a previous diploma mill operation, and currently operates the University of North America using a Missouri address). His employee, Clarence Franklin, left to establish American National University, and was later indicted by a federal grand jury. Degrees of all kinds were sold for $1,600 to $2,500, whether or not the required eight-page dissertation was written. No longer in operation. American International resurfaced briefly in 1987, using a Kansas City, Missouri, address which was a mail forwarding service.
American Legion University U.S. location unknown. Identified as a degree mill by E&T.
American Management Institute See: International Universities Consortium.
American Medical College (Burma) Rangoon, Burma. Identified as a degree mill by COE.
American Medical College (Idaho) Nampa, Idaho. Doctor of Medicine degrees have been awarded by this apparently non-existent school. A student there (with a diploma mill undergraduate degree) provided what appears to be a letter from the Idaho superintendent of public instruction confirming that the school is appropriately registered with his office. There is no listed telephone for them in Nampa.
American National University (AZ) Phoenix, Arizona. The university was established by Dr. Clarence Franklin, a California chiropractor formerly associated with American International University, and who was subsequently indicted by a federal grand jury for operating this school. Degrees were offered on payment of fees in the vicinity of $2,000. Accreditation was claimed from the National Accreditation Association, which had been established by Franklin and a colleague in Maryland. Apparently stopped operations in 1983 or 1984. Franklin was convicted of violation of federal law a few years later. A new and unrelated American National University was authorized in California in 1987.

American School of Metaphysics Location unknown. Identified as a degree mill by COE.
American University (CA) San Diego, California. Degrees of all kinds were offered on payment of a fee of $1,500 to $2,500. The claim was made that all degrees were "registered with the government" in Mexico, where the school was allegedly located. No longer in business.
American West University See: California Pacifica University. One of the many fake schools of Ernest Sinclair.
American Western University Operated from a mail drop in Tulsa, Oklahoma, in the early 1980s by Anthony Geruntino of Columbus, Ohio, who later went to federal prison for this school and his next venture, Southwestern University. American Western's mail delivery was stopped in late 1981 by the U.S. Postal Service, at which time a new address was utilized. Affiliated schools included the National College of Arts and Sciences, Northwestern College of Allied Science, Regency College, and Saint Paul's Seminary.
Amritsar University Amritsar, India. Identified as a degree mill by COE.
Anglo-American College of Medicine See: National College
Anglo-American Institute of Drugless Medicine See: National College
Aquinas University of Scholastic Philosophy New York. Identified as a degree mill by E&T.
Argus University Fairplay, Colorado. A fictitious university formed apparently just for fun in 1977. Its stated purpose is selling Doctorates to dogs and their humans. The founder writes that Argus "will confer a degree to any dog whose owner sends a check for $5 to Argus University." Same fee for humans, apparently.
Arya University Srinigar, India. Identified as a degree mill by COE.
Atlanta Southern University Atlanta, Georgia. Another of Ernest Sinclair's degree mills. See California Pacifica University. The president of a large respectable university used to tell people his degree was from Atlanta Southern; he doesn't any more.
Atlantic Northeastern University Their address in New York was a mail forwarding service. They offered all degrees, using well-designed and printed promotional materials, almost identical to those used by Pacific Northwestern and Atlantic Southern universities. Fake (but realistic-looking) transcripts were available for an additional fee. Apparently no longer in business.
Atlantic Southern University Operated briefly from addresses in Atlanta, Georgia, and Seattle, Washington. The materials look identical to those of Pacific Northwestern University. Newspaper publicity in 1980 apparently caused them to cease operations.
Atlantic University (NY) New York. As a promotional gimmick once, Atlantic Monthly magazine offered an honorary Doctorate from Atlantic University to new subscribers. A harmless gag, perhaps, but I have now seen two instances in which Atlantic University appeared on a job application resume.
Australian Institute See Bureau for Degree Promotions
Avatar Episcopal University London, England. Identified as a degree mill by E&T.
Avatar International University London, England. Identified as a degree mill by COE.
Ben Franklin Academy and Institute For Advanced Studies Washington, District of Columbia. They offered Bachelor's, Master's and Doctorates through correspondence study. "Deserving Americans" could request honorary Doctorates, which required a donation. They claimed to be "not just another degree mill, but a fully accredited degree-granting institution." The accreditation was from the American Association of Accredited Colleges and Universities which I could never locate. The former address (P.O. Box 1776) and former phone number (USA-1776) were the best part; at least it shows they had influence somewhere in Washington.
Benchley State University See: LTD Documents
Benson University Same management as Laurence University (Hawaii).
Bettis Christian University Arkansas. In the mid 1980s, Ph.D.'s were sold for $800 by two inmates of the Arkansas State Prison. Another instance of a "University Behind Walls."
Beulah College of Nigeria and Texas, in 1990, offered to award an honorary Doctor of Humanities to anyone sending them $500.
Bible University Ambuhr, North Arcot, India. Identified as a degree mill by COE.
Bonavista University Douglas, Wyoming. All degrees were sold for a fee of $500 to $700. Other Bonavista literature had been mailed from Sandy, Utah, and Wilmington, Delaware. No longer in business, at least at those locations.
Bosdon Academy of Music See: ORB
Boston City College See: Regency Enterprises
Bradford University Same management as Laurence University (Hawaii).
Brantridge Forest School See: Sussex College of Technology
Bretton Woods University New Hampshire. Diplomas of this alleged institution have been sold for $15 by a "collector of elite unit militaria" who says they were "obtained through various unknown third parties . . . Some are original unawarded certificates, while others could be reproductions."

British College of Soma-Therapy England. Identified as a degree mill by E&T.

British Collegiate Institute London, England. They used to sell degrees of all kinds for a fee of $100 to $300, through the London address, and an agent in Inman, Kansas. The provost was listed as Sir Bernard Waley, O.B.E., M.A., D.Litt. See also: College of Applied Science, London.

Broadhurst University See: West London College of Technology

Brownell University Degrees of this "University that does not now exist" were sold for $10, both by Associated Enterprises of Jacksonville, Florida, and Universal Data Systems of Tustin, California. An extra $5 bought a "professional lettering kit" so you can add any name and date you wish. School rings, decals, and stationery were sold as well. Since the sellers in Tustin (apparently two schoolteachers) slammed the door on a "60 Minutes" crew some years ago, the degrees have apparently not been sold.

Brundage Forms Georgia. Brundage sells blank forms for all purposes. His college degree form, which you can fill in yourself, costs less than a dollar. His motto is "No advice, just forms." My motto is: "You can get in just as much trouble with a phony 50¢ Doctorate as with a phony $3,000 Doctorate."

Buckner University Texas. All degrees, including some in medicine, were sold for $45 each. They claim there is a real Buckner in Texas. There isn't. The literature says, "We believe this modestly-priced yet extremely impressive document will give you great enjoyment, prestige, and potential profitability." It is also likely to give you the opportunity to meet some nice people from your district attorney's office. The degrees were sold by University Press of Houston, and by Universal Data Systems of Tustin, California (which also sold Brownell and other fake diplomas).

Bureau for Degree Promotions in Holland is selling the fake degrees of Addison State University, Atlantic Southeastern University, the Australian Institute, American Institute of Technology, and International University of India for $50 to $100, and knighthoods at $500.

Calgary College of Technology Calgary, Alberta, Canada. One of Canada's most ambitious degree mills offered the Bachelor's, Master's, and Doctorate for fees up to $275. The literature included a lengthy profile of the dean, Colonel R. Alan Munro, "Canada's premier Aeronaut." A recent book of heraldry lists "Colonel the Chevalier Raymond Allen Zebulon Leigh Munro, C.M., G.C.L.J., C.L., K.M.L.J., S.M.L.J., A.D.C., C.O.I., C.O.F., M.O.P., B.S.W., M.H.F., LL.B., M.A., LL.D., D.Sc.A., C.D.A.S., F.R.S.A., F.S.A. Scot, A.F.C.A.S.I., C.R.Ae.S., A.F.A.I.A.A., M.A.H.S., M.C.I.M., M.C.I.M.E." Could this be the same person? The Calgary catalogue even included a telephone number. That phone was answered, "Spiro's Pizza Parlor." Truly. Could "Ph.D." stand for "Pizza, Home Delivery"?

California Christian College See: R/G Enterprises

California Institute of Behavior Sciences California. Humorous but well-designed Doctorates were awarded, at least in the 1960s, with the title of Doctor of Image Dynamics, citing "mastery of Machiavelian Manipulations . . . discovery of the failsafe Success Mechanism, and the fail un-safe Failure Mechanism . . . ."

California Institute of Higher Learning See: London Institute for Applied Research

California Pacifica University Hollywood, California. Widely advertised degree mill, operated by Ernest Sinclair. Degrees were sold for $3,500, from California Pacifica or almost any other school one wanted. The slick catalogue showed photos of faculty and staff, all fictitious. Sinclair was the main subject of a CBS "60 Minutes" exposé in April 1978. He pleaded guilty to 3 of the 36 counts on which he was arrested. While his trial was on, he opened yet another fake school, Hollywood Southern University. Sinclair's advertising was regularly accepted by the New York Times and other major publications. Two years after he was arrested, California Pacifica was still listed in the official California directory of authorized schools! Mr. Sinclair once sued me for $4 million for calling his degree mill a degree mill, but he went to prison before we went to trial. One report had it that he continued to sell degrees while in federal prison—if true, the first known instance of a "University Behind Walls" program.

Canadian Temple College of Life of the International Academy Burnaby, British Columbia, Canada. Identified as a degree mill by COE.

Capital College See: National Certificate Company

Cardinal Publishing Company Florida. They publish a variety of fake diploma forms and blanks.

Carlton University Same management as Laurence University (Hawaii).

Carnegie Institute of Engineering See: Regency Enterprises

Carolina Institute of Human Relations Sumter, South Carolina. Identified as a degree mill by COE.

Carroll Studios Illinois. In 1988, they were selling "College Diploma" forms for $2 each, in which the buyer must letter not only his or her own name but the name of the school and degree earned. Two dollars also buys you a marriage certificate, a birth certificate, a divorce certificate, and, if devastated by all of the above, a last will and testament.

Central Board of Higher Education India. Identified as a degree mill by COE.

Central School of Religion England, the U.S., Australia. Identified as a degree mill by E&T.
Central States Research Center Ontario, Canada. They sold well-printed fake diplomas "in memory of famous names." The samples they sent out included Christian College, the Ohio Psychological Association, and Sussex College of Technology. Another address in Columbus, Ohio.
Central University See: National Certificate Company
Charitable University of Delaware Identified as a degree mill by E&T.
Chartered University of Huron Identified as a degree mill by COE.
Chicago Medical College Fort Pierce, Florida. Their literature says that "Your beautiful 11 x 15 graudate (sic) diploma is printed on the finest sturdy parchtone .... It will add prestige and beauty to your office." Or cell. The price of their medical degree is a mere $450.
Chillicothe Business College Ohio. Identified as a degree mill by E&T.
Chirological College of California Identified as a degree mill by COE.
Christian College See: Central State Research Center
Christian Fellowship Foundation See: Lawford State University
City Medical Correspondence College London, England. Identified as a degree mill by E&T.
Clayton Theological Institute California (the address appears to be a private home). Their Doctorate was awarded on completion of a dissertation of at least 25 words and a fee of $3. When this was done (my dissertation was 27 words; I worked extra hard), I got a nice letter saying that I have indeed been awarded their Doctorate, but if I wanted the actual diploma, it would cost $50 more. Recent letters to the institute have been returned as undeliverable.
Clemson College See: R/G Enterprises
Clinton University Livonia, Michigan. For years, they sold fake degrees of all kinds for $25 and up, offering "a masterpiece so perfect, it absolutely defies detection." Mail to their address is now returned as undeliverable.
Colgate College See: R/G Enterprises
College of Applied Science London London, England. The college exists on paper only, but, like Brigadoon, it was real (well, almost real) for one day. As reported by a German magazine, a wealthy German industrialist bought a fake Doctorate from this place, and insisted that it be presented in person. The president, "Commander Sir" Sidney Lawrence enlisted the aid of his friend, "Archbishop" Charles Brearly, who runs several universities in Sheffield. They rented a fancy girls' school for the day, installed carpets and candelabra, and rented costumes for their friends, who dressed up as "counts hung around with medals, an abbess in a trailing robe . . . and the knights of the Holy Grail." The German arrived in a Rolls Royce, and received his degree in an impressive ceremony, which only cost him $15,000. Sir Sidney, incidentally, appends a rubber stamp to his letters saying, "Hon. Attorney General U.S.A."
College of Divine Metaphysics England. Identified as a diploma mill by E&T.
College of Franklin and Marshall See: Regency Enterprises
College of Hilton Head See: University of East Georgia
College of Homeopathy Missouri. Identified as a diploma mill by E&T.
College of Journalism West Virginia. Identified as a diploma mill by E&T.
College of Life Florida. Honorary Doctorates were sold for $2, but they went away.
College of Natural Therapeutics See: International University
College of Naturatrics Missouri. Identified as a diploma mill by E&T.
College of Nonsense Nevada. "You can fool your friends and tell them you have a Doctorate degree. If they don't believe you, you can show your friends your Doctor degree." I bought a Doctor of Politics for $2. A Doctor of Martyrism, Cheerleading, or Nose Blowing would have been 50¢ extra. Silly stuff, but a better-printed diploma than many legitimate schools provide.
College of Spiritual Sciences England. Identified as a diploma mill by E&T.
College of Universal Truth Chicago, Illinois. Identified as a diploma mill by E&T.
Collegii Romanii See: International Honorary Awards Committee
Collegium Technologicum Sussexensis Britannia See: Sussex College of Technology
Colorado Christian University Subject of a landmark court case in which the state of New York successfully sued to prevent them from selling their degrees to New Yorkers, or to advertise in publications distributed from New York. No connection whatever with the accredited Rockmont College which changed its name in 1989 to Colorado Christian University.
Columbia School Unknown U.S. location. Identified as a diploma mill by COE.
Commercial University Delhi, India. Listed as a degree mill by COE. The Ministry of Education writes that it is a "coaching institution" whose degrees are "not recognised for any purpose." However a reader in Malaysia maintains that their B.Com. degree exam is comparable to those of University of London, and that at least one

graduate has had his degree accepted by the Malaysian government.

Commonwealth School of Law Washington. Identified as a diploma mill by COE.

Commonwealth University California. Degrees of this non-existent school were sold by mail for $40. Also sold by the same firm: Eastern State University.

Constantinia University In 1989, a mailing went out to Italian businessmen, offering them the opportunity to earn a doctorate from this apparently non-existent school, in association with the accredited Johnson & Wales University (which denied any knowledge of the scheme). For $3,000, they would spend a week in New York, see Niagara Falls, and go home with a doctorate. According to one source in Italy, more than 100 people signed up.

Continental University In 1990, a reader in Japan sent me a copy of a diploma (dated 1989) from the non-eixtent school, allegedly in Los Angeles.

Cranmer Hall Theological College Identified as a diploma mill by E&T.

Creative University of Southeast London London, England. Identified as a diploma mill by E&T.

Cromwell University London, England. This diploma mill was one of many run for years by the Fowler family of Chicago, five of whom were sentenced to prison in late 1987 for these activities. Cromwell sold degrees of all kinds for $730, through a mail forwarding service. Accreditation was claimed from the non-existent Western European Accrediting Society of Liederbach, West Germany.

Dallas State College Dallas, Texas. One of the earliest heavily advertised diploma mills, Dallas State flourished in the early 1970s under the guidance of at least one of the Fowler family of Chicago. In 1975, the attorney general of Texas permanently enjoined Dallas State from operating in that state.

Darthmouth College See: Regency Enterprises

De Paul University (France) Paris, France. A diploma mill operated for years by the Fowler family, from a mail forwarding service in Paris. Operations ceased following five Fowlers' sentencing to prison in 1987. Degrees of all kinds were sold for $550, and accreditation was claimed from the Worldwide Accrediting Commission, allegedly of Cannes, France. Other addresses used in Clemson, South Carolina and Santa Monica, California.

Delaware Law School Identified as a diploma mill by E&T and I'm sorry the people at the genuine Delaware Law School of Widener University are upset, but don't blame me if some diploma mill operators choose to use the same name.

Diplomatic State University See: R/G Enterprises

Diplomatic University See: National Certificate Company

Earl James National University College Toronto, Canada. Identified as a diploma mill by COE.

Eastern Missouri Business College The non-existent school established by the Attorney General of Missouri, in a 'sting' operation. During its one day of existence, the head of the International Accrediting Commision for Schools, Colleges and Theological Seminaries visited the one-room office in St. Louis, overlooked the school officers named Peelsburi Doobuoy and Wonarrmed Mann, overlooked the fact that the marine biology text was *The Little Golden Book of Fishes*, but did not overlook the accreditation 'fee' he was handed, and duly accredited the school.

Eastern Orthodox Universtiy India. **Identified as a diploma mill by COE.**

Eastern State University See: Commonwealth University

Eastern University See: National Certificate Company

Ecclesiastical University of Sheffield See: University of Sheffield

Elysion College They used to offer degrees from various addresses in California, although the proprietor was in Mexico. Several book reports or essays and $500 were required to earn the degree. When the proprietor died, his daughter continued the operation from her home in San Francisco. She told authorities she was not operating the school, but an FBI analysis of her garbage revealed that she was, and after her indictment by a federal grand jury, and her guilty plea, Elysion College faded away.

Emerson University California. Identified as a diploma mill by COE.

Empire College of Ophthalmology Canada. Identified as a diploma mill by COE.

Episcopal University of London London, England. Identified as a diploma mill by E&T.

Episcopal University of Saint Peter Port Frankfurt, Germany. Identified as a diploma mill by E&T.

Études Universitaires Internationales Leichtenstein, Luxembourg. Identified as a diploma mill by COE.

Eugenia Institute of Metaphysics See: ORB

European College of Science and Man Sheffield, England. Identified as a diploma mill by E&T.

Evaluation and Management International Inglewood, California. These folks have sent out a three-page, unsigned letter saying that on receipt of $2,100 they will arrange for the degree of your choice to be issued to you. They require 50% down before they reveal the name of the school that is to be your alma mater. Can anyone ever have fallen for this?

Evergreen University In 1989, large ads appeared in civil service and other newspapers, offering the degrees of

this school, allegedly in Los Angeles. By the time I learned of it, just a month after the ads ran, the three phone numbers had all been disconnected, and mail was returned as undeliverable.
Faraday College England. Identified as a diploma mill by E&T.
Felix Adler Memorial University Charlotte, North Carolina. Identified as a diploma mill by E&T.
Florida State Christian College Fort Lauderdale, Florida. They used to advertise nationally the availability of Bachelor's, Master's, Doctorates, and honorary Doctorates, until both the postal service and the state of Florida acted to shut them down. They also operated Alpha Psi Omega, a professional society for psychological counselors.
Forest Park University Chicago, Illinois. Identified as a diploma mill by COE.
Four States Cooperative University Texas. Identified as a diploma mill by COE.
Franklin University Same management as Laurence University (Hawaii).
Geo-Metaphysical Institute New York. "Here's a great way to get instant status," said their national advertising, offering an ornate personalized and totally phony honorary Doctorate in geo-metaphysics for $5.
Georgia Christian University Georgia. The first pyramid scheme diploma mill. When you "graduate" (buy a degree), you become a professor and can sell degrees to others. When your students buy degrees and become professors, you become a dean and share in their profits, and so on, up the academic ladder.
German-American Dental College Chicago, Illinois. Identified as a diploma mill by COE.
Golden State University (CA, CO) Operated from addresses in California and Colorado in the 1950s and 1960s. Exposed as a degree mill on Paul Coates' television program in 1958. No connection with the legitimate school of the same name that opened in 1979.
Gordon Arlen College England. Identified as a diploma mill by E&T.
Gottbourg University of Switzerland See: ORB
Graduate University See: National Certificate Company
Great Lakes University Higgins Lake, Michigan. One of several degree mills operated by W. (for Wiley!) Gordon Bennett. Degrees were sold for $200. Also used addresses in Chicago; Dearborn and Berkley, Michigan.
Gulf Southern University Louisiana. The literature is identical to that used by several other mills, such as Pacific Northwestern and Atlantic Northeastern. Degrees were sold for $45 to anyone but Louisiana residents.
Hamburger University This is the training school for McDonalds, and they award the Doctor of Hamburgerology to graduates. Of course it's not a diploma mill; in fact, it has even been licensed to grant real Associate's degrees. But I am mentioning it here, because I am convinced that anything that can be misused will be misused (see Atlantic University, above, for instance).
Hamilton State University Arizona. Sold degrees of all kinds for $50 or less. The fake diploma says they are in Clinton, New York, home of the old and respectable Hamilton College. See also: Regency Enterprises and R/G Enterprises.
Harley University London, England. When I visited the university, I found it in a tiny corner of the London College of Beauty Therapy. The receptionist for the beauty salon was the registrar of the university. Ph.D. degrees were awarded for completion of a few home study courses and a dissertation of less than 20 pages. After an earlier edition of this book appeared, the co-proprietor of Harley U. (who had previously refused to tell me the source of his own Ph.D.) wrote to me that "the details in your booklet are totally untrue in every respect. The content of the study, cost and proprietors are not as you state." The detailed questions I put to him in my reply to that letter were never answered. Harley University apparently is no more. Its proprietor later established Saint Giles University College and Somerset University.
Hartford Technical Institute See: Regency Enterprises
His Majesty's University of Polytechnics Sacramento, California. Used to sell honorary Doctorates in all subjects (but "no profanities or obscenities") for all of $5. But the "university" closed down many years ago, so please stop trying to write to them, so the former proprietor won't have to write me any more annoyed letters.
Hollywood College California. Identified as a diploma mill by E&T.
Hollywood Southern University See: California Pacifica University
Holy Toledo University American Educational Publishers has offered the delightful and humorous Doctorates of Holy Toledo U., offering the Doctor of Philosophy in Adorableness, Defrosting, Worrying, and other fields. They are nicely designed (the gold seal says, in small type, "My goodness how impressive!") and sold for $12 a dozen.
Honoré College See: ORB
Humberman University College Identified as a diploma mill by E&T.
Idaho College of Commerce See International Universities Consortium.
Illinois State University See: Regency Enterprises
Imperial Philo-Byzantine University Madrid, Spain. Identified as a diploma mill by COE.

Independence University Missouri. Flourished in the late 1970s, offering degrees by correspondence, until an exposé in the Chronicle of Higher Education and a Chicago newspaper, helped close them down. The Tribune reported that the headmaster of a prestigious Chicago private school resigned "after disclosures that he was using the office there as a center of activity for the diploma mill." A community college president in Chicago subsequently lost his job for using an Independence Doctorate. There apparently is also a humorous and unrelated Independence University, offering realistic-looking diplomas from its school of hard knocks, and signed by "A. Harry World."

Independent Study Programs, Inc. Missouri. Degrees of all kinds sold in the late 1970s. No longer there.

Independent Universal Academy See: Independent University of Australia

Independent University of Australia Morwell, Victoria, Australia. Identified as a diploma mill by E&T. However, I am persuaded by material sent by persons familiar with the school that it was a legitimate and sincere attempt to establish an alternative university, over the constant objections of the educational establishment. It survived from its founding in 1972 until the death of founder Ivan Maddern. Name changed to Independent Universal Academy after the government forbade use of the word 'university.'

Indiana State University See: Regency Enterprises

Institut Patriarcal Saint Irenée Beziers, France. Granted honorary Doctorates to the founder's American colleagues and perhaps others. See: Inter-State College, this chapter.

Institute of Excellence Florida. All degrees, including medical and dental, at $10 each. The fake diplomas are very poorly printed, and say, in small type, "for novelty purposes only."

Inter-American University (Italy) Rome, Italy. Identified as a diploma mill by COE.

Inter-State College England, France. Established by Karl Josef Werres, granting honorary Doctorates from England. One of the recipients claims that the college is "legally chartered" to do this, but all that means is that in their corporate charter, they give themselves the right. See also: Institut Patriarcal Saint Irenée.

Intercollegiate University Incorporated in Kansas before World War II. As American Mercury reported, "Intercollegiate specialized in hanging its M.A. on some of England's minor men of God—for $50; and for a few dollars more, it was willing to bestow a dazzling D.C.L. Before the war this had grown into a roaring and profitable trade, but when wartime law prohibited sending money out of England, the Intercollegiate professors were obliged to suspend their work of international enlightenment."

Internation University USA. Identified as a diploma mill by E&T.

International Academy for Planetary Planning See: International Honorary Awards Committee

International American University Rome, Italy. Identified as a diploma mill by COE.

International College of Associates in Medicine Texas. Used to offer a Ph.D. and a Doctor of Medical Letters on payment of modest fees.

International Honorary Awards Committee California. They sold a wide range of Doctorates and other awards, mostly for $100 or less. The well-designed Doctoral diplomas come from Collegii Romanii, the International Academy for Planetary Planning, Two Dragon University, and the Siberian Institute. One can also buy diplomatic regalia including the Grand Cross of the Imperial Order of Constantine and the Sovereign Order of Leichtenstein, complete with rosettes, medals, and sashes. The late Francis X. Gordon, founder of all these establishments, had a delightful sense of humor about his work. His widow apparently carried it on.

International Protestant Birkbest College England. Identified as a diploma mill by E&T.

International Universities Consortium Missouri. In 1989, help wanted ads appeared in the academic press, soliciting faculty for a consortium of non-traditional schools. Being of the suspicious sort, I fabricated a resume of the most outrageous sort, under an assumed name, and submitted it. Shortly thereafter, my *nom de plume* was appointed to the faculty of what was alleged to be a group of eight 'universities' —one a long-established diploma mill (London School for Social Research), one a school I have been suspicious about for years (Northern Utah University), and six new ones, characterized by the common theme that they do not appear to exist (no listed phones). They are Southwestern University (allegedly in New Mexico), St. Andrews University (allegedly in Baha [sic] California, Mexico), Northwestern Graduate Institute (allegedly Montana), University of the West (allegedly Wyoming), Idaho College of Commerce (allegedly Idaho), and American Management Institute (no location given). Northern Utah actually issued a catalogue, complete with the 'faculty' names of all those boobs who answered the ad and signed up to be on the staff, no questions asked. But the address and phone numbers in the catalogue are not working. I truly have no idea what is going on here, and my letters to consortium president Warren H. Green have not been answered.

International University (Greece) Athens, Greece. The literature claims that the Doctorates are non-academic, but nonetheless fully recognized as educational and professional degrees by the republic of Greece. The embassy of Greece has written to me that this is not a correct statement. The president is listed as a "Right Reverend Bishop Doctor." There apparently was an affiliation with International University (Missouri).

International University (India) Degrees of this institution are sold for $50 to $100 each by the Bureau for Degree Promotion in Holland.

International University (Louisiana) Louisiana. Opened in the early 1980s, offering degrees of all kinds. Accreditation was claimed from the North American Regional Accrediting Commission, which I have never been able to locate. Following a stern letter from the Louisiana Proprietary School Commission, International University apparently faded away. It was incorporated by relatives of a man who has run several large correspondence law schools.

International University (Switzerland) Zurich, Switzerland. One of the many diploma mill operations of Karl Xavier Bleisch, this one selling Bachelor's, Master's, and Doctorates for $500 to $1,000. The literature has a photocopy of a San Jose State College diploma awarded to Celia Ann Bleisch in 1967. What can this mean?

Jackson State University Los Angeles, Nashville, Reno, Chicago. Sold degrees of all kinds for $200. The postal service issued "false representation orders" and stopped their mail years ago, and the perpetrators finally were sentenced to federal prison in 1987. No connection whatsoever with the legitimate school of this name in Mississippi.

Janta Engineering College Karnal, India. Identified as a diploma mill by COE.

Japan Christian College Tokyo, Japan. Identified as a diploma mill by COE.

Jerusalem University Tel Aviv, Israel. Degrees of all kinds are sold for $10 to $40 from this non-existent university. Buyers must sign a statement that they will not use the degrees for any phony purpose.

Johann Keppler School of Medicine There are very few people daring or stupid enough to start a fake medical school. This was one of the most ambitious, complete with catalogues, and an alleged faculty in Switzerland, Canada, and Mexico. The claim was made that the degrees were recognized in many countries. When I asked their representative (who telephoned to make sure I would put them in this book) which countries, he thought a while and then said, "Well, Mauritius for one." All addresses used were mail forwarding services. Accreditation was claimed from the American Coordinated Medical Society, a fake organization started by L. Mitchell Weinberg, who has been to prison several times for fake medical school operations, and who was involved with Keppler as well. Operations ceased in the wake of the FBI DipScam operation in 1983. Weinberg was indicted and sentenced to prison again.

John Quincy Adams College Portland, Oregon. A totally phony school, selling any degree for $250. Later used addresses in Illinois and Nevada. Operated by the Fowler family, five of whom were sentenced to prison in 1987.

Kentucky Christian University Ashland, Kentucky. They offered degrees in everything from chemical engineering to law at all levels for a $300 fee. Same auspices as Ohio Christian and Florida State Christian, all now defunct.

Kentucky Military Institute See: Bretton Woods University

Kenwood Associates Long Green (honestly!), Maryland. For $15 each or three for $30, they will sell Bachelor's, Master's, or Doctorates, in the name of any school, with any degree and any date. Then you can buy, for $12, a Jiu Jitsu Master Instructor certificate to flash when the authorities come to take you away.

Kingsley University See: Bradford University

Lafayette University Amsterdam, Netherlands, through a mail forwarding service. One of many fake schools operated by the Fowler family, five of whom were sentenced to prison for operating diploma mills, in late 1987. Degrees of any sort, with any date, were sold for $725. Accreditation was claimed from an equally fake accrediting agency, the West European Accrediting Society of Liederbach, West Germany.

Lamp Beacon University See: California Pacifica University

Laurence University (HI) Hawaii. All degrees in all fields except medicine and law, for a fee of $45. The literature says, "We are confident you will find the benefits you can obtain with a degree from Laurence University are very valuable indeed." The main benefit I can think of is a period of room and board at government expense. The same seller, Associated Enterprises, also issues the fake degrees of Benson University, Carlton University, Kingsley University, Buckner University, Franklin University, and Bradford University. There is, of course, no connection with the legitimate school formerly called Laurence University (now University of Santa Barbara) in California.

Lawford State University Maryland. They used to sell degrees of all kinds for $6.99 from a post office box in Baltimore, now closed. The other school names were Université de Commerce de (sic) Canada and the Christian Fellowship Foundation. The hard-to-decipher signatures on the quite realistic-looking certificates were "Thoroughly Fake, Ph.D." and "Too Much Fun, Jr."

Libera Universita di Psico-Biofisica Trieste, Yugoslavia (that's what their literature says, even though Trieste is now in Italy). Identified as a diploma mill by E&T.

Life Science College California and Oklahoma. The proprietors were arrested in 1981 for an array of charges, including selling Doctor of Divinity degrees, and income tax evasion through the operation of the college and the associated Life Science Church.

Lincoln-Jefferson University See: California Pacifica University
London College of Physiology England. Identified as a diploma mill by E&T.
London College of Theology England. Identified as a diploma mill by E&T.
London Educational College England. Identified as a diploma mill by E&T.
London Institute for Applied Research London, England. All right, I did it (as I've been saying in this book for 17 years). In 1972, while living in England, I was involved with fund-raising for a legitimate school. I figured that since major universities were "selling" their honorary degrees for millions, why not use the same approach on a small scale. We created L.I.A.R. and ran ads in the U.S.: "Phony honorary Doctorates for sale, $25." Several hundred were sold, but we also seemed to upset half the world's educational establishment. (The other half thought it was a good gag.) So L.I.A.R. was retired. Then an offer came from a Dutchman living in Ethiopia (You must believe this; I mean, who would make up such a story.) who wanted to trade 100 pounds of Ethiopian ear pickers and Coptic crosses for our remaining L.I.A.R. certificates. Now he's selling them (from Holland) for $100, without humor, and has added a bunch more fake school names. And if anyone would like some Ethiopian ear pickers and crosses, have I got a deal for you! (Honestly.)
London School for Social Research London, England. The well-prepared literature offers degrees of all kinds for fees of up to $2,000. The address is in a dingy little building off Leicester Square. I climbed five flights of stairs so narrow I had to go up sideways, and at the top found the little one-room office of Archangel Services, a mail forwarding service that told me they forward the London School mail to Miami. Some literature has been mailed from Phoenix. See also: International Universities Consortium.
London Tottenham International Christian University England. Identified as a diploma mill by E&T.
Loyola University (France) Paris, France. Using a mail forwarding service, degrees of all kinds were sold for a payment of up to $650. The brochure claimed that "Many of our successful graduates have used their transcripts to transfer to other colleges and universities in the U.S.A." If this happened, it is only because of confusion of name with the four legitimate Loyolas in the U.S. The perpetrators of this Loyola were sentenced to federal prison in 1987.
LTD Documents New York. Extremely well-done, thus especially dangerous, fake diplomas, with the name of any school whatsoever and any degree imprinted, for $69.50. Also the preprinted degrees of the non-existent San Miguel College and Benchley State University for $49.50. They even explain how to "age" a certificate to make it look older.
Lyne College England. Identified as a diploma mill by E&T.
Madison State University See: R/G Enterprises
Marcus Tullius Cicero University San Francisco, California. A Swiss company advertised in the International Herald Tribune that they could provide the "registered legal degree" of this so-called university for a mere $3,000. The diploma indicates that the university is "officially registered" with the secretary of state which, if true, simply means it is a California corporation. Checks are to be made payable to The Knights of Humanity. There is, of course, no such university in California or, presumably, anywhere else.
Marlowe University New Jersey and Florida. Active during the 1960s and 1970s, selling all kinds of degrees for $150 or less.
Marmaduke University California. Degrees of all kinds were sold for $1,000 and up. The literature reports that "usually the student qualifies for more advanced study than he initialy [sic] expected." Mention was made of a 30-day resident course in the use of lie detectors, but the voice on the phone (answered, "Hello") said it has been cancelled "because of the building program." Marmaduke was once actually authorized by the state of California, back in the days (late 1970s) when such things were vastly easier.
Martin College Florida. They used to sell degrees of all kinds for $200. Graduates were required to pass some tough exams. They even gave an example in their literature: "True or false—the Declaration of Independence was signed on the 4th of July 1776 by British Royalty."
Meta Collegiate Extension Chartered in Nevada before World War II, they sold the Ph.D. degree for $50, less 20% for cash.
Metropolitan Collegiate They sell all degrees, including medical and dental, for $100 or less. The address is a mail forwarding service which told me they forward the mail to Yorkshire. It is hard to imagine that such things can be tolerated, but this place has been going for years. (I have a little fantasy, in which the prime minister becomes gravely ill on a trip abroad, and the doctor who is summoned has his M.D. from Metropolitan Collegiate.)
Millard Fillmore Institute In 1966, the year I earned my real Doctorate (from Michigan State University), Bob Hope received one of his first honorary Doctorates, after making a large gift to Southern Methodist University. I was aware that Millard Fillmore, our great 13th president, was the only president who routinely turned down offers of honorary degrees, including one from Oxford. That was the inspiration for creating the fictitious Millard Fillmore Institute, to poke fun at the way universities trade honorary degrees for money. The ornate diploma read,

"By virtue of powers which we have invented . . . the honorary and meretricious" title was awarded, "magna cum grano salis" (with a big grain of salt). Many were given away, and some were sold, complete with a cheap plastic frame, for five bucks. Most people thought it was amusing, but a few saw it as a threat to civilization as we know it, and so, after a few years, the fictitious gates of the institute were closed, perhaps forever.

Miller University Philadelphia, Pennsylvania. Identified as a diploma mill by E&T.

Milton University Maryland and New York. Identified as a diploma mill by E&T.

Ministerial Training College Sheffield, England. Identified as a diploma mill by COE.

Montserrat University California. Degrees of all kinds were sold for $10 or $20 from a Post Office Box in San Francisco in this name and the equally fake Stanton University and Rochfort College.

Morston-Colwyn University England and Canada. Identified as a diploma mill by E&T.

Mount Sinai University USA Identified as a diploma mill by E&T.

Nassau State Teachers Colleges See: Regency Enterprises

National Certificate Company New York. These people sold the degrees of eight non-existent universities at $20 to $30 each, and also sold a "make your own" kit consisting of a blank diploma and press-on letters. The eight fake schools are Diplomatic University, Central University, Capital College, Adams Institute of Technology, Eastern University, Western College, Graduate University, and the Southern Institute of Technology. Buyers must sign a statement saying they will not use them for any educational purpose. Suuuuure.

National College Kansas and Oklahoma. Doctorates of all kinds, including medical, were sold by "Dr." Charles E. Downs. Accreditation claimed from a bogus accrediting association established by "Dr." Weinberg, founder of several fake medical schools himself. See also: East Coast University.

National College of Arts and Sciences Once a very active mill, finally closed down by authorities in Oklahoma in 1982. Same ownership as American Western, Northwestern College of Allied Science, and other fake schools. A quite wonderful event in the annals of degree mills occurred when a state official in New York innocently wrote to National College to verify a Master's degree claimed by a job applicant. National College misinterpreted the letter, and sent a Master's degree to the state official, in his own name, complete with a transcript listing all the courses taken and grades received!

National Ecclesiastical University Sheffield, England. Identified as a diploma mill by E&T.

National Stevens University California. Identified as a diploma mill by E&T.

National University (Canada) Toronto, Canada. Identified as a diploma mill by COE.

National University (India) Nagpur, India. Identified as a diploma mill by COE.

National University of Colorado Denver, Colorado. Identified as a diploma mill by COE.

National University of Dakota South Dakota. Identified as a diploma mill by E&T.

National University of Sheffield Sheffield, England. Identified as a diploma mill by COE and E&T.

Nebraska College of Physical Medicine England. Degrees in chiropractic and osteopathy are sold to people who, according to newspaper articles, are said to use them to practice medicine.

New Christian Institute of New England See: ORB

New York State College See: R/G Enterprises

Newcastle University England. Not to be confused with the legitimate University of Newcastle. Identified as a diploma mill by E&T.

North American College of the Artsy With the purchase of the Complete Conductor Kit, the Portable Maestro of St. Paul, Minnesota, awards a Master's degree from the North American College of the Artsy and Somewhat Musically Inclined.

North American University Utah. Formerly University of North America. Operated at least until Spring, 1990 by Edward Reddeck, who has twice gone to prison for educational frauds. A great many people were defrauded by this "school" largely because national publications like *USA Today* kept accepting his advertising. Formerly called University of North America.

Northern Utah University/Northern Utah Management Institute They have been around for years, but now are apparently a part of the International Universities Consortium, described elsewhere in this chapter. The phone listed in Salt Lake City is not in service, and mail was returned as undeliverable in 1990.

Northwest London College of Applied Science London, England. Same location as the College of Applied Science, London. Also known as Northwest London University. Links with several medical degree mills, including Keppler and the Chicago Medical School. The signature of Karl Josef Werres, founder of Inter-State College and Institut Patriarcal Saint Irenée (described in this chapter), and past officer of two large American non-traditional schools, appears on their diploma. Professor Werres wishes people to know that he has nothing to do with this school, and that his name has been forged. Done.

Northwest London University See: Northwest London College of Applied Science

Northwestern College of Allied Sciences Oklahoma City, Oklahoma. Authorities in Oklahoma closed this mill down in 1982. Under the same management as American Western, National College, and several other fake schools, operated under the cloak of the Disciples of Truth. They were operated by James Caffey from Springfield, Missouri. Caffey was indicted by a federal grand jury in 1985, pleaded guilty, and was sentenced to prison.

Northwestern Graduate School Allegedly in Montana. See: International Universities Consortium.

Obura University London, England. Identified as a diploma mill by E&T.

Ohio Central College See: Regency Enterprises

Ohio Christian College One of the more active degree mills in the 1960s and 1970s, they sold degrees of all kinds for fees of $200 and up. Literature identical to that of Florida State Christian University, which was closed by authorities in that state. They claimed to be a part of Calvary Grace Christian Churches of Faith, Inc.

Ohio Saint Mathew University Columbus, Ohio. Identified as a diploma mill by E&T.

Open University (Switzerland) Zurich, Switzerland. One of the many diploma mills operated by Karl Xavier Bleisch.

ORB Virginia. A supermarket of phony degrees, which offered diplomas from eight non-existent institutions at fees of $5 to $65 each. The more authentic-sounding, the more expensive. They include Bosdon Academy of Music, Eugenia Institute of Metaphysics, Gottbourg University of Switzerland, Honoré College of France, New Christian Institute of New England, Royal Academy of Science and Art, Taylor College of England, and Weinberg University of Germany. ORB (other literature reveals that it stands for Occult Research Bureau) has been operated by Mr. Raymond Buckland, author and former curator of the Buckland Museum of Magick.

Oriental University Washington, District of Columbia. Identified as a diploma mill by COE.

Oxford College of Applied Science Oxford, England. A diploma mill, selling degrees of all kinds. Apparently operated from Switzerland by Karl Xavier Bleisch, who has been involved with many other degree mills.

Oxford College of Arts and Sciences Canada. Identified as a diploma mill by E&T.

Oxford Institute for Applied Research London, England. Fake honorary Doctorates sold for $250.

Pacific College They sold everything from high school diplomas to Doctorates for $75 because they believe that "everyone has the right to live and experience life according to his or her own convictions." This presumably includes convictions for fraud.

Pacific Southern University (NJ, CA) New Jersey and California. No connection whatsoever with the legitimate, state-authorized school of the same name in Los Angeles; this Pacific Southern operated from various Post Office boxes, and offered "degrees you can be pround [sic] of" at $250 each.

Pacific States College Degrees of this non-existent school have recently been sold for $5 if blank, and $15 if professionally lettered. The literature describes them as "some of the finest, most authentic looking college degrees on the market. It is almost impossible to distinguish them from the real thing."

Palm Beach Psychotherapy Training Center See: Thomas A. Edison College (FL)

Pensacola Trade School See: Regency Enterprises

People's National University USA. Identified as a diploma mill by E&T.

Philo-Byzantine University Madrid, Spain. Identified as a diploma mill by E&T.

Phoenix University (Italy) See: Accademia di Studi Superiori Phoenix

R/G Enterprises Florida. They sold degrees from 10 schools with almost-real names at prices up to $37.50. Colgate College, Clemson College, Tulsa College, New York State College, California Christian College, Alabama Christian College, Hamilton Institute of Technology, Hamilton State University, Madison State University, and Diplomatic State University. The literature says, "This offer not valid in states where prohibited by law." That doubtless means all 50 of them.

Regency College See: American Western University

Regency Enterprises Missouri. They used to sell degrees with the names of real schools, often slightly changed, such as Stamford (not Stanford) University, and Texas University (not the University of Texas). Others included Cormell University, Indiana State University, Boston City College, the University of Pittsburg, Illinois State University, Rockford Community College, Hartford Technical Institute, Carnegie Institute of Engineering, Stetson College, Nassau State Teachers College, Darthmouth College, Ohio Central College, College of Franklin & Marshall, and Pensacola Trade School. A blank diploma with a lettering kit was also sold for $20. Buyers were asked to sign a statement that they will not use these phony documents for any fraudulent purposes. It is hard to imagine any others to which they could be put. Don L. Piccolo of Anaheim, California, was indicted by a federal grand jury in 1985 for running Regency, and entered a guilty plea.

Rhode Island School of Law Identified as a diploma mill by E&T, which believed it to be in Wyoming.

Rochfort College See: Montserrat University

Rockford Community College See: Regency Enterprises

Roosevelt University (Belgium) Degrees of any kind were sold for a "tuition" of $400 to $600. Also used an address in Zurich, Switzerland. Five of the proprietors of this enterprise were sentenced to federal prison in late

1987.

Royal Academy of Science and Art See: ORB

Royal College of Science Identified as a diploma mill by E&T. Apparently affiliated with, or the same as, Empire College of Ophthalmology.

Saint Andrews Correspondence College Identified as a diploma mill by E&T.

Saint Andrews Ecumenical Foundation University Intercollegiate Identified as a diploma mill by E&T.

Saint Andrews University Allegedly in Mexico. See: International Universities Consortium.

Saint John Chrysostom College London, England. Identified as a diploma mill by E&T.

Saint John's University (India) Identified as a diploma mill by COE.

Saint Joseph University New York. They offered Bachelor's, Master's, Doctorates, and law degrees. Some of the literature was well done; some of it was ludicrous, in which the name "Saint Joseph" had been inserted in gaps where clearly some other school name once appeared. The location was variously given as New York, Louisiana, and Colorado, even in the same catalogue. Degrees cost from $2,000 to $3,000.

Saint Stephens Educational Bible College Los Angeles, California. The president of this institution, a Baptist minister, pleaded guilty to forgery and grand theft for issuing illegal credentials. He was fined $5,000 and placed on probation for five years, and Saint Stephens is no more.

San Francisco College of Music and Theater Arts In 1987, a San Francisco man began advertising this apparently non-existent school in Chinese and African newspapers. Somehow, it was certified as legitimate by the Immigration and Naturalization Service. The *San Francisco Chronicle* reports that three Chinese dancers came to San Francisco to train at the school, and ended up being forced to work as servants for its founder.

San Miguel College See: LTD Documents

Sands University Yuma, Arizona. They sold degrees of all kinds in the mid-1980s. Its proprietor, Wiley Gordon Bennett, operating from Tennessee, was convicted and sentenced to prison, thanks to the FBI DipScam operation.

School of Applied Sciences London and New York. Identified as a diploma mill by E&T.

School of Psychology and Psychotherapy England. Identified as a diploma mill by E&T.

Self-Culture University India. Identified as a diploma mill by COE.

Siberian Institute See: International Honorary Awards Committee

Sir Edward Heyzer's Free Technical College Hong Kong. An association with the National University of Canada. Identified as a diploma mill by COE.

South China University Hong Kong, Macau. Identified as a diploma mill by E&T.

South Eastern Extension College Essex, England. All degrees but medicine or law, at £20 for one, or £45 for three. "Our degrees are indistinguishable from degrees issued by other colleges in the traditional way," the sales letter says. Same ownership as Whitby Hall College.

Southern California University California. One of many fake school names used by the Fowler family, five of whom were sentenced to prison in 1987 for their part in running diploma mills worldwide. Degrees of all kinds were sold for $200 and up.

Southern Eastern University London, England. A diploma mill operated by "Professor Swann-Grimaldi" and claiming the late Princess Grace of Monaco as patron. The address used was that of the prestigious Royal Commonwealth Society, whose members can collect their mail there. Degrees were sold for fees of about $1,000 and up. Application forms were to be sent to the professor's parent's home in Essex.

Southern Institute of Technology See: National Certificate Company

Southwestern University Tucson, Arizona, and St. George, Utah. The university had its own impressive building in Tucson, with many of the trappings of a real school. But after they sold degrees to an FBI agent, several administrators were indicted by a federal grand jury, as part of the FBI's DipScam operation. President Geruntino pleaded guilty, and served a term in federal prison. The names of more than a thousand Southwestern "alumni" were made public, and a many jobs were lost as a result, including some in NASA and the Pentagon. Many students enrolled following a glowing recommendation of Southwestern by an educational guidance service in Columbus, Ohio, run also by Geruntino.

Southwestern University Allegedly in Albuquerque, New Mexico. See: International Universities Consortium.

Specialty Document Company California. In 1988, they were selling fake diplomas for a Doctor of Medicine, Doctor of Veterinary Medicine, Bachelor's, and Ph.D. certificates (no school specified) at $1 each, or 100 for $15. Imagine that, a medical degree for 15¢!

Spicer Memorial College India. Identified as a diploma mill by COE.

Stanton University See: Montserrat University

Staton University In the early 1980s, music teachers in North America received an invitation to join the American Guild of Teachers of Singing, upon which they would be awarded an honorary Doctorate from this non-existent school, which was supposed to be in Ohio.

Stetson College See: Regency Enterprises

Sussex College of Technology Sussex, England. Perhaps the oldest of Britain's degree mills, Sussex is run by "Dr." Bruce Copen from his home, south of London. At the same address, but with different catalogues, are the Brantridge Forest School and the University of the Science of Man. Each offer "earned" degrees for which a few correspondence courses are required, and "extension awards" which are the same degrees and diplomas for no work at all. Honorary Doctorates are offered free, but there is a $100 engraving charge. "Professor Emeritas" [sic] status costs another $100. A recent flyer admits Sussex is not "accrediated" [sic] but goes on to say that "No student who has taken our courses and awards have to date had problems." This statement would not be accepted by, among many others, a former high-level state official in Colorado who lost his job when the source of his Doctorate was discovered. Sussex continues to advertise extensively in newspapers and magazines in the U.S. and worldwide. In 1988, a new British law came into effect, forbidding such 'schools' to accept students who enrolled after May 1st. Sussex's solution to this minor annoyance was to offer to back-date all applications to April 30th, 1988—a creative response that British law apparently hasn't caught up with yet.

Taurus International University California. The claim is that the Taurus International Society was established in 1764 by James Boswell. The Ph.D. is sold for all of $2, and the Doctor of Whimsey for $1.

Taylor College of England See: ORB

Taylor University of Bio-Psycho-Dynamic Sciences was established in Chattanooga, Tennessee, in the early 1920s by some of that city's "most respected citizens, including a philanthropic capitalist, merchant prince, a dentist...and a woman of high intelligence." The Doctorate sold for $115, or $103.50 cash in advance.

Temple Bar College Identified as a diploma mill by E&T.

Tennessee Christian University Tennessee. Affiliated with Ohio and Florida State Christian in the sale of fake degrees.

Texas Theological University Texas. Identified as a diploma mill by E&T.

Texas University See: Regency Enterprises

Thomas A. Edison College (Florida, Arkansas) Totally fake school run by the Rt. Rev. Dr. George C. Lyon, M.D., Ph.D., LL.D., D.D. After twice being fined heavily and sentenced to prison for running fake schools in Florida, he moved to Arkansas, arriving with an entourage in a red Mercedes and a green Rolls-Royce, and bought a vacant church for cash. But the FBI's DipScam operation caught up with him again, and Lyon, now in his 80s, went off to federal prison once again. Thomas A. Edison College managed to fool an awful lot of people over the years, and not just because it sounds like the legitimate non-traditional Edison in New Jersey. This Edison was listed in many otherwise reputable college guides (like Lovejoy's) as a real school for years. Lyon's other nefarious enterprises have included the Palm Beach Pychotherapy Training Center, the Florida Analytic Institute, and an involvement with two phony medical schools, United American Medical College and the Keppler School of Medicine.

Thomas Jefferson University (Missouri) In the early 1980s, catalogues were mailed from this school, allegedly in St. Louis (the address was a private home), but there was never a listed phone, and the postmark was Denver. Degrees at all levels were offered for $1,500 on up. The catalogue was almost identical to that used by a legitimate California school. Letters were never answered. With the catalogue came a Servicemen's Allotment Account form, for military people to have the "university" paid directly each month from their paycheck, into a bank account in New York.

Thomas University Pennsylvania. They used to sell fake degrees for up to $1,000. They claimed accreditation from the fake Middle States Accrediting Board.

Trinity Collegiate Institute England, Switzerland. The London mail service forwards the mail to Karl Bleisch, an operator of many diploma mills in Switzerland. According to an expose in the Times of London, Bleisch told the forwarding service that Trinity was a language school only, with "no question of awarding degrees." Within two months, he was handing out degrees in subjects from beer marketing to scientific massage. (One alumnus went on to start Inter-State College and Institut Patriarcal Saint Irenée.)

Tuit University Georgia. The Doctorates, sold for $10, are amusing when you read the small print, which says, for instance, that the recipient "has not had the time to do the necessary work leading to the degree of Doctor of Philosophy . . . ."

Tulsa College See: R/G Enterprises

Two Dragon University See: International Honorary Awards Committee

United American Medical College A medical degree mill, operated from the apartment of its founder in Louisiana, and from a mail forwarding service in Canada. The approach was almost identical to that of the Johann Keppler School of Medicine, described earlier. When owner L. Mitchell Weinberg was first arrested (1977) for violating Louisiana school laws, he maintained the school was fully accredited by the American Coordinated Medical Society in California. Indeed, said society wrote that "we of the accreditation committee feel that

U.A.M.C. has the highest admission requirements of any medical college in the world . . . due to the great leadership of it's [sic] President, L. Mitchell Weinberg." The founder and proprietor of the American Coordinated Medical Society is L. Mitchell Weinberg. In 1982, Weinberg pleaded guilty to charges of selling medical degrees and was sentenced to three years in federal prison.

United Free University of England Identified as a diploma mill by E&T.

United States University of America Washington, Florida. The 11-page typewritten catalogue actually listed names of some legitimate faculty who had been duped into doing some work for "Dr." Frank Pany and the school he ran from his Florida home, using a Washington, DC mail forwarding service. One of the faculty, the "Chairman of the Marriage Counseling Department," whose Doctorate was from U.S.U.A. was more candid. "You're in California," he said on the phone. "Why not deal with a degree service closer to home?" In the wake of an FBI visit, and a grand jury indictment in February 1986, "Dr." Pany departed suddenly for Italy.

Universal Bible Institute (AL) Birmingham, Alabama. The state declared it was a diploma mill, and ordered it closed, because Doctoral degrees could be acquired in less than two months on payment of appropriate fees, and the school was not affiliated with any religious organization. According to Alabama authorities, the institute's president moved to Florida, taking all the records with him, as the Alabama investigation began.

Universal Ecclesiastical University Their Doctorates were offered in any field but law or medicine for a 10-page dissertation, and honorary Doctorates to anyone with "good moral character" plus $200 to spend. My last letter to Professor Gilbert at the university's address in Manchester, England, was returned with the word "Demolished" written in big blue crayon letters across the front. Let us hope they were referring to the building, not the professor.

Universidad Brasileira Rio de Janeiro, Brazil. Identified as a diploma mill by COE.

Universidad Indigenista Moctezuma Andorra's only diploma mill—identified as such by COE.

Universidad Latino-Americana de La Habana Havana, Cuba. Identified as a diploma mill by COE.

Universidad Sintetica Latina y Americana El Salvador. Identified as a diploma mill by COE.

Universidad Tecnológica Nacional Havana, Cuba. Identified as a diploma mill by COE.

Universitaires Internationales Liechtenstein, India, Sudan, Morocco, Japan, etc., etc. Identified as a diploma mill by E&T.

Universitas Iltiensis England, Switzerland. Identified as a diploma mill by E&T.

Universitas Internationalis Studiorum Superiorium Pro Deo In 1989, they began offering 'honoris causa' doctorates from an address in New York, under the imprimatur of the Titular Archbishop of Ephesus.

Universitates Sheffieldensis See: University of Sheffield

Université de Commerce de Canada See: Lawford State University

Université des Science de l'Homme France. Same as University of the Science of Man. See: Sussex College of Technology.

Université International de Paris Paris, France. Identified as a diploma mill by COE.

Université Nouvelle de Paris Paris, France. Identified as a diploma mill by COE.

Université Philotechnique Brussels, Belgium, and Paris, France. Identified as a diploma mill by COE.

Université Voltaire de France Marseilles, France. Identified as a diploma mill by COE.

University College of Nottingham See: Whitby Hall College

University del Puerto Monico Panama. Degrees of this non-existent institution were sold by Neil Gibson & Company in England, who also represent University de la Romande. They say that "the degree certificates are excellently presented and make a superb and unusual wall decoration. They are for self-esteem only but remain very popular indeed."

University in London Same as Obura University. Identified as a diploma mill by E&T.

University of Cape Cod A school of this name was promoted in eastern Massachusetts in the early 1980s.

University of Corpus Christi Reno, Nevada. Affiliated with the Society of Academic Recognition. Identified as a diploma mill by E&T. No connection with the legitimate school formerly known as University of Corpus Christi but now a part of Texas A & I University.

University of Coventry England. Identified as a diploma mill by E&T.

University of East Carolina See: University of East Georgia

University of East Georgia Georgia. Degrees in all fields, including medicine, psychiatry, surgery, and neurology sold for $500 and completion of a thesis on "a subject and length of your own choosing." I am embarrassed that I was duped by the first literature I received from proprietor John Blazer in 1975, but his game soon became clear. He also operated the University of the Bahama Islands, the College of Hilton head, the University of East Carolina, and the University of Middle Tennessee. In 1984, Blazer was indicted by a federal grand jury as a result of the FBI's, DipScam operation, pleaded guilty to a charge of mail fraud, and was sentenced to prison.

University of Eastern Florida Chicago, Illinois. Degrees of all kinds except medicine and law were sold for $40

each. They claimed to be a "state chartered university" in Florida (not true) whose purpose is "to grant degrees to persons with actual experience." No new-born babies need apply.

University of England See: University of England at Oxford

University of England at Oxford London, England. Also known as the University of England. Degrees of any kind were sold for about $200. In 1987, the American proprietors were indicted by a federal grand jury. Five of them were found guilty, and sentenced to prison. The founder of Western States University claims a degree from this institution (the university, not the prison).

University of Independence A realistic-looking diploma was given or sold as a promotional piece to independent businesspeople. The Ph.D. came from the "university's" School of Hard Knocks. A reader sent a photo of a well-known author and lecturer, that appeared in a national magazine, with the diploma prominently on his wall. Only the school name, the man's name, and "Doctor of Philosophy" are readable. This is one way that even "gag" fake diplomas can be misused.

University of Man's Best Friend A lovely $2 Ph.D. in Love and Loyalty, with paw prints as signatures.

University of Middle Tennessee See: University of East Georgia

University of North America Diploma mill operated by Edward Reddeck from a mail forwarding service in Missouri in the late 1980s. After he was fined $2,500,000 for this operation, he fled to Utah, changing the name of the school slightly, to become North American University (see separate listing).

University of Pittsburg See: Regency Enterprises

University of Rarotonga Fictitious university whose paraphernalia are sold on this South Seas island.

University of Saint Bartholomew After I gave some talks on diploma mills on Australian radio, a number of people called or wrote to mention a school of this name, in Oodnadatta, Australia that merrily sold its fake product to Europeans.

University of Sealand Identified as a diploma mill by E&T.

University of Sheffield Sheffield, England. There is a legitimate and traditional University of Sheffield, and then there is this fake one, run (according to an article in the Times of London) by Charles Brearly, an auto mechanic who calls himself Ignatius Carelus, successor to Cardinal Barberini of Rheims. Alternate names: Universitates Sheffieldensis, or Ecclesiastical University of Sheffield. He is a sometime associate of "Sir" Sidney Lawrence, proprietor of the College of Applied Science, London. I have received a stern letter from the academic registrar of the real University of Sheffield, suggesting that "in order that our academic standing should not be endangered, I would ask that your publication make it quite clear in future that the college mentioned has no connection whatsoever with this institution." Done, and thanks for thinking that my little book could endanger your large, old, and well-established university.

University of Sulgrave England. Identified as a diploma mill by E&T.

University of the Bahama Islands See: University of East Georgia

University of the Eastern United States Identified as a diploma mill by E&T.

University of the New World Arizona, Europe. Identified as a diploma mill by E&T.

University of the Old Catholic Church Sheffield, England. Presumably the same management as the fake University of Sheffield. Identified as a diploma mill by E&T.

University of the President Utah. They have sold honorary Doctorates in iridology, psionics, macrobiotics, endogenous endocrinotherapy, and dozens more, in exchange for a $25 "donation."

University of the Republic A fictitious school, started by Arizona Republic newspaper reporters Jerry Seper and Rich Robertson, as part of a series of articles on degree mills, to prove how easy it was to do such things in that state. Public outrage led to a tough new school-regulating law being passed.

University of the Science of Man See: Sussex College of Technology

University of the West See: International Universities Consortium

University of Walla Walla California. Advertising in a national women's magazine offered a Doctor of anything ending in "ologist" for $18.90.

University of Winchester London, England. Same address as the London School of Social Research. The $15 diplomas have been widely advertised as "completely spurious, nonetheless as impressive as genuine."

University of Wyoming Of course there is a real one in Laramie, but there is also a fake one. A man named Cunning, using an address in London, England, and literature printed in German, has been selling Ph.D.'s, law degrees, and, alarmingly, M.D. degrees of the University of Wyoming, for about $500. I wrote to the general counsel of the real University of Wyoming, thinking they might have interest, but no response.(Since another purveyor of fake degrees, such as Great Lakes University, is Wiley Bennett, one wonders if these two will ever get together, and form a Wiley and Cunning partnership.)

Vocational University India. Identified as a diploma mill by COE.

Washington International Academy New York. Identified as a diploma mill by E&T.

Webster University (Georgia) Georgia. Identified as a diploma mill by E&T. (There is an accredited school of the same name in Missouri. No connection, of course.)
Weinberg University of West Germany See: ORB
West London College of Technology London, England. Advertisements appearing in African magazines offered a 12-month correspondence program leading to various qualifications, including the M.B.A., "in association with Broadhurst University." The address given is a mail receiving and forwarding service in London, and there is no telephone. I can find no evidence of the existence of either the West London College or of Broadhurst University.
Western Cascade University California. Degrees of all sorts at $45 each. The address is a mail forwarding service. In an apparent effort to avoid prosecution, they will not sell their product to California residents.
Western College See: National Certificate Company
Western Orthodox University Glastonbury, England. Identified as a diploma mill by E&T.
Western Reserve Educational Services For years, they sold diplomas that they claimed to have "salvaged" from "genuine schools that have gone out of business" from an Ohio post office box. The proprietor, Robert Kim Walton, claimed to have been commended by the Sacred Congregation in Rome—not, one dares hope, for selling fake degrees.
Western University (CA) One of the early American degree mills, operating from southern California (San Diego and Jacumba) in the 1940s and 1950s. A Western University with addresses in Georgia, Montana, Colorado, and Delaware has been identified as a diploma mill by E&T. And one in India has been identified as a diploma mill by COE.
Whitby Hall College Essex, England. Dr. M. Palmer offers degrees of almost any kind for about $100, earned for your resume and a poem, a story, or a two-page book review. His other school names are the University College of Nottingham, and South Eastern University.
Williams College Idaho. When the late Lane Williams left New Mexico to move his "college" to Mexico, he changed its name from Williams to Elysion. But Williams was apparently left in other hands, and continued to operate, selling Bachelor's and law degrees for about $300 each. See also: Elysion College.
Wordsworth Memorial University England and India. Identified as a diploma mill by E&T and by COE.

23. Honorary Doctorates

Why anybody can have a brain. That's a very mediocre commodity. Back where I come from we have universities—seats of great learning—where men go to become great thinkers. And when they come out they think deep thoughts, and with no more brains than you have. But they have one thing you haven't got: a diploma! Therefore by virtue of the authority vested in me by the Universitatis Committatum E Pluribus Unum, I hereby confer upon you the Honorary Degree of Th.D. That's, uh, er, ah, Doctor of Thinkology.

—L. Frank Baum (The Wizard of Oz speaking to the Scarecrow)

The probable origin of the honorary Doctorate was discussed in chapter 3. The persistence of this "degree"—indeed, its usage has grown tremendously, with more than 50,000 being awarded by major universities in the last decade—is one of the mysteries of the academic world, for there is nothing whatever educational about the honorary Doctorate. It is, purely and simply, a title that some institutions have chosen for a variety of reasons to bestow upon certain people (and a few animals).

That the title given is "Doctor"—the same word used for academic degrees—is what has caused all the confusion, not to mention most of the desirability of the honorary Doctorate. It is exactly as if the government were to honor people by giving them the title of "Senator" or "Judge." Whatever the reason, honorary Doctorates have become highly valuable, even negotiable commodities.

Not everyone takes them seriously, however. When a German university handed its Doctor of Music diploma to the composer Handel, he rolled it into a dunce cap, placed it on the head of his servant, and said, "There! Now you're a Doctor, too."

Poet Robert Frost expressed particular delight at the announcement of his 40th honorary Doctorate (from Oxford), because he confessed that he had been having the decorative hoods given with each award made into a patchwork quilt, and now it would all come out even. He revealed this en route to England "to collect some more yardage."

When artist Thomas Hart Benton accepted an honorary degree from Rockhurst College, he gestured to the graduating class and said, "I know how those boys behind me feel. They're thinking 'I worked four years for this, and that bum gets it free.'"

One of the curiosities of honorary Doctorates is that the titles given rarely have much relevance to the qualifications of the recipient. Hence we have actor Fess Parker getting a Doctor of Letters (from Tennessee, after portraying Davey Crockett), Robert Redford a Doctor of Humane Letters (from Colorado; he said it is "as important to me as my Oscar"), Times Square restaurant owner Dario Toffenetti a Doctor of Laws (from Idaho, for promoting the baked potato), and the late industrialist Clarence Mackay a Doctor of Music (but there was a logical reason for this: his daughter had married Irving Berlin).

Perhaps Mark Twain said it best:

> It pleased me beyond measure when Yale made me a Master of Arts, because I didn't know anything about art. I had another convulsion of pleasure when Harvard made me a Doctor of Literature, because I was not competent to doctor anybody's literature but my own . . . . I rejoiced again when Missouri University made me a Doctor of Laws because it was all clear profit, I not knowing anything about laws except how to evade them and not get caught. And now at Oxford I am to be made a Doctor of Letters—all clear profit, because what I don't know about letters would make me a millionaire if I could turn it into cash.

Not all titles have been inappropriate, of course. In 1987, Mr. Rogers received a Doctor of Humanities (Bowling Green), and led the audience in singing "Won't you be my neighbor." Admiral Byrd received a Doctor of Faith and Fortitude. Charlie McCarthy, the impertinent ventriloquist's dummy, received a Master of Innuendo from Northwestern. Antioch University gave a Master of Communication to a campus switchboard operator, and Brooklyn College, which averages only one honorary degree every four years, gave a Doctor of Delectables to a long-time campus hot dog vendor. A heroic seeing eye dog named Bonzo received a Doctor of Canine Fidelity from Newark University. And so it goes.

WHY HONORARY DOCTORATES ARE GIVEN

1. To attract celebrities to campus

These humorous (or, some say, ludicrous) examples illuminate one of the four major reasons that honorary Doctorates are given: to bring publicity to the graduation ceremonies of the school. If a small college can lure a baseball star, a movie or television personality, or even the wife of a famous politician to the campus, the commencement is more likely to make the evening news, and the next morning's papers, which may help student or faculty recruiting, fund raising, or memberships in the alumni association. It may even increase the chances that a top high school quarterback will come to the school next year. Indeed, when John Carroll University awarded an honorary Doctorate to Miami Dolphins coach Don Shula, it almost certainly was not for his academic achievements. And that is why we have Dr. Marlon Brando, Dr. Henry Fonda, Dr. Dave Winfield of the Yankees, Dr. Bob Hope (at least 40 times over), Dr. Captain Kangaroo, Dr. Michael Jackson, Dr. Ed McMahon ("Watch for a diploma in your mailbox") and thousands of similar doctors.

Sometimes the publicity is not the kind the school had in mind. St. Joseph's College, a Catholic school, offered its honorary Doctorate to columnist Ann Landers, then created a big flap by withdrawing it after Landers wrote a pro-abortion column. And as Louisiana Tech was presenting its honorary Doctorate to former football quarterback Terry Bradshaw, outraged alumni flew over the ceremony and dropped a cascade of leaflets protesting the award.

There is nothing new going on here. During the Revolutionary War, Harvard gave an honorary degree to Lafayette. When he heard this, Baron von Steuben urged his troops, then approaching Cambridge, to ride through town "like the devil, for if they catch you, they make a doctor of you."

IS THERE A DOCTOR IN THE HOUSE?

Doctor Michael Jackson	Doctor Dan Rather	Doctor Ella Fitzgerald
Doctor Doctor Seuss	Doctor Stan Musial	Dr. Mike Tyson
Doctor Roger Maris	Doctor Charles Addams	Doctor Mr. Rogers
Doctor Captain Kangaroo	Doctor Margot Fonteyn	Doctor Robert Redford
Doctor Stevie Wonder	Doctor Bob Hope	Doctor Dolores Hope
Doctor Marvin Hamlisch	Doctor J. Edgar Hoover	Doctor Dave Winfield
Doctor Bing Crosby	Doctor Norman Mailer	Doctor James Earl Jones
Doctor Leontyne Price	Doctor "Doctor J" Erving	Doctor Duke Ellington
Doctor Ted Williams	Doctor Max Factor	Doctor John Wayne
Doctor Kirk Douglas	Doctor Ozzie Nelson	Doctor Marcel Marceau
Doctor Arthur Ashe	Doctor Mrs. Anwar Sadat	Doctor Frank Sinatra
Doctor Sammy Davis Jr.	Doctor Jane Pauley	Doctor Bryant Gumbel
Doctor Walter Cronkite	Doctor Terry Bradshaw	Doctor Ed McMahon

Doctor "Captain" Gavin MacLeod, and at least 50,000 more . . . .

2. To honor distinguished faculty and administrators

Honorary degrees are often given to honor distinguished faculty at the donating school, or other schools. This is perhaps the most academically defensible reason. In American society, there is nothing equivalent to the national honors of many European countries (e.g., the Queen's Honours List in Britain, at which hundreds of people each year become knights, ladies, Members of the British Empire, etc.). The honorary Doctorate remains one of the few honors we have to bestow. And so, each June, from 40% to 60% of all honorary degrees go to unknown academics, often, it is said, in the hope that their school will honor someone from our school next year.

This practice has resulted in a new world record. In 1982, then-president of Notre Dame, Father Theodore Hesburgh, collected his 90th honorary title, eclipsing Herbert Hoover's record of 89. The good Father now has more than 100.

3. For political reasons

American presidents, British prime ministers and other statesmen are regularly so honored, and often take the opportunity to make major speeches. Winston Churchill used the occasion of receiving an honorary degree in Missouri to deliver his famous "iron curtain" speech, and General George Marshall announced the Marshall Plan while receiving an honorary Doctorate.

Although every American president has collected some honorary Doctorates (George Washington had seven), none caused quite the furor of Harvard's award of an honorary Doctor of Laws to President Andrew Jackson. The

Sons of Harvard erupted in anger. John Quincy Adams wrote about how his alma mater had degraded herself, "conferring her highest literary honors on a barbarian who could not write a sentence of grammar and could hardly spell his own name." Harvard president Josiah Quincy responded, "As the people have twice decided that this man knows enough law to be their ruler, it is not for Harvard College to maintain they are mistaken."

The ceremony itself must have been quite extraordinary. After Jackson had been given the sheepskin and expressed his thanks in a few short remarks, an aide reminded him that he was expected to make a speech in Latin. Thereupon, according to biographer Robert Rayback, he bellowed out, in tones of thunder, all the Latin he knew: "E pluribus unum, sine qua non, multum in parvo, quid pro quo, ne plus ultra." So much for Dr. Jackson.

Haverford College made a rather dramatic political statement when they awarded honorary Doctor of Laws degrees to the 3,000 inhabitants of a French village that helped save the lives of 2,500 Jews during World War II.

Withholding of honorary Doctorates has also been used to make political statements. In 1987, the governing body of Oxford University voted 738 to 319 to withhold an honorary Doctorate from Prime Minister Thatcher, because of her role in cutting university research funds. And the proposed awarding of degrees to Richard Nixon has caused controversies in more than a few places—including his alma mater, Duke University, which ultimately turned him down. Indeed, one report had it that during the final days of Watergate, someone in the Nixon administration had the idea that an honorary Doctorate would give Nixon some favorable publicity for a change. The only school they could find that would agree to do it was General Beadle State College, and that is why Air Force One descended into South Dakota one day in the spring of 1974. (General Beadle subsequently changed its name to Dakota State, but denies there was any connection with the Nixon visitation.) And in 1988, it was revealed that the faculty of Dan Quayle's alma mater voted overwhelmingly to deny him an honorary doctorate, largely because of his poor academic record, but they were overruled by the administration.

4. For money

Although schools sanctimoniously deny there is any connection whatsoever, they have regularly awarded Doctorates to academically undistinguished folks who "just happened" to donate a bundle of money. How long has this been going on? Well, in *A Distant Mirror*, Barbara Tuchman writes that in the 14th century, the University of Paris "had taken to selling degrees in theology to candidates unwilling to undertake its long and difficult studies . . . ."

A few centuries later, George Baker gave Harvard millions for a new business school. Harvard gave George Baker a Doctor of Laws along with their hearty thanks. John Archbold contributed a new football field to Syracuse University. Soon after, he was doctored by Syracuse University. William Randolph Hearst "traded" $100,000 and 400 acres of land to Oglethorpe University for an honorary Doctorate.

Not long ago, a British dry goods merchant named Isaac Wolfson gave about $10 million to Cambridge University, and they not only gave him an honorary Doctorate, they named a college of the university for him. Then he made the same gift to Oxford, and they too both doctored him and named a college for him. Thus, as one London paper wrote in a caustic editorial, only two men in all history have had a college named for them at both Oxford and Cambridge: Jesus Christ and Isaac Wolfson.

The Shah of Iran made a $1 million gift to the University of Southern California, whose president hand-carried his honorary Doctorate to Iran. Around the same time, the University of Wisconsin exchanged an honorary Doctorate for a $2.5 million gift from oil millionaire C. George Weeks.

John Hope Franklin of the National Humanities Center worries, with many others, about "the delicate matter of honorary degrees. One cannot help wondering in how many ways some institutions sell their souls in conferring them . . . . Better that a university cease to exist altogether than sell its soul."

One solution to this matter is to award the honorary degree first, in the hopes that the recipient will give the school his thanks in the form of a check or other favors. This approach made headlines a while back when the *Washington Post* uncovered the "Koreagate" scandal, in which 11 U.S. congressmen had accepted, among other favors, honorary Doctorates from Korean universities, complete with all-expense luxury trips to Korea to collect them, in an apparent effort to win congressional approval of the Korean regime.

To their credit, three congressmen rejected the honorary Doctorates. But it is rare indeed when an honorary Doctorate is turned down. Oxford University used to have a policy, before Richard Nixon came along, of offering an honorary Doctorate to every outgoing U.S. president. Of all those to whom it was offered, only good old Millard Fillmore turned it down, saying that he felt he had done nothing to merit it, and besides, the diploma was in Latin and he never accepted anything he couldn't read.

HOW TO GET AN HONORARY DOCTORATE

How, then, does the ordinary person, who is not a movie star, an athlete, or a millionaire, acquire an honorary

Doctorate? There is no simple way, other than buying one from a less-than-respectable institution, or having one printed to order at the neighborhood print shop. Nonetheless, here are five possibilities:

1. Donate money. The question naturally arises, how little money does it take to buy an honorary Doctorate from a major, accredited university? If the school is in financial trouble, as little as $10,000 has been said to turn the trick. The cheapest case I personally know about is $50,000 from an Arab businessman to an accredited California university whose building fund was in trouble.

A Los Angeles businessman once ran a small ad in *The New Republic* magazine, offering to donate $10,000 to any accredited school that would give him an honorary degree. When I contacted him, he told me he had gotten the degree, but refused to name the school.

2. Perform a valuable service. Honorary Doctorates have gone to heads of fund-raising committees, who never gave a dime themselves; to real estate brokers who "put together" a big deal to acquire more land or to refinance a mortgage for the school; to friends of friends of celebrities who managed to get the Senator or the Star or the Second Baseman to speak at the commencement; to a nurseryman who wangled the donation of hundreds of trees and supervised their planting on campus; to a golf pro who donated his time to the college team; and so on.

Lawyers sometimes are rewarded, too. When Cecil Rhodes died in 1902, he left money for scholarships for "white American boys from all 13 states." The lawyer who got this legal mess untangled, and persuaded Parliament to come up with funds for "white American boys" from all the other states, got a Doctor of Civil Law from Oxford for his efforts.

Perhaps the most valuable service one can perform is finding a cash donor. Remember that $50,000 honorary Doctorate for an Arab businessman, just described? Well, the man who found that donor for the university in question also got an honorary Doctorate, as a finder's fee.

3. Capitalize on trends. Honorary Doctorates seem to be rather trendy things. Trends seem to run for three to five years. For instance, in the late 1950s, space science was in vogue, and people ranging from Wernher von Braun to the founder of a local rocketry society were being honored. In the 1960s, it was the Peace Corps. Sargent Shriver, its first director, set a record that still stands by accepting seven Doctorates in one month (June, 1964), and a lot of other Peace Corps people and other youth workers were in demand on commencement platforms.

The 1980s seemed heavy on jazz and classical musicians, medical researchers, people who work with the handicapped, the very elderly (several people over 100 got them for no apparent reason other than survival), Vietnam veterans, economists, and public interest lawyers.

Recently, more than a few kudos have gone to authors of children's books, radio talk show hosts, AIDS researchers or counselors, investigative reporters, coaches of non-major sports (lacrosse, rugby, field hockey, volleyball), and schoolteachers.

Some people have reported success by directly or, more often, indirectly contacting a school that has given a certain honorary degree this year, suggesting they may wish to consider a similar one next year.

4. Buy one. If all you really want is a fancy but meaningless document to hang on the wall (actually, all honorary Doctorates fit that description, but some may be perceived as more meaningless than others), many of the schools described in chapters 21 and 22 would be more than pleased to dispense an honorary Doctorate on payment of a fee that can range from 50¢ to over $1,000.

But you'll do just as well at the local print shop, where you can have the type set for the diploma of your choice. Just don't get carried away and have a whole batch printed for sale to the public.

5. Wait. A few years ago, I wrote that "I think it is inevitable that one or more well-known, respectable, fully-accredited colleges, faced by the cash crunch that is upon so many worthy institutions, will face reality and openly put their honorary Doctorates up for sale." A few years later, it happened. A small, accredited college took out a national ad, suggesting a donation of $25,000. The accrediting agency got quite upset at this, and the offer was withdrawn. But later, the well-respected Embry-Riddle Aeronautical University bought a *Wall Street Journal* ad offering a Trusteeship of the University in exchange for a $1 million donation. That, too, caused a furor.

So maybe I was premature in saying, "Wait." It may be that the deals will continue to go on just below the surface for a while longer.

THE ETIQUETTE OF SOLICITING DEGREES

Here's one that Emily Post never had to deal with. How straightforward should one be in letting it be known that one would like an honorary Doctorate? There is no way to know. My feeling is that in the majority of situations, the direct approach is inappropriate. One must work through intermediaries—friends of school officials or trustees, who drop hints. But there are some schools and awards committees who seem to find the blunt approach refreshingly candid. These are people who realize and admit that what they are really doing is selling honorary degrees, so why not be up front? The president of a small eastern college told me that he was once approached by a second-rate actor who really wanted an honorary Doctorate, "just like Marlon Brando and Henry Fonda." They negotiated terms, and the degree was awarded the following June—presumably after the check cleared the bank.

On the other hand, a high air force official in Europe got a lot of unfavorable publicity when *Stars and Stripes* revealed that he had solicited honorary Doctorates for himself and some associates, from universities that were doing contractual work for the air force. Two of the universities (Southern California and Maryland) turned him down. "It wasn't appropriate to ask for it, and it wasn't appropriate to give it," one school official said. But the third university gave it to him.

The army's counterpart in Europe, when asked if *he* would solicit honorary Doctorates, replied, "You've got to be out of your tree."

"We find you acceptable, sir. You will be issued a halo, a set of wings, and an honorary doctorate in the subject of your choice."

24. Glossary of Important Terms

When ideas fail, words come in very handy.
—J. W. Goethe

academic year: The period of formal academic instruction, usually from September or October to May or June, divided into semesters, quarters, or trimesters.

accreditation: Recognition of a school by an independent private organization. Not a governmental function in the U.S. There are more than 100 accrediting agencies, some recognized by the Department of Education and/or COPA, and some unrecognized, some phony or fraudulent

ACT: American College Testing program, administrators of aptitude and achievement tests.

adjunct faculty: Part-time faculty member, often at a non-traditional school, often with a full-time teaching job elsewhere. More and more traditional schools are hiring adjunct faculty, because they don't have to pay them as much or provide health care and other benefits.

advanced placement: Admission to a school at a higher level than one would normally enter, because of getting credit for prior learning experience or passing advanced placement exams.

alma mater: The school from which one has graduated, as in "My alma mater is Michigan State University."

alternative: Used interchangeably with *external* or *non-traditional;* offering an alternate, or different means of pursuing learning or degrees or both.

alumni: Graduates of a school, as in "This school has some distinguished alumni." (The word is technically for males only; females are *alumnae.* The singular is *alumnus* (male) or *alumna* (female).

alumni association: A confederation of alumni and alumnae who have joined together to support their alma mater in various ways, generally by donating money.

approved: In California, a level of state recognition of a school, generally regarded as one step above *authorized* and one step below *accredited.*

arbitration: A means of settling disputes, as between a student and a school, in which one or more independent arbitrators or judges listen to both sides, and make a decision. A means of avoiding a courtroom trial. Many learning contracts have an arbitration clause. (See *Binding Arbitration; Mediation.*)

assistantship: A means of assisting students (usually graduate students) financially by offering them part-time academic employment, usually in the form of a teaching assistantship or a research assistantship.

associate's degree: A "two-year" degree, traditionally awarded by community or junior colleges after two years of residential study, or completion of 60 to 64 semester hours.

auditing: Sitting in on a class without earning credit for that class.

authorized: In California, a form of state recognition of schools, authorizing them to exist, to accept students, and to grant degrees; starting in 1990, this category is being phased out.

bachelor's degree: Awarded in the U.S. after four years of full-time residential study (two to five years in other countries), or earning from 120 to 124 semester units by any means.

binding arbitration: Arbitration in which both parties have agreed in advance that they will abide by the result and take no further legal action.

branch campus: A satellite facility, run by officers of the main campus of a college or university, at another location. Can range from a small office to a full-fledged university center.

campus: The main facility of a college or university, usually comprising buildings, grounds, dormitories, cafeterias and dining halls, sports stadia, etc. The campus of a non-traditional school may consist solely of offices.

chancellor: Often the highest official of a university. Also a new degree title, proposed by some schools, to be a higher degree than the doctorate, and requiring three to five years of additional study.

CLEP: The College-Level Examination Program, a series of equivalency examinations given nationally each month.

coeducational: Education of men and women on the same campus or in the same program. This is why female students are called coeds.

college: In the U.S., an institution offering programs leading to the Associate's, Bachelor's, and possibly higher degrees. Often used interchangeably with *university* although traditionally a university is a collection of colleges. In England and elsewhere, *college* may denote part of a university (Kings College, Cambridge) or a private high school (Eton College).

colloquium: A gathering of scholars to discuss a given topic over a period of a few hours to a few days. ("The university is sponsoring a colloquium on marine biology.")

community college: A two-year traditional school, offering programs leading to the Associate's degree and, typically, many non-credit courses in arts, crafts, and vocational fields for community members not interested in a degree. Also called *junior college.*

competency: The philosophy and practice of awarding credit or degrees based on learning skills, rather than time spent in courses.

COPA: The Council on Postsecondary Accreditation, a private non-governmental organization that recognizes accrediting agencies.

correspondence course: A course offered by mail, completed entirely by home study, often with one or two proctored, or supervised examinations.

course: A specific unit of instruction, such as a course in microeconomics, or a course in abnormal psychology. Residential courses last for one or more semesters or quarters; correspondence courses often have no rigid time requirements.

cramming: Intensive preparation for an examination. Most testing agencies now admit that cramming can improve scores on exams.

credit: Units used to record courses taken. Each credit typically represents the number of hours spent in class each week. Hence a 3-credit or 3-unit course would commonly be a class that met three hours each week for one semester or quarter.

curriculum: A program of courses to be taken in pursuit of a degree or other objective.

degree: A title conferred by a school to show that a certain course of study has been completed.

department of education: In the U.S., the national agency concerned with all educational matters not handled by the Departments of Education in the 50 states. In other countries, commonly the Ministry of Education.

diploma: The certificate that shows that a certain course of study has been completed. Diplomas are awarded for completing degree studies or other, shorter courses of study.

dissertation: The major research project normally required as part of the work for a Doctorate. Dissertations are expected to make a new and creative contribution to the field of study, or to demonstrate one's excellence in the field. *See also* Thesis.

doctorate: The highest degree one can earn (but *see* Chancellor). Includes Doctor of Philosophy, Education, and many other titles.

dormitory: Student living quarters on residential campuses. May include dining halls and classrooms.

early decision: Making a decision on whether to admit a student sooner than decisions are usually made. Offered by some schools primarily as a service either to students applying to several schools, or those who are especially anxious to know the outcome of their application.

ECFMG: The Education Commission for Foreign Medical Graduates, which administers an examination to physicians who have gone to medical school outside the U.S. and wish to practice in the U.S.

electives: Courses one does not have to take, but may elect to take as part of a degree program.

essay test: An examination in which the student writes narrative sentences as answers to questions, instead of the short answers required by a multiple-choice test. Also called a *subjective test.*

equivalency examination: An examination designed to demonstrate knowledge in a subject where the learning was acquired outside a traditional classroom. A person who learned nursing skills while work ing in a hospital, for instance, could take an equivalency exam to earn credit in obstetrical nursing.

external: Away from the main campus or offices. An external degree may be earned by home study or at locations other than on the school's campus.

fees: Money paid to a school for purposes other than academic tuition. Fees might pay for parking, library services, use of the gymnasium, binding of dissertations, etc.

fellowship: A study grant, usually awarded to a graduate student, and usually requiring no work other than usual academic work (as contrasted with an *assistantship*).

financial aid: A catch-all term, including scholarships, loans, fellowships, assistantships, tuition reductions, etc. Many schools have a financial aid officer.

fraternities: Men's fraternal and social organizations, often identified by Greek letters, such as Zeta Beta Tau. There are also professional and scholastic fraternities open to men and women, such as Beta Alpha Psi, the national fraternity for students of accounting.

freshman: The name for the class in its first of four years of traditional study for a Bachelor's degree, and its individual members. ("She is a freshman, and so is in the freshman class.")

glossary: What you are reading now. But is anyone reading it? Let's have a readership survey: To help me determine whether to keep this section in the book, I will send a dramatic volcano eruption postcard to anyone who writes to tell me they have seen this notice. John Bear, Box 1717, Hilo, Hawaii 96721, USA.

grade point average: The average score a student has made in all his or her classes, weighted by the number of credits or units for each class. Also called G.P.A.

grades: Evaluative scores provided for each course, and often for individual examinations or papers written for that course. There are letter grades (usually A, B, C, D, F) and number grades (usually percentages from 0% to 100%), or on a scale of 0 to 3, 0 to 4, or 0 to 5. Some schools use a pass/fail system with no grades.

graduate: One who has earned a degree from a school, or the programs offered beyond the Bachelor's level. ("He is a graduate of Yale University, and is now working on his Master's in graduate school at Princeton.")

graduate school: A school or a division of a university offering work at the Master's or Doctoral degree level.

graduate student: One attending graduate school.

GRE: The Graduate Record Examination, which many traditional schools and a few non-traditional ones require for admission to graduate programs.

honor societies: Organizations for persons with a high grade point average or other evidence of outstanding performance. There are local societies on some campuses, and several national organizations, the most prestigious of which is called Phi Beta Kappa.

honor system: A system in which students are trusted not to cheat on examinations, and to obey other rules, without proctors or others monitoring their behavior.

honorary doctorate: A non-academic award, given regularly by more than 1,000 colleges and universities to honor distinguished scholars, celebrities, and donors of large sums of money. Holders of this award may, and often do, call themselves "Doctor."

junior: The name for the class in its third year of a traditional four-year U.S. Bachelor's degree program, or any member of that class. ("She is a junior this year.")

junior college: Same as *community college.*

language laboratory: A room with special audio equipment to facilitate learning languages by listening to tapes. Many students can be learning different languages at different skill levels at the same time.

learning contract: A formal agreement between a student and a school, specifying independent work to be done by the student, and the amount of credit the school will award on successful completion of the work.

lecture class: A course in which a faculty member lectures to anywhere from a few dozen to many hundreds of students. Often lecture classes are followed by small group discussion sessions led by student assistants or junior faculty.

liberal arts: A term with many complex meanings, but generally referring to the non-scientific curriculum of a university: humanities, the arts, social sciences, history, and so forth.

liberal education: Commonly taken to be the opposite of a specialized education; one in which students are required to take courses in a wide range of fields, as well as courses in their major.

licensed: Holding a permit to operate. This can range from a difficult-to-obtain state school license to a simple local business license.

life experience portfolio: A comprehensive presentation listing and describing all learning experiences in a person's life, with appropriate documentation. The basic document used in assigning academic credit for life experience learning.

LSAT: The Law School Admission Test, required by most U.S. law schools of all applicants.

maintenance costs: The expenses incurred while attending school, other than tuition and fees. Includes room and board (food), clothing, laundry, postage, travel, etc.

major: The subject or academic department in which a student takes concentrated coursework, leading to a specialty. ("His major is in English literature; she is majoring in chemistry.")

mentor: Faculty member assigned to supervise independent study work at a non-traditional school; comparable to *adjunct faculty.*

minor: The secondary subject or academic department in which a student takes concentrated coursework. ("She has a major in art and a minor in biology.")

MSAT: The Medical School Admission Test, required by most U.S. medical schools of all applicants.

multiple-choice test: An examination in which the student chooses the best of several alternative answers provided for each question; also called an *objective test* for some peculiar reason. ("The capital city of England is (a) London, (b) Ostrogotz-Plakatz, (c) Tokyo, (d) none of the above.")

multiversity: A university system with two or more separate campuses, each a major university in its own right, such as the University of California or the University of Wisconsin.

narrative transcript: A transcript issued by a non-traditional school in which, instead of simply listing the courses completed and grades received, there is a narrative description of the work done and the school's rationale for awarding credit for that work.

non-traditional: Something done in other than the usual or traditional way. In education, refers to learning and degrees completed by methods other than spending many hours in classrooms and lecture halls.

non-resident: (1) A means of instruction in which the student does not need to visit the school; all work is done by correspondence, telephone, or exchange of audiotapes or videotapes; (2) A person who does not meet residency requirements of a given school and, as a result, often has to pay a higher tuition or fees.

objective test: An examination in which questions requiring a very short answer are posed. It can be multiple choice, true-false, fill-in-the-blank, etc. The questions are related to facts (thus objective) rather than to opinions (or subjective).

on the job: In the U.S., experience or training gained through employment, which may be converted to academic credit. In England, slang for "having sex," which either confuses or amuses English people who read about "credit for on-the-job experience."

open admissions: An admissions policy in which everyone who applies is admitted, on the theory that the ones who are unable to do university work will drop out before long.

out-of-state student: One from a state other than that in which the school is located. Because most state colleges and universities have much higher tuition rates for out-of-state students, many people attempt to establish legal residence in the same state as their school.

parallel instruction: A method in which non-resident students do exactly the same work as residential students, during the same general time periods, except they do it at home.

pass/fail option: Instead of getting a letter or number grade in a course, the student may elect, at the start of the course, a pass/fail option in which the only grades are either "pass" or "fail." Some schools permit students to elect this option on one or two of their courses each semester.

PEP: Proficiency Examination Program, a series of equivalency exams given nationally every few months.

plan of study: A detailed description of the program an applicant to a school plans to pursue. Many traditional schools ask for this as part of the admissions procedure. The plan of study should be designed to meet the objectives of the *statement of purpose.*

portfolio: *See* Life Experience Portfolio.

prerequisites: Courses that must be taken before certain other courses may be taken. For instance, a course in algebra is often a prerequisite for a course in geometry.

private school: A school that is privately owned, rather than operated by a governmental department.

proctor: A person who supervises the taking of an examination to be certain there is no cheating, and that other rules are followed. Many non-traditional schools permit unproctored examinations.

professional school: School in which one studies for the various professions, including medicine, dentistry, law, nursing, veterinary, optometry, ministry, etc.

PSAT: Preliminary Scholastic Aptitude Test, given annually to high school juniors.

public school: In the U.S., a school operated by the government of a city, county, district, state, or the federal government. In England, a privately owned or run school.

quarter: An academic term at a school on the "quarter system," in which the calendar year is divided into four equal quarters. New courses begin each quarter.

quarter hour: An amount of credit earned for each classroom hour spent in a given course during a given quarter. A course that meets four hours each week for a quarter would probably be worth 4 quarter hours, or quarter units.

recognized: A term used by some schools to indicate approval from some other organization or governmental body. The term usually does not have a precise meaning, so it may mean different things in different places.

registrar: The official at most colleges and universities who is responsible for maintaining student records and, in many cases, for verifying and validating applications for admission.

rolling admissions: A year-round admissions procedure. Many schools only admit students once or twice a year. A school with rolling admissions considers each application at the time it is received. Many non-traditional schools, especially ones with non-resident programs, have rolling admissions.

SAT: Scholastic Aptitude Test, one of the standard tests given to qualify for admission to colleges and universities.

scholarship: A study grant, either in cash or in the form of tuition or fee reduction.

score: Numerical rating of performance on a test. ("His score on the Graduate Record Exam was not so good.")

semester: A school term, generally four to five months. Schools on the semester system will usually have two semesters a year, with a shorter summer session.

semester hour: An amount of credit earned in a course representing one classroom hour per week for a semester.

A class that meets three days a week for one hour, or one day a week for three hours, would be worth 3 semester hours, or semester units.

seminar: A form of instruction combining independent research with meetings of small groups of students and a faculty member, generally to report on reading or research the students have done.

senior: The fourth year of study of a four-year U.S. Bachelor's degree program, or a member of that class. ("Linnea is a senior this year, and is president of the senior class.")

sophomore: The second year of study in a four-year U.S. Bachelor's degree program, or a member of that class.

sorority: A women's social organization, often with its own living quarters on or near a campus, and usually identified with two or three Greek letters, such as Sigma Chi.

special education: Education of the physically or mentally handicapped, or, often, of the gifted.

special student: A student who is not studying for a degree either because he or she is ineligible or does not wish the degree.

statement of purpose: A detailed description of the career the applicant intends to pursue after graduation. A statement of purpose is often requested as part of the admissions procedure at a university.

subject: An area of study or learning covering a single topic, such as the subject of chemistry, or economics, or French literature.

subjective test: An examination in which the answers are in the form of narrative sentences or long or short essays, often expressing opinions rather than reporting facts.

syllabus: A detailed description of a course of study, often including the books to be read, papers to be written, and examinations to be given.

thesis: The major piece of research that is completed by many Master's degree candidates. A thesis is expected to show a detailed knowledge of one's field and ability to do research and integrate knowledge of the field.

TOEFL: Test of English as a Foreign Language, required by many schools of persons for whom English is not the native language.

traditional education: Education at a residential school in which the Bachelor's degree is completed through four years of classroom study, the Master's in one or two years, and the Doctorate in three to five years.

transcript: A certified copy of the student's academic record, showing courses taken, examinations passed, credits awarded, and grades or scores received.

transfer student: A student who has earned credit in one school, and then transfers to another school.

trimester: A term consisting of one third of an academic year. Some schools have three equal trimesters each year.

tuition: In the U.S., the money charged for formal instruction. In some schools, tuition is the only expense other than postage. In other schools, there may be fees as well as tuition. In England, tuition refers to the instruction or teaching at a school, such as the tuition offered in history.

tuition waiver: A form of financial assistance in which the school charges little or no tuition.

tutor: *See* Mentor. A tutor can also be a hired assistant who helps a student prepare for a given class or examination.

undergraduate: Pertaining to the period of study from the end of high school to the earning of a Bachelor's degree; also to a person in such a course of study. ("Barry is an undergraduate at Reed College, one of the leading undergraduate schools.")

university: An institution that usually comprises one or more undergraduate colleges, one or more graduate schools, and, often, one or more professional schools.

25. Advice for People in Prison

The vilest deeds, like poison weeds, bloom well in prison air.
It is only what is good in man that wastes and withers there.
—Oscar Wilde (Ballad of Reading Gaol)

NOTE: More than a few readers and users of this book are people who are institutionalized. For this edition, I have invited a man who has completed his Bachelor's and Master's from prison, and who consults often with inmates and others around the country, to offer his thoughts and recommendations. There is some very useful advice for non-institutionalized persons as well.

Arranging Academic Resources for the Institutionalized

by Douglas G. Dean

One obstacle for any institutionalized person interested in pursuing a degree is limited resources: availability of community faculty, library facilities, phone access, and financial aid. To overcome these, it helps to streamline the matriculation process. Time spent in preparation prior to admission can help avoid wasted effort and time when in a program, thereby reducing operating expenses and cutting down the number of tuition periods.

A second obstacle is finding ways to ensure that a quality education can be documented. Because courses are generally not pre-packaged, it is the student's responsibility to identify varied learning settings, use varied learning methods, find and recruit community-based faculty, provide objective means to appraise what has been learned, and indeed design the study plan itself.

Find a flexible degree program

Most well-established degree programs grant credit for a variety of learning experiences. In terms of cost and arrangements required, equivalency examinations and independent study projects are the most expedient. Credit for life experience learning is another option sometimes offered. If a degree program does not offer at least these first two options, it is unlikely that the program as a whole will be able to accommodate the needs of the institutionalized student.

Write a competency-based study plan

The traditional method of acquiring credits is to take narrowly focused courses of two to four credits each. Since the non-traditional student must enlist his or her own instructors, find varied learning methods, and quantify the whole experience, the single course approach creates much needless duplication of effort.

A better approach is to envision a subject area which is to be studied for 9 to 12 credits (e.g., statistics). As an independent study project, the student identifies what topics are germane to the area (e.g., probability theory, descriptive statistics, inferential statistics); at what level of comprehension (e.g., introductory through intermediate or advanced); how the topic is to be studied (e.g., directed reading, programmed textbooks), and how the competencies acquired are to be demonstrated (e.g., oral examination, proctored examination including problem solving). This way, a single independent study project can take the place of a series of successive courses in a given area (e.g., statistics 101, 201, 301).

Designing the curriculum

Every accredited degree program has graduation requirements. These requirements broadly define the breadth of subject areas that comprise a liberal arts education and the depth to which they are to be studied. It is the responsibility of the external student not only to identify a curriculum fulfilling these requirements, but in most cases to design the course content that will comprise each study module.

But how does a student know what an area of study consists of before he or she has studied it? The answer lies in meticulous preparation.

Well in advance of formally applying for an off-campus degree program, the prospective student should obtain course catalogues from several colleges and universities. Look at what these schools consider the core curriculum, and what is necessary to fulfill the graduation requirements. With the broad outline in mind, the student can begin to form clusters of courses fulfilling each criterion. This helps shape the study plan academically rather than touch it up later as an afterthought.

Next, decide which subjects are of interest within each criterion area. Compare topical areas within each subject as described in the course listings and commonalities will emerge. From there, it is simply a matter of writing to the various instructors for a copy of their course syllabi. These course outlines will provide more detailed information about the subject matter and identify the textbooks currently used at that level of study.

Means of study

Having decided what is to be studied, the student must then propose various ways to study it.

Equivalency exams enable the student to acquire credits instantly, often in core or required areas of study. This helps reduce overall program costs by eliminating the need for textbooks and tuition fees. More importantly, it helps reduce the number of special learning arrangements that must otherwise be made.

"Testing out" of correspondence courses (taking only the examinations, without doing the homework assignments) is another excellent way to acquire credits quickly. This can, however, be an expensive method since full course fees are still assessed. Nonetheless, if a student studies on his or her own in advance according to the course syllabus, and if the instructor can then be convinced to waive prerequisite assignments, it can be an efficient and cost-effective method to use.

Independent study projects should form the balance of any study plan. With the topical areas, learning objectives, and learning materials identified, an independent study project allows the student to remain with the same instructor(s) from an introductory through an intermediate or advanced level of study. This eliminates the need for new arrangements to be made every two to four credits. An independent study project can take the form of simple directed reading, tutorial instruction, practicum work, or a combination of these methods, culminating in the final product.

Independent study projects require the aid of qualified persons to act as community faculty, and to oversee personally the progress of the work. Therefore it is highly advantageous to line up faculty in advance of entering the degree program, and to have alternates available in the event an instructor is unable, for any reason, to fulfill his or her commitment. It is better to anticipate these needs at the preparatory stage than to be scrambling for a replacement while the tuition clock is running.

Multiple treatments of subject matter

The external student is without benefit of lecture halls, interactions with other students, or readily-available academic counseling services. For the institutionalized student, picking up the phone or stopping in to see a faculty member for help with a study problem is not an option. This is where alternate methods of study are so valuable.

One approach is to use several textbooks covering the same subject matter. If something does not make sense, there is a different treatment of the subject to turn to.

Programmed textbooks make especially good substitute tutors. A programmed text breaks the subject matter into small segments requiring a response from the reader with periodic tests to check progress. Such texts are now available in many subject areas, but are particularly useful for the sciences. Titles can be learned from the subject guide to *Books in Print*, or by writing directly to textbook publishers.

Audio-visual materials can, to some extent, make up for college life without lectures and classes. Writing to A-V (audio-visual) departments at large universities often yields a catalogue of materials available for rental. When using such materials, it is best to work through the school or social service department of the student's institution of residence.

Some large campuses have lecture note services, in which advanced students attend introductory lectures, and take copious lecture notes, which are then sold to students. Aside from their insights into good note-taking, these published notes are an additional treatment of course content. Such notes are especially recommended for new students.

Documenting study

The administrators of a degree program must be convinced that there are acceptable ways to document what has been learned, and what levels of subject mastery have been achieved, without taking the student's word for it. Community faculty members may be asked to provide written or oral examinations, but it does not hurt to make their jobs easier.

Most professions (accounting, psychology, law, medicine, etc.) have licensing and/or board certification examinations that must be taken. An industry has built up around this need, providing parallel or actual past examinations to help prepare students. By agreeing to take a relevant sample examination under proctored conditions, and negotiating a "pass" score in advance, the community faculty member is relieved of having to design his or her own objective examination for just one student. This approach adds validity to the assessment process, and provides a standardized score that has some universal meaning. This is an optional approach but may be worth the effort.

Recruiting community faculty

Just as it is easier for a student to organize a study plan in blocks of subject areas, a competency-based study plan of this sort makes it easier for a prospective instructor to visualize what is being asked of him or her.

A typical independent study project would define for the instructor what specific topics are to be studied, what levels of mastery will be expected of the student, what textbooks or other materials will be used, and what is expected of the instructor.

Many traditional academics are unfamiliar with external degree programs. Consequently, they tend to assume that their role as instructor will require greater effort and time on their part than for the average student, who may expect their services in many roles, from academic advisor to tutor. The more an institutionalized student can do up front to define clearly the role and expected duties of the community faculty member, the more successful a student will be in enlisting instructors for independent study projects.

Instructors may sometimes be found on the staff of the institution where the student resides. They may also be found through a canvas letter sent to the appropriate department heads at area colleges, universities, and technical schools. The same approach may be used to canvas departments within area businesses, museums, art centers, hospitals, libraries, theaters, zoos, banks, and orchestras, to name but a few. People are often flattered to be asked, providing it is clear to them exactly what they are getting into.

The more a student can operate independently, and rely on community faculty for little more than assessment purposes, the more likely a student will be successful in recruiting help, and thereby broadening the range of study options.

"Revealing" your institutionalized status

It is generally proper and appropriate to inform potential schools and potential faculty of one's institutionalized status. (Many institutions now have mailing addresses that do not indicate they are, in fact, institutions.) Some schools or individuals may be "put off" by this, but then you would not want to deal with them anyway. Others may be especially motivated to help.

Financing the educational process

Unfortunately, there are virtually no generalizations to be made here, whatsoever. Each institution seems to have its own policy with regard to the way finances are handled. Some institutionalized persons earn decent wages, and have access to the funds. Others have little or no ability to pay their own way. Some institutions permit financial gifts from relatives or friends, others do not. Some schools make special concessions or have some scholarship funds available for institutionalized persons; many do not. One should contact the financial aid office of the school to ask this question.

In conclusion

Institutionalized students must be highly self-directed, and honest enough with themselves to recognize if they are not. Because the student lives where he or she works, it takes extra effort to set aside daily study time, not only to put the student in the right frame of mind, but also to accommodate institution schedules. It can mean working with a minimum number of books or tapes to comply with property rules. It means long periods of delayed gratification, in an environment where pursuing education is often suspect. And it is the greatest feeling in the world when it all comes together.

26. Bending the Rules

Any fool can make a rule, and every fool will mind it.
—Henry David Thoreau

One of the most common complaints or admonishments I get from readers takes the form of "You said thus-and-so, but when I inquired of the school, they told me such-and-such." Often, a school claims that a program I have written about does not exist. Sometimes a student achieves something (such as completing a certain degree entirely by correspondence) that I had been told by a high official of the school was impossible.

One of the open "secrets" in the world of higher education is that the rules are constantly being bent. But, like the Emperor's new clothes, no one dares point and say what is really going on, especially in print.

The purpose of this brief essay is to acknowledge that this sort of thing happens all the time. If you know that it happens regularly, then at least you are in the same boat with people who are benefiting already by virtue of bent rules.

Unfortunately, I cannot provide many specific examples of bent rules, naming names and all. This is for two good reasons:

1. Many situations where students profit from bent rules would disappear in an instant if anyone dared mention the situation publicly. There is, for instance, a major state university that is forbidden by its charter from granting degrees for correspondence study. But they regularly work out special arrangements for students, who are carried on the books as residential students, even though all work is done by mail, and some of the graduates have never set foot on the campus. If this ever "got out," the Board of Trustees, the accrediting agency, and all the other universities in that state would probably have conniptions, and the practice would be suspended at once.

2. These kinds of things can change so rapidly, with new personnel or new policies, that a listing of anomalies and curious practices would probably be obsolete before the ink dried.

Consider a few examples of the sort of thing that is going on in higher education every day, whether or not anyone will admit it, except perhaps behind closed doors or after several drinks:

☛ A friend of mine, at a major university, was unable to complete one required course for her doctorate, before she had to leave for another state. This university does not offer correspondence courses, but she was able to convince a professor to enroll her in a regular course, which she would just "happen" never to visit in person.

☛ A man in graduate school needed to be enrolled in nine units of coursework each semester to keep his employer's tuition assistance plan going. But his job was too demanding one year, and he was unable to do so. The school enrolled him in nine units of "independent study" for which no work was asked or required, and for which a "pass" grade was given.

☛ A woman at a large school needed to get a certain number of units before an inflexible time deadline. When it was clear she was not going to make it, a kindly professor turned in grades for her, and told her she could do the actual coursework later on.

☛ A major state university offers non-resident degrees for people living in that state only. When a reader wrote me to say that he, living a thousand miles from that state, was able to complete his degree entirely by correspondence, I asked a contact at that school what was going on. "We will take students from anywhere in our correspondence degree program," she told me, "But for God's sake, don't print that in your book, or we'll be deluged with applicants."

☛ If we are to believe a book by a member of Dr. Bill Cosby's dissertation committee at the University of Massachusetts (*Education's Smoking Gun* by Reginald Damerell), the only class attendance on Cosby's transcript was one weekend seminar, and the only dissertation committee meeting was a dinner party, with spouses, at Cosby's house.

☛ Part way through my supposedly-definitive final doctoral oral exam, a key member of my committee had to leave for an emergency. He scrawled a note, and passed it to the Dean who read it, then crumpled it up and threw it away. The grueling exam continued for several hours more. After it was over and the committee had congratulated me and departed, I retrieved the note from the wastebasket. It read, "Please give John my apologies for having to leave, and my congratulations for having passed."

☛ A man applied to a well-known school that has a rigid requirement that all graduate work (thesis or dissertation) must be begun after enrollment. He started to tell an admissions officer about a major piece of independent research he had completed for his employer. "Stop," he was told, "Don't tell me about that. Then you will be able to use it for your Master's thesis."

☛ My eldest daughter was denied admission to the University of California at Berkeley because of some "irregularities" on her high school transcript. (It was a non-traditional high school.) The high school's records had been destroyed in a fire. The former principal checked with the University, discovered that the admissions people would be glad to admit her, once the computer said it was OK. He typed up a new transcript saying what the computer wanted said. The computer said OK, and three years later, said daughter graduated Phi Beta Kappa. But how many other applicants accepted the initial "No," not knowing that rules can often be bent?

Please use this information prudently. It will probably do no good to pound on a table and say, "What do you mean I can't do this? John Bear says that rules don't mean anything, anyway."

But when faced with a problem, it surely can do no harm to remember that there do exist many situations in which the rules have turned out to be far less rigid than the printed literature of a school would lead one to believe.

27. Bibliography

What! Another of those damned, fat, square, thick books!
Always scribble, scribble, scribble, eh, Mr. Gibbon?
—Duke of Gloucester, Gibbon's patron, on being presented with Vol. III
of *Decline and Fall of the Roman Empire*

Most of these books are available in bookstores and libraries. Some are sold only, or primarily by mail. In those cases, I have provided the address of the publisher or distributor.

DIRECTORIES OF SCHOOLS

•*The H.E.P. Higher Education Directory* (Higher Education Publications, 2936 Sleepy Hollow Road, Suite 2E, Falls Church, VA 22044). I listed this first because it is the one I use the most. Until 1982-83, the U.S. Department of Education published a comprehensive directory of information on colleges and universities. When President Reagan announced his intention to shut down the Department of Education, their publication was discontinued. H.E.P. began publishing an almost identical directory, which emerges toward the end of each year, and gives detailed factual information (no opinions) on all accredited and a few other schools. They used to list California-approved schools, but stopped in 1988. About 530 pages, about $30.

•*Peterson's Higher Education Directory.* In 1988, Peterson's Guides jumped on this particular bandwagon, with a nearly identical directory at a nearly identical price. The main difference is that Peterson's criteria for inclusion are broader: schools accredited by agencies recognized by both the Department of Education and the Council on Postsecondary Accreditation. The H.E.P. Directory uses only the Department of Education-recognized accreditors. Both directories have a separate listing (over 150 pages) of the names and phone numbers of administrators at all schools. H.E.P. lists 55,000; Peterson's lists 65,000.

•*Accredited Institutions of Postsecondary Education* (American Council on Education, One Dupont Circle N.W., Washington DC 20036). The standard reference book for accredited schools, issued each year (about mid-year), listing every accredited institution and candidates for accreditation. This is the book most people use to determine conclusively whether or not a given school is accredited.

•*Barron's Profiles of American Colleges* (Barron's Educational Series), a massive two-volume 1300-page description of every accredited college and university in America, with lists of majors offered by each school.

•*Comparative Guide to American Colleges,* by James Cass and Max Birnbaum (Harper & Row). One of the "standard" directories of traditional schools. Unlike Lovejoy's and Barron's, however, it is both factual and opinionated, a good feature. More than 700 pages of school descriptions and statistical information.

•*Directory of External Graduate Programs* by Mary C. Kahl (Regents College, Cultural Education Center, Albany NY 12230). Twenty-six typewritten pages; a page on each of 20 programs, with a bit more information on each than in my book.

•*Directory of United States Traditional and Alternative Colleges and Universities* by Dr. Jean-Maximillien De La Croix de Lafayette. This large $30 volume contains much useful information on schools. Universities are rated by number of stars. Among the small number of top-rated schools in the U.S. is Andrew Jackson University, established by Dr. De La Croix de Lafayette.

•*How to Earn a College Degree Without Going to College* by James P. Duffy (Stein & Day). A 1982 book, much along the lines of this one, but describing fewer than 100 programs, and not distinguishing between accredited and unaccredited, or between good and bad schools.

•*How to Earn a University Degree Without Ever Leaving Home* by William Ebbs. A 54-page book selling for $20, with an astonishing number of errors of fact. Identifies the University de la Romande as the most outstanding non-traditional school in the world. William Ebbs is the pseudonym of Raymond Seldis, administrator, at the time, of the University de la Romande. What an amazing coincidence! The now-defunct California University for Advanced Studies is identified as the second best school in the world.

•*The Independent Study Catalogue* (Peterson's Guides). In effect, a master catalogue, listing all 12,000 courses offered by the 71 U.S. and Canadian institutions offering correspondence study. Only the course titles are given, so it is still necessary to write to the individual schools for detailed information.

•*International Handbook of Universities and Other Institutes of Higher Education.* Published every two years by the International Association of Universities in Paris. 1,264 pages, and an amazing $140 price tag. Gives detailed information on virtually every college, university, technical institute, and training school in the world, with the exception of the British Commonwealth and the U.S., which are covered in two companion volumes.

•*Lovejoy's College Guide,* by the late Clarence E. Lovejoy (I wonder if I will keep writing my book years after I'm dead?)(Simon and Schuster). Briefer descriptions than other guides. In the past, the usefulness of Lovejoy's has been marred by the listing of some real clinkers: totally phony diploma mills that somehow managed to get past the editors.

•*National Directory of External Degree Programs* by Dr. Alfred W. Munzert. This was a very helpful directory, but it is now more than 10 years old, and so its usefulness is minimal.

•*Peterson's Annual Guides to Graduate Study* (Peterson's Guides). Five large books, each describing in detail opportunities for residential graduate study in the U.S. Volumes cover social science and humanities, biological and agricultural sciences, physical sciences, engineering, and there is a summary volume.

•*Peterson's Annual Guide to Undergraduate Study* (Peterson's Guides). Another massive directory (over 2,000 pages), covering traditional accredited schools only.

•*Thorson's Guide to Campus-Free College Degrees* by Marcie K. Thorson (Careers Unlimited). The well done book covers the same territory as this one, but accredited schools only.

•*Best's External Degree Directory*by Thomas J. Lavin. Much more detail than this book on many fewer schools. At $50 for under 300 pages, a bit pricey.

•*Who Offers Part-time Degrees* by Patricia Consolloy (Peterson's Guides). Very brief descriptions of more than 2,000 colleges (including junior colleges) offering degree programs for part-time students.

•*Worldwide Educational Directory* by Mohammad S. Mirza (International Educational Services, P.O. Box 10503, Saddar, Karachi 3, Pakistan). Nearly 400 typewritten pages (in English) listing degree and non-degree-granting schools. Most of the data are accurate, but some less-than-wonderful schools are included, without warning, along with the good ones. Lack of index or alphabetized listings makes it very difficult to use.

•*World-Wide Inventory of Non-Traditional Degree Programs* (UNESCO, c/o Unipub, P.O. Box 433, New York, NY 10016). A generally useful United Nations report on what many of the world's nations are doing in the way of non-traditional education. Some helpful school descriptions, and lots of detailed descriptions of evening courses offered by workers' cooperatives in Bulgaria and suchlike.

CREDIT FOR LIFE EXPERIENCE LEARNING

•*Creditable Portfolios: Dimensions in Diversity* (Council for Adult and Experiential Learning [CAEL], 10840 Little Patuxent Parkway, Suite 203, Columbia, MD 21044, $85 for all seven; $65 for any four). A looseleaf portfolio containing nine actual student portfolios from seven schools, including rationales for the procedures used, and credit awarded.

•*Earn College Credit for What You Know* by Susam Simosko (CAEL; see above; $8.95). How to put together a life experience portfolio: how to gather the necessary information, document it, and assemble it.

•*National Guide to Educational Credit for Training Programs* and

•*Guide to the Evaluation of Education Experiences in the Armed Forces* (American Council on Education, One Dupont Circle NW, Washington DC 20036). Many non-traditional programs use these four large volumes to assess credit for non-school learning. They describe and make credit recommendations for hundreds of corporate and military training programs.

•*Self-Assessment and Planning Manual* by Linda Headley-Walker, et al (University of the State of New York, Cultural Education Center, Albany, NY 12230). While prepared primarily for potential Regents College students this inexpensive and splendid 72-page manual could benefit anyone uncertain whether to pursue a non- traditional degree, and, if so, how to go about it. Guided exercises help the reader determine if he or she really needs a degree, how to assess prior educational experience, how to plan financially, and so forth.

•*Using Licenses and Certificates as Evidence of College-Level Learning* by Harriet Cabell (CAEL; see above; $3). A five-page summary of Dr. Cabell's doctoral research, examining the practices of schools that award credit based on applicants' licenses and certificates.

•*Your Hidden Credentials* by Dr. Peter Smith (Acropolis Books, 2400 17th St. NW, Washington DC 20009). Dr. Smith, the founder of Vermont Community College and later the lieutenant governor of Vermont, has written a charming and very useful book on matters related to earning credit for non-school learning (which, he points out, accounts for 90% of what an adult knows). Many inspiring case histories of adults who pursued this path, plus appendices that help one identify and describe out-of-school learning.

FOREIGN SCHOOLS

•*Guide to Education Abroad* by I. B. Chaudhary. Published from a now-closed P.O. Box in Bombay, this is an illegal pirated copy of my book. If anyone ever sees an ad for this dreadful product, please let me know, so I can commence proper legal action. Thank you.

•*How Foreign Students Can Earn an American University Degree without Leaving their Country* by Jean-Maximillien De La Croix de Lafayette. (Academia Press, P.O. Box 30054, Bethesda, MD 20814; $28 in U.S.; $50 overseas). Comparable in scope to my book, described next.

•*How to Earn an American University Degree Without Ever Going to America* by John Bear. This was the "foreign" version of the book you are now holding. It has now been replaced by an 80-page supplement to this book, *Information for People Outside the United States,* which is sold along with this book by its distributors, Costedoat & Bear, Box 826, Benicia, CA 94510.

•*UNISA: Information on the University of South Africa for Prospective American Students* by Karyn Holmes. UNISA is one of the few major universities in the world offering degrees through the doctoral level entirely by correspondence study. However the process of dealing with them can be extremely complex and frustrating. Ms. Holmes has written a detailed guide to the process of applying to, enrolling in, and working at the University. If you are considering UNISA, her 110-page single-spaced typewritten report may save time and anguish. It is available from the author for $12 (includes postage). (At presstime, I did not have the author's address. If you want this book, send me a self-addressed stamped envelope or an addressed postcard and I'll do my best to get it to you. John Bear, Box 826, Benicia CA 94510.

•*World Guide to Higher Education* (Bowker Publishing Co.). A comprehensive survey, by the United Nations, of educational systems, degrees, and qualifications, from Afghanistan to Zambia.

MEDICAL SCHOOLS

•*Foreign Medical Schools for U.S. Citizens* by Carlos Pestana, M.D., Ph.D. (P.O. Box 790617, San Antonio, TX 78279, $13 including postage). An essential book for anyone considering studying medicine at one of the Caribbean, Philippine, or other foreign medical schools. Dr. Pestana points out (and I agree) that "perhaps the greatest contribution of these modest 176 pages is that they offer an unbiased opinion . . . not tainted with obvious self interest (as you get from the owners and operators of the foreign schools) or with blind anti-foreign-medical-school prejudice." Originally published in 1983, but a current update of about 10 pages is included.

•*The Medical School Applicant: advice for premedical students* by Carlos Pestana, M.D., Ph.D. (see immediately above; also $13). Another wonderful book by Dr. Pestana, bringing his unique perspective to all the usual matters that books on medical schools have, and a great deal more, including a remarkable chapter on "Special angles: the dirty tricks department—a frank analysis of...unconventional pathways to a medical education."

FINANCIAL AID

•*Finding Money for College* by John Bear (Ten Speed Press, $7). I collected all the information I could find about the non-traditional and unorthodox approaches to getting a share in the billions of dollars that go unclaimed each year, including barter, real estate and tax gambits, negotiation, creative payment plans, obscure scholarships, foundations that make grants to individuals, etc. Some of the addresses are a bit out of date, but the strategies are good as new. Please don't write to me for this book; it will have to come from your bookstore or directly from the publisher at Box 7123, Berkeley, CA 94707. Add $1 for shipping.

•*The Scholarship Book* by Daniel Cassidy and Michael Alves; *The Graduate Scholarship Book* by Daniel Cassidy; and *The International Scholarship Book* by Daniel Cassidy (Prentice Hall, $19.95 each). A complete printout of the data banks of information used by Cassidy's National Scholarship Research Service, described in Chapter 8. Tens of thousands of sources are listed for undergraduate and graduate students, for study in the U.S. and overseas.

•*Your Own Financial Aid Factory* by Robert Leider (Octameron Associates, P.O. Box 3437, Alexandria, VA 22302). Contains an immense amount of useful information and good advice compacted into 140 pages.

MISCELLANY

•*Killing the Spirit: Higher Education in America* by Page Smith. In 1990, one of my writer-heroes [*A People's History of the United States*] issued this extraordinary book about everything that is wrong in higher educaion. From page 1: "The major themes might be characterized as the improverishment of the spirit by 'academic fundamentalism,' the flight from teaching, the meretriciousness of most academic research, the disintegration of the disciplines, the alliance of the universities with the Department of Defense...etc., and last but not least, the corruptions incident to 'big time' collegiate sports." Read this wonderful book.

•*College on Your Own* by Gene R. Hawes and Gail Parker (Bantam Books). This remarkable book, which unfortunately may be out of print, serves as a syllabus for a great many fields, for people who want to do college-level work at home, with or without the guidance of a college. Contains a brief overview of each field (anthropology, biology, chemistry, history, etc.) and a detailed reading list for learning more about the field. Quite valuable in preparing learning contracts.

•*The External Degree as a Credential: Graduates' Experiences in Employment and Further Study* by Carol Sosdian and Laure Sharp (National Institute of Education). I mention this 1978 report because it is probably the most often misquoted and misinterpreted educational survey ever published. Many schools (some good, some not) cite the findings (an extremely high satisfaction level of external students and an extremely high acceptance level of external degrees) without mentioning that the study related only to fully accredited undergraduate degrees, and may have little or no relevance to their unaccredited graduate degrees.

•*The Ph.D. Trap* by Wilfred Cude (Medicine Label Press, RR2, West Bay, Nova Scotia B0E 3K0 Canada). The author was treated very badly in his own graduate program, which turned him into a reformer . . . Farley Mowat writes that he is "the kind of reformer this world needs. Humane, literate, reasonable, and utterly implacable, he has just unmasked the gruesome goings on in the academic morgue that deals in doctoral degrees. Any student contemplating the pursuit of a doctorate had better read The Ph.D. Trap as a matter of basic self-preservation...."

•*This Way Out: A guide to alternatives to traditional college education in the U.S.* by John Coyne and Tom Hebert (E. P. Dutton). A delightful, if out-of-date book that describes a small number of alternatives in detail, with inspirational interviews with participants. Includes an intriguing essay on self-education by hiring tutors, and sections as diverse as how to study, how to hitchhike successfully, what to do when revolution breaks out in the country in which you are studying, and how to deal with large universities worldwide.

•*Winning the Ph.D. Game* by Dr. Richard W. Moore (Dodd, Mead & Co.).A light-hearted, extremely useful guidebook for current and prospective doctoral students. Covers the entire process, from selecting schools to career planning. Moore's aim is to "describe the folk wisdom passed from one generation of graduate students to the next (in order to) make the whole process less traumatic." He succeeds admirably. Sadly, the book may be out of print.

DIPLOMA MILLS

•*Diploma Mills: Degrees of Fraud* by David W. Stewart and Henry A. Spille (Macmillan Publishing). Originally this book was going to provide a lot of details on specific diploma mills, but sadly, it turned out to be a mildly interesting survey of the history of the problem, with a useful summary and evaluation of the current school laws in all 50 states.

•*Diploma Mills: The Paper Merchants* by Jerry Seper and Richard Robinson. This is a reprint of a lengthy series of articles that ran in the Arizona *Republic* newspaper in 1983, describing many of the institutions they chose to call diploma mills, then operating in Arizona. Many have since relocated to other states. The newspaper has stopped distributing the booklet, alas, but you can get a photocopy from me for $5 (including first class postage). John Bear, P.O. Box 826, Benicia, CA 94510.

JOURNALS

There are at least five journals or periodicals that have articles on non-traditional or alternative or external education:

•*The American Journal of Distance Education*, which started in 1987, published by the Office for Distance Education, College of Education, Pennsylvania State University, University Park, PA 16802.

•*The Journal of Non-Traditional Studies*, originally called *Alternative Higher Education*, which used to be published by Human Sciences Press in New York, but apparently by another publisher now.

•*Distance Education*, the journal of ASPESA, the Australian and South Pacific External Studies Association, Deakin University Press, Geelong, Victoria 3217, Australia.

•*Bulletin of the International Council for Distance Education*, published by Open University, North West Region, 70 Manchester Road, Chorlton-cum-Hardy, Manchester M21 1PQ, England.

•*Journal of Higher Education*, published by Ohio State University Press, 2070 Neil Ave., Columbus, OH 43210.

28. Help Wanted

Two helping one another will do as much as four singly.
—Spanish Proverb

In this section, I ask for two kinds of help from my readers:

1. Help in checking out schools

Situations regularly arise in which I attempt to learn more about a certain school. Sometimes I am hindered by distance. Often one can learn more from a brief inspection of a school than by hours of research or communication (such as, in an extreme but not uncommon case, when it turns out to be a mail-forwarding service). Sometimes I am hindered by notoriety. Some schools simply won't communicate with me at all, or won't answer my questions about their programs.

I do have an informal array of "pen pals" in a number of cities around the world who have been very helpful in checking out schools for me, either in person or by correspondence. But more are always needed. If you would be willing to do this from time to time, please drop me a card or note to let me know. If you live in one place but regularly travel to another place, let me know that, too. Thank you. (John Bear, P.O. Box 1616, Hilo, Hawaii 96721)

2. Help in learning more about certain specific schools

I am regularly asked for information on certain schools, by law enforcement officials, personnel officers, reporters, alumni, or interested members of the public. Often I can help, but many times I cannot. What follows is a list of schools in my "Need More Information" file. If you are familiar with any of these, even if it is only a scrap of information or a bit of hearsay, please let me know. Thank you again.

ATLANTIC UNIVERSITY A correspondent sent me a recent class schedule of this university, but I have no details of its operation. Apparently associated with Edgar Cayce's Association for Research and Enlightenment in Virginia.

AVON UNIVERSITY Several Bible school administrators have listed degrees from this school, which one said was founded in Boston in 1897, but I have been unable to locate it.

BLAKE COLLEGE A reader asks for information on this school, which he believes operated both in Mexico and in Eugene, Oregon.

COMMENIUS INTERNATIONAL UNIVERSITY A 1981 article in Monato, an Esperanto language magazine, featured an interview with the founder of Commenius International University, apparently located in San Diego. Mail to that address was neither answered nor returned as undeliverable, and there is no listed phone. The claim in the article that the university is "officially approved" by the state of California is not correct.

CONCORIA INSTITUTE La Verne, California. Offers a B.A. in business administration, and claims an affiliation with Nova College in Canada. The director's Doctorate is from Elysion College, a now-closed California diploma mill.

COOPERATING UNIVERSITY OF AMERICA Wilson, North Carolina. Plans were announced to establish a university of this name, by a retired professor. The plan was to offer European students the opportunity to study in the U.S. in order "to prevent them from studying in Communist countries." They were to be taught by retired professors. I cannot learn whether it ever happened, but it does not seem to be happening now.

CREATIVE DEVELOPMENT INSTITUTE Manila, Philippines. An American reader reports that he was awarded a Ph.D. by this Filipino school, based entirely on his career experience and writings, and without going to the Philippines. He says many other such degrees have been awarded. I have not been able to locate the school.

CYBERAM UNIVERSITYMiami, Florida. Their literature (in Spanish) offered degrees of all kinds, from psychology to music to astrology, for fees of $150 to $300. They claimed to be licensed by the Spanish Ministry of Education and Science. The diplomas issued were quite beautiful, if not of value. Also known as the Universidad Medico Naturalista Hispano-America.

DARWIN UNIVERSITY A correspondent reports a degree mill of this name, but no further information was given.

EMMANUEL COLLEGE OXFORD Oxford, England. The claim is made that the degrees will be awarded solely on completion of a Master's thesis (about 100 pages) or Doctoral dissertation (about 400 pages) and payment of about $1,800. They have not responded to my inquiries, and I am concerned about the lack of telephone, the absence of any names on the literature I have seen, and the spelling, several times, of "Ph.D." as "P.hD." Somewhat reassuring is the policy of not asking for any money until after a proposal has been approved and a faculty advisor assigned; and the note, typed onto the flyer, that tells us they are not part of the University of Oxford, and have no Royal Charter.

ESCUELA DE MEDICINE DR. EVARISTO CRUZ ESCOBEDO Saltillo, Mexico. One of the more controversial Mexican medical schools, they have received a lot of bad press and have not responded to three inquiries as to their present situation. Formerly known as Universidad Interamericana, and as Escuela de Medicina Benito Juarez-Abraham Lincoln.

ESSENES RESEARCH FOUNDATION San Diego, California. They have awarded Ph.D. degrees, through the Graduate School Consortium for the Religious Arts and Sciences. I have never been able to find an address or telephone number in University City, San Diego.

EUREKA FOUNDATION A correspondent reported that "an open university known as the Eureka Foundation has commenced advertising in Australia." I have not been able to learn more about them.

FREE UNIVERSITY I have seen a diploma—a spectacular huge diploma—on a wall. It awarded the "Academic degree of Bachelor of Dentistry" of the Free University for the recipient's exploits on a geographical expedition. I have never been able to locate the university, which was a part of the International Federation of Scientific Research Societies. Possibly the same Free U. identified as a diploma mill by E&T Magazine.

FREEDOM UNIVERSITY A correspondent asks about this school, which she says is in Albuquerque, New Mexico. But there is no listed phone there, nor can I find any information, or whether it is connected with the Freedoms in Florida and Colorado.

FREEMAN UNIVERSITY Las Vegas, Nevada. I found them in the Las Vegas phone book, but I can't find them in any school directory, nor have my letters to 4440 S. Maryland Pkwy. been answered.

FREMONT COLLEGE Officers of one university list Doctorates from this school, which they say is or was in Los Angeles, but I can find no evidence of it.

GALATIA UNIVERSITY Salem, Oregon? A correspondent saw an advertisement and wrote for a catalogue. He received a postcard saying they were temporarily out, and one would be sent soon. Nothing more was heard, and he has lost the address.

GRIFFITH UNIVERSITY Queensland, Australia. A reader writes that they have introduced a "new kind of B.A. degree" but details have not been forthcoming.

HALLMARK UNIVERSITY San Bernardino, California. All I know about this is that an advertisement was run in the Los Angeles Times, offering "University for sale."

INSTITUTE OF PARANORMAL SCIENCE Fremont, California. Announced the intention of offering a degree program in the early 1980s.

INSTITUTE OF SCIENCE AND MATHEMATICS Registered with the Louisiana Board of Regents, an automatic, non-evaluative process. Has not responded to my inquiries.

JAMILIAN UNIVERSITY Full-page advertisements in Omni Magazine (and that ain't cheap) in 1987 and 1988 heralded the arrival of Jamilian University, Reno, Nevada, in which a "much-talked-about but little known group of mystics is offering to share" the "age old secrets for prolonging life and expanding intelligence." I chose not to invest $25 in the admissions package, and they chose not to send me a catalogue, so you will have to learn the secrets for yourself.

JEAN RAY UNIVERSITY A reader inquired about this school, allegedly in Namur, Belgium, from which a prominent person in his community had claimed a Doctorate, but I can find nothing about it.

KELTIC UNIVERSITY A reader in England inquires about Keltic University, but my letters to 3 Vicarage Close, Kirby Muxloe, Leicestershire have not been answered. There is certainly no recognized school of this name in England.

KENT COLLEGE OF LOUISIANA Apparently started in New Orleans in 1988 (4714 Earhart Blvd., 70125). In the absence of a catalogue or other information (requested but not sent), I can only report on the letterhead: it says Kent is "an international consortium of resident/non-resident studies." The seal depicts a large letter "K" wearing a mortarboard hat, standing on an open book with blank pages. When I drove by the address in 1990, I found an empty building. State records show it may be affiliated with LaSalle University (Louisiana).

KRISSPY UNIVERSITY I have been sent a transcript, showing a Master's degree from Krisppy University of Bayamon, Puerto Rico, but cannot locate such a school. (Is it possible they merged with Rice University?)

LAWYER'S UNIVERSITY In late 1987, a law officer was trying to locate a school of this name, possibly in Los Altos, California, or in Florida. I could find no trace.
LINCOLN UNIVERSITY (New Guinea) The degrees are based on writing up to 10 papers in a given field. Established in Arizona when school laws were non-existent there, then in London, England, in 1987 where the address was a mail forwarding service. The university has travelled with its founder, who has now brought it to New Guinea. He seems to be a sincere scholar, and indeed Lincoln has achieved some level of acceptance. The alumni include the head of government for the Kingdom of Lesotho and the former minister for education and culture of Ghana.
LOYOLA SOUTHWERSTERN UNIVERSITY A telephone caller insisted that there is a school of this name, located in Baton Rouge, Louisiana, but neither I nor authorities in Louisiana have heard of it or can find it.
MANX UNIVERSITY Isle of Man. In 1987, an announcement was made that a university of this name was to be established on the Isle of Man, to open in 1992. A multimillion pound fund-raising appeal was said to have begun. The people behind the endeavor chose to remain anonymous. Anyone making a donation, however small, will become a trustee of the university, at least for a while.
MARQUIS GUISEPPE SCICLUNA INTERNATIONAL UNIVERSITY FOUNDATION In 1987, the Universal Intelligence Data Bank of America, in Independence, Missouri, wrote to businessmen in Asia, offering them the honorary doctorate of the above-named institution, on receipt of a $500 payment. They identify the issuer of the degree as "one of the world's most respected university foundations." The coat of arms on the letterhead is identified as that of the Dingli-Attard family. Baron Marcel Dingli-Attard is a vice president of International University, which is located in Independence, Missouri. Could there be a connection here?
NATIONAL CHRISTIAN UNIVERSITY There was once one located in Richardson, Texas, and another in Dallas. Then some ads appeared for the National Christian University of Missouri, but one was to write to the dean of theology in Oklahoma City. National Christian also appears on the Council of Europe's list of degree mills. So far, I am confused.
NORTH CONTINENTAL UNIVERSITY They have used a P.O. box in Santa Rosa, California, but my inquiries have never been answered.
NORTHWEST UNIVERSITY OF METAPHYSICS Listed as the source of a degree for a faculty member of a traditional school. Have not been able to locate it.
OCCIDENTAL INSTITUTE OF CHINESE STUDIES A reader asks about their degrees; he believes they are somewhere in Florida.
ORANGE UNIVERSITY OF MEDICAL SCIENCES Tustin, California. A major article in the Los Angeles Times in 1982 anounced the highly controversial impending opening of this investor-owned for-profit medical school. I often wonder what happened, but haven't been able to find out.
PEOPLE'S UNIVERSITY OF THE AMERICAS A correspondent has reported that such a university exists, with an address at a post office box in Solna, Sweden, from which no response has been heard.
PHOENIX UNIVERSITY The president of a Bible school lists, among his credentials, a Ph.D. from the Bari Research Center of Phoenix University for archaeological research, bestowed by its president, His Serene Highness Prince Francisco D'Aragona. I am unfamiliar with this institution. See (I suspect) Accademia di Study Superiori Phoenix.
PRACHATHIPOK UNIVERSITY Thailand's open university was announced as a totally non-residential correspondence university, with courses by mail, by radio, and by television. It is unclear to me if Sukhothai Thammathirat Open University in Bangkok, opened in 1980 and now with over 150,000 students, is the same as Prachathipok.
PROFESSIONAL SCHOOL FOR HUMANISTIC STUDIES Listed as the source of a degree for a faculty member of a traditional school. Have not been able to locate it.
RADVIS UNIVERSITY Canada? A correspondent asks about it, and I can find no information.
REM INSTITUTE A reader has inquired about non-traditional Doctorates in psychology issued by this establishment, possibly in South Euclid, Ohio, but I could find no evidence.
SAINT PAUL COLLEGE AND SEMINARY A reader asks about an honorary Doctorate that a co-worker claims from this institution, apparently in Rome.
SCHOOL OF BOTANY A reader has inquired about an honorary degree a colleague of his was using. Possibly in Spain.
SEQUOIA UNIVERSITY Califonia or Oklahoma. In 1984, a judge in Los Angeles issued a permanent injunction against Sequoia University and its president to cease operations until it complies with the state education laws. The university offered degrees in osteopathic medicine, religious studies, hydrotherapy, and physical sciences.
SHELTON COLLEGE Cape May, New Jersey. The college, founded by fundamentalist radio preacher Carl McIntire, challenged New Jersey's school licensing law, claiming that it should be exempt from licensing under

freedom of religion and speech precedents. New Jersey maintained that any exceptions to its right to license would diminish the value and integrity of degrees in the state. I was still researching this case at press time.

SOUTHERN BIBLE COLLEGE Correspondent reports they offer a Bachelor's program of Christ-centered education for Christian missionaries, entirely through evening study. Have not responded to any of my six inquiries since 1982.

SUNSHINE UNIVERSITY Florida. Probably (but I've never been sure) a gag or promotional diploma. The Ph.D. they sent me is quite attractive and appears to be signed by the mayors of three Florida cities and the chairman of the Pinellas County Commission.

TEACHERS UNIVERSITY A reader asks about this school, which she believes used to exist in Miami, but I can find no evidence of them.

TRI-STATE COLLEGE AND UNIVERSITY Oxon Hill, Maryland. Several readers asked about this institution, but my letters to Dr. J. Roy Stewart at the address provided were never answered, and there was no listed telephone.

UNIFICATION THEOLOGICAL SEMINARY Barrytown, New York. Reverend Moon's Unification Church was denied the right to grant the Master of Religious Education degree at its seminary. By a 4 to 3 margin, New York's highest court determined that the board of regents acted on bonafide "deficiencies" and not discrimination when they denied a degree-granting license.

UNIVERSITY COLLEGE ACADEMY CHRISTIANS INTERNATIONAL In 1987, I was sent a document submitted by a clergyman in Puerto Rico, to document a degree claimed from this entity. The document, purporting to be a certification by the state of New York that "University College" is legitimate and accredited, is clearly a fake. It has a number of misspellings, and it simply is not true.

UNIVERSITY COLLEGE OF NORTHERN CYPRUS I have seen help wanted ads, in which they sought a campus director for their "accredited American Degree programmes in business administration." But I have not yet been able to learn the particulars.

UNIVERSITY OF AZANIA The name has been registered in England by Dr. Bernard Leeman (see Lincoln U ni versity [New Guinea]), in the hope and expectation of establishing a school that would ultimately be located in a "free South Africa." (Azania is the name that black South Africans have used for their country.)

UNIVERSITY OF NAIROBI A plan was announced in the early 1980s for an External Degree Programme, but some years later, it had not yet started due to "unforeseen problems." The address is P.O. Box 30197, Nairobi, Kenya.

UNIVERSITY OF NATUROPATHY A reader inquires about a school of this name that he believed might be operating in East Orange, New Jersey, but there is no listed phone number there.

UNIVERSITY OF PSYCHIC SCIENCE Someone sent me a business card for this school, located in National City, California, but I have not been sent information on what they do. Perhaps they haven't picked up the request I have been transmitting.

UNIVERSITY OF THE WORLD A reader says that in 1988, it existed in La Jolla, California, but I can't find it.

WHITMAN UNIVERSITY Morelia, Michoacan, Mexico. I received a "prototype" 1985–1986 bulletin, offering Bachelor's, Master's, and Doctorate degrees through guided independent study and writing of essays and papers. Accreditation is claimed from the International Association of Non-Traditional Schools (England), an organization I have not been able to locate. Students are requested to pay tuition ($200 for the Ph.D., $600 for the B.A.!) in cash, wrapped in carbon paper and sent in a thick envelope. My letters asking for more information have not been answered.

WILLIAM DARREN UNIVERSITY A correspondent asks for information on such a school, apparently in, or formerly in Phoenix. I can find no record of them.

29. Goodbye Index

It's more than just an easy word for casual goodbye;
It's gayer than a greeting, and it's sadder than a sigh.
—Don Blanding (Aloha Oe: Its Meaning)

The "Goodbye" index is a list of schools that were in previous editions, but are not in this one, along with, in most cases, a brief explanation of why. Some schools appear in this index without ever having appeared in the book, since they appeared and disappeared in the time since the last edition.

I have taken to heart the many letters I have received urging that the "Goodbye" index include all schools that have ever appeared in this, back to 1974, or indeed all schools that have ever existed and subsequently gone out of business. I would like to do this, and am working slowly toward it, with a new computer system. Meanwhile, I have included a number of significant schools that were listed in the 7th and/or 8th editions that are no longer operating.

GOODBYE

Academic Credit University Started by the former president of Southland University and Ethiopian colleagues; mail returned as undeliverable.

Academy of Open Learning They used to offer a Bachelor of Arts in valuation sciences for appraisers, but now mail is not answered, and there is no listed phone.

Advanced School of Herbology They were in Sacramento, California, but I cannot locate them now.

American Floating University In the 1930s, they offered Bachelor and Master of World Affairs to students who studied while traveling on ocean liners. Now they have sunk from view. Constantine Raises of San Francisco was in charge.

Beacon College Washington, District of Columbia. Beacon probably had the most flexible, most non-traditional Master's degree ever to achieve traditional accreditation, which was granted in 1981. Accreditation was subsequently lost due to licensing difficulties and the school appears to be out of business. Former name: Campus-Free College, established in Boston.

Bedford University Operated briefly in Arizona. Offered degrees at a time when Arizona had no laws regulating schools. Closed in 1983. Had offered degrees in conjunction with the Academy of Technical Sciences of Beirut, Lebanon. According to the *Arizona Republic* newspaper, clients of the Educom Counseling Service in California were referred to Bedford as "the school most suited" to their needs. Educom was run by Bedford's founder, later an officer of Clayton University, and his daughter.

Berea School of Theology Linton, Indiana. Letters returned as undeliverable.

Berean Christian College A correspondent writes that he sent money to a Berean at an address in Long Beach, California, but soon after, his mail was returned and the phone was disconnected.

Blackstone School of Law Chicago, Illinois. For many years, they offered law degrees by correspondence study. The degrees permitted holders to take the California bar exams. This permission expired in December, 1983.

Borinquen University Medical School Mail returned as undeliverable; cannot locate.

California Christian University Los Angeles, then Adelanto, California. The university was established in by the Reverend Bishop Doctor Walter G. Rummersfield, B.S., Ms.D., Ps.D., GS-9, D.D., Ph.D.M., Ph.D., D.B.A., S.T.D., J.C.D., J.S.D. Formerly called California Christian College of Los Angeles; once authorized by the state of California to grant degrees. Honorary Doctorates were awarded on payment of a donation of "$1,000 or less." Dr.Dr.Dr.Dr.Dr.Dr.Dr.Dr.Dr. Rummersfield apparently transferred control to new management in the 1980s, but no one answers my letters, and there is no longer a listed phone in Adelanto.

California University for Advanced Studies Petaluma, California. During 1989, they lost their state authorization, and closed. The school maintains they were harrassed out of existence. The state will not comment, other than to say that the school no longer met the requirements for authorization. Most enrolled students were allowed to complete degrees.

Christian Congregation, Inc. They used to issue honorary Doctorates in divinity, in return for a donation. They invited donors to be as generous as circumstances and conscience permitted. Mail to the last address I have, in Monroe, North Carolina, has been returned as undeliverable.

CIFAS School of Medicine Santo Domingo, Dominican Republic. This large Caribbean medical school, primarily serving Americans, was found to be offering a legitimate education through the front door, and selling M.D. degrees for up to $27,000 out the back door. Several administrators went to prison for so doing.

Clarksville School of Theology Clarksville, Tennessee. They offered Bachelor's, Master's, and Doctorates in theology under the guidance of Dr. W. Roy Stewart, a popular evangelist. In 1988, there was no longer a listed telephone number for the school.

College of Clinical Hypnosis Honolulu, Hawaii. They used to offer a degree in clinical hypnosis through a $350 correspondence course. The founder and president "earned" his degree from Thomas A. Edison College, a notorious degree mill. In 1988, the phone had been disconnected, and there was no new listing.

College of Oriental Studies Los Angeles, California. They used to offer Bachelor's, Master's, and Doctorates in philosophy and religion, but they appear to have moved on.

Colorado Technical College Colorado Springs, Colorado. Used to offer a program through The Source, a computer correspondence system, but it was discontinued.

East Carolina University Greenville, North Carolina. The M.A. in elementary education with a large element of independent study is no longer offered.

East Coast University They offered Master's and Doctorates in many non-religious subjects, with literature identical to the National Graduate School, National College, and National University. Their address was an apartment hotel in St. Louis. When I asked for them there, the man at the desk acknowledged they got their mail there, but would say no more. They have used addresses in Mobile; Tampa; Dade City, Florida (also called Roger Williams College there); Brooksville, Florida; and Sweet Springs, Missouri. But recent mail to their various addresses has been returned as undeliverable. They were fully accredited by the International Accrediting Commission for Schools, Colleges and Theological Seminaries, an unrecognized agency which was enjoined from operating by the State of Missouri.

Florida Institute of Remote Sensing Marianna, Florida. Offered correspondence programs and, apparently, a degree in this field, involving interpretation of aerial photos and other technologies. No longer in existence, as best I can determine.

Frank Ross Stewart University System Centre, Alabama. The university has offered some courses from time to time, all taught by Mrs. Stewart. Honorary Doctorates have been offered to those who have inquired about courses. Mrs. Stewart writes that "we do not find it attractive nor necessary" to be in this book. Well lah-dee-dah.

Freedom College Colorado Springs, Colorado and Santa Ana, California. Established in 1957 by Robert LeFevre, a well-known libertarian author. Later named Rampart College. Destroyed by heavy rains (was this a message?) in 1965, re-opened in 1968, and closed for good in 1975. Later, LeFevre became president of Southwestern University, an Arizona degree mill.

Graduate School of the Suggestive Sciences El Cajon, California. They offered Mas ter's and Doctorates in what they called "Hypnoalysis," but letters have been returned as undeliverable.

Great Lakes Bible College Correspondence courses leading to a degree are not offered.

Gulf States University Established in 1977 as Southeastern University, in South Carolina. Moved to Louisiana a few years later. Offered Doctoral programs requiring several weeks of summer residency in New Orleans. Following financial problems, the university closed in 1987, with many of the current students transferring to the University of Sarasota.

Highland University Athens, Tennessee. They offered a 25-month Ed.D. program involving three four-week summer sessions with independent study in between. Originally chartered in North Carolina, and in Sweetwater, Tennessee, before going to Athens. Now mail has been returned, and there is no listed phone number in Athens.

Holistic Life University Flourished in San Francisco in the late 70s and early 80s, but no longer findable there. They offered coursework that they said could be applied to degree programs at Antioch, Redlands, or Sonoma State.

Holy Cross Junior College Merrill, Wisconsin. When the original school of this name went bankrupt, others began offering a Ph.D. program in psychology or education, from the Institute of Learning of Holy Cross Junior College. After a newspaper "exposé," holders of the degree (most of them school administrators and psychologists) maintained they had done substantial work and truly earned their degrees. Critics disagreed, and the school faded away.

Horizon University Established in Shelburne, Ontario, Canada, to offer off-campus degrees based on independent study, with credit for prior learning. Apparently a victim of a 1984 provincial law strictly regulating universities. At least I cannot locate them now.

Indiana Northern Graduate School of Professional Management They offered a Master of Professional Management degree, primarily through independent study, with some class meetings in various cities in northern Indiana. Originally called Indiana Northern University. The "University" designation and the Doctoral programs were dropped by agreement with the state of Indiana which accredited the school. Run by the Most Reverend Bishop Dr. Gordon Da Costa, Ph.D., Ed.D., D.Sc., D.C., whose only earned degrees were from Indiana Northern. Ceased operations in 1985.

Institute for Management Competency San Francisco, California. An unaccredited but state-authorized Master's program has been discontinued.

Institute of Human-Potential Psychology Palo Alto, California. Offered an external Ph.D. program for a while. Name changed to Psychological Studies Institute, but that, too, seems to have faded away.

Instituto de Estudios Iberoamericanos Saltillo, Mexico. Offered Bachelor's, Master's, and Doctorates, mostly to Americans, with a five-week summer session in Mexico plus independent study. No longer in operation.

International College Los Angeles, California. Alas, this splendid idea did not survive. They offered Bachelor's, Master's, and Doctorates through private study with tutors, worldwide. Apparently many of the well-known tutors (Lawrence Durrell, Yehudi Menuhin, Ravi Shankar, Judy Chicago, etc.) had very few (or no) students. Many of the students transferred to William Lyon University.

International Graduate School I.G.S. was established in St. Louis as the Doctoral-level affiliate of the accredited World University (Puerto Rico) in 1980, offering the Doctorate in business or education. They received candidacy for accreditation with the North Central Association in the remarkably short time of one year. However the candidacy was withdrawn in late 1987, and in 1988 the school told the state of Missouri that it would be closing down.

International Graduate University They offered Ph.D. degrees in clinical psychology and behavioral science, through an affiliation first with American College of Switzerland and later with Florida Institute of Technology, but no longer.

International Studies in Humanistic Psychology In the 1970s, they offered a non-resident Ph.D. in their field, from Cotati, California.

James Tyler Kent College of Homeopathic Medicine Offered a five-year program in homeopathic medicine, but mail was returned and there is no listed phone in Phoenix.

Juarez-Lincoln Bilingual University Austin, Texas. Letters returned as undeliverable.

Keichu Technological Institute Registered with the Louisiana Board of Regents for 1988, but mail to the registered address is returned as undeliverable, and there is no listed phone. President Karl Marx was affiliated with Andrew Jackson University, formerly of Baton Rouge.

Kripalu Institute Summitt Station, Pennsylvania. They offered a Master's in humanistic studies. There was a connection with an International University in Kayavorahan, India. But the phone is disconnected and mail is returned as undeliverable.

La Salle Extension University This huge correspondence university discontinued operations in 1982, not long after losing their accreditation from the National Home Study Council. They had been owned for many years by Macmillan Publishing Company of New York.

Lyle University They operated for a while in the mid-1980s from New Orleans and Metairie, Louisiana, offering Bachelor's, Master's, and Doctorates at $750 for a complete program. Started by a Columbia Pacific University graduate, and quite similar in approach to C.P.U. No longer registered with the board of regents in Louisiana, and therefore presumably no longer in business.

Maranatha Bible Seminary The seminary was apparently in St. Petersburg, Florida, but all correspondence and money had to go to the president in South Carolina. Degrees of all kinds; fee of $475. When they raptured, the mailing list was turned over to International Bible Institute and Seminary.

Metropolitan University Operated in Glendale, California, in the 1950s, apparently quite legitimately, offering degrees with substantial life experience credit. Long gone.

Millikin University No longer offers degrees through the Evening Division.

Ministry of Life Church Delavan, Wisconsin. One of the pioneers in offering ordination and divinity degrees by mail, at least since the 1960s. "We're not out to make a fast buck; our work is to wake up a few people so they will go out to tell it like it is," they said, but the Church did not survive the demise of its founding bishop.

Modular Education Bethany, Oklahoma. Red University of Biblical Studies..

National College for the Natural Healing Arts Birchdale, Minnesota. Offered programs leading to Bachelor's, Master's, and Doctorates in naprapathy, reflexology, iridology, homeopathy, acupuncture, cancer research, and so forth, possibly through non-residential study. Mail has been returned and there is no listed phone number in Birchdale.

North American College of Acupuncture Vancouver, British Columbia, Canada. Offered cor res pondence studies in Chinese medical philosophy and principles of diagnosis. Mail has been returned.
North American Colleges of Natural Health Science San Rafael, California. Offered professional career education in holistic natural health sciences. Mail has been returned; no listed telephone.
Ocean University At one time, they were authorized to grant law and other degrees in California, but no longer. Addresses in Lancaster and Santa Monica.
Open Door Baptist Bible College Kansas City, Kansas. They used to offer degrees through a correspondence program, but evolved into a traditional residential college with no correspondence study.
Phoenix Medical School Phoenix, Arizona. Incorporated and began recruiting students in 1984, even though the university existed, as an article in the *Arizona Republic* reported, only "on a few pieces of paper stacked on a rented credenza under a rented scenic picture in a small office [in] Mesa." President Gloria Coates announced an opening date for the university, but apparently it never came to pass.
Prometheus College Tacoma, Washington. They arose in the mid–1970s, rather quickly became a candidate for accreditation, and then suddenly they were gone, perhaps back to Olympus.
Psychological Studies Institute Palo Alto, California. Formerly Institute of Human-Potential Psychology, but no longer findable under either name.
Quimby College Alamagordo, New Mexico. Offered a B.A. in life arts and an M.A. in spiritual studies and counseling. Locally controversial (in part, perhaps, because of the focus on aura balancing, and the assertion that the college had its start when the thoughts of a New England watchmaker who died in 1866, Phineas P. Quimby, were transmitted to an Alamagordo woman). No longer findable in Alamagordo.
Rochdale College This legitimate, if unorthodox institution in Toronto, Canada, used to "award" honorary degrees as a fund-raising tool for the college, to those who made modest donations. The honorary Ph.D. had an imprinted watermark on the paper, so that when you held it to the light, you saw "Caveat Emptor."
Rockwell University Scottsdale, Arizona. They offered degrees of all kinds by correspondence study. The only requirement was writing a thesis. A former president of Loyola (Louisiana) was claimed to be one of the five founders. "An education for the 1980s" was their slogan, but they didn't make it through the 80s themselves.
Sacred Heart College A program offering a very short residency Bachelor's in management and criminal justice has been cancelled, at least for the time being.
Saint Andrew's Collegiate Seminary London, England. In the late 1950s, Saint Andrew's was a small and apparently sincere and legitimate seminary, offering Master's and Doctoral work in theology and counseling. Later, to raise funds, the seminary offered honorary Doctorates to clergy and others who made donations. This evolved into awarding non-residential degrees for life experience in the name of the Saint Andrew's Ecumenical Church Foundation Intercollegiate. This further evolved into a worldwide effort, again awarding degrees entirely based on resumes, called the International Free Protestant Episcopal University. None of these entities survives.
Saint Andrew's Ecumenical Church Foundation Intercolle giate See: Saint Andrew's Collegiate Seminary
Saint Bonaventure University Degrees through evening study no longer available.
Saint Giles University College England. They offered non-resident Bachelor's, Master's, Doctorates, and certificates in psychology, physiatrics, teacher training, and science. The Doctor of Science program, for example, consisted of three lessons: (1) factors influencing children's sweet eating, (2) psychiatry and psychology, and (3) radiation and human health. The same gentleman was the moving force behind Saint Giles, Harley University, and Somerset University.
Saint John's College London, England. A division of City Commercial College, they did not offer their own degrees, but conducted the coursework leading to a Bachelor's or an M.B.A. from an unspecified-in-their-literature non-traditional school in California. They apparently closed down in the wake of student protests.
Saint John's University Edgard, Louisiana. A very small school, established by District Court Judge Thomas Malik, they used to offer non-resident degrees, but that program was discontinued. No connection with the other Saint John's University in Louisiana.
San Francisco Theological Seminary San Anselmo, California. They have discontinued their Doctor of the Science of Theology offered through summer sessions, and do not wish me to describe their non-residential Master of Arts in Values program because "we are in the process of curriculum changes and it would be difficult to express the substance and location of programs at this time."
Santa Barbara University Goleta, California. They appeared in the 1986 directory of schools put out by the state of California, as offering Master's and Doctorate's in business, but in 1988, there was no telephone listing. Presumably not the same as University of Santa Barbara (formerly Laurence).
Santa Fe College of Natural Medicine Santa Fe, New Mexico. They offered non-residential Bachelor's, Master's, and Ph.D. programs along with residential studies. Now there is no response to letters, and the telephone has been disconnected.

Seattle College Appeared briefly in Seattle in the early 1980s, offering very short courses leading to the Bachelor's, Master's, or Ph.D. at a cost of $20. Diplomas of the students' own design were awarded. Graduates "can legitimately represent yourself as a college instructor.... It will justify higher fees and profile. You will be an AUTHORITY and treated as such."
Sedona College/Sedona University Sedona, Arizona. According to an article in the *Arizona Republic*, an application to operate this school was made in Arizona by two men, one a former employee of Southwestern University (whose owner was imprisoned for selling degrees); the other the police chief of Sedona, whose Doctorate is from De Paul University, a degree mill whose owners were sentenced to prison in 1987. According to a spirited defense of Sedona College in the *Sedona Times* newspaper (September 19, 1984), James H. Smith of California "purchased Sedona College from its founder, Ted Dalton," (president of Newport University). I am uncertain as to whether Sedona ever accepted students, but there is no listed phone for them in Sedona now. I have been told that there were actually two schools, perhaps quite independent of each other: Sedona College and Sedona University.
Sonoma Institute Bodega, California. Offered the training for an M.A. in humanistic and transpersonal psychology through a cooperative relationship with the University of Redlands. Apparently longer in operation.
Southern California Christian University No longer in business, at least at the address I had in Los Angeles.
Southland University California and Arizona. Ceased operations. La Salle University in St. Louis subsequently opened under the same management with the similar programs, including some law materials sent to students bearing the Southland name.
Stratton College Navan, Ireland. An external degree program was announced by the college, then the college was taken over by the Institution of Maintenance Engineering, and then the degree program was cancelled.
Synthesis Graduate School for the Study of Man San Francisco, California. An ambitious-seeming endeavor, offering M.A. and Ph.D. in psychology and medical synthesis. Buckminster Fuller and a Nobel laureate in medicine were on the board of advisors. Most faculty were disciples of Roberto Assagioli. But now they are gone, as best I can determine.
Tennessee Southern University The Tennessee Southern University and School of Religion was established in late 1981 for the purpose, according to its founder, Dr. O. Charles Nix, of "developing students with a special sense of social responsibility, who can organize and apply knowledge for human betterment." They have temporarily suspended operations, awaiting action on a state permit, and hope to reopen soon after 1990.
University of California, Riverside Their off-campus Master of Administration program has been discontinued.
University of California, San Diego Their non-residential Bachelor of Arts program has been discontinued.
University of California, San Francisco The M.S. in nursing which could be earned through evening study has apparently been discontinued.
University of California, Santa Cruz Their B.A. in community studies, offered through evening study, has apparently been discontinued.
University of Canterbury Los Angeles, California. In the late 1970s, they offered graduate degrees in psychology and other fields with a four-week residency requirement, but within a few years, they were gone.
University of Central Arizona Tempe, Arizona. Operated in the late 1970s, offering Doctor of Art in education and Doctor of Business Management, based on readings, examinations, and writing a dissertation. The two founders agreed to a consent judgment and stopped awarding Doctorates.
University of Central California Sacramento, California. They once offered degrees of all kinds by correspondence, typically by responding to 100 to 200 multiple-choice, true-false, and essay questions to demonstrate competency; then independent study, a thesis, and an examination. They were authorized by the state of California, but both the authorization and the university are no more.
University of Hartford They have some innovative programs that I would like to list in the book, but they must have all the students they need, because Ms. Carole Olland, director of admissions, wants them left out, so I am leaving them out.
University of Mid-America A consortium of 11 midwestern universities, which was to establish the American Open University, spent $14 million from the National Institute of Education in organizing, and then went out of business in 1982 when NIE shut its purse.
University of Saint Lucia School of Medicine The medical school was started on the Caribbean island of Saint Lucia by self-styled "Crazy Eddie" Antar, New York electronics magnate. But the school closed abruptly a year later, in early 1984, stranding students and faculty alike. Saint George's University in Grenada agreed to take qualified students, but only 37 of Saint Lucia's 127 were accepted there. No connection with Saint Lucia Health Sciences University.
University Without Walls/New Orleans Offered Bachelor's degrees. Now mail is returned, and no phone listed.
University Without Walls/Project Success North Hollywood, California. In the mid-1980s, their literature

described Bachelor's, Master's, and Doctorates in evolutionary systems design, but they are no longer there.

Valley Christian University Fresno, then Clovis, California. Degrees in many fields at all levels by correspondence. Letters neither answered nor returned; no listed telephone.

Video University Jackson, Mississippi. In the early 1980s, a major marketing effort was launched for Video U., ultimately to offer many training courses. Now the phone has been "temporarily disconnected."

Washington International College Washington, District of Columbia They offered a B.A. with two weeks' residency, achieved candidacy for accreditation, and then went out of business in 1982.

Wellsgrey College Greeley, Colorado. Advertisements appeared in business publications offering the M.B.A. by computer, but mail was not answered, and now there is no phone listing.

Western Colorado University Grand Junction, Colorado. They offered non-resident degrees in many fields at all levels, accredited by the unrecognized National Association for Private Non-traditional Schools and Colleges, with whom they shared staff and office space. Financial problems set in, and the doors were closed in the mid-1980s.

Western Scientific University Opened in the early 1980s as a "Christian internal, external alternate degree program," offering M.D. (homeopathic), and various Bachelor's, Master's, and Doctorates. Original name: Western University. No longer there.

Windsor University One of the first of California's non-traditional schools, Windsor opened in Los Angeles in 1972, soon became a candidate for accreditation, and had an affiliation with Antioch. But things fell apart in the wake of claims of misleading statements and falsified credentials, and Windsor is no more.

World University In the early 1980s, I received quite a few inquiries about the World University. The "world headquarters of the secretariat" was in Tucson, Arizona. There was a joint degree-offering venture with Columbia Pacific University. One transcript I saw identified it as "affiliated with University Danzig, USA." But now there is no listed telephone, and my letters to President H. John Zitko have not been answered.

World University Santo Domingo, Dominican Republic. It was a medical school, incorporated in Puerto Rico, affiliated with the then-accredited International Institute of the Americas, and recognized by the World Health Organization. But the phone has been disconnected, and mail has been returned.

World University There used to be a fully accredited World University, with headquarters in Hato Rey, Puerto Rico, and various branches or alliances in places around the U.S., including International Graduate School, St. Louis, and World University of Florida. But they are no longer accredited, if indeed they are there at all.

30.Index to Non-Resident and Short Residency Schools

ACCREDITED SCHOOLS WITH NON-RESIDENT PROGRAMS

School	Degrees
American Open University	B
Arts and Science University	B
Athabasca University	B
Beijing Broadcasting and Television University	
Bemidji State University	B
Berean College	B
British Columbia Open University	B
California College for Health Sciences	M
California State University Dominguez Hills	M
Canadian School of Management	B, M
Central Michigan University	B, M
Charter Oak College	B
City University	B, M
College for Human Services	B, M
College of New Rochelle	B
Colorado State University	M
Columbia Union College	B
Darling Downs Institute	B, M
Deakin University	B
Durham University	M
Dyke College	B
Eastern Illinois University	B
Eckerd College	B
Elizabethtown College	B
Embry-Riddle Aeronautical University	B
Empire State College	B, M
Evergreen State College	B, M
Everyman's University	B
Fernuinversitat	M, D
Ferris State College	B
Flaming Rainbow University	B
Framingham State College	B
Goddard College	B, M
Governors State University	B
Grantham College of Engineering Technology	B
Heriot Watt University	M
Indiana University	B
Indiana University of Pennsylvania	D
Indiana University Southeast	B
Instituto Politecnico Nacional	B
International Academy of Management and Economics	M, D
Iowa State University	B, M
Kansas State University	B
Loretto Heights College	B
Madurai University	B, M
Mind Extension University	B, M
Ohio University	B
Open University (England)	B, M, D
Open University of the Netherlands	B, D

Prescott College	B
Queens University	B
Shimer College	B
Thomas A. Edison State College	B
Troy State University	B
Universidad Estatal a Distancia	B, M
Universidad Mexicana del Noreste	B
Universidad Nacional Abierta	B
Universidad Autonoma Nactional de Mexico	B
Universidad Nacional de Educacion a Distancia	B
Universidad National de Educacion 'Enrique Guzman y Valle'	B
University of Delhi	B, M
University of East Asia	B, M
University of Idaho	M
University of Iowa	B
University of London	B, M, D, L
University of Massachusetts-Amherst	B, M
Universidy of Mindanao	M
University of Minnesota	B
University of New England	B, M
University of Northern Iowa	B
University of Phoenix	B, M
University of South Africa	B, M, D
University of the State of New York	B
University of Waterloo	B
University of Wisconsin-Madison	Certificate
University on the Air	B
Villareal National University	M, D
Western Illinois University	B

ACCREDITED SCHOOLS WITH SHORT RESIDENCY PROGRAMS

Allama Iqbal Open University	B, M
American College	M
American Technological University	M
Antioch University	M
Atlantic Union College	B
Bard College	B
Boricua College	
Brigham Young University	B
Burlington College	B
Caldwell College	B
Chicago State University	B
Columbia University	D
Dartmouth College	M
Fielding Institute	M, D
Lesley College	B, M
Liberty University	B, M
Maine Maritime Academy	M
Mary Baldwin College	B
Marywood College	B
Mercy College	B, M
Metropolitan State University	B
Mitchell College of Advanced Education	B
Murray State University	B
New Hampshire College	B, M

Northeastern Illinois University	B, M
Northwood Institute	B
Norwich University	B, M
Nova University	B, M, D
Oklahoma City University	B
Oral Roberts University	B
*Ottawa University	B
Ramkhamhaeng University	B
Rikkyo University	D
Riverina College of Advanced Education	B
Saint Joseph's College	B, M
Saint Mary-of-the-Woods College	B, M
Saybrook Institute	M, D
Skidmore College	B, M
Sonoma State University	B, M
Southwestern Adventist College	B
Sri Lanka Institute of Distance Education	B
State University College	B
Stephens College	B
Syracuse University	B, M
Technion Institute	M
Union Institute	B, D
University of Alabama	B, M
University of Maryland	B
University of Missouri-Columbia	B
University of New Hampshire	B, M
University of Oklahoma	B, M
University of Pittsburgh	B
University of Sarasota	M, D
University of South Florida	B
University of Wales	M, D
University of Warwick	M
University of Wisconsin-Green Bay	B
University of Wisconsin-Superior	B
Upper Iowa University	B
Walden University	D
West Virginia Board of Regents B.A.	B

UNACCREDITED SCHOOLS WITH NON-RESIDENT PROGRAMS

American Graduate University	M
American Institute for Computer Sciences	B, M
American Pacific University	B, M, D
American University of London	B, M, D
Andrew Jackson University College	B, M, D
Australian College of Applied Psychology	Diplomas
Bernadean University	D, L
Beta International University	B, M, D, L
California Coast University	B, M, D
California Pacific University	B, M
Century University	B, M, D
Chadwick University	B, M
City University Los Angeles	B, M, D, L
Clayton University	B, M, D
Columbia Pacific University	B, M, D, L
Columbia State University	B, M, D, L

Cook's Institute of Electronics Engineering	B
Eula Wesley University	B, M, D
Eurotechnical Research University	D
Fairfax University	B, M, D
Freie und Private Universitat	D
Gestalt Institute of New Orleans	Diplomas
Greenwich University	B, M, D, L
Heed University	B, M, D, L
Honolulu University	B, M, D
Institute for the Advanced Study of Human Sexuality	M, D
International Institute for Advanced Studies	B, M
Internationan School of Business and Legal Studies	B, M, D
International University (MO)	B, M, D
International University (NY)	D
Kennedy Western University	B, M, D, L
Kensington University	B, M, D, L
La Jolla University	B, M, D
La Salle University	B, M, D, Law
Newport University	B, M, D, L
Northland Open University	B, M
Nova College	B, M, D
Open University of America	B, M, D
Pacific Southern University	B, M, D
Pacific Western University	B, M, D
Saint John's University (LA)	B, M, D
Saint Martin's College and Seminary	B, M, D
Somerset University	B, M, D
Southern California University for Professional Studies	B, M
Southwest University	B, M, D
Summit University	B, M, D
Susan B. Anthony University	B, M, D
University de la Romande	B, M, D
University for Humanistic Studies	B, M, D
University of America	B, M, D
Washington College of Law	M, D
West London University	B, M, D
Western States University	B, M, D
William Lyon University	B, M, D

UNACCREDITED SCHOOLS WITH SHORT RESIDENCY PROGRAMS

American College of Finance	M
California American University	M
Pacific States University	M, D
Sierra University	B, M, D
University of Santa Barbara	M, D

31. Subject Index

For years, a frequent complaint from readers of this book has been that there was no subject index. There are three excellent reasons why this is the case:

1. A great many schools offer study in a huge number of subjects, sometimes over 200. To list every subject offered by every school would mean an index that could be 50 pages long.

2. The same subject might be called a dozen different things at various schools: business, business administration, administration, management, business studies, professional studies, etc. etc. etc. The amount of cross-indexing necessary would be immense.

3. The amount of time and effort it would take to compile such an index is huge. Contrary to many readers' beliefs, I am not a conglomerate. I am one person, without a secretary, sitting at one small computer, doing the best I can. [Pause for violins.]

Still, I acknowledge the value of such an index, especially for more unusual fields. Everybody and his brother (and her sister) offers business degrees or English degrees, for instance... but if your field is community mental health, it would be great to know that American Open University offers it, without having to read through 100 pages of school descriptions.

Here is my compromise for this edition; things may get better in the future:

What follows is a brief subject index, *but only for a select number of specialized subjects.*

- ➤ It covers only the schools in Chapter 16—not schools of law, theology, or health sciences.
- ➤ It most specifically ***does not*** cover popular fields of study, which are offered by dozens and dozens of schools, such as business, psychology, social sciences, education, English, history, computers, religion, humanities, etc. You will just have to browse through Chapter 16 for those.
- ➤ It is most emphatically **not complete.** For instance, the first listing is for accounting at three schools, that indicate in their literature they specialize in this. But there are probably 100 other schools in chapter 16 where you could pursue accounting studies; many of them are just identified in Chapter 16 by saying "many fields" under subject areas. So don't take this section as definitive, but only as a starting point. Thank you.

accounting	City University Marywood College Upper Iowa University
addictionology	St. John's University (LA)
agriculture	Colorado State University University of London
applied science	Darling Downs Institute Thomas A. Edison State College
art therapy	University of Norwich
biology	British Columbia Open University
Canadian studies	Athabasca University
chemistry	Eurotechnical Research University

	University of the State of New York
nutritional science	Clayton University
performing arts	Goddard College
philosophy	University of Waterloo
physical education	Atlantic Union College
physics	Eurotechnical Research University
professional arts	Saint Joseph's College
public administration	Nova University Upper Iowa University
social work	Athabasca University New Hampshire College
technology	Open University (England) Thomas A. Edison State College University of the State of New York
women's studies	Goddard College Greenwich University
writing	University of Norwich Goddard College

32. Index to Schools

A

B

C

M

N

O

P

Q

R

S

T

U

V

W

X

Y

Z

Won't someone start a non-traditional school starting with a "Z"—then there would be schools starting with all 26 letters of the English alphabet.

About the Personal Counseling Services Available

If you would like personal advice and recommendations, based on your own specific situation, a personal counseling service is available, by mail. I started this service in 1977, at the request of many readers. The actual personal evaluations and consulting are done by two friends and colleagues of mine, who are leading experts in the field of non-traditional education.

For the modest consulting fee of $50, these things are done:

1. You will get a long personal letter (usually four to six typewritten pages), evaluating your situation, recommending the best degree programs for you (including part-time programs in your area) and estimating how long it will take and what it will cost you to complete you degree(s).

2. You will get answers to any specific questions you may have, with regard to any programs you may now be considering, institutions you have already dealt with, or other relevant matters.

3. You will get detailed, up-to-the-minute information on institutions and degree programs, equivalency exams, sources of the correspondence courses you may need, career opportunities, resumé writing, sources of financial aid, and other topics, in the form of prepared notes (some 30 pages of these) and a large 16-page booklet.

4. You will be able to telephone or write the service, to get as much follow-up counseling as you want, to keep up-dated on new programs and other changes, and to use the service as your personal information resource.

If you are interested in this personal counseling, please write or call and you will be sent descriptive literature and a counseling questionnaire, without cost or obligation.

Once you have these materials, if you wish counseling, simply fill out the questionnaire and return it, with a letter and resumé if you like, along with the fee, and your personal reply and counseling materials will be prepared and airmailed to you.

For free information about this service, write or telephone:

Degree Consulting Services
P. O. Box 3533
Santa Rosa, California 95402
(707) 539-6466

NOTE: Use the above address only for matters related to the counseling service. For all other matters, write to me at P.O. Box 1717, Hilo, Hawaii 96721. Thank you.

—John Bear, Ph.D.

NOTES

(Often at the back of a book, you will find pages headed "Notes." The reason is that books like this are printed in units ('signatures') of 16 pages, so the total number of pages must be a multiple of 16. When there are pages left over, there is little that can be done, short of either rewriting the book to make it a little longer or shorter, or leaving the extra pages blank or putting 'Notes' at the top. All appropriate ecological apologies for this—so perhaps you really could use this and the next three pages for notes. Thank you.)

NOTES

NOTES

NOTES